HEGEL AND THE METAPHYSICS OF ABSOLUTE NEGATIVITY

Hegel's doctrines of absolute negativity and "the Concept" are among his most original contributions to philosophy and they constitute the systematic core of dialectical thought. Brady Bowman explores the interrelations between these doctrines, their implications for Hegel's critical understanding of classical logic and ontology, natural science, and mathematics as forms of "finite cognition," and their role in developing a positive, "speculative" account of consciousness and its place in nature. As a means to this end, Bowman also re-examines Hegel's relations to Kant and pre-Kantian rationalism, and to key post-Kantian figures such as Jacobi, Fichte, and Schelling. His book draws from the breadth of Hegel's writings to affirm a robustly metaphysical reading of the Hegelian project, and will be of great interest to students of Hegel and of German Idealism more generally.

BRADY BOWMAN is Assistant Professor of Philosophy at the Pennsylvania State University. His recent publications include *Sense Certainty: On the Systematic Pre-History of a Problem in German Idealism* (2003).

MODERN EUROPEAN PHILOSOPHY

ROBERT B. PIPPIN, *University of Chicago*
GARY GUTTING, *University of Notre Dame*
ROLF-PETER HORSTMANN, *Humboldt University, Berlin*

Otfried Höffe: *Kant's Cosmopolitan Theory of the Law and Peace*
Béatrice Longuenesse: *Hegel's Critique of Metaphysics*
Rachel Zuckert: *Kant on Beauty and Biology*
Andrew Bowie: *Music, Philosophy, and Modernity*
Paul Redding: *Analytic Philosophy and the Return of Hegelian Thought*
Kristin Gjesdal: *Gadamer and the Legacy of German Idealism*
Jean-Christophe Merle: *German Idealism and the Concept of Punishment*
Sharon Krishek: *Kierkegaard on Faith and Love*
Nicolas de Warren: *Husserl and the Promise of Time*
Benjamin Rutter: *Hegel on the Modern Arts*
Anne Margaret Baxley: *Kant's Theory of Virtue*
David James: *Fichte's Social and Political Philosophy*
Espen Hammer: *Philosophy and Temporality from Kant to Critical Theory*
Robert Stern: *Understanding Moral Obligation*

HEGEL AND THE METAPHYSICS OF ABSOLUTE NEGATIVITY

BRADY BOWMAN

Pennsylvania State University

CAMBRIDGE UNIVERSITY PRESS
Cambridge, New York, Melbourne, Madrid, Cape Town,
Singapore, São Paulo, Delhi, Mexico City

Cambridge University Press
The Edinburgh Building, Cambridge CB2 8RU, UK

Published in the United States of America by Cambridge University Press, New York

www.cambridge.org
Information on this title: www.cambridge.org/9781107033597

First published 2013

Printed and bound in the United Kingdom by the MPG Books Group

A catalogue record for this publication is available from the British Library

Library of Congress Cataloguing in Publication data
Bowman, Brady.
Hegel and the metaphysics of absolute negativity / Brady Bowman,
Pennsylvania State University.
pages cm. – (Modern European philosophy)
Includes bibliographical references and index.
ISBN 978-1-107-03359-7 (hardback)
1. Hegel, Georg Wilhelm Friedrich, 1770–1831.   I. Title.
B2948.B664 2013
193–dc23
2012036033

ISBN 978-1-107-03359-7 Hardback

CONTENTS

ACKNOWLEDGMENTS

This book is my attempt to arrive at a general understanding of Hegel's theoretical philosophy. I have been occupied with this task for longer than my doubtless very imperfect degree of success at it would indicate. The origins of the project go back to my doctoral studies at the Freie Universität Berlin, in the 1990s, and its basic conception and character have been shaped by the German community of Hegel scholars among whom I began my career. I owe a tremendous debt of gratitude to my *Doktorvater*, Andreas Arndt; through my work on this book especially I have come to appreciate how much I learned from him. At an early stage in my career I received important impulses from Walter Jaeschke. My philosophical friendship with Albrecht Heil, also in Berlin, continually reminds me of why I got into this business to begin with. Klaus Vieweg, at the Friedrich-Schiller-Universität Jena, recruited me into my first job; traces of the work I did with him on skepticism can be found throughout these pages. When I look back at the years I spent in Jena, they appear to me as an unbroken philosophical conversation – above all with Ralf Beuthan, my flatmate, fellow Hegelian, and constant interlocutor. Surely almost all the ideas in this book were, at one stage or other, topics of discussion with him and with our friends and colleagues Tommaso Pierini and Christian Spahn. In this context I would also like to mention my former colleague Jonas Maatsch. Dietmar Heidemann and Ulrich Schlösser, who were frequent guests at the department, have both also contributed to the ideas in this book in substantial ways. My association with Birgit Sandkaulen, who has since left Jena for Bochum to head the new *Forschungszentrum für klassische deutsche Philosophie*, was of decisive importance in broadening my vision of the sources and forces that shaped German thought around 1800; the philosophical exchange I enjoyed with her and her students, such as

Daniel Althof, Sandra Frey, and Oliver Koch, is continued in this book. Through my position in Jena I also had the privilege of getting to know a number of philosophers who have made decisive contributions to the study of Hegel and post-Kantian philosophy more generally. In ways the book makes obvious, I have drawn inspiration and insight from the work of Michael Forster, Dieter Henrich, Rolf-Peter Horstmann, Anton Friedrich Koch, John McDowell, Terry Pinkard, and Robert Pippin.

The ideas that began to take shape in Germany came to fruition in the United States. I have profited immeasurably from the openness and diversity of the American academy in general and from the supportive and stimulating climate among my colleagues at Penn State in particular. I am grateful to our head of department, Shannon Sullivan, for working to help maximize the time available to me for research and smoothing my path in other ways, as well. My heartfelt thanks go to Dennis Schmidt, my faculty mentor, and to Leonard Lawlor and Robert Bernasconi for their invaluable help and advice. Vincent Colapietro has also been a mentor and friend since before my arrival at Penn State and is now a trusted neighbor as well. Following Vincent's suggestion, Chris Lauer and I led a faculty–graduate student reading group on Hegel from 2007 till 2009 in which Vincent participated; a number of the views expressed in Chapters 3 and 4 on Hegel and natural science originated in our discussions there. John Christman, Paula Droege, Mark Fischer, and Jennifer Mensch have been great friends and partners in conversation on all things philosophical, and in this place I would also like to thank Jeffrey Wilson, who was there before it all began. I am also grateful to the students who took part in my seminar on the *Phenomenology of Spirit* in spring 2011; our discussions were instrumental in elaborating the views I present in Chapter 6.

Concurrently to my work on this book, I had the pleasure of working closely with Eckart Förster on the English translation of *The Twenty-Five Years of Philosophy*, which greatly expanded both my knowledge of many facets of classical German philosophy and my understanding of its systematic development. Some of what I learned surfaces explicitly in the pages to come; a larger portion implicitly informs my discussions of the subject matter; more importantly, though, Eckart Förster's philosophical rigor and seamless interweaving of intellectual history with systematic argumentation are ideals to which I have hoped to aspire.

Dalia Nassar read a substantial portion of the original draft of this book and provided valuable feedback and encouragement. As my fellow panelist at a conference on German Idealism organized by Weimin Shi at Tunghai University, Taiwan, in March 2011, where I presented a version of Chapter 5, she helped me further refine my ideas and recognize important parallels between Hegel and Schelling.

During the final phase of revisions to the manuscript, I was able to take advantage of an Erasmus Mundus "Master Mundus" stipend to spend a semester working with Dietmar Heidemann at the University of Luxembourg. This allowed me adequate time to polish the manuscript and was also felicitous in affording me the opportunity to make several new philosophical acquaintances. My thanks to Dietmar for his gracious invitation and to Dean Susan Welch of the Penn State College of Liberal Arts for kindly granting me a leave of absence on impossibly short notice.

I am especially grateful to Hilary Gaskin and Wayne Martin of Cambridge University Press for their support and encouragement while I was preparing the manuscript for its final review. My thanks also to the two anonymous reviewers of the original manuscript who read and commented on it with extraordinary care. Without their incisive criticism and helpful suggestions, this would have been a far less successful project than it has, I hope, become in the end.

To Katja Stuckatz I am grateful for the world she means to me. Du, Deiner, Dich Dir, ich Dir, Du mir – das gehört beiläufig nicht hierher!

A NOTE ON CITATIONS AND TRANSLATIONS

I cite Hegel's texts according to the historical critical edition, *Gesammelte Werke*, edited by the Academy of Sciences of Nordrhein-Westfalia (Hamburg: Meiner 1968–). In referring to the *Phenomenology of Spirit*, I also give the paragraph numbers of the translation by A. V. Miller. Kant's works are cited according to the *Akademie-Ausgabe*, except for the *Critique of Pure Reason*, which I conventionally cite by reference to the A or B edition. In the case of the most frequently cited texts by Kant and Hegel, the standard English translations include the pagination of these editions for ease of reference. I have made use of Norman Kemp Smith's translation of Kant's First Critique. For Hegel's writings, I have consulted the translations by Miller (*Phenomenology of Spirit*), Harris and Cref (*The Difference between Fichte's and Schelling's System of Philosophy, Faith and Knowledge,* and *The Relation of Skepticism to Philosophy*), di Giovanni (*Science of Logic*), and Brinkmann and Dahlstrom (*Encyclopedia, Part I*). For full details, please refer to the bibliography, where references to translations of less frequently cited authors will also be found. Throughout, I have tacitly modified translations as needed, and supplied my own where no authoritative English edition yet exists.

ABBREVIATIONS

6:12	*Kant's gesammelte Schriften* (Akademie Edition): volume and page number
A/B	First/second edition, Kant's *Critique of Pure Reason*
CSM	*The Philosophical Writings of René Descartes*, ed. Cottingham, Stoothoff, and Murdoch
Disc. Prael.	Wolff, *Discursus Praeliminarius*, trans. and ed. Gawlick and Kriemendahl
Dt. Log.	Wolff, *Vernünftige Gedanken von den Kräften des menschlichen Verstandes und ihrem richtigen Gebrauche in Erkenntnis der Wahrheit*, in *Gesammelte Werke*, Abteilung I, vol. I, ed. Arndt
Dt. Met.	Wolff, *Vernünftige Gedanken von Gott, der Welt und der Seele des Menschen, auch allen Dingen überhaupt*, in *Gesammelte Werke*, Abteilung I, vol. III, ed. Corr
E	Spinoza, *Ethics*: part, definition, axiom, proposition, corollary, and/or scholium, in *Collected Works*, vol. I, ed. Curley
ENC	Hegel, *Encyclopedia of the Philosophical Sciences* (1830 edn.). References are given by section (§) and indicate remarks (R) and additions (A)
FHJW	Jacobi, *Werke: Gesamtausgabe*, ed. Hammacher and Jaeschke
GA	Fichte, *Gesamtausgabe der Bayrischen Akademie der Wissenschaft*
GW	Hegel, *Gesammelte Werke* (Akademie Edition); for GW 9 (*Phenomenology of Spirit*), the section number (§) is also given
HA	Goethe, *Werke* (*Hamburger Ausgabe*), ed. Trunz

HBr	Hegel, *Briefe*, ed. Hoffmeister
KStA	Hölderlin, *Sämtliche Werke* (*Kleine Stuttgarter Ausgabe*), ed. Beißner
Ontol.	Wolff, *Philosophia prima, sive Ontologia*
PPC	Spinoza, *Principles of Cartesian Philosophy*, in *Collected Works*, vol. I, ed. Curley
SW	Schelling, *Sämmtliche Werke*, ed. K. F. A. Schelling
TIE	Spinoza, *Treatise on the Emendation of the Intellect*, in *Collected Works*, vol. I, ed. Curley
TW	Hegel, *Werke in zwanzig Bänden*, ed. Moldenhauer and Michel

INTRODUCTION: "A COMPLETELY ALTERED VIEW OF LOGIC"

... application of the categories to the unconditioned, i.e., metaphysics.

(ENC §46)

0.1. Hegel's metaphysical project

Logic, Kant had famously proclaimed in the *Critique of Pure Reason*, has not been forced to retrace a single step since the time of Aristotle, nor has it been able to advance a single step, and it is to all appearances "a closed and completed body of knowledge" (Bviii). Hegel, looking back over the development of German philosophy some thirty years later, suggests that the failure of logic to advance a single step in the space of two thousand years ought to have prompted Kant to draw the opposite conclusion: logic is in need "of a total reworking." In a related passage he credits Kant himself, alongside Jacobi, with having shown the necessity of such a "completely altered view of logic" (GW 21:35; 15:25). Hegel's proclamation is clearly at odds not only with Kant's understanding of logic, but with Kant's view of his own place in the history of logic. How are we to understand this discrepancy? What is the substance of this altered view, and how might Kant, unbeknownst to himself, have shown the necessity for it?

The short answer to these questions is that from Aristotle's time down to the emergence of post-Kantian idealism, philosophers had exclusively thematized what Hegel calls "the ordinary logic of the understanding," which is concerned only with "relations among finite things" (TW 19:241). This logic is constitutive of *finite cognition* and by its very nature it tends to obscure the conceptual structures that are truly at work in our knowledge of reality. Kant, and in a different, complementary way Jacobi too, demonstrated that the logic of finite cognition is marked by an essential negativity which, if we do not take pains to become aware of it, divides reason against itself. But to understand the nature of that negativity, and the necessity with which the logic of finite cognition must inevitably arise, a different logic is required that can both trace its genesis and delimit its scope, resolving the distortions inherent to it. This alternative, "speculative" logic can work with theoretical resources that were unavailable to the tradition prior to Hegel; in particular, it can draw on a conception of *absolute* negativity that can both explain and overcome the *aporiae* that arise in the philosophical application of the traditional categories and so-called laws of thought. Thus despite the fact that neither Kant nor Jacobi was willing to embrace the positive alternative of a completely altered view of logic, their criticism of the traditional philosophical use of logic served to demonstrate the necessity of such an alternative if the nature of knowledge and the place of mind in reality were to be grasped. In short, they demonstrated the necessity of a complete revision of metaphysics and philosophical methodology.

This short answer describes a result. As such, it can be fully comprehended and adequately appraised only in light of the arguments and interpretations that make up the substance of this book. On the other hand, the discussions in the coming chapters rely in part for their intelligibility on a broader view of Hegel's project and its place in the development of classical German philosophy, and in part also on a clear articulation of the basic concepts and assumptions that structure my approach to Hegel's philosophy. In this introductory section I try to give an account of these basic concepts and assumptions, together with an indication of the trajectory that the following chapters will take.

In the context of recent North American scholarship, one of the more controversial aspects of the interpretation put forward here is perhaps the underlying assumption that Hegel is a metaphysical thinker. Some of his most sympathetic and most influential recent commentators have sought to demonstrate that Hegel can be read as espousing no metaphysical doctrines at all, that as a post-Kantian thinker he thoroughly respected Kant's interdiction against transcendent incursions into the noumenal realm.[1] However, as I will argue at length in

---

1 The most forceful proponents of this reading in the Anglophone world are Robert Pippin, Terry Pinkard, and, in a different way, Robert Brandom (given their immense

Chapter 1, I do not think that recognizing Hegel as a post-Kantian thinker commits us *eo ipso* to the belief either that Hegel adopted any of Kant's positive doctrines or that he was engaged in a project that is best described as a "continuation" or "completion" of the project begun by Kant. I do not deny that Hegel *in fact* owes a significant debt to Kant (often via Fichte's reformulation of transcendental idealism, which colors many of Hegel's own pronouncements): central concep-tions such as Kantian pure reason, transcendental apperception, the intuitive understanding, and the primacy of freedom for both prac-tical *and theoretical* philosophy are indisputable cases in point,[2] and I draw attention to more deeply embedded structural parallels further on in this Introduction. Moreover, there are numerous ways in which Hegel may be seen to give a deeper grounding or more rigorous elab-oration of Kantian ideas such as transcendental affinity between the intellect and the empirical manifold. What I do deny is the implication that to be a philosopher self-consciously working in the wake of Kant's "fortunate revolution"[3] is necessarily to be engaged in a project that is continuous with transcendental idealism or one that needs to recog-nize the peculiar limitations Kant sought to impose on thought. *Post Kant* is not necessarily *propter Kant.*[4]

contributions to reintroducing Hegel as a serious thinker to mainstream Anglophone philosophy, this goes virtually without saying). For a critical, but even-handed overview of their "nonmetaphysical" readings versus "traditionalist" views of Hegel, see James Kreines, "Hegel's Metaphysics: Changing the Debate," *Philosophy Compass* 1:5 (2006): 466–80.

2 Cf. Béatrice Longuenesse, *Hegel's Critique of Metaphysics* (Cambridge University Press 2007), 167–88.

3 Karl Leonard Reinhold, *Briefe über die Kantische Philosophie* (Mannheim: Bender 1789), 1 of the unpaginated Preface.

4 In his overview "Philosophy of Language and Mind: 1950–1990" (*Philosophical Review* 101 [1992]: 3–51, esp. 9), Tyler Burge argues that contrary to Quine's own intentions, the effect of his devastating critique of logical positivism was to have "reopened a path to the traditional fundamental problems of philosophy. The positivists did not succeed in placing any questions … off limits from rational inquiry." Such cases are not rare in the history of philosophy. Certainly, Jacobi's detailed criticism of Spinoza did more to ignite a whole generation's interest in metaphysical monism than to quell their passion for systematic philosophy, despite his intentions. I am suggesting that Kant holds a similar place in relation to Hegel, who saw him as having devastated the traditional mode of metaphysical cognition in its very foundations and thus to have opened the path to a different, speculative approach to the problems of philoso-phy. (A similar point is made by Birgit Sandkaulen, "Die Ontologie der Substanz, der Begriff der Subjektivität und die Faktizität des Einzelnen: Hegels reflexionslogische 'Widerlegung' der Spinozanischen Metaphysik," *Internationales Jahrbuch des Deutschen Idealismus* 5 [2007]: *Metaphysics in German Idealism* [Berlin and New York: de Gruyter 2008], 235–75, esp. 237–41.)

In German scholarship, *affirmative* readings of Hegel as a metaphysical thinker are hardly unusual.[5] But neither in the Anglophone literature is such an approach as marginal or as provocative as it might have seemed as recently as five years ago. Several recent publications point to a nascent consensus that Hegel's philosophical concerns and systematic approach exhibit greater continuity with pre-Kantian metaphysical lines of thought than some of his more sympathetic recent commentators have wished to countenance – affinities that might seem obvious in light of the controversies that shaped German Idealism during Hegel's own formative period in the 1790s (e.g. the Pantheism Controversy, the debate about the philosophical theology implied by the new idealism, or the rift between Fichte and Schelling about the legitimacy of *Naturphilosophie*).[6] Hegel's philosophical contribution can be adequately appraised only in light of the metaphysical debates into which he intervened. For that matter, recent scholarship on Kant has also underscored continuities between pre-critical metaphysics and the doctrines of the *Critique of Pure Reason*;[7] and as a general observation, mainstream Anglo-American philosophy has

5 See, e.g., the representative collections of Henrich's essays on Hegel and German Idealism in *Selbstverhältnisse: Gedanken und Auslegungen zu den Grundlagen der klassischen deutschen Philosophie* (Stuttgart: Reclam 1982); Rolf-Peter Horstmann, *Die Grenzen der Vernunft: Eine Untersuchung zu Zielen und Motiven des Deutschen Idealismus* (Frankfurt am Main: Anton Hain 1991); Anton Friedrich Koch, "Die schlechte Metaphysik der Dinge. Metaphysik als immanente Metaphysikkritik bei Hegel," *Internationales Jahrbuch des Deutschen Idealismus* 5 (2007): 189–210.

6 In addition to Longuenesse, *Hegel's Critique*, see, e.g., Paul Franks, *All or Nothing: Systematicity, Transcendental Arguments, and Skepticism in German Idealism* (Cambridge, MA: Harvard University Press 2005); Stephen Houlgate, *The Opening of Hegel's Logic: From Being to Infinity* (West Lafayette, IN: Purdue University Press 2006); Robert Stern, *Hegelian Metaphysics* (Oxford University Press 2009).

7 See, e.g., Martin Schonfeld, *The Philosophy of the Young Kant: The Pre-Critical Project* (Oxford University Press 2000), which emphasizes continuities between Kant's pre-critical metaphysics on the one hand and the critical project and the *Opus postumum* on the other. Alison Laywine (e.g. *Kant's Early Metaphysics and the Origins of Critical Philosophy*. North American Kant Society Studies in Philosophy 3 [Atascadero, CA: Ridgeview 1993]) has similarly demonstrated the ways in which Kant's pre-critical metaphysics positively illuminate central doctrines of the *Critique of Pure Reason*. Eric Watkins, *Kant and the Metaphysics of Causality* (Cambridge University Press 2005), shows the extent to which Kant's later views on causality remain positively embedded in a framework specific to German metaphysical discussions of his time. In a different manner, Rae Langton combines interpretation of Kant's pre-critical doctrines with concerns from contemporary (e.g. Lewisian) metaphysics in *Kantian Humility: Our Ignorance of Things in Themselves* (Oxford University Press 1998).

now re-embraced metaphysics as an indispensible field of inquiry to such an extent that it no longer seems necessary to make apologies for being a metaphysician, either on one's own behalf or on that of any historical figure.[8] In light of these developments we might well speak today of Hegel's rehabilitation as a metaphysician, just as Karl Ameriks cautiously spoke of his rehabilitation as an epistemologist twenty years ago on the cusp of the most powerful renaissance of Hegelian thought in recent memory.[9]

But what does it mean in this context to insist that Hegel is a metaphysician? What, precisely, is called metaphysics? Given the long history of the term "metaphysics" and its status, at least since Kant's time and especially in the twentieth century, as an essentially contested concept, no definition I could offer here is likely to meet with universal recognition. Moreover, the somewhat pejorative senses that Hegel associates with the term differ from the neutral sense in which I use it to describe Hegel's own thought. I understand by "metaphysics" that field of *a priori* inquiry which is concerned with the fundamental structure of reality as a whole.[10] I contrast it with, among other fields of philosophical inquiry, epistemology, which is concerned with the right definition and proper standards of certainty and knowledge.

Hegel's idealist metaphysics can be summed up in the thesis that mind and reality as a whole are of essentially the same structure. In this respect, it might appear after all that Hegel effectively reduces general metaphysics to philosophy of mind, thus continuing a broadly Kantian trend. This appearance is not altogether misleading as long as we remember that Hegel's thesis differs from Kant's in that it is not restricted to the finite mind, excludes any doctrine of independently existing things in themselves, and is compatible with a philosophy of nature which seeks, inter alia, to demonstrate the necessity with which the finite mind emerges in the physical world. The usual way of expressing this is to say that Hegel espouses an *objective idealism*. He himself expresses allegiance to such a view when, for example, at the beginning of the *Science of Logic* he appeals to Anaxagoras as the first

---

8 For example Brian Ellis, *The Philosophy of Nature: A Guide to the New Essentialism* (Montreal and Kingston: McGill-Queen's University Press 2002), and E. J. Lowe, *The Four-Category Ontology: A Metaphysical Foundation for Natural Science* (Oxford University Press 2006).

9 Karl Ameriks, "Recent Work on Hegel: The Rehabilitation of an Epistemologist?," *Philosophy and Phenomenological Research* 52:1 (March 1992): 177–202.

10 Here I am taking a page from E. J. Lowe, *A Survey of Metaphysics* (Oxford University Press 2002), 2–3.

to have articulated the thought "that *Noûs*, thought, is the principle of the world, that the essence of the world is to be defined as thought" (GW 21:34). From his arrival in Jena in 1801 until the completion of the *Science of Logic* in 1816, Hegel's main philosophical efforts were directed towards the demonstration of this thesis; it was only in the years after 1817 that he increasingly returned to the themes that had occupied him prior to his arrival in Jena: religion, history, politics, and aesthetics.

The sense in which I understand Hegel to be a metaphysician gains in distinctness when we consider his own use of the term "metaphysics." In the narrower sense, Hegel uses it to refer to pre-critical or "older" rationalist metaphysics, particularly in its incarnation as the *Schulphilosophie* or "scholasticism" of Wolff and his followers. As he himself emphasizes, however, there is also a broader sense in which "metaphysical" thought is present in every historical period, namely as the belief "that it is *through thinking things over* that the *truth comes to be known* and that what objects truly are is brought before consciousness" (ENC §26). Hegel finds nothing exceptionable in this conviction that to be and to be intelligible are synonymous. The weakness of the metaphysical attitude lies in its uncritical assumption that the form of thought by which the truth is known is the form of the "finite thought-determinations" or, more familiarly, the categories of traditional ontology. This conception of the fundamental, intelligible structure of reality as made up of distinct categories (predicates, as Hegel says) and hence as having an objective existence fundamentally distinct from that of thinking as such is what Hegel finds to be untenable.[11]

Metaphysics in Hegel's pejorative sense is therefore any attitude toward reality which takes the categories of traditional ontology (a) as the exclusive and irreducible forms of objective cognition and (b) as the basic forms of the substantially real itself. These commitments need not be held explicitly, nor does Hegel always hold commitment to both to be a necessary condition of the metaphysical attitude. Traditional rationalists, for example, subscribe to both, yet though their critic Kant embraces only (a) while rejecting (b), I will argue

---

11 Cf. ENC §§28–29. The sense in which the conception of being as a realm of objects or *entia* follows from commitment to the categories as the irreducible forms of being is a topic to be discussed in Chapter 2 of this book; until then, the "hence" in the sentence above is a promissory note.

later that this is sufficient in Hegel's eyes to brand him as a metaphysician. Borrowing P. F. Strawson's well-known distinction, we may say that "metaphysics" in Hegel's pejorative sense denotes commitment to the categorial scheme that underlies ordinary everyday and scientific discourse about reality, the scheme that we make explicit through "descriptive metaphysics."

By contrast, Hegel's own *speculative* metaphysics is emphatically *revisionary*, as I will be arguing throughout this book. When Hegel affirms Anaxagoras' insight that "*Noûs* is the principle of the world," he is not affirming the notion that the categories of traditional ontology (e.g. quality, quantity, identity, substance, cause and effect, and so on) limn the fundamental structure of reality. Hegel introduces his own unique set of concepts in order to explicate both that structure and the necessity that it appear to the finite mind under the derivative and ultimately inadequate forms of the traditional categories. Chief among these uniquely Hegelian concepts are, first, the concept of the Concept itself, and second, the concept of (absolute) negativity. As I will argue, all of Hegel's operative concepts (for instance determination, determinate negation, sublation, thought-determinations, indifference, Conceptual movement, realization, reflection, and the Idea) can and ought to be understood as so many modifications of the Concept and absolute negativity. So although on my reading Hegel does intend a derivation of the traditional categories and forms of thought that guarantees their necessity and validity within certain well-defined limits, his more fundamental aim is to demonstrate that neither the meaning of those categories, nor the fundamental structure of reality, nor the relation of those categories to reality can be made out prior to a thoroughgoing "speculative" revision of our natural categorial scheme. And in this sense I agree with Hans Friedrich Fulda when he describes Hegel's metaphysics as "a metaphysics without ontology."[12] Speculative philosophy is a systematic critique and overcoming of traditional ontological (categorial) thought in service of an alternative, revisionary metaphysics Hegel calls "speculative science."

---

12 Hans Friedrich Fulda, "Ontologie nach Kant und Hegel," in D. Henrich and R.-P. Horstmann (eds.), *Metaphysik nach Kant?* (Stuttgart: Klett-Cotta 1987), 44–82, here 49. Contrast Stern's view of Hegel as restoring a form of ontology in the introduction to Stern, *Hegelian Metaphysics*, 20–34.

0.2. The argument of this book

Here I would like to pull together the main questions and claims of the chapters to follow, and to exhibit them as constituting a single, unified chain of argument. I should also like to emphasize, however, that although the chapters are linked by a sustained argument, the individual chapters also focus on specific subject matter and treat it in a relatively self-contained manner. This should allow readers with particular interests to focus on the topics they find relevant without too much searching and cross-referencing.

0.2.1. Absolute negativity as the essence of the Hegelian Concept

Chapter 1 introduces the book's conceptual center of gravity, the notion of *absolute negativity*, by situating it in the framework of an essentially *critical* project.[13] Hegel recognized Kant and Jacobi as having equal share in demonstrating the necessity of a "completely altered view of logic"; they represent the true threshold between pre-critical logic and metaphysics and a new form of critical philosophy.[14] The meaning of this claim is more complex, however, than the standard historiography of German philosophy would immediately suggest; neither is Hegel's conception of critical philosophy the same as Kant's, nor does Kant end up as standing unambiguously on the critical side of the break with pre-critical logic and metaphysics. In specifically different ways, Kant and Jacobi succeed merely in showing the *necessity* of an altered view of logic. From the Hegelian perspective, Kant's demonstration that the categories and logical forms of the understanding lead to antinomies when applied to the unconditional demonstrates that they are not in fact the authentic and fundamental structures of intelligibility, but must themselves be interpreted and reconstructed on the basis of a deeper, dialectical logic that Kant failed to recognize.

13 To some extent, my focus coincides with that of Karin de Boer, *On Hegel: The Sway of the Negative* (Basingstoke: Palgrave Macmillan 2010), who also puts negativity at the center of her interpretation. Contrary to my approach, de Boer takes a critical view of absolute negativity precisely to the extent that it serves as a principle of systematic totality. She argues that Hegel recognized a principle she calls "tragic negativity" early in his career, but then shut his eyes to it when he turned to the "speculative science" that ushers in his mature thought. De Boer finds this principle of "tragic negativity," along with a concomitant "logic of entanglement," to be free of the dangers of domination and subordination she associates with Hegel's own explicit principle of absolute, dialectical negativity (cf. de Boer, *On Hegel*, 4–5, 11, and 222n.). I am inclined to take a more positive view than de Boer.

14 Cf. GW 21:35, GW 15:25.

Jacobi's critique of scientific rationality as issuing in hard determinism and nihilism ("Spinozism") shows in turn that that form of rationality inevitably tends to conceal and undermine its very presuppositions: the existence of scientific activity as the expression of free and metaphysically robust, personal minds cannot be grasped according to the model of explanation explicitly favored by scientific activity, traditionally conceived. But Jacobi does not recognize the possibility for an alternative form of rationality that would be equal to such a task; indeed, his narrow identification of rationality as such with functional analysis (*avant la lettre*) and explanation leads him to reject it absolutely as a mode of self-understanding. On Hegel's view, then, both thinkers embrace unnecessarily narrow conceptions of rational cognition, thereby overestimate the scope of their critique, and thus fail to see the true significance of their results as pointing toward a different conception of thought, a completely altered view of logic. They fail to be truly critical philosophers in the full sense of the term.

A truly critical philosophy would elaborate a deeper logic (a logic of "reason") on whose basis the logic of the "understanding," toward which Kant and Jacobi were exclusively oriented, could be genetically derived and its scope defined, even as its incapacity for cognizing the real is systematically exposed. "Finite cognition" would thus be replaced by, and become the critical object of, a higher form of cognition, "speculative science." Since Hegel believes that speculative science has consequences for central concerns such as the nature of truth, the place of mind in the natural world, or the possibility and reality of human freedom, it is fair to say that it is a doctrine equally of logic and of metaphysics. Differently from Kant's analysis (in the *Critique of Pure Reason*) of the forms of understanding, which issues in theoretical agnosticism about these questions of human concern, and differently from Jacobi's, which issues in fideism and a theoretically unstable intuitionism, Hegel sees speculative science in a position to give substantive and rigorously argued answers.

It is in this broader, in part historically defined context that we must understand the meaning and systematic role of the notion of absolute negativity. In the middle sections of Chapter 1, I draw on work by Dieter Henrich and Rolf-Peter Horstmann to argue for what is, to my knowledge, an original thesis. Horstmann has given a detailed analysis of what Hegel refers to as "the Concept," showing it to be a complex self-relational structure which has for its elements relations that are isomorphic to the whole.[15] The details of his

15 The details of Horstmann's analysis make up the content of Chapter 1, section 1.3.2.

account are fleshed out in Chapter 1. The important point here is that both the whole and the elements of this relational structure of the Concept can be derived from the logic of autonomous negation first analyzed by Dieter Henrich, that is, the logic of what Hegel himself calls absolute negativity.[16] This is significant because it allows us to identify the Concept with absolute negativity: they are two views or aspects of a single, fundamental reality – the former a static view, the latter a dynamic one: structure versus process. The larger claim is that Hegel holds precisely this structural-cum-dynamic unity to be the unique form of intelligibility. The large tract of cognitive activity critically analyzed by Kant and Jacobi that Hegel calls finite cognition exhibits forms of intelligibility in a merely derivative way. Both the scope and the limits of finite cognition are meant to be chartable by reference to this deeper logic. Put most strongly, the methodological function of absolute negativity is to effect a reduction of the categories and forms of finite cognition to "moments" of the logic of autonomous negation, such that the prima facie content of those forms is fundamentally transformed. Finite cognition is not holistically justified in the *Science of Logic*, but subjected to skeptical critique and revision.

0.2.2. *The critique of finite cognition*

Chapters 2 through 5 are concerned primarily with Hegel's *critique of finite cognition*. They are organized according to the three *a priori* sciences identified by Kant: metaphysics, pure natural science, and mathematics, and I seek to show the ways in which each of these sciences manifests limitations that are interpretable by reference to the logic of absolute negativity. Chapter 6 takes a more positive approach. There I show how the logic of absolute negativity is integral to a Hegelian theory of representational content that simultaneously tackles the Kantian problem of the sensible manifold and the significantly parallel Spinozist problem of the determinateness of substance. Together, these five chapters present a sustained investigation of the ways in which absolute negativity and its derivative concepts such as mediation or determinate negation come together to constitute a powerful metaphysical interpretation of truth and knowledge. They constitute the heart of the book.

16 I discuss Henrich's reconstruction in Chapter 1, section 1.4.2.

More specifically, Chapter 2 begins by arguing that we should see Hegel's project of speculative science as continuous with Wolff's endeavor to elaborate a unified, systematic exposition of rationalist logic and metaphysics. Indeed, even Kant's mature philosophy exhibits far deeper affinities with the school of Wolff than with the empiricist and popularist streams of philosophy that came to dominate German thought in the middle decades of the eighteenth century. For Kant and *a fortiori* for Hegel, diagnosing the fatal weaknesses of classical metaphysics is a step towards its rehabilitation, not its elimination. The two thinkers differ, however, in where to locate those weaknesses. Put most simply, Kant identifies the source of error in the Leibniz–Wolff school's failure to recognize that sensibility and the understanding are different in kind, paired with their lack of insight into the ultimately subjective status of space and time.[17] Hegel, by contrast, focuses on their privileging of the *categories* (or "predicates," as he also sometimes says) as the basic forms of ontology. They failed to see that the individual categories are subordinate fixations or expressions of a more fundamental, dynamic unity (the Concept, absolute negativity) which they systematically distort as long as this essential link goes unrecognized.

By this accounting, Kant is on the pre-critical side of the logical revolution that Hegel calls for. Even so, he goes beyond his rationalist predecessors in recognizing that the categories must, on the one hand, be grasped as rooted in a single, underlying structure (the synthetic unity of apperception) and, on the other, that the categories systematically lead into forms of error when we try to apply them to the unconditioned, i.e. to what exists in itself and independently of external relations. In other words, he grasped that the categories could not be identical with the structures of transcendental reality. Nevertheless, this insight did not lead him to consider alternative forms of intelligibility – at least not as available to the human mind – but rather to restrict cognition of what is intelligible to mere appearances.

For Hegel, this represents an *uncritical* move insofar as Kant does not go on to examine the purely categorial content of the categories (as opposed to the sensible content furnished by the imagination).[18] Had

---

17 For Kant's analysis of Leibnizians' failure to distinguish between intuitions and concepts and its consequences see "The Amphiboly of Concepts of Reflection" (B316–46).

18 Most recently, Sally Sedgwick has undertaken a sympathetic reconstruction of Hegel's criticisms of Kant's practical and theoretical philosophy, focusing inter alia on the charge of formalism and seeking to defend its cogency: see *Hegel's Critique of Kant: From Dichotomy to Identity* (Oxford University Press 2012). Sedgwick's book came out just as my manuscript was going into production.

he done so, Hegel believes, he would have recognized the dialectic that is immanent in the categories and seen that it does not arise primarily or exclusively with their application to the unconditioned. He would thereby have recognized that the categories cannot, even when limited to finite or conditional applications, truly be considered to be forms of intelligibility inasmuch as they are burdened by irresolvable contradictions. Furthermore, Hegel finds Kant's restriction of cognition to mere appearances to be self-undermining in a way that affects the very concept of truth. So while we may accurately describe Kant as the end of pre-critical metaphysics, we should see that, from Hegel's perspective, anyway, Kant represents an ending that falls within the metaphysical period itself. Kant is the metaphysical end of pre-critical metaphysics, not a complete overcoming of pre-critical metaphysics.

Analogous points can be made about Jacobi. He too grasped the impossibility of classical, pre-critical rationalist metaphysics, but he did so from a standpoint that ultimately remained internal to that very tradition. Because he did not entertain the possibility of an alternative view of logic, he ran athwart a false alternative: Either we embrace the demand for unlimited intelligibility with its "Spinozist" consequences, or we abandon it entirely. But here the conception of intelligibility has been taken over uncritically from the tradition with which Jacobi seeks to break, and in consequence he can do no more than gesture at some standpoint outside scientific metaphysics; but he cannot positively identify it. So both Kant and Jacobi might be described as having achieved a fully explicit consciousness of the *aporiae* that were already present in a more or less inchoate manner in pre-critical metaphysics, but to have found no other response to them except rejection or the restriction of the scope of cognition.

Hegel's positive alternative emerges from his concept of absolute negativity. Pre-critical metaphysics, with its focus on ontological categories as the most general forms of *things*, is the product of sustained reflection on the world as it is revealed in finite cognition. Finite cognition as such, however, is not limited to a particular epoch; it is the omnihistorical manifestation of a structure cutting across the mind–world distinction that Hegel calls the *Concept*.

The task of a critique of finite cognition is therefore coextensive with the project of its metaphysical derivation as a moment in the unfolding of the Concept. This is a project Hegel sometimes describes as the "overcoming of consciousness" (e.g. GW 4:20–23). By "consciousness" he means our ordinary view of how we are related to the world in cognition, namely as individual minds over against a sphere of independently existing, individual things available to us in sense perception, largely amenable to our attempts to explain them, and with which we causally interact. This is the natural interpretation of our relation to objectivity that metaphysics seeks to make rigorous. The task of speculative science is not to demonstrate its falsity, but to exhibit it as embedded in a structure (the Concept) that shines through the forms of finite cognition, but which these same forms tend to distort and obscure.

The complexity of Hegel's undertaking stems in part from the nuances of this interpretation of finite cognition. At the deepest level, speculative science *replaces* the categories and explanatory forms of the ordinary view with the structural moments of the Concept and the logic of absolute negativity they embody. However, it does not replace them by simply exchanging them for a distinct set of categories and forms (the way Bacon, for example, seems to have viewed the relation between his methods and those of untutored, natural cognition[19]). Instead, speculative science might be described as *reducing* the categories and forms of finite cognition to iterations of the logical dynamic of absolute negativity. Reduction, unlike elimination, implies a limited *justification* of the reducible forms or entities: although they prove not to possess the logical or ontological dignity initially ascribed to them, they are also shown to be actually grounded at a level that is logically or ontologically independent. To this extent, the speculative project supports readings of Hegel that see him as giving a transcendental, holistic, or similarly constituted justification of the forms of ordinary knowledge claims.

At the same time, however, we must not forget the specific character of Hegelian reduction, namely its reinterpretation of finite cognition as belonging within the dynamic of absolute negativity to the moment of difference, relation-to-other, or determinate negation. This leads to an assessment of finite cognition as an essentially self-external aspect of the Concept – one that is entailed by the logic of absolute negativity, but whose scope and validity is thereby limited. In all its forms, finite cognition is therefore subject to *aporiae*, contradictions, indeterminacy, and foundationlessness that are ineliminable within the framework of finite cognition. To this extent, anti-realist, anti-foundationalist, deconstructive, and otherwise

---

19 Cf. Francis Bacon, *The New Organon*, ed. L. Jardine and M. Silverthorne (Cambridge University Press 2000), e.g. aphorisms 2 and 37–52 (33, 40–46).

skeptical readings also find support in Hegel's project. But like their more dogmatic counterparts, we must recognize that they capture only one aspect of it. The structure of the Concept that constitutes the framework of Hegel's critique of finite cognition is not intended to be open to the kinds of broadly skeptical strategies that are effective within the limited sphere of finite cognition, just as it is not adequately describable in the categorial terms for which it provides a limited justification.[20]

Finite cognition is not simply a stance toward the world that is at the same time external to the world; it represents a state of affairs that is of the same metaphysical order as the world. Hegel's *critical metaphysics* thus consists in folding knowledge as ordinarily conceived into an explanatory scheme that posits no ultimate difference in kind between the activity of knowing and the being of what is known. This opens the way to a positive interpretation of finite cognition and its *aporiae*. In principle, it becomes possible to assert a continuity between thought and being, and hence also to assert infinite intelligibility, without needing to overstep the limits set down by Kant. Indeed, understanding the necessity of such limits to *finite* cognition and their positive significance in the structure of the Concept is one of the chief tasks of speculative science.

Chapters 3 and 4 draw out the ramification of this doctrine for general metaphysics and for the metaphysics of natural science in particular. In Chapter 3 I revisit an aspect of Hegel's Kant critique only touched on before, namely his rejection of transcendental idealism. I hinted above that Hegel believes that when Kant restricts cognition to mere appearances, he undermines the notion of truth at its root. Here I begin to elaborate on that claim by considering John McDowell's realist interpretation of Hegelian thought and his argument for its superiority over the subjectivism and psychologism that follow Kant's idealism like a shadow. I agree with McDowell that Hegel rejects the idea that the forms of sensibility and understanding are in any way external to things themselves; in this sense, Hegel must surely be accounted a robust epistemological realist. Given the notion of absolute negativity as a dynamic that cuts across the mind–world

20 This point is made in Michael Forster, *Hegel's Idea of a Phenomenology of Spirit* (University of Chicago Press 1998), esp. 126–92; see also Michael Forster, *Hegel and Skepticism* (Cambridge, MA: Harvard University Press 1989).

distinction, lying indeed at the very origin of that distinction, this real-ist implication should be unsurprising. By the same token, though, we should expect that the same characteristics that show up as antinomies and other *aporiae* in finite cognition will therefore also manifest them-selves in the objects specific to finite cognition. This is the core of the position that Robert Stern has characterized as Hegel's *idealism of the finite*. In Hegel's words:

> The idealism of philosophy consists in nothing else than in recogniz-ing that the finite has no veritable being [*ein wahrhaft Seiendes*] ... This is as true of philosophy as of religion, for religion equally does not rec-ognize finitude as a veritable being [*ein wahrhaftes Sein*], as something ultimate and absolute or as something underived, uncreated, eternal. The opposition between idealistic and realistic philosophy is therefore without meaning. (GW 21:142)

In a deeper sense, then, the objects of finite cognition truly are *mere appearances*. This status is conferred upon them, however, not primarily by the fact that they are merely ways some otherwise existent and inde-pendently determinate being appears to a finite subject. Of course, it is part of the concept of appearance that there is a subject *to whom* something is appearing. This is not being denied. What is specific to Hegel's view, however, is that the existence of a subjectivity character-ized as finite by its inherent antinomies and other *aporiae* is constituted by the numerically identical structures that constitute the objects of nature as transitory, context-dependent, partially indeterminate, and subject to vagueness and various forms of incompleteness. What we ordinarily take to be flaws or shortcomings of cognition are not merely that; rather, when we take the broad view they become interpretable as indications of the finitude of nature itself – indications that it "is not a true being." Therefore, in Chapter 4 I turn to Hegel's views on the metaphysics of natural science in order to draw attention to the classificatory vagueness, gaps, nomological underdetermination, and related aspects he believes to be immanent features of nature itself. Here again, the phases in the dynamic of absolute negativity contrib-ute to an understanding of how, on Hegel's view, nature or finite being objectively corresponds to the limitations of finite cognition. This does not tend to erase those limitations, as Kantians might wish to object, but rather to reconceive the impossibility of a complete natural science, for example, as a metaphysically necessary and significant fact about the world.

If Chapters 2 through 4 have been devoted primary emphasis to metaphysical questions posed by Hegel's relations to Kant and pre-Kantian rationalism, Chapter 5 examines Hegel's methodological views on the rationalist ideal of mathematical rigor as a paradigm for all knowledge, including philosophical cognition. Here Jacobi's impact once again comes to the fore. Whereas Hegel viewed Kant as having shown the limits of finite cognition with respect to its content (the nature of the unconditioned), he located Jacobi's importance in the critique of deductivist, "geometrical" ideals of method. Though Hegel concurs with Kant in rejecting the *mos geometricus* as an appropriate model for philosophic cognition, his reasons for doing so diverge from Kant's in every particular, and prove to be closer to Jacobi's in spirit if not in the letter.

Both in the *Phenomenology* and in the *Logic*, Hegel ascribes privileged status to geometry. On the basis of textual evidence, I argue that he views it as the highest form of knowledge within the sphere of finite theoretical cognition. In the first half of the chapter, I analyze Hegel's notion of a *real* (as opposed to nominal) definition and locate it in a tradition reaching at least as far back as Leibniz. The organizing role of such real definitions is what secures geometry its privileged status in the system (and not apodictic certainty, as for Kant). In the second half, I examine the reasons that nevertheless cause him to exclude it as a genuine form of speculative cognition. As in the case of empirical science, these reasons center on the concept of self-externality.

The section concludes by inferring, from Hegel's critique of geometry, the positive outlines of what he calls speculative cognition. At this point in the book, the doctrine of the Concept re-emerges in positive form. I show that when the self-externality of cognition in its specifically "geometrical" form is overcome, the resulting complex of relations (relation-to-other as an integral moment of relation-to-self) is identical to the structure of the Hegelian Concept explicated in Chapter 1. This observation sheds interesting light on Hegel's mature attitude to Jacobi: he agrees with Jacobi that finite cognition at its best distorts the nature of the unconditioned in ways that lead to determinism and nihilism; however, he also insists that the right kind of logical reflection on finite cognition is able to reveal its origin in the structure of the absolute itself, and thereby to provide insight into the nature of the absolute.

*0.2.3. Kant and Spinoza: the metaphysics of intentionality
meets the metaphysics of substance*

Hegel repeatedly insists that the *Science of Logic* is distinguished from the formal logic of the tradition partly in virtue of its being a *logic of content*, where the notion of content is further specified as *truth*. For example in the Preface to the second edition:

> The inadequacy of this [traditional, purely formal] way of regarding thought which leaves truth on one side, can only be remedied by bringing the content into the thinking consideration, and not merely what is customarily credited to the external form. It soon becomes obvious that the content that superficial reflection ordinarily distinguishes from the form is not in fact formless and indeterminate in itself (in that case it would be a vacuity, for instance the abstraction of the thing-in-itself); rather, the content proves to be form in itself, indeed it is only by virtue of form that it has animation and substantial content, and we see that the form itself is what changes into the illusion of a content and thus also into the appearance of a merely external aspect of this appearance. By thus introducing content into logical consideration, it is not *things* that become its object, but the *reality* [*Sache*], the *Concept* of things. (GW 21:17)

Chapter 6 seeks to articulate the core conception of speculative logic as a *logic of content*, and to show that the logic of content *just is* the logic of absolute negativity.

The key terms in the passage above are *Sache* (which for reasons presently to be discussed I have translated as "reality") and *Begriff* ("Concept"). Hegel obviously intends them as co-referential expressions: the reality of things is identical to their Concept. Equally obviously, they denote distinct aspects of this common referent. In order to have a form of words that captures both the identity of reference and the distinctness of aspect, I introduce the traditional metaphysical expressions, "formal reality" and "objective reality." In the Cartesian usage on which I base my employment of the terms, "formal reality" denotes non-representational or intrinsic being: to exist formally is to be a substance, an attribute, or a mode (or the mode of a mode, etc.). This category stretches across the distinction of substances into mental and non-mental: just as material substances with their spatial attributes and the particular modes of those attributes exist formally, so do minds with their cognitive and volitional attributes and their particular modes (thoughts and desires). "Objective reality" in turn denotes a way of being specific to mental substance: it is the representational content of thoughts and desires, where either material substance (consciousness) or mental substance (self-consciousness) can be the intentional correlate of the content. In this framework, "truth" may be said to denote the adequate correspondence between objective reality and the formal reality it represents.

As introduced here, "objective" and "formal reality" originally belong to a dualist metaphysics that Hegel would find unacceptable. Therefore, the terms must be reinterpreted in order to become serviceable. Now, as will have been spelled out in detail in Chapter 1, the Hegelian Concept is emphatically not the representation (*Vorstellung*) of some referent supposed to be distinct from it, so it cannot be straightforwardly identified with objective reality, classically construed. The Concept is a relational structure cutting across the mind–world distinction such that mind (the structure of finite cognition) and world (the structure of finite being) are at once both (a) relational structures in themselves that are homomorphic to each other and (b) elements within a higher-order relation (the Concept in its totality) to which they are *also* homomorphic. So objective reality qua representational content (finite cognition) and formal reality qua intrinsic being (finite being) must be construed as themselves moments of or elements within the structure of the Concept that Hegel, in the passage cited above, identifies with the *Sache*. Since the German word *Sache* corresponds to the Latin *res*, and *Sachhaltigkeit* to *realitas*, I propose to understand the Hegelian *Sache* as the unqualified reality of which objective and formal reality are distinct aspects. This accords with what has just been said about the structure of the Concept and with the fact that Hegel clearly intends to treat "Concept" and *Sache* as synonymous.

The task of a speculative logic of content may therefore be defined as the task of analyzing the structure of objective reality (basically: intentionality and representational content) and explaining the possibility and the nature of the relation in which it stands to formal reality (intrinsic being), where that relation is constitutive of what is called *truth*. Equivalently, but viewed from the opposite perspective, the task of speculative logic is to analyze the structure of intrinsic being or substance, and to explain the necessity of its appearing – the necessity with which being expresses itself as the content of determinate thought, where that relation of being to its representation in thought is constitutive of what is called *truth*. Hegel's revolutionary idea is to have conceived of formal and objective reality (substance and subject) as moments that achieve determinate existence solely through the unfolding of a unique logic: the logic of absolute negation. The speculative logic of content is therefore nothing other than the logic of absolute negativity.

As Hegel says above, once we embrace this innovative logic of content:

> [I]t soon becomes obvious that the content that superficial reflection ordinarily distinguishes from the form is not in fact formless and *indeterminate* in itself – in which case it would be a *vacuity*, for instance the abstraction of the thing-in-itself; rather, the content proves to be form in itself, indeed it is only by virtue of form that it has animation and content, and we see that the form itself is what changes into the *illusion* of a content and thus also into the appearance of a merely external aspect of this appearance. (GW 21:17; emphases added)

Consideration of this remark reveals a further advantage of the traditional expressions "formal" and "objective reality" as instruments of interpretation: it allows us to bring together two superficially distinct Hegelian concerns: the critique of Spinoza's substance monism and the critique of Kant's transcendental idealism.

One of Hegel's recurring criticisms of Spinozist metaphysics is that it leaves reality – substance – ultimately indeterminate. There are two sides to this. On the one side, the form in which the determinateness of reality immediately appears, that is as the existence of a manifold of distinct, qualitatively individuated substances, is assumed as given while at the same time it is denied that such existence reflects any real multiplicity in substance: the determinateness that is given by the one hand is taken by the other. On the other side, Spinoza indicates no internal principle or ground of determination for substance: that it should go out of itself and "finitize" itself as the perspective that a finite understanding has upon it, remains a brute fact. Here is how Hegel puts it in his review of the second volume of Jacobi's collected works, composed just after the completion of the *Science of Logic*:

> An even more obvious requirement would be to demonstrate some transition from the absolute unity to the divine attributes, for it has merely been *assumed* that there are such attributes, just as the existence of a finite *understanding* or *imagination* and of particular, finite things was assumed. Their being is constantly being revoked as something untrue and immersed in the infinity of substance, yet despite this recognition of their negativity they retain the status of a *given point of*

departure. Conversely, absolute substance is not understood as the point
of departure for distinctions, particularization, individuation, or whatever form distinctions may take, be it as attributes and modes, as being
and thought, understanding, imagination or what have you. And hence
everything is merely submerged and perishes in a substance which
remains motionless within itself and out of which nothing ever resur-
faces. (GW 15:10)

Hegel immediately goes on to explain that this *aporia* of Spinozist
substance monism can only be addressed if the determinateness of
substance is conceived as arising on the basis of active *self-determination*,
and that the self-determination of substance must be conceived as
a logic of absolute negation. Yet the full significance of Hegel's proposed solution emerges only when we recognize its place in a speculative logic of content. The metaphysical problem of the source of
determinateness in reality is the same as the problem of the metaphysics of intentionality. Hegel contends that the determinateness of
substance (i.e. of formal reality) *just is* the existence of subjectivity:
the basic structure of reality is such that determinateness in general
(let's call it: the substance-attribute model of reality) arises together
with and is ultimately identical to the structure of intentionality, that
is, *appearance*. Outside of appearance, there is no determinateness,
no "things in themselves" that could be some way or other independently of appearance, and that means independently of beings capable
of representation. The metaphysics of intentionality is not a special
branch of metaphysics, a particular ontological problem; rather, it is
coextensive with the study of being qua being (assuming, that is, that
purely indeterminate being – a being devoid of qualities – is nothing
at all).[21]

Once it has become clear that Hegel's solution to the weaknesses of
Spinozist substance monism is coextensive with an analysis of intentionality, it should no longer come as a surprise that his engagement
with Spinoza is continuous with his engagement with Kant's model
of the cognitive mind. A recurring criticism he makes of Kant (and
of Fichte too, in this regard) is that Kant treats being in itself, that is
being as it is independently of our cognitive relation to it, as for all
intents and purposes *formless*. Consider for example this passage from
Faith and Knowledge (1802):

---

21 This, of course, is the moral of the opening section of the *Science of Logic* with its dia-
    lectic of being, nothing, and becoming: GW 21:68–104.

Such a formal identity [of the abstract ego] is immediately confronted with an infinite non-identity over against or beside itself with which it must in some incomprehensible way coalesce. And so we have on the one side the I with its … formal unity of the manifold posited in isolation, and on the other an infinitude of sensations and, if you will, of things in themselves, which realm can be nothing else than a formless clump in the absence of the categories, even though according to the *Critique of the Power of Judgment* it is supposed to contain within itself, as a beautiful realm of nature, determinations in relation to which the power of judgment can only be reflective and not subsumptive. (GW 4:332)[22]

In light of the foregoing, it is easy to recognize the affinity with Hegel's critique of Spinozist substance as having no immanent determinations, but only the determinateness projected onto it by an external, finite understanding or imagination whose existence is not adequately derivable from the infinite substance itself. More importantly, however, this passage begins to articulate the problem of how there can be any determinate consciousness or representational content at all, given Kant's model of the cognitive mind. On the one side we have pure consciousness of self-identity with no determinate content, since all such content must be provided by sensibility. On the other side we have a manifold of sensations with no internal structure of their own, and *a fortiori* without the structure of intentionality that would characterize them as contents of consciousness. On this model, it is not clear that apperception could even count as consciousness since there is nothing for it to be consciousness *of*.

To see this more clearly, consider Kant's somewhat puzzling idea of the "sensible manifold in general." According to a widely held interpretation, Kantian intentionality is thoroughly conceptual. "It must be possible for the 'I think' to accompany all my representations; for otherwise something would be represented in me which could not be thought at all, and that is equivalent to saying that the representation would be impossible, or at least would be nothing to me" (B131–32). At the same time, though, the relation to the identity of the subject (to *my* self-consciousness) comes about

only in so far as I conjoin one representation with another, and am conscious of the synthesis of them. Only in so far, therefore, as I can unite a manifold of given representations in *one consciousness*, is it possible for me to represent to myself the identity of the consciousness in these

22 For the corresponding criticism of Fichte, see GW 4:394, 396.

representations ... Combination does not, however, lie in the objects, and cannot be borrowed from them, and so, through perception, first taken up into the understanding. On the contrary, it is an affair of the understanding alone, which itself is nothing but the faculty of combining *a priori*, and of bringing the manifold of given representations under the unity of apperception. (B134)

The understanding, in turn, is an essentially judgmental (propositional) and thus *conceptual* capacity (cf. B92–94). Therefore, nothing can be a representation *for me*, i.e. embedded in the structure of intentionality, prior to or independently of conceptualization.[23]

This view of intentionality as *essentially* conceptually mediated renders the notion of the sensible manifold in general somewhat puzzling. Kant does state in more than one place that the manifold of sensible intuition is given prior to all thought (e.g. B132). But it is difficult to grasp what a pre-conceptual sensible manifold could be. Under the description "*sensible* manifold," an essential relation to consciousness, an intentional character, is clearly implied. Yet under the description "pre-conceptual," the manifold is clearly excluded from the structure of intentionality: outside the structure of intentionality, however, the characterization as sensible would appear to be empty; the pre-conceptual manifold could be nothing but the concrete determinateness of things without the mind, which is what I have been calling formal reality.

Furthermore, it is difficult to see how the mere synthesis or combination of such determinations could suffice to embed them in the structure of intentionality, thereby transforming them into representational content. Kant himself states that "the representation of this unity [of the manifold as belonging to an identical self-consciousness]

---

23 This view of Kant is widely held, but it has recently been the subject of debate. R. Hanna attributes to Kant the view that the objective content of some conscious experience is thoroughly nonconceptual in nature (see Robert Hanna, "Kant and Nonconceptual Content," *European Journal of Philosophy* 13:2 [2005]: 247–90, and more recently "Kantian Non-Conceptualism, Rogue Objects, and the Gap in the B-Deduction," *International Journal of Philosophical Studies* 19:3 [2011]: 397–413), a similar position is represented by Lucy Allais, "Kant, Non-Conceptual Content, and the Representation of Space," *Journal of the History of Philosophy* 47:3 (2009): 383–413. Hannah Ginsborg has argued against the strong nonconceptualist interpretation in "Was Kant a Nonconceptualist?," *Philosophical Studies* 137:1 (2008): 65–77, and in "Kant and the Problem of Experience," *Philosophical Topics* 34:1/2 (2006): 59–106. A somewhat weaker version of nonconceptualism ("state nonconceptualism") is attributed to Kant by Stephanie Grüne, *Blinde Anschauung: Die Rolle von Begriffen in Kants Theorie sinnlicher Synthesis* (Frankfurt am Main: Klostermann 2009).

cannot ... arise out of the combination" (B131). Equally mysterious, however, is how combination *as such* is supposed to transform the manifold into representational content, any more than tying sticks into a bundle transforms them into a sign or sentence.

Therefore, if the conceptually mediated structure of intentionality is not already present in the manifold, now taken as the manifold determinations of formal reality, it is unclear how that manifold could ever come to *appear* to a mind; and if consciousness of self arises "only insofar as I *conjoin* one representation with another" (B133), it is unclear how there could be any determinate consciousness if it did not already belong to formal reality as part of its essential structure. In light of this reflection, we can see that the *aporia* at the heart of Kant's model of the cognitive mind is really the flip side of the *aporia* at the heart of Spinoza's substance monism. Formal reality requires objective reality in order to be determinate, that is, in order to be something (*Etwas*), that is, to be anything at all.[24] Conversely, objective reality (intentionality) requires formal reality in order to be determinate and thereby to be consciousness of anything at all; and since all consciousness is consciousness *of something*, without an appropriately structured formal reality, there could be no consciousness.

This is a somewhat more elaborate way of expressing Hegel's basic insight that the absolute must be grasped not only as *substance*, but equally as *subject*. And the logic that Hegel uses to model the way substance (formal reality) and subject (objective reality, content) mutually necessitate each other, is the logic of absolute negativity.

Thus we come once again to appreciate the unique character of Hegelian idealism as it will emerge repeatedly over the course of the book. Chapter 2 will argue that Hegel broke most decisively with Kant and the pre-critical tradition by rejecting the idea that the basic forms of intelligibility and/or of being are categorial in nature. Prior to ontology is a deeper metaphysical account of negativity designed to explain *both* the emergence of a finite cognitive mind that finds itself over against a categorially structured world of finite things, *and* the specific limits finite cognition encounters in trying to render that world intelligible to itself. Ultimately, the structure of the Concept and the dynamic of absolute negation serve to integrate the two great models from which post-Kantian philosophers drew their inspiration: Spinoza's monism and Kant's idealism. They do so by supporting a

24 Cf. GW 21:99–104.

unified account of the source of determinacy in nature and intentionality, that is, by identifying a single structure that is at once the structure of being and the structure of thought.

0.2.4. Absolute negativity and the history of logic
The final chapter begins by spelling out the continuity of Hegel's
speculative logic of content with his often cited commitment to the
necessarily systematic form of philosophical truth. The larger part of
the chapter is devoted, however, to considering the place of Hegel's
notion of absolute negation in the history of logic and philosophical
theories of negation. I adopt Lawrence Horn's distinction between
symmetricalist and asymmetricalist theories of negation to argue that
Hegel occupies a unique place among them. Horn himself counts
Hegel among the asymmetricalists, that is, among those who believe
true negations ultimately presuppose and may be reducible to true
affirmative propositions or states of affairs.[25] His reasons for doing
so have to do with Hegel's concept of determinate negation. I argue
that close analysis of determinate negation proves it to depend on the
master concept of absolute negativity for its specific content and oper-
ational significance. Because absolute negativity is conceived by Hegel
as being prior to and generative of affirmation or being, Hegel cannot
be classified as an asymmetricalist in the classical sense defined by
Horn; negation neither presupposes nor is it reducible to affirmation.
For the same reason, however, neither can we understand Hegel as a
symmetricalist, that is, as someone who conceives negation and affirmation as independent and equiprimordial logical acts. I therefore suggest that we create a new category of theories about negation, namely,
negative asymmetricalism, which is distinguished from positive asymmetricalism by the claim that affirmation ultimately presupposes and
is in some sense reducible to negation. In the history of thought on
negation, therefore, Hegel is *sui generis*.

His relation to classical logic is less straightforward. Although he
himself apparently took the logic of absolute negation to ground
classical logic, I think we should rather see it as a powerful and theoretically fruitful hypothesis about the relation of thought and reality that presupposes classical logic in order to use it as a medium of

---

25 Cf. Lawrence R. Horn, *A Natural History of Negation* (Stanford: Center for the Study
   of Language and Information (CSLI) 2001 [originally University of Chicago Press
   1989]), esp. 1–5 and 45–79.

representation. On this view, dialectic and classical logic are not competing enterprises. My reasons for this view are drawn in part from consideration of an objection that could be raised against absolute negation on the basis of Henrich's classic analysis of its unique logic: absolute negation appears to be parasitical upon the logic it is supposed to ground and generate. This objection can be met, but only at the price of deflating Hegel's stronger *logical* claims for the status of absolute negativity. However, this leaves his metaphysical and methodological claims for it untouched. In somewhat the same way as Minkowski space depends on three-dimensional spatial relations for its representation, yet without for that reason compromising the scientific claim that reality consists in a four-dimensional manifold called space-time, Hegelian negativity may be said to depend on classical logic as a medium for the demonstrations carried out in accord with dialectical logic, yet without for that reason compromising the metaphysical claim that thought and reality must be conceived as structured in ways that diverge from the categorial view and its associated logical forms. The chapter concludes with a brief recapitulation of the major results of the preceding chapters, and an appreciation of the power and contemporary relevance of Hegel's core philosophical conception.

THE HEGELIAN CONCEPT,
ABSOLUTE NEGATIVITY, AND
THE TRANSFORMATION OF
PHILOSOPHICAL CRITIQUE

1.1. Introduction

This chapter introduces the figures and themes that the rest of the book will go on to develop in greater detail. It begins with the thesis that Hegel was committed to a particularly strong form of rationalism that identifies being with intelligibility, a position that had come under attack by Kant and Jacobi. Serious commitment to rationalism therefore requires its defense against this attack. I argue that Hegel mounts his defense by first accepting key points made by Kant and Jacobi: the categories of the understanding are unsuited to cognizing being as it is in itself, that is, the unconditioned, and unqualified commitment to rationalist ideals of demonstrative certainty in metaphysics leads to nihilist consequences incompatible with our human certainty of freedom, agency, and substantial individuality. Kant's response to his insight, I argue, was to hold on to the categories of the understanding as the unique and fundamental forms of intelligibility, and to deny that (finite, human) intelligibility can be legitimately identified with being as it is in itself, the unconditioned. Hegel, by contrast, holds on to the equation of being with intelligibility, but denies that the categories are truly forms of intelligibility; indeed, as the Kantian antinomies show, they reveal their irrationality as soon as they are employed in the cognition of being as it is in itself.

Jacobi, in turn, responded to his insight by holding on to mathematical forms of analysis and demonstration as the unique form of scientific rigor, while denying that the subjective certainty of freedom and agency in which science itself is grounded can ever be made the object of scientific knowledge; on pain of nihilism, there can be no self-grounding science. Hegel, by contrast, maintains the ideal of a self-grounding *speculative* science; doing so, however, entails the rejection of the geometric method as an appropriate methodological ideal in favor of a new form of *dialectical* demonstration in philosophy. Here, and analogously in the case of Kant, Hegel redefines what it means for metaphysics prior to Jacobi to have been "pre-critical": commitment to the uniqueness of the very forms that Kant and Jacobi identify with intelligibility is what characterizes metaphysics as pre-critical. So while these two threshold figures demonstrate the necessity of transforming pre-critical logic and metaphysics, their thought remains continuous with pre-critical philosophy in important respects.

This basically historical claim is paired with a systematic thesis that takes us to the center of Hegelian metaphysics and methodology: what Hegel calls "the Concept" is identical to what he calls absolute negativity, and his entire philosophy is organized around this identity. To show this, I build on Rolf-Peter Horstmann's analysis of the relational structure of the Concept and Dieter Henrich's analysis of the logic of absolute negation, in order then to argue for the original thesis that they must be conceived as static and dynamic aspects, respectively, of a single underlying reality. This unified, dynamic structure provides the conceptual resources for Hegel's transformation and rehabilitation of the rationalist tradition. The structure of the Concept allows him to reinterpret the traditional categories as partial and inadequate representations of a reality that is fundamentally non-categorial in character, while deploying the logic of absolute negation in order to supplant the classical ideal of the geometric method and to maintain its rigor while obviating its nihilist consequences. This new conception also allows Hegel to redefine philosophical critique as a critique of *finite cognition*, by which he understands a necessary phase or expression in the unfolding of the Concept (or equivalently, in the logic of absolute negativity). In this way Hegel can account both for the seemingly natural attitude towards intelligibility reflected in rationalism and for the ways in which that attitude systematically distorts reality.

The chapter concludes with this conception of the philosophical critique of finite cognition, thereby setting the stage for the chapters to come, in which that critique is fleshed out in greater detail.

1.2. Kant's and Jacobi's challenge to rationalism
and Hegel's response

"*Noûs*, thought, is the principle of the world ... the essence of the world is to be defined as thought." With this proposition, Hegel writes, Anaxagoras

> laid down the foundation for an intellectual view of the universe, the pure shape of which must be *logic*. Logic has nothing to do with a thinking that is *about* something that is supposed to exist for itself outside of thought; nor does it have to do with forms meant to provide the mere *marks* of truth; rather, the necessary forms of thinking, and its specific determinations are themselves the content and the highest truth. (GW 21:34)

If to be is to be intelligible, there can be no difference between the investigation into the fundamental structure of reality: metaphysics, and the investigation into the fundamental structure of thought: logic. Hegel is committed to a rationalist tradition in Western philosophy that stretches from Anaxagoras to Leibniz and Wolff and which teaches the unboundedness of scientific knowledge.

By the end of the eighteenth century in Germany, however, maintaining this position had become more difficult than ever before. Independently from each other, Immanuel Kant and Friedrich Heinrich Jacobi had elaborated a critique of classical rationalism that was as deep as it was influential. The *Critique of Pure Reason* (1781/87) had persuaded many of Kant's contemporaries that reason operated within strict bounds of intelligibility – bounds set by the structure of discursive reason itself – and that the price of overstepping them was the irrationality of self-contradiction. The chief casualty of this attack on rationalism was traditional metaphysics and its commitment to the knowability of the unconditioned, of being as it is in itself. "I have ... found it necessary to deny knowledge, in order to make room for faith" (Bxxx), Kant wrote in the Preface to the second edition of the *Critique*. One could say with equal accuracy that he found it necessary to deny knowledge, in order to create a reservation for intelligibility, now confined to a realm of mere appearances.

Jacobi's work *On the Doctrine of Spinoza, in Letters to Moses Mendelssohn* (1785/89), was addressed to Germany's greatest living proponent of rationalism and argued that its defining commitment to the principle of sufficient reason also entailed the denial of human freedom, a personal God, and ultimately even that of the existence of any finite beings at all: nihilism. Fichte's philosophy is the earliest systematic attempt to integrate Jacobi's critique of rationality into a positive account of reason by subordinating the theoretical faculty to practical reason, but Jacobi rejected Fichte's attempt as a form of "inverted Spinozism" whose monism of subjectivity leads to the same baleful, self-undermining consequences as the monism of substance (see FHJW II, 1:195). He therefore asserted that reason itself, if it is to be conceived as humanity's possession and not as humanity's possessor, must be grounded in a rationally unrevisable faith in the reality of one's own freedom, of a world and other minds outside oneself, and of a personal God.[1] Jacobi can therefore be understood as accepting a mitigated form of "irrationality," namely the rejection of the world-view logically entailed by the efficacious methodology of scientific rationality, in order to resist what he saw as the immeasurably more harmful irrationality of denying one's own reality as a rational moral agent in a world of one's fellows.[2] Jacobi's proverbial leap consists in just this rational resistance to an overweening, unlimited rationality, and like Kant, his doctrine is one of self-limitation in the interest of self-preservation: "Whoever does not seek to explain the inexplicable, but only to know where the limit begins and to recognize that it is there: that is who I believe will make the most room in himself for authentic human truth" (FHJW I, 1:29).

Kant and Jacobi both sought, therefore, to set limits to what philosophical rationalism had conceived as infinite intelligibility, not least in order to avoid what each saw as a specific form of irrationality that arose from ignorance of those limits. Logic could therefore no longer be conceived as basically identical with metaphysics. Kant insisted that "the proud name of an Ontology that presumptuously claims to supply, in systematic doctrinal form, synthetic *a priori* knowledge of

---

1 "Does man possess reason or does reason possess man?," is a question posed by Jacobi in the seventh supplement to the *Doctrine of Spinoza in Letters to Moses Mendelssohn*: FHJW I, 1:259.

2 The scare quotes around "irrationality" are meant to alert the reader that I am not hereby imputing any form of *irrationalism* to Jacobi. Against the view of Jacobi as a counter-Enlightenment irrationalist see Birgit Sandkaulen "'Oder hat die Vernunft den Menschen?' Zur Vernunft des Gefühls bei Jacobi," *Zeitschrift für philosophische Forschung* 49:3 (1995): 416–29, esp. 420. Also see George di Giovanni, "The Unfinished Philosophy of Friedrich Heinrich Jacobi," in *Friedrich Heinrich Jacobi: The Main Philosophical Writings and the Novel Allwill* (Montreal and Kingston: McGill-Queen's University Press 1994), esp. 43.

things in general ... must, therefore, give place to the modest title of a mere Analytic of pure understanding" (B303), that is, transcendental logic. Jacobi insisted that intuitive certainty of freedom, personality, and agency guide us in seeking to "unveil and to reveal existence": Metaphysics is the expression of "sense," whereas logic is merely an instrument for manipulating intrinsically non-rational givens.[3]

Still, both philosophers remained basically committed to an image of logic and rationality they shared with classical, "pre-critical" rationalists. For Kant, transcendental logic was fundamentally an investigation into the *categories* in which experience becomes intelligible; for Jacobi, rationality was fundamentally an explanatory endeavor guided by the *principle of sufficient reason* and a notion of *truth as tautology* (e.g. FHJW I, 1:258–59).[4] They rejected the pretensions of logic, not the traditional picture of it. It is therefore of the utmost significance when Hegel states, in a review of Jacobi's collected works written shortly after he had completed the *Science of Logic*, "It is hardly deniable that it is the shared achievement of Jacobi and Kant to have put an end to the older metaphysics, not so much in regard to its content as to its method of cognition, and thus to have shown the necessity of a completely altered view of logic" (GW 15:25).[5]

It is doubtful that Hegel intended his statement to capture the way Jacobi and Kant themselves thought of their place in the history of modern philosophy, which was to have shown the necessity of limiting the scope of logic or pure thought, not the necessity of revolutionizing its very shape. But it is also clear that if commitment to the identity of being and intelligibility, of metaphysics and logic, was to be maintained in the face of their critique, it was necessary to revise the traditional understanding of both. The *Science of Logic* is Hegel's most elaborate attempt to reaffirm the rationalist thesis not by ignoring the critique of Kant and Jacobi, but *by reinterpreting its significance.*

The flip side of every historical rupture is historical continuity, and the break with the rationalist tradition represented by the Critical

---

3 The phrase "to unveil and to reveal existence" also occurs at FHJW I, 1:29. Jacobi discusses the character and fundamental role of what he calls "Sinn" at FHJW II, 1:90. On the purely instrumental nature of logic, see FHJW I, 1:248–49, 259.

4 Jacobi's critical view of scientific truths as tautologies is presumably a response to Leibniz's "concept-containment" theory of truth.

5 Cf. Fichte's "*Sonnenklarer Bericht*," where he declares that the whole tendency of his philosophy is the same of that of Kant's (despite the latter's repudiation of the *Wissenschaftslehre*) "and the same as that of a *reformer of philosophy contemporaneous with Kant,* Jacobi ... Hence, it is the tendency of all *recent* philosophy which understands itself and knows what it wants" (GA I, 7:194; emphases added).

Philosophy and Jacobi's philosophy of faith is no exception. Kant sacrificed the traditional commitment to the knowability of the unconditioned in order to maintain the tradition's commitment to the *categorial* form of intelligibility. Jacobi sacrificed the traditional commitment to the rational demonstrability of freedom and divine personality while maintaining the tradition's commitment to the principles of identity, non-contradiction, and sufficient reason as the basic forms of intelligibility. Hegel ought to be understood as rejecting the traditional commitment to the categorial form of intelligibility and its grounding in the principles just named, in order to maintain commitment to the identity of being and thought. He therefore accepts the diagnosis of Kant and Jacobi, while rejecting their cure. He agrees that the traditional view of logic or the conception of intelligibility is indeed incompatible with insight into the unconditioned, but he sees Kant and Jacobi misplacing their conservativism with that traditional view. Being *is* intelligibility, but intelligibility is not what we thought it was – nor, for that matter, is being.

From this perspective, it is natural that Hegel would conceive of logic as identical with metaphysics since what is at stake is the identity of thought and being. It is equally clear that as the master discipline of Hegelian philosophy, the *Science of Logic* has a twofold task. On the one hand, it must re-enact the critical gesture of Kant and Jacobi, only now the point is not to show how the unconditioned – the true, as Hegel sometimes says – fails to be intelligible, but rather how the traditional categories and logical forms fail to represent intelligibility. On the other hand, the *Logic* needs to give a positive account of the unconditioned that does not fall prey to the forms of irrationality identified by Kant and Jacobi. Depending on whether one regards this twofold task from the standpoint of a Kantian or from that of Jacobi, the desiderata will need to be specified in distinct, though ultimately complementary, ways. The following two sections work out these complementary formulations and show how they are unified in a new conception of philosophical critique.

1.3. The Hegelian Concept and the transformation of the categorial structure of intelligibility

In a passage from the final volume of the *Science of Logic*, *The Doctrine of the Concept* (1816), Hegel describes the importance of Kant's and Jacobi's critique of pre-critical metaphysics:

[T]he whole style of the former metaphysics as well as its method was done away with by Kant and Jacobi. As for **the content** of that metaphysics, Kant has in his own way shown that it leads by strict demonstration to *antinomies* ... But Kant did not reflect on the nature of such demonstration itself, which is bound up with finite content; but the one must fall with the other ... While Kant attacked the former metaphysics mainly from the side of its matter, Jacobi attacked it especially from the side of its **method of demonstration** and, with great clarity and profundity, he put his finger on precisely the point at issue, namely that such a method of demonstration is strictly bound to the cycle of rigid necessity of the finite and that *freedom*, i.e. the *Concept* and with it *everything that truly is*, lies beyond it and is unattainable by it. (GW 12:229; emphases in bold added)

Depending, therefore, on whether the task of speculative logic is approached from the Kantian or the Jacobian perspective, a slightly differing formulation will result.

From the Kantian perspective, speculative logic pairs a critique of the categorial content of traditional logic and metaphysics with the positive exposition of an alternative, fundamentally non-categorial structure that explains the scope and limits of traditional categories and which Hegel calls the *Concept* or, in its fully realized form, the *Idea.* "Concept" denotes a *singulare tantum*, the unique "entity" whose various modifications and degrees of manifestation constitute the whole of reality.[6] Thus Hegel is clearly not using the term "Concept" to mean what we ordinarily mean by it, and in the *Science of Logic* he explicitly acknowledges his deviation from ordinary usage, criticizing the latter: "When we speak of the *determinate concept*, what we ordinarily mean is precisely just this abstract universal. Even by the *concept* as such, what is generally understood is only this concept void of concept [*begriffloser Begriff*], and the *understanding* is designated as its faculty" (GW 12:40).

This remark makes it obvious that Hegel considers our ordinary concepts (his examples are "human being, state, animal, etc."), to be in some sense *abstract* and divorced from what he thinks of as

---

6 The expression *singulare tantum* is from Hans Friedrich Fulda, "Hegels Dialektik als Begriffsbewegung und Darstellungsweise," in R.-P. Horstmann (ed.), *Seminar: Dialektik in der Philosophie Hegels* (Frankfurt am Main: Suhrkamp 1978), 124–74, here 129. Talk of "entities" must be taken in this context with a sizeable grain of salt. As I discuss in the next chapter, Hegel eschews pre-critical metaphysics partly just because it is concerned with *entia* rather with the self-reflexive process of the concept in which they are grounded. Thus, calling the Concept an entity is something of a malapropism.

the authentic concept of the Concept. Yet beyond specifying that a non-abstract concept would be one whose determinacy was at the same time the "*principle*" of its content-distinctions, the remark does not go very far in providing us with a notion of what the Concept is supposed to be and how it differs from ordinary concepts.[7] Indeed, he insists that the "content and determination" of the Concept "can be proven only on the basis of an immanent deduction which contains its genesis, and such a deduction lies behind us" (GW 12:16), namely, the whole *Science of Logic* itself, from whose Preface the remark is taken.

1.3.1. The science of logic as a critique of categorial thought

To gain a clearer understanding of the Hegelian Concept, we will therefore do well to consider the overall organization of the *Science of Logic*. It comprises two parts, the "Objective Logic" and the "Subjective Logic." The Objective Logic is itself subdivided into two books (the *Doctrine of Being* and of *Essence*, respectively) that treat of a list of categories corresponding roughly to those of pre-critical metaphysics and those Kant investigates in the Transcendental Analytic of the *Critique of Pure Reason*.[8] These are the categories or "thought-determinations"

---

7 See GW 21:41. The idea of a non-abstract concept being one which contains the principle of its own content-distinctions seems to be best interpreted along the lines suggested by Robert Stern. According to him, Hegel's ontology is directed against the atomist-pluralist view that objects are composed of (and hence can be reduced to) collections of distinct property-universals or predicates. Instead, Hegel is said to propose a model of genuine objects as constituting irreducible unities. According to Stern, this is because an object "is primarily an exemplification of a substance-universal (such as man, dog, or whatever)" (*Hegel, Kant, and the Structure of the Object* [London and New York: Routledge 1990], 75; cf. Stern, *Hegelian Metaphysics*, 153–58). However, the examples given by Hegel in the passage above seem to contradict Stern's view. Some qualification to that view may therefore be necessary.

8 Hegel himself explains (GW 11:31) that the content of what he calls "objective logic," i.e. the examination of the categories of Being and Essence comprising the first part of the *Logic*, corresponds pretty closely to what Kant calls *transcendental logic*, and the parallels are clearly discernible in the text: determinate being corresponds roughly to the Kantian categories of quality: reality, negation, and limitation; Kant's categories of quantity (unity, plurality, totality) are taken up in the chapter on being-for-self; under the heading "Quantity," Hegel provides a discussion parallel to Kant's axioms of intuition and anticipations of perception. In Book II of the *Logic*, the *Doctrine of Essence*, Hegel addresses the concept of reflection in general and the specific concepts of reflection: identity, difference, opposition, the inner and outer, form and content – corresponding to Kant's discussion of the Amphiboly of the Concepts of Reflection – and adds to them the concept of contradiction, which Kant treats under the heading "The highest principle of all analytic judgments."

that constitute the sphere of finite *objects*: hence the label "Objective Logic." Hegel's ordering of the categories and the thematic connections he draws between them diverge markedly from the tradition. Hegel's diverging treatment of the topics of special metaphysics (rational cosmology, psychology, and theology, albeit in altered form) should also be noted. In the Wolffian tradition, these were dealt with immediately following the treatment of the categories of general metaphysics or ontology; similarly, Kant makes them the topic of a "transcendental dialectic" following on the critical discussion of the categories in the "transcendental analytic." Hegel, by contrast, relocates them to a section of the so-called Subjective Logic or *Doctrine of the Concept*, which is otherwise devoted to what would traditionally have been considered formal and applied logic.[9]

As I have already indicated, the Objective Logic has two tasks to perform, one critical or destructive, the other constructive. The assumption which Hegel subjects to critical scrutiny is that each of the categories of traditional ontology has a distinct and independently graspable content and that each makes a notionally separable contribution to the constitution of the objects of which they can be predicated. Were each category graspable in and through itself, then it could be said to be absolute or to have a substantial content in and for itself: in Hegelian terms, it would be *true*.[10] Hegel's critical procedure is to demonstrate of each such category that, when taken in itself, it turns out to be notionally incomplete and thus bound up with other categories into which it "passes over" or in which it is "reflected."[11] To the extent that the content of each category is essentially related to that of another, on which it relies for its complete conceptual determinacy, each category of the Objective Logic may be said to be "finite," that is, to be bounded and thereby determined by a category superficially distinct from it.

While only this dialectical procedure can manifest the content-dependency and "passing over" of the objective categories, the non-

---

9 The roots of this structure go back at least as far as the so-called *Zweiter Jenaer Systementwurf* of 1804/5 (see GW 7). See the discussion in Rolf-Peter Horstmann, *Ontologie und Relationen: Hegel, Bradley, Russell und die Kontroverse über interne und externe Beziehungen* (Königstein im Taunus: Athenäum 1984), 92–97.

10 Cf. ENC §28R. My talk of *substantial content* is motivated by Spinoza's definition of substance at E1d1, as that which is in itself and can be conceived through itself.

11 Hegel identifies "passing over" (*Übergehen*) and being reflected (or "shining") in(to) another as modes of transition specific to the Logic of Being and the Logic of Essence, respectively. Cf. ENC §161/161A.

dialectical or natural attitude is to take them as semantically distinct and independent. In other words, in our ordinary conception of the categories we have already unconsciously *abstracted* from the necessity with which their content is a continual passing over, and thereby apprehended them in a purely *formal* manner. Compare for example this explanation from the *Doctrine of the Concept*:

> Qualitative determinateness [i.e. the categories of Being] and also the determinations of reflection [i.e. the categories of Essence] are essentially *limited* and have, in their limit, a relation to what is *other* than them, and hence the *necessity* of their transition and perishing. But the universality they possess in the understanding gives them the form of reflection-into-self, removing them from their relation-to-other and making them imperishable. Now although this eternality belongs to the pure Concept by nature, its abstract determinations are eternal essentialities in their *form* alone; but their content is not appropriate to this form and therefore they are not truth and imperishability … [T]he form of the limited understanding is for this reason itself imperfect universality, that is to say, *abstract* universality. (GW 12:41)

This clarifies what Hegel means, in the passage cited above, by saying that ordinary concepts, including the pure concepts of the understanding, are *abstract universals*: they are extracted from the passing over and passing away that characterizes their content. Even so, it is tempting to believe that although the categories are semantically incomplete and bound to pass away when we take them *separately*, those same categories will fare better when we view them *holistically* and take them in their totality.[12] As an interpretation of Hegel, however, this belief would be mistaken. Consider, for instance, how he envisions the *Logic* in its relation to the two *Realphilosophien* of spirit and nature that emerge from it:

---

12 Robert Brandom has given the most elaborate reading of Hegel as providing a holistic explanation of the objective validity and determinacy of (broadly) the kinds of categories investigated in the Objective Logic; see *Tales of the Mighty Dead: Historical Essays in the Metaphysics of Intentionality* (Cambridge, MA: Harvard University Press 2002), 178–209, e.g. 207: "The objective world is a holistic relational structure, determinate just insofar as it is articulated by modally robust relations of material incompatibility. Such a structure is in principle intelligible only by means of … holistic role abstraction ascending from immediacy through mediation to immediacy as expressive of purely mediated contents." In a sense, I wholly agree with this characterization of how, on Hegel's view, the objective world is constituted (modulo qualifications introduced by Hegel's "strong individuational holism," which Brandom rejects). However, I think that it is crucial for the interpretation of the historical Hegel to see (a) that

> These concrete sciences do attain to a more real form of the Idea than
> logic does, but not because they have turned back to the reality which
> consciousness abandoned as it rose above the appearance of it to sci-
> ence, or because they have again resorted to the use of such forms as
> are the categories and determinations of reflection, the finitude and
> untruth of which were demonstrated in the logic. The *Logic* rather
> exhibits the rise of the Idea up to the level from which it becomes the
> creatrice of nature. (GW 12:25)

The most natural way to read this passage is to construe it as rejecting
lock, stock, and barrel the forms of the Objective Logic: They are not,
in the final analysis, descriptive of reality and they do not provide an
adequate instrument for philosophical reflection.

Speaking once more from the Kantian perspective, then, the
intended result of the Objective Logic is the destruction of the categorial forms of finite thought and hence the demonstration that they
are not in fact the true forms of intelligibility that Kant took them to
be. The result is important in that it necessitates a *transformation of
the content* of traditional logic-cum-ontology. Or rather, to the extent
that ontology is actually defined as an investigation into the most
general *categories* or predicates of things, the result necessitates that
ontology itself be rejected as a discipline capable of limning the true
structure of reality.[13] But if this is the critical result, what is the aim

---

rearticulation of the determinations of the objective world in these holistic terms
changes their meaning to a significant degree: they become "moments in the unfolding of the Concept"; and (b) that the objective world as such in fact *is not fully determinate,* but metaphysically incomplete. I argue for this interpretation in Chapter 3.

13 Cf., e.g., Alexander Gottlieb Baumgarten, *Metaphysica,* 7th edn. (Magdeburg:
Hemmerde 1779), §4(2): "*Ontologia ... est scientia praedicatorum entis generaliorum.*"
I take Fulda to be expressing this insight when he describes Hegel's philosophy as
"metaphysics without ontology." Accordingly, I agree with de Boer when she states
that "Kant's critique of former ontology by no means implies that he abandoned
the investigation of those concepts that determine the ways in which something
can become an object at all. I will use the term "ontology" to refer to the mode of
philosophy that is concerned with such concepts" (*On Hegel,* 36–37). I disagree, however, with her view that "former general metaphysics, Kant's transcendental analytic,
and Hegel's objective logic constitute three different modes of ontology. Each in its
own way investigates the ontological perspectives that ground our actual knowledge
of objects, regardless of whether they are used to determine empirical representations, ideas of reason, or reality as such." Though very different in its motivations
and orientation, and despite the fact that Hegel's speculative idealism itself belongs
to the history of ontology Heidegger seeks to destroy (see *Sein und Zeit* [Tübingen:
Max Niemeyer 2001], §6, 19–27.), there is a sense in which Hegel intends a destruction of ontology every bit as radical as Heidegger's and just as little concerned with

of the constructive task of the Objective Logic? We have seen what it means for ordinary concepts to be *abstract*, but what does it mean for the Concept to be *concrete*?

1.3.2. Horstmann's analysis of the Hegelian Concept as a relation of relations

There is no way to answer the question just posed that does not lead directly to the core of Hegel's system. In *Ontologie und Relationen* (1984), Rolf-Peter Horstmann has provided an illuminating analysis of Hegelian metaphysics as a *relationslogischer Monismus der Subjektivität* whose center is formed by the Hegelian *Concept*.[14] The unique character of the Concept lies in its being constituted wholly by *relations* which themselves are metaphysically prior to any relata that might appear to realize those relations. This can best be understood by starting with the case of self-consciousness, which Hegel himself identifies as "the Concept when it has progressed to a concrete existence which is itself free" (GW 12:17). It was pointed out in the Introduction that Kantian apperception or self-conscious spontaneity depends essentially on there being some given sensible manifold that it can combine (see B133). Another way of saying the same thing is that for Kant, the relation-to-self that constitutes the "highest point" (B134n.) of transcendental philosophy is mediated by a relation-to-other. Two relata are essentially involved such that the first is itself a relation (self-consciousness) and the second some given term (the sensible manifold) to which the first term must be related in order to relate to itself and thereby constitute the self-relation it essentially is. Recall, though, that the manifold qua *sensible* is itself defined by way of its *relation* to (self)consciousness. So what we have is a complex structure whose elements are defined in purely relational terms such that the whole structure is itself a relation.

This "Kantian" picture of the structure is not yet the whole picture of the Hegelian Concept. Hegel introduces a further relational element into the Concept: the term represented above by the sensible manifold is to be understood as itself constituted by a relation that is homomorphic to the relation represented by self-consciousness. So if self-consciousness (relation-to-self) is essentially mediated by a term

---

vindicating the self-(mis)-interpretation that reason gives itself in the form of the understanding with its categorial outlook.

14 See Horstmann, *Ontologie und Relationen*, e.g. 104. The following account follows 90–92.

that is external to it (relation-to-other), that "other" is itself mediated by its relation to self-consciousness and hence it is *relational in itself.* We therefore arrive at a picture in which an overarching relation (call it R) obtains between two relata (r_1, r_2), while r_1 and r_2 mirror both each other and the overarching relation to which they belong. To retranslate this into a basically Kantian framework, (*finite*) self-consciousness is a relation-to-self that is distinct but inseparable from the relation-to-other that characterizes object-consciousness; however, the object of consciousness – the other of self-consciousness – is neither an unstructured manifold nor an unstructured unity (thing-in-itself). Rather, that other must also be interpreted as constituting a relation: namely, a relation to itself that is also essentially mediated by the relation-to-self (i.e. self-consciousness) that it stands in relation to. Therefore, call r_1 *finite self-consciousness* and r_2 *nature.* The Hegelian Concept is identical to the overarching relation R that is metaphysically prior to finite self-consciousness and nature, that is, the relation that constitutes them in the first place. When that relation R is made fully explicit, it constitutes what Hegel calls the *Idea* and what we may characterize in contrast with finite self-consciousness as *infinite self-consciousness* or absolute knowing.[15] To the extent that the Concept is all reality, therefore, reality itself is structured like knowledge.

The structure of the Concept is thus what underlies Hegel's provocative remark that the *content* of the *Science of Logic* is the "exposition of God as he is in his eternal essence before the creation of nature and of a finite spirit" (GW 21:34). It also distinguishes him from Kant and Fichte, who had no room for a philosophy of nature *in independence from the forms of self-conscious cognition*; the structure of the Concept can explicitly accommodate an essentially Schellingian philosophy of nature seeking to derive the relation-to-self that is self-consciousness from an initially unconscious realm of physics. Most importantly in the present context, however, the non-explicit Concept or the Concept as it is outside its full realization in the Idea, represents the *true* content of the finite thought-determinations whose critical destruction is carried out in the Objective Logic. The *Logic*'s constructive task is to transform the abstract determinations of finite thought into concrete determinations of the Concept.

---

15 Hegel identifies the Idea with the realized Concept at ENC §242, for instance.

1.3.3. The role of the Hegelian Concept in constructing a positively
determinate absolute

To begin to flesh out this highly schematic statement, let's first
recall what is *wrong* with the categories or so-called *finite* thought-
determinations. Their finitude and untruth was said to consist in the
fact that, although they display the form of independently determinate identity and hence an *absolute* character (which Hegel explicates
as *relation-to-self*), in fact they have their determinate content only via
their *relation-to-other*, into which other they therefore pass over and
pass away. So finitude is here glossed as relation-to-other, while infinitude and eternality are to be understood as relation-to-self. Thus it
would seem that what distinguishes the Concept from the merely finite
thought-determinations is its instantiation of pure relation-to-self or,
as Hegel also calls it, the relation of infinity (since not to be related to
any term other than itself is not to be bounded by any other term and
hence to be non-finite). And in fact, the absoluteness of the Concept
needs to be understood in just this quite traditional way.

However, the problem facing Hegel is that he is also committed to
the principle (somewhat misleadingly attributed to Spinoza) that all
determination is essentially negation: *omnis determinatio est negatio*.[16]
Since negation is an essentially relational operation, to be determinate is to stand in a relation-to-other. As a consequence, to conceive
the absolute exclusively as relation-to-self is to define it as completely
indeterminate – as lacking all determinations and hence unknowable
in the sense that beyond the sheer fact of its indeterminacy, it possesses no determinate content that could be content for knowledge.
Readers familiar with Hegel will recognize in this logical construct
the category of pure being, determined merely as wholly indeterminate, with which the *Logic* opens. The positive task of the *Logic*, therefore, is to demonstrate that pure being (substance) is in truth *infinite*
self-consciousness (the realized Concept: the Idea). By this standard
the *Logic* would fail if the exclusive determination of the Idea qua

---

16 Cf. GW 21:101; ENC §91A; see also TW 20:164–65. The attribution of this principle
to Spinoza is due to Jacobi: see FHJW 1, 1:100. Jacobi takes the formula out of context, promoting it to a systematic status it may not in fact have. Whether it may be
described as a general metaphysical principle to which Spinoza actually subscribed
appears doubtful when we consider that the proposition occurs only once in his published works, in a letter, in discussion of a very specific point regarding the nature
of geometrical figures: see Spinoza's Letter 50 (to Jelles, June 2, 1674), in Baruch
de Spinoza, *Complete Works*, ed. M. L. Morgan, trans. S. Shirley (Indianapolis, IN:
Hackett 2002), 892.

realized Concept were relation-to-self. In other words, determinateness and hence relation-to-other have to be integrated into the infinite self-relation of the Concept, a logical property Hegel calls *absolute* or *infinite determinateness*.[17]

Therefore, the success of Hegel's endeavor depends on his being able to interpret determinacy (= relation-to-other) as an internal aspect or moment of absoluteness (= relation-to-self). It does not, however, indicate how it might be possible for him to do so. This is where the relational structure of the Concept comes in.

To begin to see how the Concept provides a solution to Hegel's problem, consider this example of a typical exposition of finite thought-determinations: Hegel's discussion of identity, difference, and ground at the beginning of the *Doctrine of Essence*. There Hegel introduces the concept of *identity* as mediated relation-to-self. He then reminds the reader that the whole sphere of essence is characterized as the negation of being (which was the thematic complex of the preceding book of the *Logic*, *The Doctrine of Being*). Thus, the self-relation constitutive of identity must be construed as a negative relation-to-self: "its repelling of itself from itself" (ENC §116). Consequently, identity qua negative self-relation is inseparable from a relation-to-other that is internal to it. This moment of otherness constitutes *difference*. A series of reflections on the nature of difference follows: As mere diversity or manifold, the others are isolated, unrelated terms that are "indifferent" to their difference; in other words, their difference falls outside of them and is thereby the first full realization of difference as exteriority. The exteriority of the difference, that is, the fact that the difference *is* exterior, now represents the *sameness* (*Gleichheit*) of the individual others that make up the manifold. At the same time, however, the very fact that the individual others manifest this exteriority in themselves represents their *unlikeness* (see ENC §117). Hegel therefore observes: "Likeness [*Gleichheit*] is an identity only of such as are *not the same*, not identical with one another, and unlikeness is a *relation* of what is not alike" (ENC §117); and since relation entails some respect in which the relata are the same, their unlikeness entails their sameness. Hegel calls this coincidence of sameness and non-sameness "*determinate* difference" (ENC §118), and very quickly identifies it with the category of *ground*, that is, "the unity of identity and difference"

---

17 Cf. GW 11:248, 256–57; 12:16; see also GW 21:235, 310–11.

(ENC §121).[18] *Ground* is therefore found to be "the truth of what the difference and the identity have turned out to be" (ENC §121).

The point of this example is to illustrate how Hegel critically reinterprets finite thought-determinations by mapping them onto the component relations of the Concept. Identity proves to correspond to relation-to-self, difference to relation-to-other. Yet identity is relation-to-self only by virtue of a relation-to-other that it includes and by which it is essentially mediated. On the other side, however, difference (i.e. the *external* or *exterior* term required for the relation-to-other on which identity depends) turns out to be an explication of the very same relational complex that identity is. These two relations are therefore reinterpreted, from one perspective, as *moments* within a higher determination ("ground") that is constituted by their relation to each other; from a different perspective, ground is reinterpreted as a more fundamental relational structure (what he calls "the *truth*" of identity and difference), of which the opposite guises of relation-to-self (identity) and relation-to-other (difference) are merely *appearances*. In this way, the finite thought-determinations *identity*, *difference*, and *ground* are shown to have no proper content of their own. They are strictly speaking only different aspects of or perspectives on a single, complex relational structure.

Now, in the immediate context in which Hegel carries out this analysis, the resulting total structure itself may be characterized as *ground*. We should remind ourselves, however, that from the broader perspective of the *Logic* as a whole, ground is identified as such purely by virtue of its determinate place within a sequence of determinations that begins with the triad *being – nothing – becoming* and ends with the fully self-explicit triad *immediacy – mediation – sublation of mediation* (equivalently: *relation-to-self – relation-to-other – relation-to-other-as-relation-to-self*) that is the absolute Idea. In other words, the very content of the thought-determination "ground" is defined in a purely relational manner as one in the sequence of iterations of the same triadic structure of the Concept. Each such iteration may be referred to as a *determination of the Concept*; and in this way, the *finite thought-determination*s are reinterpreted as *moments* in the increasingly rich *Concept-determinations*.

18 Since this development is intended to serve as an illustration for a more general point, here is not the place to go into all the intermediate steps. However, it is helpful to note that the definition of "ground" as a unity of identity and non-identity becomes a commonplace in German Idealist thought after Fichte: cf. GA I, 2: esp. 272–74. But the general idea can be found in Spinoza: see E1p3, for instance

Herein lies the positive or constructive side of the Objective Logic: the *destruction* of the finite thought-determinations coincides with their *reduction* to the uniquely instantiated relational complex called the Concept. As I warned above, it is tempting to view this positive dimension of the Objective Logic as vindicating the categories of traditional ontology *rightly understood*, namely as determinations of the Concept. But this view would be mistaken. In reducing the categories of *metaphysica generalis* to determinations of the Concept, and thus reformulating their content in terms of a structure that they either fail entirely to exhibit in their ordinary employment or at best succeed in exhibiting only in an inadequate way, Hegel is effectively transforming the ordinary meaning of those categories and hence making them into concepts different from those as which they started out.[19]

A remark from the Preface to the *Science of Logic* sheds light on this fact. Hegel writes:

> The divisions and headings of the books, the sections and chapters given in this work, as well as the explanations associated with them, are made for the purposes of a preliminary overview, and ... strictly speaking they are of only *historical* value. They do not belong to the content and body of the science but are rather compilations of an external reflection which has already gone through the whole of the exposition, therefore knows the sequence of its moments in advance and anticipates them before their emergence from the matter itself [*Sache selbst*].[20]

Considering that the books, sections, and chapters of the *Logic* are oriented toward the traditional *titles* given to the various categories and forms of thought, it is fair to interpret Hegel as saying that, *in principle*, we could dispense with such terms and hence with any reference at all to the traditional content associated with those terms, and instead grasp the content of the *Logic* purely as a tightly ordered sequence of iterations of the basic structure of the Concept.

Hegel's early American commentator William Torrey Harris seems to have recognized this revolutionary aspect of Hegel's *Logic*. In defending Hegel against Trendelenburg's influential objection that Hegel is forced, against his express declaration, to draw on experience even in order to enter into his speculative logic,[21] Harris makes the

---

19 I examine the *skeptical* significance of Hegel's procedures in Chapters 3 and 4.
20 GW 21:39.
21 The main charge that Friedrich Adolf Trendelenburg brings against Hegel, and the one that recurs throughout his detailed criticism of Hegel's logic, is that the

following observation about Hegel's use of traditional logical names such as being, nothing, quality, quantity, and so forth:

> This naming proves that Hegel understands his logic to have two parallel lines of thought. One reflects upon the pure thought and discerns the determination implicit in being: the second line of thought compares this new determination with experience and discovers its identity with some category already used and named. Deriving thus the names of his dialectically discovered categories he shows the practical application of his logic to clearing up the problems of experience. Thus there is a line of *a priori* thinking and a line of *a posteriori* thinking combined in one, in the logic.[22]

Our path has thus brought us to an initial answer to the question how Hegelian metaphysics must be structured if it is to serve as a proof and vindication of Anaxagoras' dictum that "*Noûs*, thought, is the principle of the world," that is, as a demonstration that "the necessary forms of thinking, and its specific determinations, are themselves the content and the highest truth" (GW 21:34). Hegel's system is a monistic metaphysics of subjectivity according to which the authentic forms of being and intelligibility are not the categories of traditional ontology, but the complex relations constitutive of the Concept.

1.4. The logic of absolute negativity and the transformation of the demonstrative ideal

The previous section set out to examine the way Hegel's speculative logic is able to pair a critique of the categorial content of traditional logic and metaphysics with the positive exposition of an alternative, fundamentally non-categorial structure that explains the scope and limits of traditional categories. The starting point for this examination was the

---

speculative dialectic surreptitiously relies on ordinary experience (e.g. of locomotion, of real opposition between empirical objects, etc.) in order to perform its putatively *a priori* operations and to concatenate its allegedly pure terms. For Trendelenburg's own compact restatement of his criticisms see *Die logische Frage in Hegels System: Zwei Streitschriften* (Leipzig: Brockhaus 1843), 12–19. As will become clear from my discussion of absolute negativity below, I think Trendelenburg is *in principle* mistaken when he explains Hegelian negation as a product of abstracting from real opposition (15–16); absolute negation is a genuinely *a priori* construction – this much has to be said for it. Trendelenburg may be right, however, that Hegel's *deployment* of negation is not always free of empirical admixture.

22 William Torrey Harris, *Hegel's Logic: A Book on the Genesis of the Categories of the Mind. A Critical Exposition* (Chicago: S. C. Griggs 1890), 132.

observation that, *from a Kantian perspective*, a "completely altered view of logic" means replacing the traditional orientation toward *categories* as the ultimate forms of intelligibility with an account that is deeper than categoriality and hence immune to the forms of irrationality that arise from the categories when we try to grasp the unconditioned by their means. It was also emphasized, however, that the *Logic's* twofold task will take a distinct, though compatible, formulation when we approach it *from the Jacobian perspective*. That formulation is the topic of this section.

1.4.1. Jacobi's critique of "Spinozism" and its legacy in Fichte and Hegel

Recall that whereas Kant directed his critique chiefly toward the *content* of pre-critical metaphysics, Jacobi is said to have "attacked it especially from the side of its method of demonstration" (GW 12:229), more specifically: its commitment to mathematical models of analysis and proof. Jacobi's critique of rationalist metaphysics is sufficiently multifaceted to resist being easily summarized, but since I will return to its details several times over the course of this book (particularly in Chapters 2 and 5), I will try for the moment to restate the position as compactly as possible.[23] Jacobi believes that metaphysical commitment to the principle of sufficient reason and methodological commitment to the ideal of mathematical rigor (epitomized for him in the system of Spinoza) leads to a number of consequences that are unacceptable in themselves and mutually inconsistent when taken together. Most obviously, commitment to the thesis that nothing is excepted from the principle of sufficient reason leads to hard determinism and the denial of freedom; but Jacobi also believes he can show that it leads to the conclusion that the supreme being itself (Spinoza's God) must be a temporal rather than a strictly eternal entity, which he finds to be both irreconcilable with a right understanding of God and inconsistent with Spinoza's own statements regarding the eternality of substance.[24]

23 For a comprehensive reconstruction of Jacobi's critique of the rationalist conception of rationality, see Birgit Sandkaulen, *Grund und Ursache: die Vernunftkritik Jacobis* (Munich: Fink 1999); also see "System und Systemkritik: Überlegungen zur gegenwärtigen Bedeutung eines fundamentalen Problemzusammenhangs," in Sandkaulen (ed.), *System und Systemkritik: Beiträge zu einem Grundproblem der klassischen deutschen Philosophie* (Würzburg: Königshausen und Neumann 2006), 11–34.

24 The *locus classicus* for Jacobi's charge of determinism is at FHJW I, 1:123: "Every path of demonstration ends in fatalism." On the temporality of God, see FHJW I, 1:93–98, 251–54. Spinoza specifies that God is eternal in the sense of strict atemporality (rather than omnitemporality) in E1d8 and in Letter 12 (to Meyer, April 20, 1663), in *Complete Works*, 787–91.

Furthermore, he believes that commitment to the ideal of mathematical rigor, when pushed to full generality, leads to a kind of formalism that denies substantiality to the objects of experience (FHJW I, 1:99–100; II, 1:61, 201). Mathematical analysis reduces *things* to pure *relations*, such that their identity is no longer conceived as rooted in intrinsic or essential properties of the things, but solely in the differences that characterize their relations to other things: *omnis determinatio est negatio*, that is, individuality "does not pertain to the thing in regard to its being; on the contrary, it is its non-being."[25] Jacobi infers from this that individual things, "insofar as they exist only in a determinate manner, are *non-entia*; and the indeterminate, infinite being is the only true *ens reale*" (FHJW I, 1:100). This conclusion he finds to be irreconcilable with our experience of ourselves as fully real, substantial beings. However, it is equally incompatible with Spinoza's own understanding of substance as infinite being. For since (on Jacobi's reading) the infinite being in no way transcends or is really distinct from the finite things that are its *modes*, neither can substance be considered to have any intrinsic, substantial determinateness of its own. Hence substance itself disappears into utter indeterminacy and thus, effectively, into nothingness.[26]

Jacobi himself located the source of these unacceptable consequences in a conflation that he held to be constitutive of rationalist metaphysics, namely the failure to distinguish between the relation of ground and consequent, which is one of logical necessitation, and the relation of cause and effect, which is rooted in action; and since the relation of cause and effect is graspable independently of the concept of logical necessitation, it is also compatible with freedom, divine as well as human (FHJW I, 1:255–56; cf. FHJW II, 1:53).[27] Yet while the major proponents of post-Kantian philosophy seem to have followed Jacobi's critique of rationalism-cum-Spinozism, they did not wholly embrace his conceptual alternative. It is a hallmark of all the systems produced by German Idealists that they conjoin a derivation of basic

---

25 Spinoza, Letter 50 (to Jelles, June 2, 1674), in *Complete Works*, 892; cited by Jacobi: FHJW I, 1:100.

26 Cf. Franks, *All or Nothing*, 170–74.

27 Cf. Sandkaulen, *Grund und Ursache*, 171–228; Sandkaulen returns to the link between action and personhood in "Das, Was oder Wer? Jacobi im Diskurs über Personen," in W. Jaeschke and B. Sandkaulen (eds.), *Friedrich Heinrich Jacobi: Ein Wendepunkt der geistigen Bildung der Zeit* (Hamburg: Meiner 2004), 217–37, esp. 227–34. Prominent instances of the failure to distinguish between the relation of ground-consequent and that of cause-effect can be found in Spinoza, E1p3, and in Wolff, Dt. Log. §29.

categories and cognitive faculties (including those constitutive of agency) with the attempt to "refute" or at least to "overcome" Spinoza. Arguably, Karl Leonhard Reinhold's *Letters on the Kantian Philosophy* were instrumental in introducing this characteristic feature into the post-Kantian discussion as it was soon to develop in Jena, for it was there that Kant's theoretical philosophy was first "injected" into the Spinoza-dispute begun by Jacobi.[28] However, its first canonical expression is to be found in Fichte's *Grundlage der gesammten Wissenschaftslehre* (1794). In its most compressed formulation, the early *Wissenschaftslehre* seeks to demonstrate that the self-conscious I is sufficient and necessary for a complete derivation of the categorial structures of objective world. In deriving a complete account of the cognitive faculties and their associated categories on the basis of an absolute I that both posits itself and exists for itself (i.e. is conscious of itself), Fichte can claim to have shown the I to be a sufficient condition. However, he claims to show by the same token that it is also a necessary fundamental condition in the sense that it is impossible to derive self-conscious experience from any putatively higher, non-self-conscious source. To the extent that Fichte identifies philosophy of Spinoza as the paradigmatic attempt to go beyond self-consciousness to a fundamentally non-subjective substance, the *Wissenschaftslehre* represents a refutation of Spinozism – or at least a demonstration of its "groundlessness" (GA I, 1:264, 280–81).

Hegel's relationship to Spinoza is more complicated than Fichte's owing to his commitment to a ground of reality higher than finite subjectivity and the related commitment to speculative philosophy of nature he shared with Schelling. With this important qualification, however, we may view the *Science of Logic* as pursuing much the same goal as the early *Wissenschaftslehre*, albeit with the further difference that the *Logic* is not concerned with deriving cognitive faculties and mental operations.[29] The very architecture of the *Logic* reflects

---

28 For a general account see Frederick Beiser, *The Fate of Reason: German Philosophy from Kant to Fichte* (Cambridge, MA: Harvard University Press 1987), 44–108. Also see Karl Ameriks, *Kant and the Fate of Autonomy: Problems in the Appropriation of the Critical Philosophy* (Cambridge University Press 2000), 134–35; George di Giovanni, "The First Twenty Years of Critique: The Spinoza Connection," in Paul Guyer (ed.), *The Cambridge Companion to Kant* (Cambridge University Press 1992), 417–48; see also di Giovanni's remarks in his "Editor's Presentation" to the volume *Karl Leonhard Reinhold and the Enlightenment* (Dordrecht, Heidelberg, etc.: Springer 2010), 1–12; the metaphor of "injecting" Kant into the Spinoza debate is taken from here.

29 Cf. ENC §193. Houlgate (*The Opening of Hegel's Logic*, 139) makes the same point.

this goal of overcoming Spinoza. Consider the terms in which Hegel frames the Subjective Logic in its introductory section, *On the Concept in General*:

> The Concept is the *truth* of substance, and since *necessity* is the determining relational mode of substance, *freedom* reveals itself to be the *truth of necessity* and the *relational mode of the concept* ... The transition of the relation of substantiality [to subjectivity] occurs through its own immanent necessity and is nothing more than the manifestation of [substance] itself, that the Concept is its truth and freedom is the truth of necessity ... The exposition in the preceding book [i.e. the *Doctrine of Essence*] as leading to the Concept is, therefore, the only refutation and the true refutation of Spinozism.[30]

When we look back over the objective logic from the vantage point of this transition from the substance (the Objective Logic) to subject (the Subjective Logic), we can recognize how Jacobi's interpretation of Spinoza is present at crucial junctures of the exposition. The discussion of pure being at the opening of the *Logic* makes repeated reference to Spinozist substance; in Determinate Being, the concept of reality is accompanied by an elucidation of Spinoza's principle *omnis determinatio est negatio* and its significance for monism; in the scholium to the category of the infinite, Hegel presents his treatment as a solution to the problem, which Jacobi posed as a challenge to Spinoza, of how the infinite becomes finite; in the section on quantity, he credits Spinoza with having formulated the concept of the true infinite; he introduces his exposition of measure with a reference to Spinoza's attributes and to pantheism more generally; and he concludes the Logic of Being with the category of absolute indifference, which he identifies as "the determination of Spinozist substance," and which initiates the transition from Being to Essence.[31] And as noted, the *Doctrine of Essence* culminates with a further exposition of Spinozist substance and the transition to subjectivity.

In turn, the pivotal second section of the *Doctrine of the Concept*, "Objectivity," moves from a view of the world-whole as mechanically determined, to a vindication of natural teleology. It opens onto section

---

30 GW 12:12, 14, 15. Thus when Hegel turns to discussion of Kantian apperception a few pages later, that discussion is already situated in the framework of another project, the refutation of Spinozism.

31 See GW 21:99–101, 140–41, 380; the problem of the transition from the infinite to the finite is raised by Jacobi and taken up by Mendelssohn: see FHJW I, 1:93–95, 171–72.

three, "The Idea," with an exposition of the Idea of Life: organic life as the immediate manifestation of the same self-relating structure or activity exhibited by cognition and, in the highest degree, by the absolute Idea itself. The main lines of the *Science of Logic* thus very naturally place it in the lineage of attempts to overcome Spinozism from within, accepting its monism and its claim to rigorous demonstration while transforming its undesirable conception of the absolute as a nexus of mechanical determinism.

For that very reason, however, we must ask how it is that Hegel believes he can match or even exceed the rigor of the geometric method without committing himself to the consequences that moved Jacobi to reject the methodology of rationalism *in toto*.[32] When I examine the details of Hegel's alternative critique of the ideal of geometric rigor in Chapter 5, it will become obvious that his views on the nature of geometric demonstration dovetail with the structure of the Hegelian Concept. In anticipation of that later discussion, here is the place to introduce the basic template of Hegelian logic, *the logic of absolute negativity*. As I now would like to show, absolute negation is both the logical figure that grounds the peculiar rigor of Hegelian demonstrations and the generative dynamic that gives rise to the structure of the Concept analyzed above.

1.4.2. Henrich's analysis of autonomous negation and its identity with the Concept

In this section I will appeal to Dieter Henrich's canonical reconstruction of Hegel's concept of negation in order to show that negativity and the Concept are identical, or rather that they are two sides of a single metaphysical conception considered in its *structural* aspect (the Concept) and then in its *dynamic* or *processual* aspect (negativity). The

32 See, e.g., Hegel's characterization of "plasticity" at GW 21:18. Catherine Malabou (*The Future of Hegel: Plasticity, Temporality, and Dialectic* [New York: Routledge 2005]) has recently made the concept of plasticity central to the interpretation of Hegel's philosophy, suggesting that it plays a key role in assessing his relevance to contemporary thought. Malabou appears not to quote the passage just cited, however, and does not view plasticity as an ideal that is intimately linked to Hegel's understanding of *mathematical rigor*. I will later suggest that Hegel's methodological ideal is characterized by a form of immanence foreign to geometrical demonstration and more akin to the phenomena of biological self-organization investigated by Evan Thompson (see *Mind in Life: Biology, Phenomenology, and the Sciences of Mind* [Cambridge, MA: Harvard University Press 2007], e.g. 180). If this is right, then my understanding of plasticity coincides with Malabou's in crucial points, who points to organic phenomena in order to illustrate the meaning of plasticity.

fundamental significance of negation in the philosophy of Hegel is unmistakable and it has indeed long been recognized. Hegel himself draws attention to its fundamental importance in numerous passages.[33] Few would therefore disagree with Dieter Henrich when he writes, "Coming to terms with the way Hegel's logic makes use of negation is the precondition for achieving an independent relationship to his theory – be it in emulation or critique."[34] However, it was Henrich himself who, in a series of related articles published between 1970 and 1978, first provided an analysis of the Hegelian concept of negation that was able both to demonstrate its peculiar logical cohesion and to reconstruct in great detail Hegel's methodical deployment of it.[35]

33 The most famous passage is GW 9:27–28/§32, where Hegel evokes the *ungeheure Macht des Negativen* – the "terrific power of the negative." But his remark at GW 15:10 is no less revealing, where he claims that in order to grasp "the internal principle of separation in substance itself" – i.e. in order refute Spinozistic substance monism and to think substance as subject – "everything depends on a correct understanding of the status and significance of negativity."

34 Dieter Henrich, "Hegels Grundoperation," in U. Guzzoni, B. Rang, and L. Siep (eds.), *Der Idealismus und seine Gegenwart. Festschrift für Werner Marx* (Hamburg: Felix Meiner 1976), 208–30, here 245.

35 Henrich initially developed his analysis of Hegelian negation in "Hegels Logik der Reflexion," in *Hegel im Kontext* (Frankfurt: Suhrkamp 1970), 95–157, and in the expanded version of the same title in *Hegel-Studien* Beiheft 18 (1978): 204–324. "Formen der Negation in Hegels Logik," (*Hegel-Jahrbuch* 1974, 245–56), and "Hegels Grundoperation" (see the preceeding footnote) offer condensed accounts of the basic results. For a competing analysis of Hegelian reflection, see Andreas Arndt, *Dialektik und Reflexion: Zur Rekonstruktion des Vernunftbegriffs* (Hamburg: Meiner 1994), 194–219. De Boer rejects Henrich's approach on the grounds that, contrary to his assumptions, "Hegel does not derive his conception of absolute negativity from a mode of negation proper to statements, but rather attempts to interpret concepts such as "not", "nothing", and "double negation" as inadequately manifesting the principle of absolute negativity" (*On Hegel*, 222, n. 1). But according to what standard does de Boer measure the degree of adequacy to which a concept manifests the principle of absolute negativity? One standard she recognizes is the degree to which a concept succeeds in incorporating its contrary determinations (see, e.g., 54). But why should precisely this be the standard? She goes on to say that this criterion determines the division of the *Logic* into the Doctrines of Being, Essence, and the Concept, respectively, which represent different "modes of negativity" (54). This is correct, but de Boer gives no account of why Hegel should embrace this criterion, or why we should think of negativity as a unity that presents itself in different "modes," or how those modes should be understood in relation to (and as *transformable into*) each other. The same is true of the remark that "absolute negativity [is] proper to the concept as such. Yet all finite concepts must submit to the absolute negativity that constitutes the element of Hegel's method" (72). Why is it proper to the Concept "as such"? And what defines a "finite concept" in contradistinction to *the* Concept? And why should a finite concept have to "submit" to absolute negativity? De Boer does not address these questions. By dismissing Henrich's approach on the grounds that he associates

Henrich's basic insight is encapsulated in the term "autonomous negation." The specifically Hegelian concept of negation is born at the moment when Hegel both radically separates it off from its native function in the logic of terms and propositions, and ceases to view it as fundamentally standing in complementary correlation to affirmation. In Henrich's phrase, Hegel "autonomizes" negation and makes it to serve as the unique basic term from which to derive all other logical determinations and indeed his whole system.[36] At the same time, though, Hegel does adapt several classical rules governing negation, in particular these three: (1) negation negates *something*; (2) negation can be applied to itself; and (3) self-referential use of negation has an affirmative result. The first rule obviously respects the classical understanding of negation as a unary logical operator, while the second two parallel the classical law of double negation. As will soon become evident, the behavior of autonomous negation only parallels that of double negation; its behavior is by no means an expression of the classical law, as similar as it may appear on the surface.[37]

With these three rules in place, a unique logic of negation unfolds. Given rule (1) together with the assumption of an originary negation wholly free of relations to distinct, external terms, we are forced to think of negation as *negating itself* (since it must negate something) – a move licensed by rule (2). As negation of itself, it furthermore stands in an original *relation to itself*. As Henrich points out, here we already see the fundamental deviation of rule (2) from classical double negation, as the latter is not self-referential: double negation classically understood involves, first, the negation of some term or proposition, and second, a negation of that negated term or proposition. The object of the first negation is therefore distinct from the object of the second negation. This is not the case with self-referential negation, and as a

Hegel's notion of negation with propositions, she neglects an important resource in explaining how absolute negativity can fulfill its manifold functions while nevertheless *demonstrably* constituting a single, unified dynamic.

36 See Henrich, "Hegels Grundoperation," 214. My discussion will closely follow and sometimes paraphrase the account in "Hegels Grundoperation," but only explicit quotations will be indicated in the notes. To my knowledge, Henrich's text is not available in English, but see Dieter Henrich, *Between Kant and Hegel: Lectures on German Idealism*, ed. D. S. Pacini (Cambridge, MA: Harvard University Press 2003), 316–33.

37 This difference is to be insisted on despite Hegel's remark (which, significantly, is a *hapax legomenon*) at TW 20:171 that "the affirmative is thus negation of negation; *duplex negatio affirmat*, according to the familiar grammatical rule."

consequence self-referential negation is not iterative, whereas double negation allows for an indefinite iteration of the negator.

Given this point of departure, two paradoxical results emerge at once. The first is this. On the one hand, since the (so to speak) *two* negations are the expression of a self-relation, it follows by definition that they are identical. The immediate product of autonomous negation is identity. (Thus here and in the next step we see the significance of rule [3].) On the other hand, the negation of negation presupposes that a difference must already have arisen between negation as self-negating and negation as what is negated. Autonomous negation therefore immediately gives rise to difference. Autonomous negation is at once both identity and difference.

The second paradox issues with equal directness. Since autonomous negation is the negation *of negation*, its immediate result is the vanishing of negation. The absence of negation is affirmation or simple being. Therefore autonomous negation is (disappears into) affirmation. (Here we see once more the presence of rule [3].)

As Henrich notes, Hegel need not be troubled by this result. What would seem to be simply the end of autonomous negation, namely its vanishing into absolute affirmation or *immediacy*, reveals itself upon reflection to be the renewed positing of autonomous negation: affirmation is itself the result of autonomous negation and thus the two terms stand to each other in a relation of difference or *mediation*. The overlapping notions of affirmation, immediacy, and being may thus be seen to arise as the expression of the identity or *relation-to-self* of autonomous negation, while at the very same moment it must be recognized as the expression of the difference or *relation-to-other* that is equally constitutive of autonomous negation. In this way a relation of synonymy is established at the very basis of Hegel's thinking between identity, immediacy, relation-to-self, and being on the one side, and between difference, mediation, relation-to-other, and negativity on the other. This fact is of the utmost importance for grasping Hegelian modes of argument in their specific rigor.

However, these steps are not yet sufficient to complete the concept of autonomous negation. For at this point a difficulty arises which, unlike the initial paradox, does need to trouble Hegel since it cannot be solved just by continued reflective analysis of what is posited in the concept of autonomous or self-referential negation. Namely, the two halves or rather moments of autonomous negation, which above were held together in a paradoxical unity, have now fallen asunder into two mutually external relata. Why so? The reason is this. Qua self-relating negation, autonomous negation immediately gives rise to a positive term (affirmation, being) to which it stands in an external relation, that is, a relation-to-other. The "movement" of autonomous negation thus ends *either* in the absence of any relation whatsoever, that is, in the vanishing of difference into simple, immediate being or identity, *or* in a relation-to-other that compromises autonomous negation's status as pure self-relation and thus the absoluteness that made it into a promising candidate for the absolute foundation of Hegelian logic and metaphysics in the first place.

How is this difficulty to be resolved? Just above I hinted that being or immediacy could be understood as realizing both sides or moments of autonomous negation at once – both the pole of identity/immediacy and the pole of difference/mediation. In order for this to be a viable interpretation, however, the relation of autonomous negation to affirmation/being/immediacy must be integrated into autonomous negation qua pure relation-to-self. That is, relation-to-other must be redescribed as (a moment of) relation-to-self. A remark is in order here that will help to clarify the nature of this move, and readers should take careful note of its particular valence. In introducing the (analytically underived) idea that relation-to-other is a moment of relation-to-self, Hegel is not making the point that something is what it is only by way of its relations to others. That thesis says that relation-to-self is *mediated by* relation-to-others, and leaves ample room for metaphysical pluralism regarding the genesis and existence of such others. But if that thought were also valid here, that is, if autonomous negation itself turned out to be mediated by relation-to-other, as it now threatens to, this would be ruinous for its status as the single basic concept from which all else follows. Hegel would be locked into a fundamental dualism.

The decisive move, therefore, in reconstructing Hegel's *Grundoperation* is to posit relation-to-other as a moment wholly internal to the relation-to-self: the relation-to-other that emerges as an analytic implication of autonomous negation has to be interpreted as, in truth, the relation of autonomous negation to itself. And here the same logic applies that kicked off the development of self-referential negation in the first place: by definition, a self-relation is one in which the relata are identical to one another. Therefore, if being/identity/immediacy is to be a realization of autonomous negation's self-relation, it must have exactly the same internal, relational structure as absolute negativity: in differing from autonomous negation, it must not be different from it but the very realization of its selfhood: in becoming two it becomes one, and in becoming one, it becomes two. As Henrich points out, this is what Hegel means when he says that the absolute is essentially *Beisichsein im Anderen*, being at one with itself in its other.[38] And it is also clearly the logical state of affairs Hegel seeks to express in his metaphor of the *Gegenstoß gegen sich* – a self-repelling that is at the same time a self-attracting.[39]

To sum up this reconstruction of absolute negativity or autonomous negation, here is Henrich's own recapitulation:

> In the beginning is negation. Thus it negates itself. With this, however, negation vanishes, and thereby negation comes to be related to its opposite by virtue of its very own self-relation, which is negative. This relation to an other can, strictly speaking, only be maintained with negation's relation-to-self if the other is in turn itself negation. But this means that the opposite of autonomous double negation must itself be double negation. Double negation can be conceived as self-relation only if it is conceived twice over ... The absolute is at one with itself only in its being-other.[40]

Here is the relevant formulation from the logic of reflection that opens the second division of the *Science of Logic*, the *Doctrine of Essence*:

> In [the sphere of] essence, therefore, the becoming ... is the *movement from nothing to nothing and thereby back to itself*. Transition or becoming sublates itself in its transition; the other which comes into being in this transition is not the nothing of a being, but the nothing of a nothing, and this, to be the negation of a nothing, constitutes being. – Being *is* only as the movement of the nothing to the nothing, and so it is essence; and essence does not *have* this movement *within itself*, rather it *is* this movement as absolute appearance [*Schein*] itself, pure negativity with nothing outside itself for it to negate, but which rather negates only its own negativity, and which exists only in this negating ... This immediacy, which *is* only as the *returning* of the negative into itself, is the immediacy which constitutes the determinateness of appearance [*Schein*] and from which the previous movement of reflection seemed to begin. But, far from being able to start from this immediacy, this immediacy

---

38 Harris gives accurate characterizations of this dynamic relational structure of the Concept at numerous points in *Hegel's Logic*, 309–27. Compare his insight that the "first principle" of Hegel's philosophy is not a proposition, but a method, an operation: 148–49.

39 See, e.g., GW 11:252; 15:12.

40 Henrich, "Hegels Grundoperation," 219.

itself exists only as the returning or as the reflection itself. Reflection is therefore the movement which constitutes that which begins or returns only by being itself the returning. (GW 11:250–51; cf. 252)

Two concluding remarks about this passage are in order. First, it is unquestionably a formulation of just the logical operation of autonomous negation as specified above. Second, we must see that it is the very structure of the Hegelian Concept that was discussed in the preceding section of this introduction. Henrich's analysis of the dynamic logic of Hegel's *Grundoperation* turns out to correspond exactly to Horstmann's relational account of the Hegelian Concept and the structure of subjectivity. The two are at bottom one and the same, considered first from the dynamic perspective, then from the static or structural perspective. The Concept *is* self-referential, autonomous negation. The Concept and absolute negativity are one and the same.

1.4.3. Hegelian terminology as representing modes of negativity

The unity and foundational character of the notions of Concept and absolute negativity also shed light on the systematic interconnections among key Hegelian terms. For instance, "determinateness" (*Bestimmtheit*) refers quite generally to standing in some relation, where in the final analysis *all* the relations considered in the *Science of Logic* are reducible to moments of the relational complex of the Concept. On the one hand, to the extent that a term fails to exhibit (in Hegelian terms: *an ihm selbst zeigen* or *darstellen*) the relation in which it stands to others as a constituent of its own content, it exhibits "finite determinateness"; to a lesser or greater extent, all the traditional categories are of this kind: they are "finite thought-determinations" (*endliche Denkbestimmungen*). On the other hand, to the extent that finite thought-determinations reveal themselves, upon dialectical analysis, as moments within triads that are structured in a way basically isomorphic to the Concept, they enter into the constitution of a "determination of the Concept" (*Begriffsbestimmung*). These determinations of the Concept are themselves finite: they point in a more or less explicit way to further determinations as co-constitutive of their content. Here again, the more explicitly they manifest such relations as constituents of their own content, the more adequate they are as determinations of the Concept: thus the categories of Being, whose relations to one another are wholly implicit and which therefore appear as "indifferent" (*gleichgültig*) to one another, go to form the least adequate determinations of the Concept; the categories of Essence, by contrast, whose mutual relations are explicitly part their content (e.g. "cause" points as part of its very meaning to "effect," "substance" to "accidence"), are more adequate determinations; and the determinations of the Concept (universality, particularity, individuality) are from the outside defined completely by their mutual relations.

Hegel's way of expressing these levels and degrees of adequacy is to speak of stages in the *realization* of the Concept. "Realization" is chosen deliberately (and not, for example, "actualization"): the Concept is realized precisely to the degree that the *content* of a conceptual determination, that is, its *realitas*, its *Sachhaltigkeit*, explicitly manifests the relations constitutive of the Concept. Throughout most of the *Science of Logic*, including the first two sections of the Subjective Logic, the determinateness of the Concept is manifested inadequately as a relation between (to some degree) "indifferently" existing terms, that is, as finite determinateness. This changes in the transition first to the Idea and then to the absolute Idea, the whole content of which is strictly defined by just the set of complex relations described above. In the Idea, the Concept exhibits "infinite determinateness," which is tantamount to saying that the Idea is the complete realization of the Concept.[41]

Since the determinations of the Concept are identically moments in the unfolding dynamic of absolute negation, technical expressions like "determinateness," "(in)-finitude," "indifference," "realization" can also be interpreted as modes of negativity. This result is particularly important with regard to the concept of determination. Whatever the sources of Hegel's belief that determinateness entails opposition, negation, and finitude, that belief is written into the very fabric of his logic of autonomous negation, and we ought to consider everything Hegel says involving those terms from the vantage point of this logic. Most importantly, *determinate negation* and *sublation* (*Aufhebung*) are terms whose proper signification can be grasped only when they are recognized as presupposing the doctrine of *absolute negation*. Determinate negation expresses a specific phase in the unfolding of absolute negativity, namely the moment of relation-to-other when conceived *as the result* of self-referential negation. Any attempt to boil it down to some adage, for instance that to know what something is entails knowing what it is not, or that worthwhile criticism ought to point to a positive

---

41   The notion of reality as *Sachhaltigkeit* will be taken up in Chapter 6.

alternative, risks trivializing the logical and metaphysical uniqueness of the conception that led Hegel to call it "determinate negation" in the first place.

Something similar is true of sublation. The idea that one can simultaneously negate and preserve some term or object rests on the logical and metaphysical construction of absolute negativity. For on the one hand, it is this construction that enables Hegel to reconceive the being or affirmation of any term or object as itself the *result* of negation, and surely this relation between negation and affirmation is the precondition for the relation between negation and preservation that sublation enacts. And on the other hand, the methodical reconception of what is negated in its apparent indifference as either (a) a positive term constituted by its opposition to and hence negation of a correlated term or (b) as an affirmative moment or expression of a underlying dynamic from which it necessarily emerges, that is, by which it is posited and in that sense *preserved*, again presupposes the logic of absolute negation sketched above.

In short, therefore, the Concept and absolute negativity are two sides of a single "speculative" coin, one structural, one dynamic; and their unity is at the same time the unity of Hegelian metaphysics and methodology. For just as the Concept cannot be adequately understood except as the structural expression of absolute negativity, neither can the methodology of Hegelian science be understood except as the finite intellect's recreation or *Nachvollzug* of the same dynamic that constitutes Hegel's monist metaphysics of subjectivity, the Concept.

1.4.4. The refutation of Spinozism and the critical self-consciousness of finite cognition

Hegel's response to Jacobi's critique of the Spinozism inherent in rationalism depends on grasping the logic that leads to (Spinozist) substance as the logic of autonomous negation, and then showing that that same logic necessarily leads beyond substance to the full-blown structure of the Hegelian Concept. In his review of Jacobi's works, published shortly after Hegel had completed the last volume of the *Logic*, Hegel is very explicit about this:

> [S]ince substance has been defined as the truth of the particular things that are sublated and extinguished in it, *absolute negativity* has effectively already been posited as its determination, and absolute negativity

is itself the source of freedom.[42] – Everything depends here on a correct understanding of the status and significance of negativity. If it is taken only to be the determinateness of finite things (*omnis determinatio est negatio*), then we are already thinking of it outside of absolute substance and have allowed finite things to fall outside of it; our imagination *maintains* them *outside of* absolute substance ... Substance, namely, is supposed to be the sublation of the finite, and that is just to say that it is the *negation of negation*, since it is precisely negation which we took to be definitive of the finite. And as the negation of negation, substance is absolute *affirmation*, and just as immediately it is *freedom* and *self-determination*. – Thus the difference between determining the absolute as substance and determining it as spirit boils down to the question whether thinking, having annihilated its finitudes and mediations, negated its negations and thus comprehended the one absolute, is conscious of what it has actually achieved in its cognition of absolute substance, or whether it lacks such consciousness.[43]

At least two things are to be taken from this passage. The first is that absolute negativity is made to do very important *metaphysical* work in Hegel's system, for it denotes the source of the fundamental structure of reality by virtue of which atheism, fatalism, and nihilism prove to be false. The second is that it contains important *methodological* specifications regarding the properly speculative mode of cognition: the overcoming of substance monism depends on *explicit self-consciousness* of the determinate negativity characteristic of finite cognition. This methodological notion of critical self-consciousness is the topic of the following section.

1.4.5. *The origin of finite cognition and Hegel's transformation of the concept of critique*

We can now recognize the unity of Hegel's response to the challenges posed to the rationalist tradition by Kant and Jacobi. The rejection of a fundamentally categorial understanding of reality is intimately linked to the formulation of a "negative" logic of philosophical demonstration that can vie in terms of rigor with the geometrical method it is intended to supplant. While accepting the threshold between pre-critical metaphysics and critical thought marked by Kant and Jacobi, Hegel significantly redefines what it is about pre-critical

42 See ENC §382, where Hegel spells out the connection between freedom and absolute negativity.
43 GW 15:10–11.

metaphysics that needs rejecting. For him, pre-critical metaphysics comes to signify any attitude toward reality which takes the categories of traditional ontology (a) as the exclusive and irreducible forms of objective cognition and (b) as the basic forms of the substantially real itself. In light of what has been said in the preceding discussion of absolute negativity and the Concept, it should now be clear that for Hegel any attitude toward reality which is committed to the categories of traditional ontology is committed to the (*per definitionem*) finite determinations of the unrealized Concept. Or to put the same thought in slightly different terms, the cognitive attitude toward reality that is constituted by the finite thought-determinations is *finite cognition*, and since the finite thought-determinations are moments of the Concept in its phase of relation-to-other or determinate negativity, *finite cognition is the determinate negativity of the Idea.*

Accordingly, the notion of critique must also be redefined as a critical account of why a form of cognition that systematically distorts the true structure of reality necessarily arises – the Hegelian analogue of Kant's transcendental dialectic. Why, in other words, should the realized Concept (the absolute Idea) give rise to the appearance of any finite thought-determinations in the first place?

The analysis of the Concept has given us a structural schema in terms of which we can understand a whole set of Hegelian terms as representing modifications or aspects of the central notion of the Concept, some of which can be ordered in terms of the increasing adequacy with which they exhibit the complete relational structure of the Concept. The question is why there should be such differences in adequacy in the first place or, in terms of a problem that structured a great deal of debate in German Idealist circles, why does the infinite go outside of itself to become finite?[44] The answer is that relation-to-other (finitude) is a moment generated internally by the dynamic of self-referential negation – Henrich's analysis shows us how. For if we conceive of autonomous negation as actually consisting in the series of steps outlined above, that is, if we conceive of it as a dynamic giving rise to and encompassing precisely those moments (including the paradoxes and apparent *aporiae*) then there is a necessary phase in its unfolding in which the elements will seem indifferent to one another despite the fact that they exist only as aspects of the underlying

44 See GW 21:139–41.

self-relation in which negation stands to itself. Such indifference will characterize the content of the so-called *Seinsbestimmungen*, the finite thought-determinations peculiar to the sphere of Being. The underlying identity of identity and difference comes out more explicitly in the determinations of Essence, whose content exhibits the inseparability of distinct terms (cause–effect, substance–accident, etc.). But the whole process of autonomous negation is only fully explicit as the content of the realized Concept, the Idea, which emerges as the result of the Subjective Logic.

This is what it means to say that the Objective Logic is the Concept in its finitude or being-other, the *merely* determinate (rather than the infinitely determinate, i.e. determinate via relation-to-self) Concept. All of the finite thought-determinations therefore have a certain reality and necessity, namely to the extent that they are *determinate negations* or incarnations of the finite phase of absolute negativity in which the Concept "loses itself in otherness." Here again, though, it is crucial to recognize that this constitutes a *clarification* of why there are finite thought-determinations, *not a vindication* of the objective validity of finite thought-determinations.

Thus we arrive at a *specifically Hegelian notion of philosophical critique.* On the assumption that cognition is inherently reflexive, there are two senses or ways in which it can be true of finite cognition that it is the determinate negativity of the Idea, either unconsciously or explicitly and self-consciously. If finite cognition is self-consciously aware of its real status as the determinate negativity of the Idea, then it has already grasped itself from the speculative standpoint and come to comprehend the scope and limits of its (merely finite) validity. To bring about the self-consciousness of finite cognition in this sense is the critical task of the *Science of Logic*. If, on the other hand, finite cognition is not self-consciously aware of its true metaphysical status, that is, if it has not yet *posited itself as* the determinate negativity of the Idea and hence as sublated in the speculative standpoint, then it is de facto in the state Hegel calls *indifference*: in itself it is constituted by negative self-relation, but it appears (to itself) to exist outside such relation, of which it is wholly unconscious. This is the case for ordinary, pre-philosophical consciousness with its natural dualism of subject and object, but also for non-speculative varieties of philosophical monism such as materialism or traditional idealism. Dualism fails to recognize the essential unity of subject and object; materialism and idealism fail to acknowledge the necessity of difference and duality; and in all these cases the fundamental reality of negative self-relation is completely absent from reflection.[45]

Pre-critical metaphysics, therefore, is the *indifferent form* which the determinate negativity of the Idea takes for *reflection*. Note that in a broader sense of metaphysics that is not restricted to the pre-critical variety, this characterization is itself a *metaphysical definition* of pre-critical metaphysics: it purports to explain the *existence* of pre-critical metaphysics as a manifestation of the deeper reality of the Concept.[46] Furthermore, when taken as an attitude toward reality, the content that is reflected by metaphysics *sensu stricto* is common to natural consciousness generally, including scientific consciousness.[47] So pre-critical metaphysics is a specific form of reflection *on* finite cognition *by* finite cognition. Now since finite cognition is itself a *reality*, its necessary emergence and place within reality falls within the purview of any inquiry into the forms of intelligibility. As we have seen, though, Hegel's metaphysics of the Concept provides a determinate place for the genesis of finite cognition, namely by virtue of the dynamic of

45 De Boer (*On Hegel*, 5) attributes to Hegel the "view that a philosophical system 'contains' assumptions it cannot completely incorporate" and on this basis she assimilates Hegel's conception of philosophical critique to the deconstructive strategy that identifies elements that are essential to the text, but which the text represses or denies in a manner that constitutes its specific textual dynamic. She supports this interpretation by reference to a well-known passage in the Preface to the *Phenomenology* (GW 12:14–15). However, I find it more natural to read this passage as saying simply that the proponent of a system is under no rational obligation to acknowledge assumptions he does not share with his critic, and that his justified refusal of such acknowledgment will place fundamental limitations on the rational persuasiveness of any critique making use of such assumptions. As far as it goes, this principle says nothing about the relation of a system to its own implicit or explicit assumptions. Fulda has suggested that the *Phenomenology* in particular is motivated by Hegel's conviction that since finite thinking is an expression of spirit, it therefore commands unconditional respect, and that phenomenological critique is an exercise primarily intended to mediate the stance of the finite thinker qua speculative scientist with the stance of that same thinker as a contingent, historical individual (see Hans Friedrich Fulda, *Das Problem einer Einleitung in Hegels Wissenschaft der Logik*, 2nd edn. [Frankfurt am Main: Klostermann 1975], 297–301). I am inclined to share this view, which places emphasis on thinkers' inherent rationality, not on their constitutive susceptibility to irrationality.

46 See Kant's distinction between *metaphysica specialis* as a (specious) body of scientific knowledge on the one hand, and *metaphysica naturalis* as a natural disposition of the human mind on the other (see B21–22 for one instance among many). Hegel's conception of pre-critical metaphysics as a manifestation of the underlying negative dynamic of the Concept is analogous to Kant's conception of metaphysics as a natural disposition, but Hegel goes further than Kant in his belief that the *necessity* of such a disposition can be demonstrated on the basis of an alternative idealist metaphysics.

47 Cf. ENC §26.

absolute negativity. Finite cognition is the Idea in its moment or phase of relation-to-other or determinate negativity. The critique of finite cognition therefore has as its goal to demonstrate the manner in which this metaphysical status is manifested in the finite thought-determinations and the objects constituted by them. In Hegelian terms: the task is to posit finite cognition as sublated.

HEGEL'S COMPLEX RELATIONSHIP TO "PRE-KANTIAN" METAPHYSICS

2.1. Introduction

Chapter 1 concluded with a discussion of the concept of finite cognition as the object of philosophical critique in a specifically Hegelian
sense. The present chapter will take up that thread in order to examine in depth the origin and structure of finite cognition and the shape
of Hegel's critique; the result will be a nuanced understanding of what
Hegel means by "metaphysics" and how he sees his relation both to
"pre-critical" metaphysics and to Kant's treatment of it. At the same
time, this chapter is the first in a sequence of four that deal with Hegel's
critique of the three *a priori* sciences identified by Kant: metaphysics,
pure natural science, and mathematics. Over the course of these next
chapters, the idea of a *critique of finite cognition* will be exemplified in
its application to the forms in which finite cognition achieves its most
highly explicit consciousness.

With this purpose in mind, the chapter begins by considering
the specific period in philosophy that Hegel most closely associates
with the label "metaphysics," namely the school of Christian Wolff.
Hegel was never exclusively a critic of metaphysical thought in any of
its manifestations, and hence neither should we assume that his relation to Wolff was lacking in complexity. Wolff introduced a standard
of rigorous demonstration and systematic organization into German
philosophy that had been absent before him; indeed, more than any
one of his great predecessors among the continental rationalists, he
integrated the insights of modern philosophy into a single, systematic
worldview. Moreover, Wolff taught philosophy to speak German; the
cultural significance of his creating a philosophical terminology in
German cannot be overestimated. I point to statements by Kant and

Hegel that indicate their appreciation of Wolff in all these respects. Above all, however, I argue that Hegel viewed the Wolffian systematization of metaphysics to represent its most characteristic and highly determinate manifestation. By understanding the several senses in which it earned this somewhat ambivalent accolade, we gain deeper insight into what Hegel understands by metaphysics both as a historical phenomenon and as an omnihistorical feature of human thought.[1]

The greater part of this chapter is devoted, however, to a discussion of what Hegel calls the *metaphysics of the understanding* and its background in Kant. A brief review of the theory of cognition presented in the *Critique of Pure Reason* serves to point up Kant's fundamental orientation toward the form of categoriality and the objects constituted according to it. Hegel will object that this orientation is necessarily committed (1) to the *finitude* of cognition, (2) to an unsystematic *mixing* of *a priori* and *a posteriori* elements, and (3) to the unexamined assumption that the basic form of reality is objectivity in the sense of *thinghood*. These commitments make it impossible for Kant to form a proper conception of the unconditioned, which he consistently assimilates to the ontological form of finite things. Consequently, Kant fails on Hegel's view to grasp the true significance of the distinction between understanding and reason that he himself introduced into philosophy.

These observations open onto an examination of the metaphysical origin and nature of the understanding or, as I also call it, finite cognition. Analysis of what Hegel calls "understanding" (*Verstehen*) shows that it rests on two basic conditions: (1) it must be rooted in a real or metaphysical unity with its object: cognition and what is cognized ("the true") must ultimately be identical; (2) the identity of cognition and the true can only be adequately realized by way of a difference inscribed into their identity: the structure of intentionality is an essential dimension of reality. As in many things, so too in his conception of knowledge, Hegel is a disciple of Spinoza. In E1p30, Spinoza states that "the finite intellect in its actuality or the infinite intellect in its actuality must comprehend the attributes of God and the affections of God, and nothing else." That is, the exclusive object of cognition is the unconditioned itself. Of course, despite ordinary, pre-philosophical commitment to the belief that we know, or can come to know, things

---

1 The significance of Hegel's relation to Wolff for understanding his conception of critique has most recently been emphasized by de Boer, *On Hegel*, 128–32.

as they truly are, we do not ordinarily think of ourselves as cognizing continuously and exclusively the unconditioned. Spinoza accounts for this lack of consciousness through his doctrine of the different kinds of knowledge. Hegel, to some extent analogously, accounts for it by reference to the categorial form that is constitutive of finite consciousness and self-consciousness. That form at once both fulfills the condition of difference between cognition and truth, and obscures the presence of the first condition of their identity. Nonetheless, the "naïve" commitment of pre-critical metaphysics to the belief that the categories it has uncovered are indifferently the forms of both cognition and being is an unconscious expression of just that first condition. It is by way of a dialectical critique of the categories, revealing their *difference* from the unconditioned, that finite cognition is brought to understand its true unity with the unconditioned and the proper form of that unity, that is, the structure of the Concept, absolute negativity.

The chapter concludes with a renewed discussion of the failure of pre-critical metaphysics to grasp the real significance of categorial thought and finite being. In their different ways, Kant and Jacobi recognized that failing, and may in that sense be said to represent the critical self-consciousness of traditional metaphysics. As I argue, however, the same *aporiae* that plagued metaphysics before Kant and Jacobi re-emerge in their own thought: although they bring pre-critical metaphysics to an end, they nevertheless remain entrapped in its paradigm. Like Moses, they were destined only to show philosophy where the desert ends, not to enter into the promised land.

2.2. The legacy of Christian Wolff

This chapter pursues the modest goal of clarifying what Hegel means by "metaphysics," and of parsing his somewhat ambiguous attitude toward "metaphysics" into distinct views. For a start, we can distinguish two main senses in which he uses the term, namely to refer to a specific historical movement in philosophy and to characterize a general approach to the basic ontological categories (e.g. quality, quantity, relation, modality). In turn, both the historical movement and the general approach exhibit positive as well as negative features, and in each case Hegel's attitude differs accordingly.

The meaning of "metaphysics," as Hegel uses the term, emerges most clearly when we begin with its more narrowly historical reference to "the former metaphysics" (*die vormalige Metaphysik*), that is, the system of Christian Wolff and his school which dominated German universities throughout the period from 1720 to 1750, and in some places (e.g. Tübingen, at Hegel's *alma mater*) longer than that.[2] Wolff was the first to produce German-language textbooks on logic, metaphysics, ethics, and other branches of philosophy (including physics, i.e. natural philosophy), thereby contributing substantially to the creation of a German philosophical vocabulary.[3] His textbook on metaphysics, *Rational Thoughts on God, the World, the Human Soul, and All Things as Such*, went through twelve editions in his lifetime; his German *Logic* went through fourteen editions, and the Latin editions enjoyed equal popularity and influence. In addition, Wolff's students also produced textbooks on metaphysics closely modeled after those of Wolff and widely used in German universities. Baumgarten's *Metaphysica* (which went through seven editions between 1739 and 1779) is still well known today, at least by name, since Kant based his lectures on it well into the 1790s, praising it as "the most useful and most thorough of all the handbooks of its kind" (1:503).[4] But it was just one of many in regular use throughout the German-speaking states.[5]

2 For an overview of the period focusing on Wolff, see Max Wundt, *Die deutsche Schulphilosophie im Zeitalter der Aufklärung* (Hildesheim: Georg Olms 1964), esp. 122–264. In Tübingen, the logician and metaphysician Gottfried Ploucquet (1716–90) made original contributions in the spirit of the Leibniz–Wolffian philosophy well into the 1780s, though Hegel, who entered the university in 1788, would not have been able to attend lectures by Ploucquet. Wundt (336) dismisses the idea that Ploucquet actually influenced Hegel or Schelling. More recently, however, Michael Franz has argued that Schelling adopted elements unique to Ploucquet's formal logic (*Schelling's Tübinger Platon-Studien* [Göttingen: Vandenhoek & Ruprecht 1996], esp. 110–17); there are also indications that Hegel was more favorably disposed toward Ploucquet's logic than his dismissive comments in the *Science of Logic* (GW 12:110) would suggest; see Riccardo Pozzo, "Ploucquet – Hegel – Hamilton: Problem- und Wirkungsgeschichte," *Hegel-Studien* 26 (1991), 449–56.

3 Nor was Wolff's creative contribution to the German language limited to philosophy. On the condition and reputation of German prior to the work of Wolff, and on the effect that he had in transforming German into an internationally recognized language of science and literature (his works were the first to be widely translated from German into other European languages), see Eric A. Blackall, *The Emergence of German as a Literary Language* (Cambridge University Press 1959), esp. 27–48, where Blackall both lists the numerous terms that Wolff either invented or was instrumental in establishing in the sciences and shows how Wolff transformed what had in many cases been an essentially *metaphorical* vocabulary, borrowed from the German mystics, into a precise and widely shared language of science. He also underscores the specifically rhetorical and literary effects of Wolff's achievement.

4 Cf. 24:205 and 9:21: "The general logic by Wolff is the best we have."

5 For an exhaustive list of logic textbooks in the Wolffian mould, see Dt. Log., 98–99.

At the center of Wolff's *specifically philosophical* achievement is the rationalization of scholasticism, its transformation from an empirical Aristotelianism into a rational Aristotelianism based on doctrines and (above all mathematical) methods adopted from Descartes, Weigel, Tschirnhaus, Leibniz, and Spinoza as well.[6] Honnefelder emphasizes that it is above all his orientation toward mathematics as a methodological ideal that constitutes Wolff's modernity; defining contents of Leibniz's philosophy, such as the theory of monads and the associated conception of substance, for example, are absent from Wolff's system, whereas the continuity with scholastic concepts and theorems is quite prominent.[7] At the same time, Wolff starkly diverges from the instrumentalist approach to logic taken by many of his Protestant contemporaries, who excluded the "art" of logic from the ranks of the true sciences. By the same token, he demonstrates his Aristotelian loyalties through "the central importance for logic he accords to the syllogism,

6 On the chronology of Wolff's reception and practical adoption of methods based on work by Descartes, Leibniz, Weigel, Tschirnhaus, and Spinoza, as well as an assessment of the degree of continuity between these methods and the scholastic tradition, on the one hand, and Wolff's employment of them, on the other, see H. W. Arndt's informative introduction to the *Deutsche Logik* in *Gesammelte Werke*, Abteilung I, vol. I, esp. 9–31, 55–92; also cf. Wundt, *Deutsche Schulphilosophie*, 151–52. Herman Jean de Vleeschauwer ("La Génese de la Méthode Mathématique de Wolf," *Revue Belge de la Philologie et d'Histoire* 11:3–4 [1932]: 651–77) demonstrates the interplay of religious, scholastic, and Cartesian influences that shaped Wolff's approach to philosophy, underscoring the decisive role of the "cartésien-spinoziste" Tschirnhaus. Wolff first reads Tschirnhaus' *Medicina Mentis* (1687) during his tenure in Jena, where he also comes under the influence of the recently deceased Erhard Weigel, professor of mathematics in Jena, Leibniz's teacher, and the author of *Analysis Aristotelis ex Euclide restituta* (1658). Wolff is, however, by no means simply dependent on his predecessors for his methodological views. For example, Vleeschauwer ("La Génese," 652–53) points out that Wolff defended the adoption of mathematics as a general methodological paradigm prior to his contact with Leibniz. Arndt (Dt. Log., 16–17) cites the passages from Wolff's autobiography and the *Ratio praelectionem* in which Wolff expresses his disappointment with Tschirnhaus' truth criterion. Also, Wolff distances himself from Descartes, for instance, for not having made better use of the geometrical method in metaphysics, and he also criticizes Spinoza's demonstrations in the *Ethics*, which he finds lacking in rigor: see Dt. Log., Preface to the first edition, 106. See Wundt, *Deutsche Schulphilosophie*, 126–27, for further references.

7 Cf. Ludger Honnefelder, *Scientia transcendens: Die formale Bestimmung der Seiendheit und Realität in der Metaphysik des Mittelalters und der Neuzeit (Duns Scotus – Suarez – Wolff – Kant – Peirce)* (Hamburg: Meiner 1990), 296–98. Cf. Disc. Prael., ch. 4, "De methodo" (§§115–39), esp. §139 on "the identity of philosophical and mathematical method." Also cf. *Ausführliche Nachricht von seinen eigenen Schrifften, die er in deutscher Sprache heraus gegeben*, in *Gesammelte Werke*, ed. J. École, H. W. Arndt, Ch. A. Corr, J. E. Hofmann, and M. Thomann (Hildesheim, Zurich, and New York: Georg Olms 1965–), Abteilung I, vol. IX, §§22–25, esp. 52–64.

his consciousness of the logical form and necessity expressed by it, the rigorous separation of logic from rhetoric, psychology, and moralist discourse, and his understanding of logic not merely as an instrument of scientific cognition, but as an object of scientific theory."[8] Wolff thus re-established continuity with the pre-Cartesian, Aristotelian tradition in metaphysics that had initially seemed threatened by the scientific revolution and the mechanical philosophy associated with it. The effect was not merely to modernize the scholastic tradition, thus revitalizing the university from which the creative thinkers who defined philosophical modernity had been alienated. At the same time, Wolff synthesized many elements of modern philosophy with those from the Aristotelian metaphysical tradition, integrating them into a coherent body of doctrine founded on precise definitions and principles, and held together by rigorous demonstration. This is something his more original predecessors had never attempted – with the obvious exception of Spinoza, whose philosophical theology made it impossible for many philosophers of the time to take an openly affirmative attitude toward his philosophy. He was thus the first modern German philosopher to aspire to an explicitly systematic form of presentation, and in at least this respect he paved the way for the achievement of Kant and the Idealists.[9]

This assessment helps put Hegel's discussions of metaphysics in context. In the First Attitude of Thought to Objectivity, for instance, Hegel remarks that metaphysical thought, especially insofar as it is limited to the "finite thought-determinations" (about which more below), finds its "most determinate ... development" in the "former metaphysics, the way it was constituted in Germany [*bei uns*] prior to the Kantian philosophy" (ENC §27). He is obviously referring to the Wolffian school, as the following sections (33–36) corroborate, where he goes on to discuss the canonical subdisciplines of metaphysics: ontology, psychology, cosmology, and theology. His remarks in the *Science of Logic* are strictly parallel. Metaphysics, he says, "in the final shape of its elaboration" comprises on the one hand "*ontology* ... intended to investigate

---

8 Dt. Log., 54. Wolff thus plays a crucial role in reviving and strengthening the Aristotelian and scholastic tradition for which the notion of a *science* of logic, as Hegel envisions it, is not in itself already an oxymoron.

9 Cf. Wundt, *Deutsche Schulphilosophie*, 164: "Wolff was thus not wrong in boasting that he was the first to have made the fundamental science [i.e. metaphysics] into a system." Hegel acknowledges the greatness of Wolff's intentions even as he excoriates the form and method: see TW 20:260–61.

the nature of *ens* in general" and on the other an attempt "to comprehend with the pure forms of thought such particular substrata, originally drawn from figurative representation, as the soul, the world, and
God" (GW 21:48–49).[10]

What is striking about Hegel's reference to Wolffian metaphysics
in both passages is that he characterizes it as the "final" form of elaboration of a more pervasive attitude of thought to objectivity: to the
extent that thought unselfconsciously sets out to cognize being as it is
in itself, and to the extent that it does so on the basis of an investigation
of categorial determinations informed by traditional (non-dialectical)
logic, that cognitive attitude finds its most adequately and completely
articulated form in the metaphysics of German *Schulphilosophie*. If this
is in fact Hegel's opinion, then surely the structure of his *Science of Logic*
is a reflection of it. The first two books, Being and Essence, comprising
the "objective logic," are explicitly said to take the place of ontology as
conceived in pre-Kantian metaphysics. Similarly, in the first section of
the *Logic of the Concept*, "subjectivity," Hegel orders his treatment of formal logic according to the three *operationes mentis*, concept, judgment,
and syllogism, a schema that harkens back to medieval scholasticism,
but which Wolff had made into the template that would determine
the structure of German logic textbooks until the revolution in logic
that set in toward the end of the nineteenth century.[11] In the Preface
to the second edition of the *Logic*, Hegel even acknowledges (in a

---

10 Cf. Ontol. §1: *Ontologia seu Philosophia prima est scientia entis in genere, seu quatenus
    ens est.*

11 Cf., e.g., the organization of Wolff's *Deutsche Logik*, which begins with a discussion of
    concepts as arising from the mental activity of representation (ch. 2), and then moves
    on to propositions (as the product of judging, ch. 3) and the various syllogistic figures
    (as the representation of inference, ch. 4). (Of course, the division of logic according
    to the concept, the proposition, and the syllogism ultimately goes back to the organ-
    ization of Aristotle's *Organon* into *Categoriae*, *De interpretatione*, and the two *Analytics*.)
    On the historical context and influence of Wolff's logic textbook, see Dt. Log. 95–99,
    and Wundt, *Deutsche Schulphilosophie*, 156. Hegel himself states that he had known
    Wolff's logic "perfectly by rote since the age of fourteen, and his definition of clear
    ideas since the age of twelve." See Karl Rosenkranz, *G. W. F. Hegel's Leben* (Berlin:
    Duncker & Humboldt 1844), 26, cited by Walter Jaeschke, *Hegel-Handbuch: Leben-
    Werk-Wirkung* (Stuttgart: Metzler 2003), 1, who also conjectures which textbook the
    young Hegel would have used. Hegel's discussion of definition, classification, proof,
    and fundamental methodological questions in the section on "The Idea" corresponds
    recognizably to the "applied logic" that had rounded out logic textbooks since Wolff
    and steadily grew in length and importance throughout the late eighteenth and nine-
    teenth centuries. The same structure is reflected in Kant's First Critique.

somewhat begrudging tone) that he found "external material" for his own presentation "in the former metaphysics and logic" (GW 21:10).[12]

A closely related point is Wolff's orientation toward mathematics as the paradigm of rational cognition, his dedication to the *mos geometricus*. As Hegel underscores in his *Lectures on the History of Philosophy*, "logical consequence, method is the principal thing" (TW 20:122; cf. 153) for metaphysics as reborn in the spirit of Cartesianism, and Wolff showed more alacrity even than Spinoza in structuring the whole of philosophy *more geometrico*. This ideal should concern us all the more, precisely because Kant and the post-Kantian idealists were so vehement in their rejection of it as an appropriate model for philosophical method. Consider Kant's emphatic praise of Wolff in the Preface to the B edition of the First Critique:

> In the execution of the plan prescribed by the critique, that is, in the future system of metaphysics, we have therefore to follow the strict method of the celebrated Wolff, the greatest of all dogmatic philosophers. He was the first to show by example (and by his example he awakened that spirit of thoroughness which is still not extinct in Germany) how the secure progress of a science is to be attained only through orderly establishment of principles, clear determination of concepts, insistence upon strictness of proof, and avoidance of venturesome, non-consecutive steps in our inferences. He was thus particularly well fitted to raise metaphysics to the dignity of a science, if only it had occurred to him to prepare the ground beforehand by a critique of the organ, that is, of pure reason itself. The blame for his having failed to do so lies not so much with himself as with the dogmatic way of thinking prevalent in his day ... Those who reject both the method of Wolff and the procedure of a critique of pure reason can have no other aim than to shake off the fetters of *science* altogether, and thus to change work into play, certainty into opinion, philosophy into philodoxy. (Bxxxvi–xxxvii)

Significantly, this passage is located in Kant's Preface, a text intended to situate the endeavor of a critique of pure reason within the broader landscape of contemporaneous philosophy. I have quoted it at length in order to bring out the fact that Kant's praise of Wolff's method *is at the same time an explicit rejection* of the unsystematic mode of thought that

---

12 Johann Edouard Erdmann asserts that "hardly a single category is to be found [in Hegel's *Logic*] that Wolff did not discuss, in his own way of course, in his ontology" (*Versuch einer wissenschaftlichen Darstellung der neueren Philosophie*, vol. IV [Stuttgart: Fromann 1932], 289); cited in Honnefelder, *Scientia*, 298.

had become dominant in Enlightenment Germany after the decline of Wolff's school.[13] Kant sees his philosophical endeavor, in respect to its claims to rigor and systematicity, as a revitalization of the Wolffian "spirit of thoroughness" that is "*still* not extinct in Germany."

It is, of course, *revitalization* that Kant is striving for, and not any straightforward restoration of Wolffian science.[14] The Enlightenment thinkers who rebelled against Wolff's rationalism and intellectualism naturally also rejected his geometric method, but they did so in order to turn to modes of presentation that rejected the ideal of rigor and systematicity as such. In order not to throw out the baby with the bathwater, it is therefore crucial for Kant and those who follow him to develop a coherent account of why the geometric method is an inappropriate means of realizing the scientific ideal for philosophy. That is the only path to the principled introduction of a truly scientific philosophical method. Critical analysis of the assumptions, ramifications, and legitimacy of the *mos geometricus* as a paradigm for philosophy will occupy idealist philosophers and their critics well into the nineteenth century.[15]

This book on Hegel is not the place for a thorough examination of Kant's methodology. However, in Chapter 5 I provide a detailed analysis of Hegel's critique of the geometric method, and in that context

---

13 I follow Hegel in my use of the term "Enlightenment"; cf. TW 20:269: "This, then, is the shape of philosophy in the eighteenth century, and French, Scottish, and German philosophy belong to this shape. The latter, especially to the extent that it is not Wolffian metaphysics, is also referred to by the expression 'Enlightenment'." As Wolff's school entered decline, the reception of English, Scottish, and French philosophy intensified. From 1750 on, the rising tide of interest in Locke, Hume (whose *Treatise* is translated twice, first in 1755 and then again in 1793), Hutcheson, Shaftesbury, Ferguson, Beattie, Reid, Montesquieu, Helvetius, Bonnet, Condillac, and Holbach is documented by the steady stream of translations. The *Spätaufklärung* is thus inseparable from an intensive reception of empiricist and materialist streams of thought from abroad (for chronological details see Wundt, *Deutsche Schulphilosophie*, 270–71.) Hegel has this *Spätaufklärung* in mind when he refers critically to "the Enlightenment": see GW 4:125; 15:8; ENC§36; cf. also Hegel's occasional references to the encroachment of "Lockeanism," GW 4:321–22; 15:8.

14 Cf. Max Wundt, *Geschichte der Metaphysik* (Berlin: Junker and Dünnhaupt 1931), 10–11.

15 Public debate on the employment of the geometric method in philosophy goes back at least as far as 1761, when the Royal Prussian Academy issued its prize essay question, "Are the metaphysical sciences capable of the same evidence as the mathematical sciences?" Kant's answer came in second after Mendelssohn's. For an account of the effect this debate had on contemporaries, among them the nineteen-year-old Jacobi, see Alexander Altman, *Moses Mendelssohns Frühschriften zur Metaphysik* (Tübingen: Mohr-Siebeck 1969), 252–62.

I will make comparisons with Kant's (and Jacobi's) views on the subject. For now, the main point is that at the beginning of the period of Kantian and post-Kantian German philosophy, the *mos geometricus* still stood as the last great attempt to transform metaphysics into a systematic, *a priori* science – undertaken seventy years before and then abandoned by the younger generation of *Aufklärer* and *Popularphilosophen* still dominant in the 1780s and 90s. "By Science," Wolff writes, "I understand a facility of the understanding for irrefutably demonstrating, through incontrovertible reasons, everything one claims" (Dt. Log. §2). The emphasis on *Wissenschaftlichkeit* (scienticity) that is common to Kant, Reinhold, Fichte, Schelling, and Hegel is to this extent a renewal of a specifically German tradition which had been interrupted, eroded, and neglected almost to the point of extinction in the preceding half-century. For all its profound differences, Hegel's *Logic*, with its self-conscious parallels to Wolffian metaphysics, is the most explicit manifestation of this spirit of renewal.

In stressing the *Wirkungsgeschichte* or "effective history" of Wolffian scholasticism in the tradition of German philosophy right down to Hegel's times, it is not my intention to downplay the extent and importance of Hegel's direct acquaintance with the writings of the more creative originators of modern rationalism, Descartes, Spinoza, and Leibniz. Dutens' edition of Leibniz in six volumes (1768) made his thought available to an extent that exceeded even what Wolff could have known, and revealed a mind very different from what had been codified in Wolff's definitions and principles. This is the edition Hegel draws on in his later lectures on the history of philosophy. This Leibniz renaissance soon expanded into the Plato renaissance that came to be so important for Schelling and the *Frühromantiker*, culminating in Schleiermacher's epoch-making translation of Plato's works.[16] Similar points can be made about the Spinoza renaissance unwittingly initiated by Jacobi's controversy with Mendelssohn; one effect of this heightened interest was Paulus' new edition of Spinoza (1802/3), on which Hegel collaborated for a brief time at the beginning of his tenure in Jena.[17] There can be no doubt about the impact

16 Wundt, *Deutsche Schulphilosophie*, 319, 339–41. See also Franz, *Schellings Platonstudien*, 45–97; Frederick Beiser, *The Romantic Imperative: The Concept of Early German Romanticism* (Cambridge, MA: Harvard University Press 2003), 56–72; Horstmann, *Grenzen der Vernunft*, 86, 219.

17 Hegel mentions his participation in TW 20:160; it seems to have been limited to comparing existing French translations of Spinoza's works.

had by this far more robust, more "speculative" rationalism on Hegel's generation of philosophers. Indeed, when Hegel speaks of the "Period of Metaphysics" in the *Lectures on the History of Philosophy*, he identifies Descartes, Leibniz, Spinoza, the French materialists, and Locke (!) as its "main protagonists," and treats Wolff primarily as the mere "systematizer" of Leibniz's philosophy (TW 20:122, 256).

What I am suggesting, however, is that parallel to his direct reception of what we today would consider the canonical figures of modern philosophy, Hegel would also have been able to organize what he read of them according to the compartmentalization, systematization, and methodical concatenation created by Wolff. So when he refers to the "former" metaphysics as it was before Kant, the sense determining that reference is importantly shaped by the Wolffian system. Therefore, appreciating Wolffian metaphysics as the paradigm case will help us to see what is at issue in both Hegel's critique and his appreciation of metaphysics as a general approach to investigating the categories. And it will help us be clear about how much rationalist metaphysics as a *form* of thought has in common with speculation, both in terms of content and in terms of its systematic aims.

2.3. Hegel's conception of the metaphysics of the understanding and its Kantian background

2.3.1. Kant on reason and the understanding: a brief review
Since Hegel closely associates metaphysics with the faculty of understanding as distinct from reason, systematic discussion of his concept of metaphysics must begin with the distinction between these two modes of cognition.

It was Kant who first introduced the distinction between reason and the understanding.[18] Let us recall the salient features of each. Understanding, according to Kant, is a *spontaneous* faculty, that is, a faculty whose activity arises from within and does not need to be produced by external impulse (B75–76). It is distinguished from sensibility by this spontaneity and more specifically as the faculty of cognition by means of *concepts*. A concept, Kant explains, is a *function*, that is, "the unity of the act of bringing various representations under one common representation" (B93). The direct implication is that concepts relate immediately to other representations, since concepts are

18 See Hegel's acknowledgment of this fact at TW 20:352.

precisely the function of unifying them, and thus only indirectly to the objects that are the content of those lower-order representations (which, at the most basic level, are intuitions). In addition to its spontaneity, therefore, the understanding is also distinguished from sensibility by its mediated character. The activity of the understanding thus consists in the formation and combination of concepts by way of *judgment*, which Kant defines as "functions of unity among our representations; instead of an immediate representation, a *higher* representation, which comprises the immediate representation and various others, is used in knowing the object, and thereby much possible knowledge is gathered into one" (B93–94).

In a word, the understanding is a spontaneously acting faculty of synthesis (conceptualization) whose content consists in other representations, these being either themselves concepts or, at the basic level of all content, spatio-temporal appearances as given to the receptive faculty of sensibility. The understanding is therefore spontaneous, but not self-sufficient: it relies for its content on a source external to it, sensibility. In Kant's famous words, "Thoughts without content are empty, intuitions without concepts are blind" (B75). The first clause of this dictum sums up the understanding's reliance on sensibility for its content. The second clause, however, formulates the equally important reliance of sensibility on the understanding in order to acquire objective import, that is, in order to come to be *about* something. Kant's most direct expression of this thought comes in the A-deduction, where he introduces the idea of the *transcendental object*:

> The pure concept of this transcendental object, which in reality throughout all our knowledge is always one and the same, is what can alone confer upon all our empirical concepts in general *relation to an object, that is, objective reality*. This concept cannot contain any determinate intuition, and therefore refers only to that unity which must be met with in any manifold of knowledge which stands in relation to an object. This relation is nothing but the necessary unity of consciousness, and therefore also of the synthesis of the manifold, through a common function of the mind, which combines it in one representation. (A109; emphasis added)

This passage brings out two important features of the understanding. First, objectivity in general, and the objectivity of empirical cognitions taken individually, is a *function of conceptual synthesis*, not something to be met with in the raw input, as it were, of sensibility.

Second, objectivity is a *function of identity*: the relation of representations to objects boils down to a relation of consciousness to itself, namely its necessary unity; the identically persisting transcendental object, toward which all empirical synthesis is oriented, is a reflection of the transcendental subject, the unity of consciousness.[19]

Pausing to sum up, we can say that the understanding is a spontaneous function of combining representations such that they constitute a unified, identically persisting consciousness, whose immediate concomitant is the object of consciousness in general and the objective import of representations taken singly. Put differently, conceptual synthesis is a two-sided, productive activity that gives rise at one and the same time to a coherent world of *things* and to an identical cognitive self in relation to that world.

To complete our review of Kant's concept of the understanding, we should note that conceptual synthesis is complex in itself; it comprises multiple functions of unity that work together to produce objective, unified representations. These basic functions of unity are the pure concepts of the understanding, which Kant identifies as substantively identical with the subset of traditional ontological categories he considers to be authentically conceptual. These he organizes into a table with four headings (quantity, quality, relation, modality), each comprising a triplet of determinations. These latter determinations, which fully specify the superordinate category, are organized such that the third determination can be read as the unification of the first two. For example, the category of quality comprises the subordinate determination *reality*, the contrary determination *negation*, and the determination *limitation*, which signifies a partially negated reality. Since, therefore, the understanding constitutes a properly objective, coherent world of things by way of these multiple functions of synthesis, that world is experienced by the cognitive subject as *structured* according to them. In more traditional terms, the fundamental ways things in the world can be experienced as being, the categorial structure of the world, have intelligibility built into them: the world is necessarily such that we can *understand* it.

Yet whereas the traditional study of these most fundamental ways things *can be experienced* was conceived as enumerating the ways things *can be*, period, Kant deflates the categories to the status of subjective

19 Longuenesse (*Hegel's Critique*, 18–27) has also analyzed this passage in its relevance for Hegel; my discussion here is partly indebted to her account.

forms imposed upon a material which, both in its spatio-temporality and its sensuous qualities, is thoroughly conditioned by the contingent nature of the human mind (B59, 72; cf. 5:402, 18:502). The categories of traditional metaphysics have thus been subjectivized, or to quote another famous Kantian dictum, "the proud name of an Ontology that presumptuously claims to supply, in systematic doctrinal form, synthetic *a priori* knowledge of things in general ... must, therefore, give place to the modest title of a mere Analytic of pure understanding" (B303).

Reason, like the understanding, is a faculty whose basic function is unity, and in one respect it is continuous with that faculty. Namely, in its purely formal or "logical employment" (B359), reason is a faculty of inference, that is, the faculty of specifying, for a given conclusion, all the premises upon which it rests; in the ongoing search for such premises, reason "endeavors to reduce the varied and manifold knowledge obtained through the understanding to the smallest number of conditions (universal conditions) and thereby to achieve in it the highest possible unity ... [M]ultiplicity of rules and unity of principles is a demand of reason," Kant goes on to say, "for the purpose of bringing the understanding into thoroughgoing accordance with itself, just as the understanding brings the manifold of intuition under concepts and thereby connects the manifold" (B361–62). In this respect, then, reason is continuous with and subordinate to the faculty of understanding.

Reason is discontinuous with the understanding, however, in respect to its "pure employment" as the *faculty of principles*. Kant distinguishes between two senses of "principle": On the one hand, any universal proposition that can serve as a major premiss in a syllogism may be called a principle; but such propositions are principles in a merely relative sense, with regard to the cases that can be subsumed under them.[20] Even the axioms of geometry, Kant points out, are principles only in relation to what can be given in intuition; hence they are not principles in and of themselves, but only in relation to the form of outer intuition which is itself, of course, non-discursive. Principles in the absolute sense, by contrast, are not subject to restriction by a specific class of objects nor do they depend for their validity on any non-conceptual component: they issue from the nature of reason itself and constitute "criteria for the attainment of such absoluteness and

20 Cf. B356.

totality as will harmonize reason with itself."[21] As Béatrice Longuenesse has emphasized, in originating its own theoretical and practical principles reason is not merely a faculty concerned with the unconditioned, but is itself an *unconditioned faculty*.[22] And in this sense it is discontinuous with and superior to the faculty of understanding.

Nevertheless, a deep analogy between reason and the understanding obtains with respect to the function of unity. Just as the various propositional functions of unifying sensible representations are reflected in the concepts of the understanding (*categories*) so too are the inferential functions of unity reflected in concepts of reason that Kant calls *ideas*. Specifically, there are three: the idea of the soul, the idea of the world-whole, and the idea of the supreme being (God). If the analytic of the understanding takes the place of traditional ontology, then Kant's theory of the necessary ideas of reason is the successor to what the tradition called special metaphysics. Whereas the concepts of the understanding actually enter into the constitution of the things we construe from experience, however, Kant believes that the concepts of reason have a merely regulative function. They guide us in the scientific pursuit and systematic explanation of experience, but they do not actually congrue with anything that could be given in experience. Hence they remain, to this precise extent, *empty*: if the theory of categories is forced to give up the name of ontology to become a subjectivized theory of the understanding, speculation about the nature of the unconditioned – metaphysics proper – has been demoted to a logic of illusion.

2.3.2. *The metaphysics of the understanding and the categorial view of reality*

Hegel restates Kant's model of the mind in succinct terms: "Understanding is thinking in finite relations, – reason, for Kant, is thinking that has as its object what is unconditioned, infinite; and he calls the unconditioned an idea, an expression from Plato."[23] It is now crucial to recognize that Hegel associates the term "metaphysics" exclusively with the understanding, that is, with thinking in finite relations. This is in stark contrast to Kant, who correlates ontology

---

21 Cf. Norman Kemp Smith, *A Commentary to Kant's Critique of Pure Reason* (New York: Humanities Press 1962), 443.
22 Cf. Longuenesse, *Hegel's Critique*, 168–69.
23 TW 20:352.

(general metaphysics) with the understanding and special metaphysics with reason. As we will now see, the central characteristics of metaphysics, as Hegel uses the term, correlate directly with features of Kantian understanding:

(1) The objects of metaphysics are distinct, independently existing essentialities, just as Kant's categories of the understanding manifest themselves as distinct, independent functions of synthesis whose internal unity and connection remains invisible, that is, they are *finite*.

(2) Metaphysical cognition is a mixture of *a priori* and empirical elements that does not rise to unadulterated systematic integrity, just as the categories of the understanding are, on the one hand, abstracted from our representations of sensible appearances and, on the other, receive their content exclusively from sensibility.

(3) Metaphysical objects are mere *things* (*entia*), just as the categories constitute *things* (*entia*) which, qua phenomena, are explicitly acknowledged as being, in the final analysis, unreal ("transcendentally ideal").

But this covers only general metaphysics or ontology, one might object; what about rational psychology, cosmology, and theology? The answer to this question holds the key to understanding how Hegel can reject the whole of what he calls metaphysics, while maintaining that the unconditioned in its three canonical forms is nevertheless accessible to scientific cognition. Hegel tells us in the Introduction to the first volume of the *Logic* that in respect to Wolff's systematization, what the Objective Logic replaces *immediately* and *in the first instance* is ontology, by which he means "that part of metaphysics intended to investigate the nature of *ens* in general" (GW 21:48). Additionally, however ("*alsdann aber*"), the objective logic is said to encompass the rest of metaphysics as well insofar as it "sought to comprehend with the pure forms of thought such particular substrata, originally drawn from imagination, as the soul, the world, and God, and in this way of viewing things the *determinations of thinking* constituted what was *essential*" (GW 21:49).

Analysis proves how informative this remark really is. Careful attention to the structure of the *Logic* shows that Hegel's substantive discussion of the content of special metaphysics comes only in the *Doctrine of the Concept*, where he deals with the world-whole, the soul, and the supreme being under the headings "objectivity," "the idea of cognition," and "the absolute idea" respectively.[24] At first glance, this would seem to contradict his remark in the Introduction assigning those topics to the Objective Logic. In fact, however, the specifically "metaphysical" treatment of the unconditioned consists in handling it as a kind of *ens*, a kind of *thing*. Hence the emphasis on the fact that traditional metaphysics took up the soul, the world, and God as substrates that it derived from representation, and sought to define them in terms of the thought-determinations provided by traditional ontology. It is certainly not in this sense that Hegel treats of those topics in the Subjective Logic, and so when he consigns *all* of traditional metaphysics to the Objective Logic, that means he will also deal there with the topics of rational cosmology, psychology, and theology *to the extent* that they can be formulated mistakenly, inadequately, in the terms of the finite thought-determinations at issue in that part of the work. In fact, not only do we find him directly addressing and criticizing traditional approaches to metaphysical topics there, but he explicitly characterizes the procedure of the whole *Logic* as producing progressively more adequate definitions of the absolute: "The logical determinations in general can be regarded as the definitions of the absolute, as *metaphysical definitions of God* ... For, to define God metaphysically means to express his nature in *thoughts* as such. But logic comprises all thoughts as they are while still in the form of thoughts" (ENC §85).[25]

Thus to the extent that traditional metaphysics had, by definition, no means of thematizing the unconditioned except by way of the finite thought-determinations (the categories of the understanding) the critical exposition of traditional psychology, cosmology, and theology belongs necessarily to the Objective Logic.

It should now be clear how Hegel can both appropriate Kant's own picture of the relation of the understanding to reason and charge Kant with having contradicted himself by reducing reason to the understanding. Consider Kant's introductory remarks to the System of Cosmological Ideas: "Reason does not really generate any concept. The most it can do is to free a concept of understanding from the unavoidable limitations of possible experience, and so to endeavor to

---

24 Cf. GW 12:127–28, 154, 192–94, where Hegel draws the parallel with these traditional metaphysical topics.

25 Cf. GW 21:73–77, 99, 326. For further discussion of this statement see Chapter 5 below.

extend it beyond the limits of the empirical, though still, indeed, in terms of its relation to the empirical" (A409).

This characterization of reason contradicts the notion that reason is the independent source of its own absolutely unconditioned principles. Rather than being a direct expression of the unconditioned itself, special metaphysics figures in this explanation as the attempt to extend forms of thought that are constitutive of and essentially tied down to the conditioned and finite, to "objects" that are essentially unconditioned and infinite. Special metaphysics is thus concerned with what Hegel would call the "unconditioned of the understanding" (ENC §46), not with the unconditioned as it realized by speculative reason. Hence we may say that theoretical reason *as Kant understands it* is essentially identical with the understanding *as Hegel understands it*.[26] And therefore "metaphysics" as understood by Kant and criticized by Hegel is essentially the metaphysics of the understanding. So Hegel clearly agrees with Kant in rejecting traditional rationalist metaphysics: the categories (the finite thought-determinations) cannot serve to determine the absolute. However, he would criticize Kant for having unconsciously and illicitly identified reason with the understanding and thereby having identified cognition *as such* with the use of the understanding.

2.4. The metaphysical origin and structure of the understanding

In this section I will address what Hegel calls *Verstandesmetaphysik* in the more strictly systematic sense introduced in the last section. Understanding and reason were certainly not intended by Kant as historically specific forms of cognition that have come about through the process of civilization and could, in whichever way, pass away leaving the human race in some new condition, be it for better or for worse. Kant intended them to be faculties belonging essentially to finite, discursive minds and to be at least as permanent as the human species itself. Hegel clearly shares this conception.[27] As he says in section 27 of the *Encyclopedia*, "This metaphysics is something *past*, however, only in relation to the history of philosophy; of itself, it is absolutely always

---

26 Cf. the discussion in Longuenesse, *Hegel's Critique*, 167–71.
27 *Pace* Tom Rockmore (*Hegel, Idealism, and Analytic Philosophy* [New Haven, CT: Yale University Press 2005], 193ff.) and de Boer (*On Hegel*, 31, 216–17).

present, as the *perspective of the mere understanding* on the objects of reason." My task in the following is to spell out with greater perspicuity the features of *Verstandesmetaphysik* that were adumbrated in the preceding comparison with Kant.

So what, according to Hegel, does it mean to *understand* something? Hegel's discussion in the 1820 Introduction to the *Lectures on the History of Philosophy*, in the section headed "The Concept of Philosophy," sheds light on this question. The immediate context bears on religion as the primary and immediate form in which humans have become aware of the unconditioned and sought to make it understandable (*verständlich*) to themselves. Understanding, he says there, includes two complementary moments, one unconscious and infinite, the other conscious and finite. On the one hand, the very possibility of becoming aware of the unconditioned (here specifically God) presupposes what might be called a basic affinity between the mind and that content. In Hegel's words, the "substantial basis" of the content of religion is "the absolute essence of spirit," and thanks to this common basis shared between the mind and its religious content, the mind finds itself "touched" (*berührt*) in its innermost; the content *resonates* with the mind: "This is the first and absolute condition for understanding; anything that is not, *in itself*, inside the mind, cannot come *into* the mind, cannot be for it – content namely that is infinite and eternal" (TW 20:493).[28]

Here Hegel insists on the necessity of an immediate, pre-reflective unity of cognition with what it will come consciously to conceive as the absolute or unconditioned, if it is to become aware of it at all. To put it strongly, to be *minded* is – prior to all being *mindful-of* – to have a relation to the unconditioned; the mind itself is that very relation.[29] This relation is non-conscious in Hegel's technical sense of "consciousness." Consciousness involves the supposition that thought, on the one hand, and that which exists substantially and in itself, on the other, are

---

28 Cf. Hegel's critique of instrumental conceptions of cognition in the *Phenomenology* GW 9:53–54/§73. We can trace the same idea at least as far back in Hegel's development as the 1801 *Differenzschrift*. Compare what he has to say there – in essentially the same terms of finitude and infinitude, consciousness and unconsciousness – about the need for philosophy and its relation to "reflection as an instrument of philosophizing" (GW 4:12–19).

29 Note the relation between this view and the structure of the Concept presented in the previous chapter: Cognition, knowing, *is itself the structure of reality*, yet in such a way that the differentiation between mind and world, form and content, is entailed by the structure of the Concept itself; in other words, the self-differentiation of cognition into finite cognition is supposed to be metaphysically necessitated.

metaphysically distinct. Hegel suggests that a deeper affinity or indeed substantial identity is a pre-condition of the mind distinguishing any putatively unconditioned content and attempting to make it understandable to itself. As a presupposition of consciousness, such affinity or identity is non-conscious.

Its non-finite status is directly related to its character as non-conscious. Frederick Beiser has rightly argued that the core of Hegelian idealism lies in the claim that the absolute is spirit, that self-consciousness is therefore an essential feature of spirit, and that absolute spirit's own self-consciousness is identical to our artistic, religious, and philosophical consciousness of it.[30] On this assumption, awareness of the unconditioned is from its very inception "infinite" in the sense that, when taken in itself, the differentiation implied by awareness, namely thought as distinguished from its unconditioned object, is just the manifestation of the unconditioned itself – thought thinking itself. Differentiation that is immediately the emergence of unity marks the structure of what Hegel calls "the infinite" (GW 21:123–37). The first basic condition of understanding, then, is "the going-together with itself of what is substantial," and this condition, says Hegel, "is met unconsciously and fulfills itself, for the very reason that, as what is substantial, the infinite, pure activity, it is not caught up [befangen] in the opposition of consciousness" (TW 20:494).

The first condition of understanding is therefore its "infinite" unity with the infinite itself. Now, before going on to the second, finite condition of understanding, let us pause to observe the parallels between this first condition and what Hegel says about metaphysics in the Encyclopedia.

There metaphysics is initially characterized in the context of a mode of thought that is unbefangen, a word that, in modern German, has a spectrum of related meanings ranging from naïve and unselfconscious through unbiased and objective to shameless and uninhibited:

> The first attitude [of thought to objectivity] is the unbefangen manner of proceeding which, still oblivious to the opposition of thinking within and against itself, contains the faith that through thinking things over the truth comes to be known and what objects truly is brought before consciousness. In this faith, thinking engages the objects directly, reproduces out

---

30 Frederick Beiser, German Idealism: The Struggle against Subjectivism 1781–1801 (Cambridge, MA: Harvard University Press 2002), 588–95; see also Horstmann, Grenzen der Vernunft, 165–87, esp. 180–81.

of itself the content of sensations and intuitions as a content of thought, and finds satisfaction in the like as the truth. All philosophy in its beginnings, all the sciences, even the daily doings and dealings of consciousness, live in this faith. (ENC §26)

When we approach this text from a "non-metaphysical" Kantian or "critical" perspective, we will be inclined to stress the naïveté and lack of critical self-consciousness betokened by the word. And this reading certainly finds support in the presence of words like "faith" (*Glauben*), "obliviousness" (*Bewußtlosigkeit*), as well as in Hegel's express view that metaphysics was in need of Kant's critique. Yet though we must not ignore the text's critical tone, nor ought we to resolve its ambivalence one-sidedly in favor of simple critique. In accord with its root *fangen*, to catch, to trap, to be *befangen* is to be in some sense unfree, hemmed in, hindered, blocked; *Unbefangenheit* can thus also denote a desirable condition. It is in precisely this sense that Hegel uses the word in the passage quoted from the *Lectures on the History of Philosophy*, where he speaks of the first condition of understanding as an "infinite, pure activity" that is "not caught up [*befangen*] in the opposition of consciousness." Hegel's further characterization harmonizes with this: "Because it has no consciousness of its opposition, it is *possible* for this kind of thinking to be both genuine *speculative* philosophizing in terms of its content as well as to dwell in *finite* thought-determinations, that is, the *as yet unresolved* opposition" (ENC §27).

This remark is of the first importance for a proper estimation of the place of metaphysics and the understanding in Hegel's thought. Using "untrammeled" to render *unbefangen* in its positive aspects, we may say that untrammeled, directly realistic thought about the world, including reflection on the unconditioned, can fulfill all the criteria of speculative philosophy *prior to and independently of any critique of reason*, and that it can do so *without necessarily abandoning the medium of "finite" thought-determinations* Hegel believes incapable of expressing the nature of truth. In this sense he repeatedly emphasizes for example the speculative nature of Plato's and Aristotle's thought, as well as of Descartes' or Spinoza's philosophy which he nevertheless locates in the "metaphysical" period.[31] And on the other hand, as we will see below, there are also elements in Locke and Kant that lead him to reckon them among the metaphysicians despite their having introduced the notion of a critique of human cognition. There is thus

31 ENC §31A; TW 19:439; 20:122, 262, 265; GW 15:8–10.

no simple line of demarcation between the critical good guys and the metaphysical bad guys.

Section 27 of the *Encyclopedia* tells us that, to the extent that philosophical understanding expresses the conviction that what is truly substantial is what is revealed in thought and is of the same nature as thought, it is authentically speculative philosophy in Hegel's affirmative sense of the word. It thereby expresses the first condition of understanding, above, namely the inner identity of the unconditioned as the content of thought, with the absolute essence of thought itself. Contrary to Kant in the *Critique of Pure Reason*, for whom the ideas of reason are really just concepts of the understanding that have been "freed" of their legitimate limitations (becoming, shall we say, *unbefangen*), Hegel obviously views the concepts of the understanding – the terms in which we strive to make the unconditioned *understandable* to ourselves – as specifications and limitations of reason's unconscious, speculative conviction of its inner affinity or indeed identity with the absolute itself. To this extent, Hegel would certainly have agreed with Hölderlin that *reason is the beginning of the understanding*, not merely a potentially illicit extension of it.[32] We may therefore expect that his critique of metaphysics as a specific form of thinking about the unconditioned will be motivated by a very different spirit from that of Kant's critique. For Hegel, metaphysical understanding of the unconditioned is not an instance of the mind overstepping its bounds, but of its failing adequately to realize what the first condition of all understanding truly is.

Let us turn, therefore, to Hegel's second basic condition of understanding. It will shed light on the *forgetfulness of reason* that specifically characterizes the form of thought Hegel calls metaphysics.

The second condition of understanding, Hegel tells us, concerns "the presence [*Dasein*] of the content of knowledge, that is, its being in consciousness" (TW 20:494). Distinguishing in purely logical terms between what is *realiter* inseparable, we may say that the mind as it is in itself is the self-relation of the unconditioned to itself (this is the substance of the first condition), but that insofar as that relation is essentially self-consciousness, it must be present *idealiter* as conscious,

---

32 Cf. Hölderlin's letter to Schiller, August 1797, in KstA 6:268. Eckart Förster has argued that in the *Opus postumum*, Kant himself moves away from his earlier doctrine toward a position that could aptly be expressed by Hölderlin's dictum. See *Kant's Final Synthesis: An Essay on the Opus postumum* (Cambridge, MA: Harvard University Press 2000), 148–74.

rational content. The identity of thought and the unconditioned must determine and realize itself through difference. The second condition of understanding is closely linked to this moment of difference:

> [T]o the extent that what is true and eternal is supposed to be *known*, that is, supposed to enter into finite consciousness and be *for* spirit, this spirit *for which* it initially is, is the *finite* spirit, and the manner of its consciousness consists in the representations and forms of finite things and relations. These forms are what consciousness is used and accustomed to; it is the universal mode of finitude, which mode consciousness has appropriated to itself and made into the universal medium of its representational activity, and everything it encounters must be reduced to this form in order for consciousness to possess itself therein and to cognize it. (TW 20:493–94)

The sense of finitude in which the "forms" through which spirit works to understand the unconditioned are said to be finite is complex, but the subject–object diremption is clearly basic to it. *Knowing* what is true and external entails setting it over against the mind as an object to be known. The German is able to bring out this connection more directly in that the noun *Gegenstand* (object) naturally suggests a connection with the verb *entgegensetzen* (to posit something over against something else). We should not, however, assume that Hegel is therefore merely playing on a contingent German etymology. The thought is that *intentional* consciousness (which is all Hegel is interested in here) involves a self-conscious distinction between the conscious self, the object of consciousness, and the way the object is present to consciousness.[33] Understanding necessarily involves such a diremption between subject and object, related to each other in some determinate way. And to be in a determinate relation to some term, some element, some *thing* that is taken as essentially opposed to oneself is to be finite in the Hegelian sense.

Now the lesson from Kant, rehearsed above, was that objectivity is a function, a product, of the synthetic activity through which consciousness brings about its own apperceptive unity. In other words, the fact that the self finds itself over against a world of *things* is bound up with

---

33 Here I am consciously echoing Reinhold's "Principle of Consciousness." For recent discussion of the principle see Eckart Förster, *The Twenty-Five Years of Philosophy*, trans. B. Bowman (Cambridge, MA: Harvard University Press 2012), 153–58; cf. the more detailed account in Beiser, *Fate of Reason*, 252–65, and Ameriks, *Fate of Autonomy*, 105–12. I return to this theme in a more substantial way in Chapter 6.

its own self-consciousness. Furthermore, the synthetic activity that unifies consciousness is complex in itself: there is a plurality of distinct, concurrently acting forms of synthesis (the categories). When we view Hegel's account of understanding from this perspective, we can see that the finitude that consists in the diremption and opposition of subject and object immediately entails a plurality of distinct, mutually opposed, and to that extent *finite* forms of synthesis, that is, determinate relations between subject and object. So the "universal mode" of finitude, that is, the basis of what we ordinarily call *understanding*, comprises at once both a relation of the (*ipso facto* finite) self to a world of things, and as the very structure of that world of things, the basic modes of finitude, that is, the categorial features and relations that properly constitute the objectivity of that world. *Understanding*, then, involves the recognition of those features and relations and their conscious reproduction *idealiter* as the content of thought – as "the true."

> [W]hether or not something is understood, whether consciousness takes possession of some content, finding and knowing itself in that which is an object for it, depends on whether it encounters it in the shape of its accustomed metaphysics. For its metaphysics constitutes its familiar relations; these form the net that stretches throughout its particular intuitions and representations, and it cognizes them only to the extent that they can be contained by it. These relations are the spiritual organ through which the mind takes in content, the sense by which something acquires and possesses sense for the spirit. (TW 20:494)

The categorial features and relations that constitute the objectivity of the finite world are thus the stuff of metaphysics, and metaphysics defines the scope and limits of what, in the broadest sense, can be understood.

It is important, however, that we distinguish here among degrees of explicitness and completeness. It should be a commonplace that in this broadest sense of understanding, the categories need by no means to be clearly formulated and conscious to those who instinctively or habitually employ them:

> Our consciousness has these representations, adheres to them as ultimate determinations, proceeds by way of their guiding connections, but it does not *know* them; it does not make them into the object and interest of reflection ... Metaphysics like this is woven into all its knowing and representing and governs it; it is the net that holds together all the concrete material that concerns us in everything we do. But in our ordinary

consciousness, this web and its nodes are submerged beneath many lay-
ers of material containing our conscious interests and the objects we
have *in front of us*. Those universal threads are not isolated and made
into the objects of our explicit reflection. (TW 20:485–86)[34]

At this implicit level of category use there is no explicit consciousness
of the categories as such, which are present to us implicitly and naïvely
as submersed in the things and events of our perceptual environment.
We can go further: bearing in mind Hegel's first, "unconscious" condition on understanding, we can say that at this implicit level there is no
consciousness of the *necessarily* finite and conditioned nature of what
we understand by means of the categories – the finitude of objectivity
as such and of the categorial forms that structure it.

It is important to see that the transition to explicit consciousness
of the categories as such, represented by ontology, does not initially
include consciousness of their finitude, that is, their role in constituting and structuring a *necessarily* finite objectivity. This is what Hegel
means in section 27 of the *Encyclopedia*, quoted above, when he says
that metaphysical thinking can be at once both genuinely speculative
and hopelessly caught up in merely finite thought-determinations *precisely because* it is unconscious of its "opposition" to being when being is
represented (as it must) as a world of things, objects.

2.5. Hegel's critique of the metaphysics of the understanding

We are now in a position to appreciate Hegel's basic critique of what
he calls metaphysics in its explicitly systematic, philosophical form.

(1) Hegel criticizes metaphysics for its basic orientation towards *things*,
entia, as the subject of philosophical thought. This is obvious in the case
of ontology, which is explicitly concerned with *onta*. However, the same
attitude also pervades rational psychology and theology as the tendency
to grasp the soul and God as kinds of substrates or things. So one of
the basic characteristics of metaphysics is its *reification* of "the true."
Metaphysical reification is the immediate consequence of the *objectification* that is the primary function of the understanding. The objects of the
understanding are not grasped as products or moments of rational activity, but as things in themselves, indeed as the very form of being in itself.

---

34 Cf. GW 21:13–15. These passages are also cited in Stern, *Hegelian Metaphysics*, 4–6.
   I agree with Stern's appraisal, although I would insist on Hegel's critical attitude
   toward the categorial view of reality.

Taking a broad perspective, we may say that Hegel's project of thinking "substance" as "subject" is one with the critique of the metaphysics of the understanding; and that to the extent that Spinoza, in making an infinite and unique substance the fundamental category and reality of his philosophy, proved himself to be the most uncompromising and most speculative of metaphysicians, the project of overcoming Spinozism is again one with that of thinking substance as subject and revealing the unconscious finitude of metaphysics. These correlations are only fully visible, however, when we grasp the specificity of what Hegel criticizes under the label "metaphysics."

(2) Hegel criticizes metaphysics for deriving its categories from *representations* (*Vorstellungen*). That it should do so is unsurprising, given our discussion so far. In Hegelian terminology, "representation" denotes a particular kind of intentional relation to a content.[35] When I represent some content, I am aware of it as *mine*, as participating in my mental life. It arises from the dimension of spatio-temporal intuition that is explicitly experienced as subjective, for example when I *pay attention* to the content of intuition. Furthermore, in contrast to what I experience as the objective dimension of intuition (the "thing" I take myself to be intuiting or to have intuited), the representation belongs to me such that I can (in principle) recall it to mind, consider it under various aspects, imagine it being differently than it is, and so on.

Hegel's term "representation" corresponds to what Kant would call the representation of a possible object, the investigation of whose conditions of possibility is the task of transcendental logic. The problem with metaphysics is that it takes up the categories *only* to the extent that they are the forms of possible objects. This feature of metaphysics cuts across the difference between realism and nominalism, realism and idealism.[36] Regardless of whether the categories are treated within logic as a set of basic concepts or predicates, or within ontology as the

---

35 Cf. ENC §§446–54. Contrast Kant's understanding of representation as the genus of all mental content (B376–77) and Longuenesse's definition of the term "representation" in *Hegel's Critique*, 48.

36 In this context it is notable that Wolff's emphasis on *possibilia*, i.e. on what is thinkable and hence on ontology as treating of the first principles of our *cognition*, is strictly speaking neutral regarding the question whether the content of the categories is mind-independent or merely ideal. For Hegel, this difference is of very subordinate importance, for regardless of whether such contents are interpreted realistically or idealistically in the traditional sense of the terms, they are always already *entia*, things, Wolff's *Dinge überhaupt*, and as such they are *finitizations*, i.e. distortions, of the underlying relation between thought and being.

basic ways things themselves can be, they are conceived as essentially related to objects (*entia*) distinct from and to this extent external to them. The same is still true of Kant: transcendental logic succeeds in taking up the categories as functions of synthesis, that is, as being *essentially* modes of intellectual activity; but Kant fails to grasp them as *more than* forms of synthesis, that is, as generating a content which is *wholly internal* to the activity of thought. The categories, for Kant, remain what they were for pre-Kantian metaphysics, forms of *possible objects*.[37]

Hegel returns frequently to this point of criticism. Metaphysics, he says in section 29 of the *Encyclopedia*, treats its "predicates" as distinct from one another, joined together only insofar as they are predicates of a single (grammatical) subject (a representation); here too, however, their content remains distinct "and they are taken up externally as opposed to one another"; they lack internal cohesion. His charge against Kant is essentially the same: he made it easy for himself by taking up the categories empirically, that is, by abstracting them from the kind of judgments we *in fact* make about things, instead of rationally deriving them and demonstrating their necessity, totality, and internal principle of cohesion.[38] So while the Kantian categories, qua functions of unity, are supposed to constitute the unity and thus objectivity of the sensible manifold as an object of possible experience, in truth they themselves are joined together only externally in the intuition of an object distinct from thought. The categories that are supposed to be the source of concretion ("synthesis") are thus themselves just products of abstraction.

Excursus: Kant's apparent failure to offer any explicit derivation of the table of categories had first been openly criticized by Reinhold, who was followed by Fichte, Schelling, and Hegel.[39] The project of supplying the missing derivation therefore became central to this strand of post-Kantian thought.

---

37 Cf., e.g., Wolff's definition of philosophy as "a science of all possible things, [and] how and why they are possible" (Dt. Log., 115). The fundamental place of possibility in Wolff's philosophy is further evidenced by its place at the beginning of Wolff's ontology ("Von den ersten Gründen unserer Erkenntniß und allen Dinge überhaupt"): see §§10–16.

38 TW 20:346, 392; ENC §42; GW 12:44.

39 See Karl Leonard Reinhold, *Beyträge zur Berichtigung bisheriger Mißverständnisse der Philosophen*, vol. i, *Das Fundament der Philosophie betreffend* (Jena: Widtmann und Mauke 1791, 313–16); for Fichte's and Schelling's formulations of the criticism, see GA i, 4:200–3, 230–1, and SW 1:87, 103ff., respectively.

Now, Michael Wolff has recently argued that contrary to the opinion of Reinhold, Fichte, Schelling, Hegel, and the majority of Kant scholars since their time, Kant did in fact supply a principle and a derivation of the unity and completeness of the table of judgments, one that is based on the possible relations between concepts in judgment.[40] If Wolff is right, then one of the central projects and sources of motivation for Hegelian logic could seem to rest on a mistake. Although space prohibits thorough discussion here, I do not think this implication holds.

It can be argued that the view Hegel elaborates in the Subjective Logic (especially the doctrine of the speculative syllogism) converges with the Kantian derivation as reconstructed by Wolff. However, this does not mean that Hegel would at best merely have reinvented the wheel. First, even in Wolff's version, the Kantian derivation relies on an admixture of traditional logic to which Hegel would have objected. Hegel believes himself not only to have eliminated these *a posteriori* elements, but also to have derived the forms of concept, judgment, and syllogism *in the proper order,* namely from an examination of the categorial forms that Kant, too, holds to be the real foundation of objectively valid judgment, rather than the other way around.

Second, Hegel seeks to derive the forms as iterations of the moments of the same logic of absolute negativity that is the motor for his derivation and critique of the categories of the Objective Logic. One peculiar consequence of this is that various forms of judgment and syllogism are indexed to the categorial levels examined in the Logic of Being and the Logic of Essence. So over the course of Hegel's elaboration of the judgments of determinate being (*Dasein*), reflection, and necessity, and then of the corresponding syllogisms, he conceives his analysis as identifying the strengths and weaknesses of the respective forms and their adequacy for grasping and expressing the structure of the Concept.

Third, Hegel seeks to demonstrate how a sequence of rigorously derived categorial contents necessarily fits into a series of logical forms that are themselves derived by the same kind of procedure as the contents; the forms are not therefore derived on the basis of any *methodical*

---

40 See Michael Wolff, *Die Vollständigkeit der Kantischen Urteilstafel* (Frankfurt: Klostermann 1995). For an overview of the most influential interpretations of the table of judgments, see Peter Baumanns, *Kants Theorie der Erkenntnis: Durchgehender Kommentar zu den Hauptkapitel der "Kritik der reinen Vernunft"* (Würzburg: Königshausen und Neumann 1994), 265–304.

presupposition of *operationes mentis*. Consequently, concept, judgment, and syllogism are presented in the first instance as arising together with objective, categorial content, not as activities carried out by finite subjects. While the same tight fit between pure concepts and subjective functions of unity that we find in Kant is thus maintained in Hegel's exposition, it takes on a decidedly "externalist" slant that contrasts distinctly with the psychologistic slant he criticizes in Kant.

For these reasons, Hegel would hardly have considered his own "completeness proof" for the list of categories and logical forms to be rendered superfluous by the discovery or reconstruction of a roughly corresponding, but essentially quite different completeness proof in Kant. *End of excursus.*

Thus, Hegel sees himself as justified in criticizing both Kant and Locke as metaphysicians because he sees them as deriving the content of the categories from given representations. In the *Critique of Pure Reason*, he complains,

> thinking, understanding stays one particular thing, sensibility another particular thing, and they are joined in an external, superficial way like a chunk of wood and a bone with a piece of string. For example, in the schematism the concept of substance becomes something permanent in time, that is, the pure concept of the understanding, the pure category, is posited in unity with pure intuition. – The representation within me is determined as an accident; it could as well be determined as effect, as a thing-in-itself, as a cause, as a plurality that presupposes unity, and so we have the whole metaphysics of the understanding. (TW 20:348)

He charges Locke with a similar failing: "The Lockean philosophy is, if you will, metaphysics: it is concerned with universal determinations, universal thoughts, and this universal is supposed to be derived from experience, from observation. The Lockean philosophy explains universal representations by abstracting what is universal from concrete perceptions" (TW 20:231; cf. 233, 290–91).

What these two remarks show is that for the critique of metaphysics, as Hegel intends it, the investigation into the origin of our (universal) representations is neither necessary nor sufficient. It is not sufficient, because regardless of whether we locate the origin of universal representations (in particular, the categories) in the spontaneous synthetic activity of the understanding or in raw sense experience, investigation into the psychological genesis of concepts fails from the outset to address their externality and abstractness and constitutive finitude.

It is not necessary, because for the purposes of critique we may just as well start with the categories themselves; Hegel's question is not whether and how the universal representations, categories, or, as he also says *predicates*, apply to objects, but "whether such predicates are something true in and of themselves, and whether the form of judgment is capable of being the form of truth" (ENC §28R).

Hegel's question, in other words, is whether the predicates investigated in their different ways by Wolffian metaphysicians, Lockean empiricists, and Kantian transcendental idealists, are suited *in principle* to be determinations of the unconditioned ("the truth"). For this question, at least as far as Hegel intends to pursue it in the *Logic*, the question of origins is irrelevant; only the possibility of logical genesis or the formulation of a generative procedure for the complete series of such determinations is relevant to Hegel's version of the critique of metaphysics. From the perspective of speculative logic, then, Kant and Locke are caught up in an abstract metaphysics of the understanding to no less a degree than Wolff, his predecessors, and his disciples were.

(3) This metaphysics is abstract precisely to the extent that it is derived from and dependent on representations for its content and its standard of accuracy. Thus Wolff's method was to "give definitions, they are the basis. On the whole they are based on our representations; they are nominal definitions. He transforms our representations into determinations of the understanding; the definition is right when it conforms to such a representation ... Our ordinary representations are thus translated into the empty form of thought" (TW 20:261, 263; cf. 286). Because the categories are derived by a process of abstraction from (putatively) given representations, they are subject to an externality that is incompatible with their supposedly *a priori* nature. Rather than being derivable immanently, according to a principle rooted in the nature of thought (or being, for that matter) itself, they are taken up on the basis of a reflection on our experience of how we use them, and that can never be conclusive.[41] This, indeed,

41 A very closely related criticism is that metaphysics constantly conflates and conjoins the *a priori* with the *a posteriori*: it consistently relies on observation and analysis either of external events or psychological facts about concept use in order to secure its content. This criticism extends to Kant. Cf. ENC §9; TW 20:121–22, 154, 261, 264, 281, 334. Honnefelder's characterization of Wolff's ontology as "rationalism *a posteriori*" may be understood as corroborating Hegel's view of Wolffian philosophy as a mixture of *a posteriori* and *a priori* elements. Honnefelder goes further than Hegel, though, in suggesting an explanation for this characteristic; according to him, Wolff should be

was the reason Kant insisted that in philosophy the definitions have to come at the end and not at the beginning.[42] Thus in addition to the lack of any systematic derivation of the content of supposedly *a priori* categories, they also fall prey to an ineliminable contingency. What they mean is constantly open to dispute, and appeal can be made to no higher standard than that which the disputants happen to believe to be the meaning of the name by which the category is known. One might as well take a poll.

Hegel is keenly aware of this difficulty and will seek to avoid it altogether by defining his concepts *constructively*. Philosophy has a right, he says, to adopt the language of ordinary life in order to designate its concepts, but there can be no question of wanting to prove that the meaning associated with them in a system of philosophy is the same as that which plays a role in ordinary life: "for ordinary life has no concepts, only representations" (GW 12:130). The *Science of Logic* is meant to generate its concepts by a strict, dialectical procedure; their content is determined by their place in the series (in this sense they are *concrete*, that is, not isolated in their content from one another); their name is chosen (arbitrarily within certain bounds) from language's "superfluity" of vaguely synonymous expressions (cf. GW 12:130).

The abstract metaphysics of the understanding, paradigmatically embodied by the system of Wolff, comes to an end with Kant. But this is not to say that Kant is not a metaphysician of the understanding in just the sense to which Hegel objects. In his orientation toward objects, in his focus and dependence on representation, and in his tendency toward abstractness and consequent failure to come to grips with the actual content of the thought-determinations in themselves, Kant continues the Wolffian tradition. As Hegel puts it in the *Lectures on the History of Philosophy*, Kantian philosophy "put an end to the metaphysics of the understanding insofar as it was an objective dogmatism, but in fact it just translated it into a subjective dogmatism, that is, a consciousness in which the same finite determinations of the understanding persist, while the question about what is true in and for itself is abandoned" (TW 20:333). So the transcendental turn is by no means sufficient to constitute a break with the "pre-Kantian" metaphysical

seen as combining the "*a posteriori*-reductive method" of the Scotist metaphysics he would have been familiar with through Suarez, with the modern mathematical ideal he adopted from Descartes, Tschirnhaus, and others. See Honnefelder, *Scientia*, 440.
42 Cf. B756.

tradition; *a fortiori*, it is insufficient (and most likely unnecessary) for a specifically Hegelian critique of metaphysics.

In his almost exclusive commitment to what Hegel calls the finite understanding, Kant belongs to the very metaphysical tradition he brings to an end. So what can Hegel mean when he proclaims Kantian philosophy to be "the foundation and the starting point of recent philosophy" (GW 21:46n.)? The next section provides an answer to this question.

2.6. The *aporiae* of pre-Kantian metaphysics and their re-emergence in Kant and Jacobi

Recall the way Hegel introduces his discussion of modern German, specifically Wolffian, metaphysics in sections 26–27 of the *Encyclopedia*. Metaphysics, as the naïve, natural, or unconscious employment of the categories of the understanding in the faith that they constitute what is truly essential in the things of experience, is an omnihistorical cognitive attitude. And neither, as an explicit philosophical movement, is metaphysics confined to a single period of intellectual history: we find it wherever the understanding's finite determinations are held to be determinations of the conditioned and the unconditioned equally, and it is not in principle incompatible with authentically speculative philosophy, as we can recognize from the cases of Aristotle or Spinoza, for instance. To the extent, however, that metaphysics in the emphatic sense concerns "the *perspective of the mere understanding* on the objects of reason" (ENC §27), it is distinct from speculative philosophy. In this narrow sense, says Hegel, metaphysics finds its "most determinate ... development" in the "former metaphysics, the way it was constituted in Germany prior to the Kantian philosophy" (ENC §27).

I suggested above that the Wolffian school earned this ambivalent distinction because it had given canonical form to modern metaphysics as a self-contained branch of human learning. Wolff formulated ontology, cosmology, and rational psychology and theology as distinct areas of metaphysical inquiry, and in his manner of synthesizing the elements he adopted from more original predecessors such as Descartes and Leibniz he exemplified the ideal of rigorously logical argumentation *more geometrico* to a degree and extent unmatched (albeit largely unsought for) even by them. Wolff's systematic drive remained paradigmatic for Kant and the idealists who came after him, even as they transformed the very method and substance of the older scholastic metaphysics.

There is, however, a further respect in which "pre-Kantian" metaphysics represents the most determinate formulation of a type of philosophical cognition that pervades intellectual history. Through the intensity of their investigations into the unconditioned purely on the basis of finite determinations of the understanding, early modern metaphysicians began to adumbrate an interlocking set of categorial oppositions and contradictions. Now Hegel understands the finite first as constituted through opposition (being this *rather than* that, this *insofar as* it is not that), and thus second as being essentially relative, that is, as being what it is only through its relation to what it is not, that is, as having its identity as what it *is* in its very relation to what it *is not*. Hegel therefore construes this essentially relational character as implying contradiction: finite things and finite determinations generally have their identity or being in an opposed other and thus are (i.e. have their being) what they are not (i.e. by virtue of their non-being).

We need not pause just here to examine the ultimate cogency of Hegel's logico-metaphysical construction of the finite. For the moment it is sufficient to point out that given (1) his conception of finitude and its relation to contradiction, and (2) his commitment to the thesis that the determinations of the understanding are by their very constitution finite, it is natural for Hegel to view the oppositions and contradictions at the core of early modern metaphysical discourse as symptomatic of the finitude of its categories and as marking the beginning of an insight into this (for Hegel) basic fact about the understanding.

Here is Hegel's general characterization of early modern philosophy:

> The shapes of philosophy that we have considered have the character of being metaphysical, of beginning with universal determinations of the understanding, but then joining them up with experience, observation, the empirical manner as such. In the case of this metaphysics, the one side is that the oppositions of thought have been brought to consciousness and interest is directed toward the resolution of the contradiction. Thought and being (extension), God and the world, good and evil, God's power, prescience, and the evil in the world and human freedom, these contradictions ... were at the center of interest. The resolution of these oppositions and contradictions is what has to be given, and the resolution is posited in God; God is therefore that in which all these oppositions are resolved ... In this modern metaphysics, the oppositions have

been developed into absolute contradictions. Though their absolute resolution is also indicated – God – this resolution remains abstract, in the beyond. In this world, all the contradictions remain unresolved in regard to their content. (TW 20:264–65)

It is not hard to recognize elements in this characterization that Hegel would presumably affirm as genuinely speculative. Hegel is here considering Leibnizian metaphysics in particular, but in the context of debates among competing positions his point extends across the breadth of early modern philosophy: these systems are oriented toward the unconditioned as an all-embracing unity that grounds the world of experience. It is in the course of trying to develop a coherent view of the unconditioned that early modern metaphysicians encounter apparent contradictions; we are not dealing with this or that random inconsistency, but with apparently irresolvable tensions arising in the concept of the world-whole and its relation to its ultimate ground. Furthermore, the unconditioned is explicitly conceived as the unity of the contradictory elements or at least as the resolution of the tension.

It is clear that this characterization is not specific to any one system. Cartesian dualism, Spinozist monism, Leibnizian monadology, and French materialism all seek to resolve the tensions named by Hegel. Whichever way the unconditioned is conceived, it is the attempt to conceive the unconditioned that gives rise to the tensions demanding resolution, and the unconditioned is conceived as resolving them, be it through some kind of synthesis or by one-sided denial of the metaphysical independence of one of the terms of opposition.

On the other hand, it is just as obvious what Hegel finds lacking in these systems and the movement from which they emerge. The oppositions and contradictions crop up willy-nilly. For instance, if the unconditioned is represented as an all-knowing, all-powerful, providential God, problems about human free will and the existence of evil in the world arise; but if there is no evident necessity to conceive the unconditioned in this way, then the apparent tensions can be resolved by denying this or that divine attribute or indeed the very notion of God. If matter is conceived as bereft of inherent force and as nothing but extension, the origin of motion and the possibility of the connection of the soul with the body become problematic; but why conceive matter just so? In short, the contradictions within and between rival systems arise inevitably and yet in a seemingly contingent way. They all emerge in the course of thinking the unconditioned, and yet they form a mere aggregate of philosophical problems, interconnected only vaguely. Early modern metaphysics achieves no insight into the necessity of the contradictions it strives in competing ways to resolve: it is unsystematically systematic.

Moreover, the resolutions provided by the various systems in their different ways have one thing in common, namely, their lack of determinateness. Beyond its function as the locus of unity and resolution, the unconditioned has little to offer in the way of concrete features, be it God, nature, or matter. In other words, the unconditioned is introduced to resolve the contradictions, but there is no satisfying account of why the contradictions seem to arise from it in the first place. So the name of the unconditioned marks the empty location of a desired resolution without actually constituting one. To put the point more forcefully, metaphysics reduplicates in the very solution to its problems the structure of finitude that gives rise to them in the first place: the unconditioned or infinite constitutes a sphere of resolution, but an empty sphere, indeterminate, abstract; opposed to it is the sphere of the conditioned, the finite, which is concrete, determinate, and saturated with lived experience, but in which the contradictions persist unresolved for those who must endure them. The infinite remains opposed to the finite, the unconditioned to the conditioned, unity to difference, the indeterminate to the determinate, and the very mode of thought for which the problems of metaphysics emerged in their full determinateness reveals the contradiction of finitude as its innermost structure.

As a matter of fact, therefore, early modern metaphysics is the *most determinate formation* of the mode of thought best characterized as the conception of the unconditioned from the perspective of the mere understanding. Its orientation toward the unconditioned is informed by contradictions that structure its very categories and by the desire to resolve those contradictions in an overarching unity; meanwhile, the structure of its attempted resolutions reduplicates the finitude and contradiction that define it as a mode of thought limited to the understanding. Needless to say, however, these *facts* about early modern metaphysics *in itself* are not part of what it is *for itself*, they are not part of its self-conception: they are not *for it* as they are for us as Hegelian critics. It lacks consciousness of the opposition that runs through it.

Kant's Critical Philosophy, by contrast, may justly be said to represent the self-consciousness of modern metaphysics. Kant was the first to try to systematize the contradictions at the core of metaphysical discourse, to derive them from the form of (finite) thought itself, and thus to show their necessity and insolubility within the framework of finite thought. And this is why Hegel views Kant as "the foundation and starting point of recent philosophy":[43]

> The Kantian antinomies will always remain an important part of the critical philosophy. They, above all, caused the downfall of the previous metaphysics and can be regarded as one of the main transitions to more recent philosophy. For they were instrumental in producing the conviction that the categories of finitude are null on the side of content. (GW 21:179–80)

Hegel repeats this assessment of the transcendental dialectic, especially the antinomies, in the *Lectures on the History of Philosophy*: "The necessity of these contradictions is the interesting side of things that Kant brought to consciousness. Common metaphysics imagines that one of the terms must be true, the other refuted; *but the necessity with which such contradictions arise is the really interesting thing*."[44]

This remark sheds light on section 32 of the *Encyclopedia*, where Hegel says that the older metaphysics "became *dogmatism* because, due to the nature of finite determinations, it had to assume that of *two opposing assertions* ... one had to be *true* while the other was *false*." In other words, its dogmatism was rooted in its commitment to the principle of non-contradiction and the law of the excluded middle. This explanation of what it means for metaphysics to have been *dogmatic* contrasts strikingly with that of Kant, who defines dogmatism as "the presumption that it is possible to make progress with pure knowledge, according to principles, from concepts alone (those that are philosophical) ... and that it is possible to do this without having first investigated in what way and by what right reason has come into possession of those concepts" (Bxxxv).

This difference again goes to show how fundamentally Hegel's conception of critique diverges from Kant's. For Hegel, dogmatism has nothing to do with the supposedly "naïve" commitment to conceptual realism (the belief that, in principle, the essence of things is as we conceive it to be); rather, he singles out that commitment as what is best in "pre-Kantian" metaphysics and as placing it on a higher level than Critical Philosophy itself![45] Neither has it to do with the belief

---

43 GW 21:46n.
44 TW 20:358; emphasis added; cf. TW 20:353.
45 Cf. ENC §28.

that genuine and substantial knowledge can be gained by meditating on philosophical concepts alone; for Hegel, it is precisely because "pre-Kantian" metaphysics continuously has recourse to experience and observation that it is subject to an ineliminable externality, contingency, and lack of properly scientific form. Nor, finally, has it anything to do with some failure to investigate the origin of the categories and the manner in which reason (that is, the understanding) has come into their possession; that kind of inquiry, as we have seen, is neither sufficient nor necessary for breaking with the tradition of *Verstandesmetaphysik*. Kant's single greatest contribution to the critique of metaphysics, as conceived by Hegel, is to have demonstrated that "the infinite cannot be made out with finite categories" (TW 20:327).

Hegel therefore rejects Kant's own explanation of why metaphysics inevitably becomes entangled in a "transcendental dialectic" when it pretends to scientific knowledge of the unconditioned. Kant's transcendental critique, he suggests, amounts to no more than a

> subjective idealism for which their [sc. the categories'] only defect is that they are subjective, not anything about what they are in themselves. In spite of its great achievement, therefore, Kant's exposition of these antinomies is very imperfect; both because it is internally awkward and eccentric and because it is skewed in its result, which *presupposes that cognition has no other forms of thought than finite categories*. In both respects, these antinomies deserve a more accurate critique, one that more closely clarifies its standpoint and method, and also extricates the main point at issue from the useless form into which it has been forced. (GW 21:181; emphasis added)

Moreover, the result that emerges from Kant's presentation of the dialectic is that the ideas of the unconditioned are merely *regulative*. This Hegel sees as the attempt at a "unification of the unconditioned with the conditioned" which, like the God of pre-Kantian metaphysics, remains merely abstract (cf. TW 20:353). Despite Kant's having begun with systematizing the contradictions inherent in the finite determinations of the understanding, and despite his having recognized the necessity with which those contradictions arise, Kant's positive doctrines failed to go a single step further than the metaphysics he brought to an end. The fundamental opposition, that between the finite and the infinite, the conditioned and the unconditioned, remains unresolved (indeed, it is represented as theoretically unresolvable), and the idea of the unconditioned remains as empty and abstract as it was in, say, Spinoza. So as far as its positive results go, Kant's (and Jacobi's) critique of metaphysics ends up at the same place as metaphysics.[46]

2.7. Kant and Jacobi between the finite metaphysics of the understanding and the speculative metaphysics of reason

Kant's philosophy marks one of the significant edges of the "metaphysical period" in Western philosophy. That being said, we must nonetheless take care to note how the sense of "former metaphysics" potentially differs from that of "pre-Kantian metaphysics." For one, Hegel is not averse, in some instances, to counting Locke among the metaphysicians, and this fact indicates that "metaphysics" is not, for Hegel, co-extensive with *rationalist* metaphysics. Furthermore, he sees important continuities between older, "dogmatic" metaphysics and Kant's transcendental philosophy: like the dogmatic metaphysicians, in his theoretical philosophy Kant is exclusively concerned with the finite determinations of the understanding; to the extent that he considers the possibility of an alternative mode of cognition (as he does in respect to the intuitive intellect), it is only to set it up as a hypothetical point of contrast to our finite, discursive understanding. Finally, the period of the former metaphysics is demarcated not by Kant alone, but by *Kant and Jacobi*, whom Hegel almost invariably mentions together in this connection.[47] This fact is significant. Jacobi is by no stretch of the imagination a transcendental philosopher. His critique of metaphysics rests on the argument that metaphysical pretensions to scientific cognition of the unconditioned necessarily end in atheism, fatalism, nihilism; differently from Kant, his emphasis lies not on proving the logical incoherence of special metaphysics, but on revealing the morally and existentially repugnant consequences of a strictly coherent metaphysical system.

From this perspective, Kant's transcendental explanation of the scope and limits of theoretical philosophy, that is, the function of the categories in constituting unified empirical consciousness of appearances and their dependence on sensible intuition for content, is not at the heart of the story. Indeed, it is impossible not to notice that Kant's

---

46 Cf. Hegel's common characterization of Kant and Jacobi at TW 20:384, who are criticized as leaving us with an "unknown God," merely "God as such, God with the determination of what is unlimited, universal, undetermined."

47 Cf. the discussion in the Introduction.

transcendental subjectivism is the subject of at least as much Hegelian polemic as Jacobi's insistence on the sufficiency of immediate certainty as a guarantor of the reality of God, freedom, and personality. Rather, the dual significance of Kant and Jacobi is that, on the one hand, both insist on the necessary relation of the finite mind to the infinite (the unconditioned), that is, on the necessity of metaphysics; this distinguishes them from the superficial *Popularphilosophie* and *Unphilosophie* of late Enlightenment psychology, anthropology, and common sense with their misguided anti-metaphysical, anti-systematic affect.

On the other hand, both insist that scientific cognition of the infinite (the unconditioned) is impossible on the basis of the cognitive forms the understanding has to rely on. Kant argues that attempts at scientific metaphysics lead the understanding into antinomies and other devastating logical embarrassments; Jacobi argues that the forms of scientific cognition necessarily construe their objects as conditioned, dependent, externally determined and thus not only falsify the objects of metaphysics (the unconditioned) in advance, but ultimately instill a perverse belief in their unreality. Therefore all that remains of the former metaphysics is its fundamental directedness toward what exists in and for itself, substantial being ("rational faith"), minus any cognitive means for moving determinately in its direction – a compass without a map to go with it.[48]

The negative effects of attempting to formulate the unconditioned in terms of our conceptual scheme motivate Kant and Jacobi, in their separate ways, to place relatively narrow limits on the scope of the categories, and this is the *germ* for the idea of a critique of the understanding, a critique of categories, a critique of our conceptual scheme *in the Hegelian sense of critique*.

By metaphysics, in its strictest sense, Hegel therefore understands the philosophical standpoint (1) for which the conceptual scheme represented by the categories (by the understanding) is ultimate and (2) which explicitly undertakes to determine the nature of the unconditioned by means of the categories. It makes no difference in this context whether the categories are understood realistically as ontologically ultimate or idealistically as (merely) epistemologically ultimate. To the extent that Kant and Jacobi deny the possibility of (2), that

---

48 Cf. Andreas Arndt, "Figuren der Endlichkeit: Zur Dialetik nach Kant," in Annett Jubara and David Bensler (eds.), *Dialektik und Differenz: Festschrift für Milan Prucha* (Wiesbaden: Harrassowitz Verlag 2001), 91–104.

is, the possibility of determining the unconditioned in terms of the categories, they initiate the project of a critique of metaphysics. To the extent, however, that their attitude towards (1), the irreducible and ultimate nature of the categories, is ambiguous, both can be seen still to have one foot in the metaphysical mode of thought.

In spite of themselves, Kant and Jacobi remain unwilling and unwitting metaphysicians. They belong to the epoch of thinking whose end they have brought about. They are basis and the starting point of a new age in philosophy, yet an age to which on Hegel's view they do not wholly belong.

3

HEGELIAN SKEPTICISM AND THE IDEALISM OF THE FINITE

3.1. Introduction

This chapter is centrally concerned with the consequences that follow when one rejects Kant's doctrine of transcendental idealism while retaining his views on the relationality of finite, conditioned objects and the antinomies of pure reason. The basic line of thought is this: transcendental idealism exposes Kant to criticisms of subjectivism and psychologism; Hegel therefore rejects it, thereby radicalizing Kant's insights into the conformity of the empirical world with the exercise of apperceptive spontaneity. However, since Hegel retains the Kantian idea that the finite things of the empirical world are entities constituted solely by relations, and since he believes Kant was right in arguing that the application of the categories to non-finite things results in contradictions, the position that results from his denial of transcendental idealism can be labeled "realism" only with heavy qualifications. It is more accurate to characterize the position as an "idealism of the finite" (as Robert Stern has done): the thesis that finite things are ungrounded in themselves and therefore have no substantial existence of their own; they are indeed merely relational and the contradictions that arise in the sphere of finite things are real. We must therefore accept that Hegel's rejection of transcendental idealism results in a maximally strong version of skepticism in regard to authentic knowledge about the things of the empirical world; for if these are ontologically deficient and less than fully grounded, adequate rational insight into particular, finite aspects within the empirical world is not possible. Since Hegel nevertheless believes himself in a position to give a satisfactory account (1) of why the finite world is constituted in this way and (2) of the structure of the unconditioned or infinite, we should understand him not, finally, as a skeptic, but as a revisionary philosopher.

Section 3.2 begins with a brief discussion of the distinctly non-Kantian perspectives that informed Hegel's reception of Kant's theoretical philosophy from the very outset, among them his sym-philosophical relations with Hölderlin and Sinclair in the second half of the 1790s, from which period his first serious engagement with Kantian epistemology and metaphysics dates. The purpose of this discussion is chiefly to remind the reader of the relative distance between Hegel's original philosophical motivations and those of Kant, so as to frame the ensuing discussion of Hegel's thoroughgoing revision of central Kantian doctrines. In particular, I will argue that Hegel espouses an unmitigated skepticism toward the objects of finite cognition that is perhaps more radical than any variety of skepticism before it.

Sections 3.3 through 3.5 approach Hegel's skepticism by way of an extended discussion of three major contemporary interpreters of Hegel: Robert Pippin, John McDowell, and Robert Stern. I agree with McDowell that it is more accurate to describe Hegel as a realist than as an anti-realist, as Pippin would have it. In fact, the most radical features of Hegel's philosophy only come to the fore once the extent to which he rejected Kant's transcendental idealism is realized. However, there is also something potentially misleading in McDowell's realist characterization of Hegel. We must not forget that he embraces Kant's insights into the dialectical nature of the categories when they are applied to the unconditioned, and that he shares certain Kantian intuitions about the relational character of finite objects. In maintaining these positions while simultaneously rejecting transcendental idealism, Hegel commits himself to the thesis that the finite world has no authentic being or existence in itself and that it is marked by a pervasive underdetermination. I follow Robert Stern in referring to this doctrine as Hegel's "idealism of the finite."

Section 3.6 deepens this interpretation by examining parallels between Kant's idealism and Spinoza's substance monism – parallels that were noticed by some of Kant's contemporaries, including Jacobi. I try to show that in rejecting transcendental idealism two alternatives are possible. Either one follows Jacobi in reaffirming an effectively "pre-critical" view of the substantiality of finite objects, or one maintains Kant's absolutely relational ontology of *substantia phaenomenon*, but without holding any kind of finite substantiality in reserve "behind" the veil of perception. The latter alternative is that taken by Hegel.

Section 3.7 draws out the consequences of this move for Hegel's conception of truth. Specifically, I argue that the specific manner in which Hegel rejects transcendental idealism also makes it impossible for him to acknowledge that there can be anything like foundationally justified empirical propositions about determinate, finite objects. This deeply skeptical consequence puts Hegel further at odds with McDowellian realism, and in section 3.8 I seek to corroborate my interpretation of Hegel as pursuing a strategy of skeptical revisionism in regard to the categorial view of reality. Section 3.9 concludes the chapter with a reconsideration of the ways in which, from a Hegelian perspective, it was the defining doctrine of transcendental idealism itself that prevented Kant's critical philosophy from achieving a critique of knowledge in the fullest possible sense.

3.2. The post-Kantian preconceptions of Hegel's Kant reception

"Philosophy is not yet at an end. Kant has provided the results; the premisses are still lacking. And who can understand results with premisses?"[1] Schelling's dictum, formulated in a 1795 letter to Hegel and frequently cited in literature, follows a pattern already well established by Kant's less orthodox heirs in Jena. Karl Leonhard Reinhold was the first to claim that Kant had failed even to hint at the basic premisses of his philosophy, much less to formulate them with the clarity appropriate to a rigorously scientific exposition.[2] Fichte adopts both Reinhold's criticism and his ambition of providing a foundation and systematic exposition of Kant's unwritten (and perhaps incompletely conceived) philosophy.[3] Common to all three is an attitude of ambivalence toward Kant's achievement: with the critical turn, Kant has initiated a new period in philosophical thought, but in the published Critiques he has given no more than the fragment of a system whose principles and method have yet to be found. This attitude, perhaps more than any specific doctrines held in common, qualifies the Jena

---

1 Schelling to Hegel, letter from January 6, 1795. On the topos of "conclusions without premises," which was first introduced by Reinhold, see Horstmann, *Grenzen der Vernunft*, 76–77, 85–91.
2 See Reinhold, *Beyträge* 1:274. Cf. *Über das Fundament des philosophischen Wissens* (Jena: Mauke 1791), 5.
3 Cf., e.g., GA I, 2:67, 335.

idealists as genuinely *post*-Kantian. They directed their energies neither toward an elaborate and detailed criticism of the Kantian "letter,"
as did Kant's detractors in the empiricist, rationalist, and *popularphilos-
ophische* camps, nor toward commentary, exegesis, and apology, as did
Kant's orthodox disciples in Königsberg and Halle. Rather, Kant's
thought was for them indicative of a new set of conceptual possibilities
that could and ought to be explored and developed independently of
Kant's specific example.

That Hegel shares this attitude need hardly be emphasized. When
analyzing and appraising his views on specific Kantian doctrines, we
must never forget that, from the outset, Hegel approached Kant's *theoretical* philosophy through the mediation of distinctly non-Kantian
perspectives. Hegel's earliest documented, independent discussion of
Kant's theoretical philosophy takes place relatively late in his philosophical development, in the fragment *Glauben und Sein* from Hegel's
Frankfurt period (1797–1800), during which his thinking was strongly
influenced by his association with Hölderlin and Sinclair.[4] There his
approach to the Kantian antinomies is informed by Jacobi's concept of
"faith" or "belief" (*Glauben*) in the *Letters on the Doctrine of Spinoza*, as well
as by Hölderlin's concept of "unification" and his philosophy of life.[5]
Hegel's selection of topics and passages from Kant's three Critiques in
the critical writings from his early Jena period (1801–3) is also clearly
dictated by the programmatic interests he pursued in common with
Schelling, and even his characterization of specific Kantian doctrines
sometimes betrays the direct influence of Fichte (for example his consistent identification of reason with the pure I).[6] Somewhat differently,
therefore, from Reinhold, Fichte, or Schelling, whose post-Kantianism
was to a far greater degree shaped by unmediated study of the letter
of the Kantian texts, Hegel may be said to have approached Kant's
philosophy with a post-Kantian perspective on its strengths and weaknesses already in place. It would be untenable to deny the importance

---

4 See Manfred Baum, *Die Entstehung der Hegelschen Dialektik* (Bonn: Bouvier 1986),
48–73. There are reasons to believe that the earlier *Manuskript zur Psychologie und
Transzendentalphilosophie* from 1794 (GW 1:167–92) depends on a compilation
of lecture notes taken by some third party, and not on direct study of Kant's text:
see Riccardo Pozzo, "Zu Hegels Kantverständnis im manuskript zur Psychologie
und Transendentalphilosophie aus dem Jahre 1794," in M. Bondeli and
H. Linneweber-Lammerskitten (eds.), *Hegels Denkentwicklung in der Berner und
Frankfurter Zeit* (Munich: Fink 1999), 15–29.
5 This is most evident in the early text *Glauben und Sein* (TW 1:251).
6 Cf., e.g., GW 4:359, 434.

of Kantian philosophy for the understanding of Hegel's thought or to suggest that Hegel was simply dependent on his predecessors for the content of his views on Kant; yet neither must we underestimate the extent to which his understanding of the stakes involved in the critical reception of Kant was determined by the advanced state of play when Hegel entered the game after considerable delay.

These remarks are made by way of prefacing discussion of the role played in the *Science of Logic* by Kant's conception of *transcendental logic*. The importance of the Kantian template for understanding Hegel's *Logic* has rightly been emphasized, most recently by Béatrice Longuenesse, who argues that down to its minutest details, "Hegel's *Logic* is literally nourished by Hegel's discussion of transcendental philosophy. It's relation to Kant's philosophy is certainly not the only source of intelligibility for Hegel's *Logic*," she concedes, "but it is the most important."[7] Longuenesse has shown the extent to which key Hegelian notions (concept, reason, truth, critique, and others) are to be understood as transformations of Kantian terms.[8] The result is an illuminating analysis of the aims and methods of Hegel's *Logic*, not least the notoriously difficult *Doctrine of Essence*. Yet though my interpretation here owes a debt to Longuenesse's acute reconstruction, I disagree with her judgment that Kant is the *single most* important source of intelligibility. As I pointed out in Chapter 1, Jacobi's very different critique of rationalist metaphysics is of equal importance for understanding the architectonic of the *Science of Logic* as well as its methodology and Hegel's basic motives for developing it.

For the present, however, I intend to focus on Kant's transcendental logic, reviewing some of the very persuasive reasons for seeing it as a kind of template for Hegel's speculative logic. I will later turn to a discussion of why, nevertheless, Hegel's logic cannot properly be said to be a transcendental logic, or Hegel to be pursuing a transcendental project in anything like the Kantian sense.

3.3. Hegel's rejection of Kantian subjectivism

"In this work," Hegel states in the first published volume of the *Science of Logic*, "I make frequent references to the Kantian philosophy (which

---

7 See Longuenesse, *Hegel's Critique*, 16. Also Robert Pippin, *Hegel's Idealism: The Satisfactions of Self-Consciousness* (Cambridge University Press 1989), 175–77.
8 Cf. Longuenesse, *Hegel's Critique*, esp. 165–81.

to many might seem superfluous) because, whatever might be said in this work or elsewhere of its precise character or of the various parts of its exposition, it constitutes the foundation and the starting point of recent German philosophy, and this is a merit of which it can boast undiminished by whatever faults may be found in it" (GW 11:31n.). As he then explains, the content of what he calls "objective logic," that is, the examination of the categories of Being and Essence that comprises the first part of the *Logic*, corresponds pretty closely to Kant's "transcendental logic," and that he will therefore be making frequent reference to the latter.

It is easy to see that many of the so-called *pure thought-determinations* of Hegel's objective logic correspond directly to the transcendental analytic of the *Critique of Pure Reason*. Of course, in light of the influence Wolffian logic exercised on Hegel's generation as well on Kant's, this high degree of correspondence between their respective treatments of logic and metaphysics should not surprise us. Both philosophers must be seen engaged in a critical transformation of a living logico-metaphysical tradition in which both were reared. This transformative aspect of their relation to the tradition is especially manifest in the relation between Hegel's subjective logic (*Logic of the Concept*) and Kant's transcendental logic. In the section entitled *Der Begriff im Allgemeinen*, Hegel again makes direct reference to Kant's path-breaking achievement: Whereas pre-Kantian expositions of logic treated concepts as representations that are merely *had* or *possessed* by minds, Kant is said to have "gone beyond this superficial relation of the understanding as the faculty of concepts and of the concept itself" and to have recognized them as essential functions or modes of activity of the I: "It is one of the profoundest and truest insights to be found in the *Critique of Reason* that the *unity* which constitutes the *essence of the concept* is recognized here as the *originally synthetic* unity of *apperception*, as the unity of the 'I think' or of self-consciousness" (GW 12:17–18).

It would be easy to extend discussion of the parallels between the *Critique of Pure Reason* and Hegel's *Science of Logic*. However, the important point within this preliminary comparison of the two is simply to recognize that both for Hegel and for Kant, the pure concepts of the understanding are not in the first instance *possessions* of thought, but *modes of synthetic activity*. In other words, the actual ground of the *content* of categorial representations is a self-directed *activity* constituting the unity of thought. Yet despite the massive parallels between the two, there are equally substantial aspects in which Kant's transcendental idealism is also absent from Hegel's methodological reflections. To these I now turn.

Robert Pippin's landmark study, *Hegel's Idealism: The Satisfactions of Self-Consciousness*, is based on the premise that "the basic position of [Hegel's] entire philosophy should be understood as a direct variation on a crucial Kantian theme, the 'transcendental unity of apperception.'"[9] As Pippin explains in a related text, not only in the *Phenomenology of Spirit* (which is directly concerned with so-called shapes of *consciousness*), but also in the *Science of Logic*, Hegel is "still adhering, roughly, to the Kantian strategy on how to establish basic or fundamental components of any conceptual scheme (or rules for any objective judgment about determinate objects), one that makes essential reference to the possibly self-conscious nature of all judgment."[10] Pippin's influential approach explicitly breaks with a long tradition of viewing Hegel either as an extravagant metaphysician who refused to heed Kant's critical admonitions or as a historicist philosopher concerned exclusively with the development of society, state, and culture.[11] Hegel is represented instead as a transcendental epistemologist, dedicated to uncovering the conditions of possibility under which we can lay claim to objective knowledge (or even formulate such claims), and committed to the unity of self-consciousness as the most basic condition of all.[12]

Pippin's interpretation has not been without its critics. In an early discussion, Terry Pinkard observed that Hegel's mature system, comprising speculative logic and philosophy of nature in addition to the philosophy of (human) mind and spirit, cannot be reconciled with the thesis that Hegel placed apperception at the center of a transcendentally oriented project.[13] More recently, Robert Stern has insisted on the

---

9 Pippin, *Hegel's Idealism*, 6, with reference (in note 14) to the passages from the *Science of Logic* quoted above (*Vom Begriff im Allgemeinen*), GW 12:17 and 23.

10 Robert Pippin, "Hegel and Category Theory," *Review of Metaphysics* 43:4 (June 1990): 839–48, here 843. The article appeared as a response to Pinkard's critical discussion of *Hegel's Idealism* in the same issue, cited below.

11 Cf. Pippin, *Hegel's Idealism*, 3ff.

12 Cf. Terry Pinkard's characterization of Pippin's view in "How Kantian was Hegel?" *Review of Metaphysics* 43:4 (June 1990): 831–32. Ameriks, "Recent Work," documents the epistemological shift in Hegel studies that took place around the turn of the decade, 1989–1990.

13 Pippin, "How Kantian was Hegel?" 833–34. Pippin might well rejoin by insisting that Hegel's philosophy of nature must be jettisoned from any successful attempt to appropriate Hegelian insights in a contemporary philosophical context, informed

weight of Pippin's own observation that Hegel "slips frequently from a 'logical' to a material mode, going far beyond a claim about thought or thinkability, and making a *direct* claim about the necessary nature of things, direct in the sense that no reference is made to a 'deduced' relation between thought and thing."[14] Stern also argues that if the upshot of Hegel's radicalization of Kant, as Pippin sees it, is to deny any sense to a mind–world dichotomy, then there is no reason left to "think of an investigation into the categories as an investigation into the conditions of *self-consciousness* at all." The I loses any real significance as the ground of the enterprise, and as a further consequence the anti-realism Pippin attributes to Hegel loses purchase: after all, the motivation for the alleged anti-realism comes mainly from the thesis that critical exploration of the categories is an exploration of *how we* as self-conscious cognizers *must take the world to be*, not how the world really is.[15]

In my view, the balance of the textual evidence is in favor of the opinion that Hegel accorded a distinctly metaphysical significance to the *Logic* (and *a fortiori* to the parts of the system comprising the *Realphilosophien* of mind and nature). Consider for example what Hegel has to say about the value of the transcendental approach as such:

> Now because the interest of the Kantian philosophy was directed to the so-called *transcendental* character of the thought-determinations, the treatment itself of such determinations came up empty. What they are in themselves apart from their abstract relation to the I, a relation which is the same for all, their determinateness and relation to each other was not made into a subject of consideration, and therefore knowledge of their nature was not in the least advanced by this philosophy. What alone is of interest in this connection comes only in the critique of the ideas [sc. of pure reason]. (GW 21:48)

Hegel immediately goes on to say that adequate knowledge of the categories will only be achieved once the form of "the I, consciousness" has been "shed" (GW 21:48).

---

by modern empirical science and philosophy of science. Sebastian Rand has recently argued, however, that Hegel's philosophy of nature plays an indispensible role in securing his currently more attractive views on human freedom and autonomy. See "The Importance and Relevance of Hegel's Philosophy of Nature," *Review of Metaphysics* 61:2 (2007): 379–400. Objections to placing apperception at the center of Hegel's project have also been raised in Houlgate, *The Opening of Hegel's Logic*, 139.

14 Pippin, *Hegel's Idealism*, 187, quoted in Stern, *Hegelian Metaphysics*, 49–50.

15 For the quotation and the line of argument sketched above, see Stern, *Hegelian Metaphysics*, 50–51.

In a similar vein, Hegel suggests that Kant's philosophy was one-sided in being focused exclusively "on the origin of our cognition insofar as it cannot be ascribed to objects" (GW 21:46; cf. ENC §§42A1–3). Even apperception, as conceived by Kant, is not allowed to stand as an unqualified result of transcendental philosophy. The "I think" is said by Kant to "accompany" all my representations; but to accompany all my representations, sensations, desires, actions, and so forth, says Hegel, is to be merely common (*gemeinschaftlich*) to them all, and this is to reduce the I as "the universal in and for itself" to an external and superficial form of universality (ENC §20; cf. B131–36). So while Kant did go further than any thinker before him by grasping apperception itself as the ground of the categories, he also went no further than the I, "the concrete existence of the entirely *abstract* universality, of that which is abstractly *free*." "Nothing then remained but this appearance of the 'I think' that accompanies all my representations – and of which we do not have *the slightest concept*" (ENC §20; GW 12:194; cf. B403–5).

As mentioned previously, Hegel followed a general post-Kantian trend in criticizing Kant for having failed to give a systematic derivation of the categories. This aspect of his criticism, taken in itself, is of course compatible with an intention to carry out and complete the Kantian project, somewhat as Reinhold or Fichte had hoped to do. The same is true of Hegel's more drastic charge that Kant failed even to investigate the nature and content of the categories as he takes them up. Kant himself says that in the *Critique of Pure Reason* he purposely omits "definitions of the categories, although I may be in possession of them ... In a system of pure reason, definitions of the categories would rightly be demanded, but in this treatise they would merely divert attention from the main object of the inquiry" (B108–9). However, Hegel's remark (quoted above) that it is only in regard to the ideas of pure reason that Kant gives any account of the determinate content and relation of concepts to one another, indicates that he does not have definitions in mind but rather what it means for the categories to have content at all, that is: what it means for them to have a relation to an object. In Hegel's eyes, therefore, Kant not only failed to derive the categories in any scientific, systematic way; he also failed to do justice to the minimal requirement of a transcendental logic, that is, to investigate concepts "that refer *a priori* to objects, and not to abstract from all the *content* of objective cognition" (GW 21:47). But here again, even this drastic charge is compatible with an intention to carry out the transcendental project that Kant perhaps envisioned, but failed to execute in a satisfactory way.

By contrast, some of the other passages quoted above indicate a fundamental incompatibility between speculative logic and Kantian transcendental logic. Kant's critical project is *defined* by the epistemological question concerning the origin, the scope, and the limits of human cognition. It is just this defining question that Hegel rejects as the fundamental error of transcendental philosophy. We must keep this fact in mind when for example Hegel characterizes the objective logic (i.e. the doctrines of being and essence in the *Science of Logic*) as "tak[ing] the place of the former metaphysics."

> Logic, however, considers these forms [sc. of pure thought] free of those substrata, which are the subjects of *figurative representation*, considers their nature and value in and for themselves. The former metaphysics neglected to do this, and it therefore incurred the just reproach that it employed the pure forms of thought *without critique*, without previously investigating whether and how they could be the determinations of the thing-in-itself, to use Kant's expression – or more precisely, of the rational. – The objective logic is therefore the true critique of such determinations – a critique that considers them, not according to the abstract form of the *a priori* as contrasted with the *a posteriori*, but in themselves according to their particular content. (GW 21:48–49)[16]

When, therefore, Hegel promises to deliver the "true critique" of metaphysics he cannot mean a transcendental critique that would go beyond Kant merely by supplying the premises he failed to formulate or the definitions he never gave. Hegelian critique is not Kantian critique. Its aim is not to vindicate the *a priori* objective validity of the categories, on the one hand, and to determine the scope and limits of that validity,

16 Rand ("Hegel's Philosophy of Nature," 385–86) takes this passage to show that Hegel explicitly rejected the *a priori/a posteriori* distinction itself as irrelevant to (his) philosophy. It is true that if Hegel's *Logic* is not primarily an epistemological undertaking, then the epistemic distinction between the *a priori* and the *a posteriori* is irrelevant to its content. But this cannot mean that the distinction itself is irrelevant to philosophy in general, since otherwise Hegel would not have criticized Kant's "merely empirical" manner of deriving the categories from a given table of judgments. In my view, Rand's interpretation misplaces the emphasis of the passage. Hegel is objecting not to the distinction between the *a priori* and *a posteriori*, but to the view (attributed to Kant) that a genuine critique need do no more than vindicate the categories as legitimate *a priori* possessions of the understanding. Hegel's point is that this formal treatment of the categories, which considers them only in their epistemic relation to a finite subject, fails to address the more important question of their content, taken in itself.

on the other. Hegel intends a critical derivation of the content of the *ontological* categories of traditional metaphysics that will effectively disqualify them as forms of authentically scientific cognition at all.

3.4. Hegel's rejection of transcendental idealism: the realist dimension

John McDowell has given us a way of addressing some of the discrepancies between Kant's transcendental idealism and Hegel's speculative idealism which, at first blush, seems to succeed in reconciling a broadly Kantian construal of Hegel's thought with the latter's harsh critique of Kant's subjectivism.[17] McDowell follows Pippin in emphasizing Hegel's indebtedness to the centrality of transcendental apperception and the spontaneity of the cognitive faculty. But contrary to Pippin he believes that Kant's transcendentalism is precisely what, in Hegel's eyes, is most deeply wrong with Kant's idealism.[18]

McDowell points to the aspects of Kantian philosophy that are closest to the idealism recommended by Hegel: the centrality of judgment and the notion that categorial unity is at once both a condition of the possibility of experience and of the possibility of the objects of experience themselves.[19] Together, these components of Kantianism add up to the idea that the "capacities that belong to apperceptive spontaneity are actualized in intuitions," or more strongly: "the way empirical thinking is beholden to the independent reality disclosed in experience ... is not, just as such, an infringement on the freedom of apperception. It constitutes what we might conceive, rather, as the medium in which that freedom is exercised ... the pursuit of knowledge as the unconditioned activity of reason."[20]

While the first formulation is Kantian, the second is distinctly Hegelian. What separates the two is the doctrine of transcendental idealism, that is, Kant's claim that space and time are purely subjective and contingently human forms of intuition. On this view of things, the spontaneity of thought is, first of all, conditioned by "a sort of brute

---

17 John McDowell, "Hegel's Idealism as a Radicalization of Kant," in *Having the World in View: Essays on Kant, Hegel, and Sellars* (Cambridge, MA: Harvard University Press 2009), 69–89.

18 For a clear statement of McDowell's divergence from Pippin in regard to the value and coherence of transcendental idealism and in regard to Hegel's estimation of it, see *ibid.*, 82–85.

19 *Ibid.*, 69–75.

20 *Ibid.*, 74 and 82, respectively.

fact about us – given from outside to the unifying powers of apperceptive spontaneity, and not determined by their exercise."[21] Moreover, the objectivity of knowledge (that is, knowledge itself) is undercut, since according to transcendental idealism what we know is not how things are, but merely how things are *insofar* as we have imposed our purely subjective forms of sensibility upon them. This is recognizably a variation on the criticism Hegel formulates in the Introduction to the *Phenomenology*: the picture of cognition as involving a medium or instrumental form specifically different from the form of the objects of cognition is self-undermining, since it finally entails that once we have, so to speak, *corrected for* the purely non-objective components in cognition, there is nothing objective left over to serve as the content of cognition. All that remains of putatively cognized reality is a fully indeterminate "thing-in-itself," or as Hegel says, only the "pure direction or a blank place" of truth (GW 9:54/§73).

In McDowell's "harsh" formulation, "though the Aesthetic purports to ground *a priori* knowledge that is objective, in the only sense we can make intelligible to ourselves, what it puts in place is indistinguishable from a subjective psychologism."[22] Far from protecting "the common-sense conception of empirically accessible reality as independent of us,"[23] Kant fundamentally alienates that view with a conception which, as Hegel says, "must seem rather bizarre to natural consciousness" (ENC §42R3).

The charge of psychologism is one that Hegel himself levels against Kant,[24] and he takes it to be unanswerable within the framework of transcendental idealism. Hegel's radicalization of Kant thus consists in "discarding the frame" of transcendental idealism in order to arrive at a picture that is both closer to the natural view of our cognitive relation to the world and which reveals "the objects of empirical intuitions" as "both genuinely objective and such that the very idea of our getting them in view requires an appeal to apperceptive spontaneity"[25] – the unconditioned freedom of reason.

---

21 *Ibid.*, 76.
22 *Ibid.*
23 *Ibid.*, 81–82.
24 Cf. TW 20: 339–53, to which McDowell also refers. Hegel makes the same point at GW 12:22: "Kantian philosophy has never got beyond the psychological reflex of the Concept and has once more reverted to the claim that the Concept is permanently conditioned by a manifold of intuition."
25 McDowell, "Hegel's Radicalization of Kant," 81.

3.5. Hegel on the non-being of the finite: objective idealism and the limits of McDowell's realist interpretation

McDowell is right that Kant's transcendental idealism is untenable, or at least that it must be judged unsuccessful by Kant's own lights and unacceptable by Hegel's standards. The doctrine fails to be fully objective in precisely the measure it fails to be properly *realistic* about the relation of the categories to experience and to the things themselves. McDowell's reconstruction of Hegel as a radicalized Kant, freed of transcendental idealism, also goes a long way toward an accurate rendering of Hegelian logic and metaphysics. It does not, however, get us all the way there. To see why not, consider that despite his rejection of transcendental idealism and the concomitant doctrine of uncognizable things-in-themselves, Hegel praises and preserves Kant's thesis that empirical cognition is cognition of *mere appearances*:

> Kant stopped halfway through in that he took appearance in a merely subjective sense, fixating abstract essence outside of it as a thing in itself, inaccessible to our cognition. To be only an appearance is the proper nature of the immediately objective world itself, and by knowing it to be such we also cognize its essence which does not lie behind or beyond appearance, but manifests itself as essence precisely by deflating it [the objective world] to mere appearance. (ENC §131A)

Thus to reject the doctrine of things-in-themselves that reduced cognition to something merely subjective without genuinely and robustly objective import is not to reinstate what Hegel elsewhere calls the *realism of finitude* (GW 4:321). Odd though the formulation may initially sound, what we *objectively cognize by way of the categories are, objectively and in themselves, appearances*, which is to say nothing in themselves.

Hegel is committed to the complex thesis that (1) the categories are constitutive of objects; (2) objects are both cognizable and independent of finite cognizers and acts of cognition; (3) objects as constituted by the categories are finite; and (4) to be finite is to have no ontologically independent (i.e. "really real") existence, that is, the finite is mere appearance.[26] The first two components of this thesis make up what we might call Hegel's *epistemological realism*:[27] the objects of

---

26 In Chapter 6, I argue that this complex thesis is required in order to resolve difficulties in Kant's theory of formal apperception and its relation to the sensible manifold.

27 I am nodding here to Kenneth Westphal. See his *Hegel's Epistemological Realism: A Study of the Aim and method of Hegel's Phenomenology of Spirit* (Dordrecht, Boston, and London: Kluwer, 1989), esp. ch. 10.

human cognition are essentially cognizable in terms of the categories[28] and their cognizability is not merely a product of impositions by finite subjects. The second two components make up Hegel's *idealism of the finite*:

> The proposition that the finite is ideal constitutes idealism. The idealism of philosophy consists in nothing else than in recognizing that the finite has no veritable being. Every philosophy is essentially an idealism, or at least has idealism for its principle, and the question then is how far this principle is actually carried out. This is as true of philosophy as of religion; for religion equally does not recognize finitude as a veritable being, as something ultimate and absolute or as something underived, uncreated, eternal. Consequently the opposition of idealistic and realistic philosophy has no significance. A philosophy which ascribed veritable, ultimate, absolute being to finite existences as such, would not deserve the name of philosophy. (GW 21:142)[29]

We can restate Hegel's position this way. What McDowell quite lucidly and correctly reconstructs as Hegel's radicalization of Kant is Hegel's cognitive or *epistemological realism*. McDowell's reconstruction seems to halt, though, before arriving at Hegel's *metaphysical idealism*: the position that the whole sphere of categorically constituted, finite objectivity is both *independent* of *finite* cognizers and radically *dependent* on an *infinite* ground that does not itself in turn fall under the categories, but is the activity of which they are manifestations.[30]

Once we recognize this second component of Hegel's position, we are in a better position to understand what he means when he says the objective logic is the "true critique" of metaphysics Kant failed to give. For we can see that, to the extent that the categories are constitutive of the merely finite (Kant's "appearances"), they cannot be properly employed as a means of cognizing the infinite (i.e. the unconditioned). But this is to say that it is neither necessarily the nature of

---

28 That is, according to the complete list of categories, not the somewhat truncated list offered by Kant.

29 Also cited in Stern, *Hegelian Metaphysics*, 57–58. Stern refers (58, n. 41) to a parallel passage at ENC §95; he also adduces reasons not to heed Pippin's warning that we ought not to read too much into this and similar passages since Hegel is just "self-consciously appropriating the language of pre-critical metaphysics" without adopting any of its outlook (57, n. 40).

30 Hegel would presumably object to applying the finite category of "ground" to describe the relation of the Idea to the categories and the finitude they constitute: cf. GW 15:26 or TW 17:496–97.

cognition as such (for example the discursivity of finite understanding) nor the objects of metaphysics (the unconditioned) as such that are the limiting factor on traditional metaphysics, but its unexamined assumption that the *categories* are the universal and exclusive form of cognition and that they could be adequate determinations of the unconditioned. This insight is the core of my interpretation of Hegel's relation to Kant and "pre-Kantian" metaphysics, and I will soon return to it in more adequate detail. Before I do so, however, I would like to indicate how this "second" component of Hegel's idealism, that is, the idealism of the finite, can also be understood, at least in part, as a radicalization of elements in Kant's Critical Philosophy.

3.6. Kant's monism of mere appearances: transcendental idealism versus Spinozism

One of the defining features of the Jena reception of Kant lay in its tendency, from early on, to combine transcendental idealism with a project of "refuting" or "overcoming" Spinoza's substance monism. Interestingly, however, and in part disconcertingly, Kant's early critics, chief among them Jacobi himself, also noticed some interesting analogies between Kant's metaphysical views and the metaphysics of Spinoza (cf. FHJW I, 1:96, n. 1).[31] As we are about to see, there are also significant disanalogies; but these prove to depend on Kant's doctrine of transcendental idealism. Thus, by rejecting transcendental idealism, Hegel also pulls down a crucial defense against Spinozist monism. The resulting view is not identical to Spinozism, however, since the tensions of transcendental idealism are not resolved in favor of transcendental realism, but in favor of Hegel's idealism of the finite. The precise meaning of this claim is the topic of this section.

Let us begin with a brief review of the relevant features in Spinoza. As understood by Jacobi, substance monism entails two interconnected claims. The first is the often-cited principle *omnis determinatio*

---

31 Paul Franks points to this passage from Jacobi and to related texts by other contemporary authors such as Schütz and Pistorius; see his "From Kant to Post-Kantian Idealism," *Proceedings of the Aristotelian Society, Supplementary Volumes* 76 (2002): 229–46, esp. 231, nn. 9 and 10, where Franks gives detailed references to the associated passages in Spinoza. My discussion here is based on Brady Bowman, *Sinnliche Gewißheit: Zur systematischen Vorgeschichte eines Problems des Deutschen Idealismus* (Berlin: Akademie-Verlag 2003), 68–73, as well as on Franks' analysis of the analogies and disanalogies between Kant and Spinoza.

est negatio. In the context of its original formulation, Spinoza explains the principle as meaning that determinateness "does not pertain to the thing in regard to its being; on the contrary, it is its non-being."[32] Jacobi rephrases the point this way: "Individual things therefore, insofar as they exist only in a determinate manner, are *non-entia*; and the indeterminate, infinite being is the only true *ens reale*, **hoc est**, *est omne esse, & praeter quod nullum datur esse* [real being, which is all things and outside of which there is nothing]" (FHJW I, 1:100). This principle is the chief basis for Jacobi's interpretation of Spinozism as nihilism: since individual things are *non-entia*, and since the infinite being in no way transcends or is really distinct from them, substance itself disappears into utter indeterminacy and thus, effectively, into nothingness.[33]

The second principle entailed by Spinozist substance monism is *totum parte prius esse necesse est*: necessarily, the whole precedes the part. Once again, here is Jacobi's gloss:

> All individual things mutually presuppose each other and relate to each other such that no one of them can be or be comprehended without all the others, nor any of the others without this one; that is, all together make up an indissoluble whole; or more properly and precisely: *they exist all together in an absolutely indivisible thing and in no other way.* (FHJW I, 1:110)

According to this pantheistic holism, the unconditioned does not have the form of an absolutely first element within a potentially infinite chain of causes and effects; the unconditioned is itself the totality of the series of conditioning and conditioned terms, not a term of the same order as the terms that make up the series of finite things, states, and events that Hegel will later call the "bad" or "spurious" infinite.[34] But while these details of (Jacobi's version of) Spinozism are all highly relevant to understanding Hegel's metaphysics, the matter at hand is to draw out the analogies between Spinoza's monism-cum-holism and Kant's own implicit metaphysics.

The first analogy is to be found in Kant's conception of *appearances in space*. Space, Kant argues in the Transcendental Aesthetic, is a single, unique, infinite, given magnitude. Like finite things for Spinoza,

---

32 Spinoza, Letter 50 (to Jelles, June 2, 1674), in *Complete Works*, 892.
33 Cf. Franks' discussion in *All or Nothing*, 170–74.
34 Cf. Franks, "Post-Kantian Idealism," 238–41. On Hegel's concept of the "spurious infinite" cf. GW 21:124–25, 137–38. Also see Houlgate's commentary in *The Opening of Hegel's Logic*, 404–13.

the spatial manifold (i.e. determinate spaces) arises solely by way of limitations being introduced into it, which manifold coexists ad infinitum and is wholly contained within the one unique space.[35] In both cases, multiplicity arises through a process of *division* rather than *addition*; number is derivative, and unity is correspondingly to be understood as original, not as arising through the combination or synthesis of an antecedently given manifold.[36] *Totum parte prius esse necesse est.*

An exactly similar analogy is to be found in Kant's conception of the *ens realissimum* or transcendental ideal. The conception is much older than the *Critique of Pure Reason*; it originates around the time of Kant's *Nova dilucidatio* (1755) and lies at the heart of *The One Possible Basis for a Demonstration of the Existence of God* (1763).[37] In the latter work, Kant premises his argument with a distinction between the formal and material elements in possibility. A thing is formally possible just insofar as its concept does not include logically incompatible (contradictory) determinations; the material element of its possibility, in turn, consists in whatever real determinations its concept does include.[38] This material element is understood as being prior to the formal element for the obvious reason that logical incompatibility is a relation between determinations, and it would seem that the content of the determinations themselves has to be given as the basis for any evaluation of their compatibility. Moreover, a possible thing with only one determination is conceivable; its possibility cannot be accounted for by appealing to logical compatibility; therefore, its possibility has to be grounded in a non-formal, material way.

On the basis of this premise, Kant goes on to argue that a supremely real being necessarily exists. The exact shape and validity of his argument has been the subject of some debate, but its basic outline looks

---

35 Cf. B39–40. As Franks points out ("Post-Kantian Idealism," 231, 234ff.), both Jacobi and Pistorius noted these analogies.

36 On these alternative conceptions of unity and number, see Förster, *The Twenty-Five Years*, 318–20.

37 Allen Wood shows how the basic assumptions and the proof-structure of *The One Possible Basis* are at work in Kant's discussion of rational theology in the First Critique: see Allen Wood, *Kant's Rational Theology* (Ithaca, NY: Cornell University Press 1978), esp. 64–79. For a more recent treatment that integrates Wood's results into an account of the subjective necessity of the idea of the *ens realissimum*, see Michelle Grier, *Kant's Doctrine of Transcendental Illusion* (Cambridge University Press 2001), 234–55.

38 The notion of a real, as opposed to a merely formal or logical, determination is at work in Kant's thesis that existence is not a real predicate. Cf. *One Possible Basis*, 2:72–75; B626.

like this.[39] All possibility is grounded in antecedently given real determinations as its material element. Now, let *impossibility* be defined
as that which cancels all possibility whatsoever. If no real determinations at all existed, then all possibility whatsoever would be cancelled.
Therefore, it is impossible that no real determinations at all exist.
That whose non-existence is impossible is necessary. Consequently,
the real determinations that ground all possibility necessarily exist.
Now, real determinations are either affirmative or negative (privative)
in character; that is, a thing may be determinate either in respect to
properties it has or in respect to those it lacks. But privations refer
essentially to the positive determinations whose absence they denote.[40]
Therefore, all determinations whatsoever are ultimately grounded in
affirmative determinations: call these *realities*, and call the set of all
such realities the *omnitudo realitatis*. The *omnitudo realitatis* therefore
exists necessarily.

The steps Kant takes from this distributive totality of all realities
to their collective totality or unity in a unique, supremely real (purely
affirmative), indivisible, unchanging, eternal being are subtle. He
argues for its uniqueness on the basis of his characterization of it as
the *ground* of all possibility (see 2:285–86). For assume there to be two
such beings; since each one is the ground of all possibility, it has no
other ground of its own possibility beyond its own existence, and it is
the ground of possibility of the other one as well. But it will also have
the ground of its possibility in the other, since the other is also assumed
to be the ground of all possibility; in other words, it will both have the
ground of its possibility in itself and not in itself, which is a contradiction. Therefore the ground of all possibility is a unique being.

Furthermore, it must be indivisible. For if it were divisible, then
either (a) its parts would also be necessary beings as the ground of
all possibility, or (b) they would be contingent beings, or (c) some

<hr/>

39 In addition to Wood (cited in note 37), see Klaus Reich, *Kants einzigmöglicher Beweisgrund
zu einer Demonstration des Daseins Gottes: Ein Beitrag zum Verständnis des Verhältnisses von
Dogmatismus und Kritizismus in der Metaphysik* (Leipzig: Meiner 1937), and Mark Fisher
and Eric Watkins, "Kant on the Material Ground of Possibility: From 'The Only
Possible Argument' to the 'Critique of Pure Reason,'" *Review of Metaphysics* 52:2 (1998):
369–95. Both Reich and Fisher and Watkins examine the question whether Kant has
reasons for rejecting the pre-critical proof that are independent of doctrines peculiar
to the critical standpoint, and come in both cases to the conclusion that he does not.
40 This thesis identifies Kant as holding an asymmetricalist view of negation. I discuss
this view in some detail in Chapter 7.

would be the ground of some possibilities while other parts would be the ground of others. The first case reduces to the assumption of a plurality of necessary beings, the absurdity of which was just demonstrated. In the second case we would have a necessary whole composed entirely of contingent parts, which is impossible. In the third case we would have a plurality of grounds of possibility such that, necessarily, at least one of them exists, but no particular one would be necessary. If this were the case, then first of all there would seem to be no ground why any particular one of the parts necessarily exists, and so each would be contingent when taken in itself; this reduces to case (b) just considered.

We reach a similar conclusion if we assume that as long as at least *some* possibilities remain, the other possibilities could be negated. If this were the case, then some things would be merely contingently possible, that is, they could have been impossible. But for something to be impossible, it must either contain a contradiction or lack any material element whatsoever in which its possibility could be grounded. However, it is not possible for the determinations of one and the same thing to be contingently incompatible; for it to become internally possible or impossible, it would have to have *different* determinations and hence would no longer be the same thing, so by the principle of self-identity whatever is formally possible is necessarily possible. Or again, if something were contingently possible in respect to its material ground, this would mean that its material ground of possibility could not have existed. But then there would be nothing in respect to which possibility or impossibility could be predicated at all; as Kant says, "it is utterly unthinkable and contradictory that something is nothing" (2:84). Therefore, whatever is possible is necessarily possible, and hence any material ground of possibility exists necessarily; and therefore, in turn, case (c) above is impossible. So since there is no case in which the divisibility of the ground of all possibility can be conceived, it must be indivisible.

The immutability and eternality of the ground of all possibility follows directly from the premise that its actual existence is the antecedent ground of its possibility. For there is no possible manner for it to exist that is not already actualized and so it cannot exist in any other way than it does. Therefore, the ground of all reality is supremely real (as containing nothing but affirmative realities), unique, indivisible, immutable, and eternal.[41]

41 For Kant's argument for the personality of this necessary being, see 2:87–90.

Now, this line of argument gives us no reason to assume that the finite things of creation lack intrinsic reality or have no determinateness beyond their limitations or their relation to other realities outside them and which they themselves lack. Indeed, the existence of intrinsically determined, finite substances is a central feature of Kant's position at the time of the *One Possible Ground*, and he thinks that a plurality of such individual substances is necessary to account for change and the existence of the spatio-temporal order.[42] It is the determinate content of these substances that grounds their form and relations to others. However, among the deep conceptual shifts separating the *Critique of Pure Reason* from the *One Possible Basis* is a fundamentally altered conception of form and content. In the pre-critical text, Kant identifies the form of possibility as consisting in the logical compatibility of internal determinations which, in turn, make up the content or material element of possibility. In the First Critique, however, Kant now warns against inferring the *real possibility* of things from the *logical possibility* of their concept (i.e. its internal consistency: B266–72).

For the critical Kant, cognition of the real possibility of an object is synthetic. For as Klaus Reich points out, "possibility, just like actuality and necessity, is never contained in a concept as a determination (predicate). Rather: 'Even if the *concept* of a thing is already complete, I can still ask of this *object* whether it is merely possible, or also actual or … even … necessary' (B266)." In other words, just as existence is not a real determination internal to an object, neither are the other modal determinations; therefore, the idea of judging whether a *thing* (in contradistinction to a mere concept) is *internally* possible loses all meaning. Instead, "the complete determination of any and every thing rests on the limitation of this *total* reality [of all predicates collectively], inasmuch as part of it is ascribed to the thing, and the rest is excluded" (B605). As Reich interprets this passage, each thing is

> represented by the principle of thoroughgoing determination "as deriving its own possibility from the share which it possesses in this sum of all

---

42 Cf. Kant's Principle of Succession in the *Nova dilucidatio*: "Substances can only experience change insofar as they are connected to others; their mutual dependence determines the reciprocal change in state. Hence, a simple substance that is free of all external connection, is in itself completely immutable … Hence, if all connection between substances is completely negated, succession and time also disappear" (1:410). The implications for space emerge in the Principle of Coexistence: cf. 1:414. For a discussion of the details of Kant's arguments, see Watkins, *Metaphysics of Causality*, 112–60.

possibilities" (B600). The size of the share in the totality of all possibility had by a particular thing, that is: the *relation* of the realities posited in it to those which it lacks, or also the relation between the realities belonging to it and the sum of all realities together, is the *form* of this particular thing with respect to its possibility.[43]

For the critical Kant, then, individual empirical things are relational entities even as regards their *essential possibility*; their determinateness lies not within them, but in their relation to what they lack: to what they are *not*. This shift to a purely relational view of possibility and object-identity is explicit in any number of passages in the *Critique of Pure Reason*, for example at B606 in the "Transcendental Ideal," where Kant explains that "all possibility of things (that is, of the synthesis of the manifold, in respect of its contents) must ... be regarded as derivative, with one exception, namely the possibility of that which includes in itself all reality."

This latter possibility must be regarded as original. For all negations (*which are the only predicates through which anything can be distinguished from the ens realissimum* [!]) are merely limitations of a greater, and ultimately of the highest, reality; and they therefore presuppose this reality and are, as regards their content, derived from it. All manifoldness of things is only a correspondingly varied mode of limiting the concept of the highest reality which forms their common substratum, just as all figures are only possible as so many different modes of limiting infinite space. (B606)[44]

Lest this way of putting the point seem to imply that finite things are actually *parts* of the supreme being, cut out of it, as it were, by varying modes of limitation, Kant emphasizes that we cannot grasp the primordial being as in any way *composed* of finite things (cf. B607). The emerging picture has on the one side a unique, individual, infinite being that is thoroughly determinate in itself (cf. B604), and on the other a sphere of manifold finite beings with absolutely no determinateness in themselves, but only a kind of positional identity determined by their mutual relations. Kant is equally explicit on this score in his discussion of the Amphiboly of the Concepts of Reflection. Contrary to the rationalist preconception of Leibniz, he argues there, it is wrong to believe that when we abstract away from all the relations an object

43 Reich, *Kants einzigmöglicher Beweisgrund*, 25; Reich refers the reader to B322.
44 See Franks, "Post-Kantian Idealism," 232–33.

bears to others, that is, its *form*, we must necessarily presuppose, as the end point of abstraction, some *matter* or *substance* as the basis of the relations. Quite the opposite: "the form is given by itself, and so far is the matter (or the things themselves which appear) from serving as the foundation ... that on the contrary its own possibility presupposes a formal intuition (time and space) as antecedently given" (B324). He concedes that it is "startling to hear that a thing is to be taken as consisting wholly of relations. Such a thing is, however, mere appearance, and cannot be thought through pure categories" (B341).[45]

If we now compare these aspects of the critical philosophy with the philosophy of Spinoza, especially as reconstructed by Jacobi, we find that the doctrines of determination as negation and of the metaphysical priority of infinite whole of reality over finite individuals correspond directly to doctrines explicitly held by Kant. However, as soon as we take into account Kant's characteristic doctrine of transcendental idealism, we also discover a significant *disanalogy* between Kant and Spinoza: Kant asserts that *things in themselves* are intrinsically individuated as real entities by unique combinations of real determinations. So while Kant may be a monist as far as appearances go, he is a pluralist when it comes to transcendental, non-phenomenal reality.[46]

Now, I argued above, with McDowell, that Hegel actually rejects Kant's transcendental idealism. In light of the foregoing analysis of Kant's views on the individuation of finite entities, rejection of transcendental idealism could in itself go in either of two directions. On the one hand, we could try to return to a version of Kant's pre-critical philosophy, or some similar position, and assert the intrinsic, substantial individuality of finite things as Jacobi does. On the other hand, though, we might also find ourselves persuaded by his insights into the dialectical character of the categories when applied to the unconditioned or by his observations on the essentially relational character of our knowledge of empirical objects.[47] In this latter case, rejection of

45 Longuenesse has emphasized the consequences of this section of the First Critique for understanding the Transcendental Ideal and its properly critical function: *Kant on the Human Standpoint* (Cambridge University Press 2005), 211–35.

46 This point is made by Franks, "Post-Kantian Idealism," 232–34.

47 On the latter point, cf. B66–67: "Now a thing in itself cannot be known by mere relations." James van Cleve discusses the way this thesis functions as a premise in Kant's argument for the transcendental ideality of space, and also shows that it supports a two-worlds reading of the duality of appearances and things in themselves: see *Problems from Kant* (Oxford University Press 1999), 48–49, 150–55.

transcendental idealism will have a very different meaning. For what the foregoing discussion has shown is that the only thing separating Kant from Spinozist monism is transcendental idealism: if Kant gives up the idea of a gap between subjectively constituted appearances and things in themselves, that is, if he ceased to consider what Hegel calls "appearance in a merely subjective sense," the monism, holism, and finally the nihilism with which Jacobi charged Spinoza would all reappear. In slightly different terms, as soon as the transcendental frame is dropped (as McDowell suggests we drop it), things as they are do indeed come into view, but as ontologically depotentiated, merely relative, wholly negative entities with no genuine reality of their own. And that is a realism of a very different stripe.

Now, McDowell rightly criticizes the thesis that what would have been most attractive to Hegel in Kant was the latter's transcendental idealism.[48] But now we find that the rejection of *transcendental* idealism has further ramifications that are distinctly at odds with the version of realism McDowell finds to be philosophically appealing. Namely, that Hegel's *speculative* idealism is not only not ultimately concerned with determinate judgments about determinate objects, but committed (as I will argue below) to the thesis that orientation toward such judgments as the paradigmatic and exclusive model of knowledge is itself misguided.

So consider once more Pippin's statement from above, according to which Hegel is "still adhering, roughly, to the Kantian strategy on how to establish basic or fundamental components of any conceptual scheme (or rules for any objective judgment about *determinate* objects), one that makes essential reference to the possibly self-conscious nature of all judgment."[49] From the Hegelian perspective, the difficulty with this view is not only that Kant's transcendental idealism renders genuinely objective judgment impossible, nor only that Kant's orientation toward apperception obscures the content of the categories taken in themselves and locks us into a one-sided consideration of the forms of thought in their relation to finite cognizers. Rather, the idea that philosophy should consist in a search for "rules for any objective judgment about *determinate* objects" makes thought beholden to a class of objects that are finite, merely phenomenal, and hence ultimately unreal.

48 See esp. McDowell, "Hegel's Radicalization of Kant," 83, n. 18.
49 Pippin, "Category Theory," 843, emphasis added.

Thus Hegel does indeed reject Kant's transcendental idealism, and he does so partly for the reasons McDowell suggests. In rejecting Kant's theory of cognition, Hegel *eo ipso* rejects any form of what in contemporary parlance might be called anti-realism: barring gross anomalies and the many common varieties of illusion and other forms of epistemic misfires, the things of our natural experience are just as they appear to us to be. Yet in rejecting anti-realism, Hegel does not thereby embrace anything like full-blooded realism about the things of experience or, for that matter, about the objects of scientific inquiry as it is usually understood (i.e. not as *speculative* science). On the contrary, once the "frame" of transcendental idealism is dropped, all commitment to the reality of finite things has lost the last leg it had to stand on, and something disturbingly similar to Spinozist monism rushes in. The categories or pure concepts of the understanding are constitutive of *objective appearances*; that is to say, they are *the form of finitude*.

3.7. "Truth" versus "correctness": is there adequate ground for true determinate judgments about finite objects?

I would like to begin this section by going back to my assertion that Hegel's speculative idealism is not only not ultimately concerned with determinate judgments about determinate objects, but committed to the thesis that orientation toward such judgments as the paradigmatic case of knowledge is itself misguided. This formulation is intended on the one hand to emphasize Hegel's distance from the broadly empiricist conception (shared by Kant) that at the most fundamental level, true judgments are those substantiated by sensible intuition, and that justification in the sciences ultimately comes down to the testimony of the senses. This point has of course been argued in different ways, and to different ends, by many interpreters of Hegel, and his distance from the empiricist tradition is obvious in any case. On the other hand, however, Hegel's skepticism regarding the ultimate justifiability of empirically oriented, determinate judgments *in any terms whatsoever* has not been as clearly seen.

Now Hegel's rejection of singular, determinate judgments about determinate objects as incapable of adequate grounding is not tantamount to rejecting objective, determinate judgments about determinate objects as worthless or without any role to play in speculative philosophy. The sphere in which such judgments do play a role – for example, the so-called formal sciences such as logic and mathematics on the one hand, and our best-founded empirical theories on the other – are themselves moments and manifestations of the reality Hegel calls the Concept, and the investigation of the forms, functions, logical constituents, and epistemic scope of judgment is thus essential to Hegel's speculative science. On the other hand, the reader may recall that Hegel draws a distinct line between the correspondence between Concept and reality he calls *truth,* and the correspondence between representations more generally and experience which he refers to as *mere correctness* (GW 12:64–65; ENC §172).[50] Given this difference, together with the fairly unproblematic observation that the judgments that play a role in science seem by and large to instantiate the "mere correctness" relation, it ought not to be surprising that Hegel is not chiefly concerned to examine the conditions of possibility of making determinate judgments about determinate objects *in this sense.* In contrast to much of traditional and mainstream contemporary philosophy, Hegel is not concerned to provide a foundation (transcendental or otherwise) for our prototypical knowledge claims, be they scientific or of the everyday variety. I will argue that in his views on the epistemology of "objective knowledge," Hegel is in fact a radical skeptic.

The dimensions of this skepticism can best be suggested by considering the relation of Hegelian logic and speculative science generally to what Hegel calls *the finite,* including finite cognition. Empirical science (including for example physics, chemistry, botany, zoology, empirical psychology, and anthropology) and *a priori* science (including traditional formal logic, arithmetic, and geometry) are limited by the finitude of their very objects. That finitude manifests itself in different ways. In the case of empirical science, it emerges for example as the so-called problem of induction, as the historical variability of taxonomies and explanatory schemes, and as the failure of natural objects to conform neatly to our categories and predictions. Hegel will view such difficulties not as limits on cognition as such, but as limits

50 This distinction is rooted in Hegel's conviction that, although it is right to define truth as the correspondence or agreement of thought with its object, it is incoherent to assume that thought (concepts) could agree with something so radically different from it as a sensible representation is. This reflection, simple yet far-reaching in its implications, limits the scope of what can properly be called truth to the agreement of thought with itself, sacrificing not only the "truth" of empirical judgments, but for the most part also that of formal logical and mathematical propositions. Cf. the discussion of Hegel's concept of truth, and its relation to the Kantian notion of truth, in Longuenesse, *Hegel's Critique,* 24–27.

arising jointly from the finite and conceptually inferior nature of the relevant objects and of the finite thought-determinations (categories) at work in those sciences.

Something similar goes for mathematics, which can escape neither a certain kind of self-externality in its objects and methods nor a moment of indemonstrability and hence irrationality in its axioms.[51] From the standpoint of speculative science, these limits of cognition are not problems to be solved (or analyzed or defined away), but inherent features of a certain level or moment in the genesis of the Idea or Spirit. By the same token, the inevitability of such limits reverberates through the whole sphere of empirical science: if the true is the whole, and if for reasons of principle there can be no whole of empirical science, then a plausible conclusion is that none of the judgments composing "finite," empirical science is true, at least not when held to the strict Hegelian standard.

In fact, this view is not so far removed from a position that one could plausibly attribute to Kant himself. If we take seriously Kant's analysis of the concept of thoroughgoing determination (discussed in the preceding section) as *transcendent* (cf. B599), this means that nothing corresponding to it can be given in experience. The corresponding Principle of Thoroughgoing Determination, according to which "Everything that exists is completely determinate" (B601), must therefore be a *merely regulative ideal*.[52] As Nikolai Klimmek points out in his discussion of the Principle, "Not everything that exists is completely determinate, but rather subject to complete determination relatively to our conceptual repertoire. But the problem seems to be that, independently of our concepts of the properties of things, we cannot even understand what it would mean for a thing to be completely determinate."[53]

This would mean that in fact *no object of experience – no appearance – is ever completely determinate*, inasmuch as appearances are by definition

51 Cf. Hegel's stringent demands on the discipline of logic in the *Encyclopedia* (§42R): "If thinking is to be capable of proving anything at all, if logic must demand that *proofs* be given, and if it wants to teach how to give proofs, then it should be capable above all of proving the content most proper to it and seeing its necessity."

52 This is actually one of several competing formulations of the Principle; for the others see B600–1; cf. Nikolai Klimmek, *Kant's System der Transzendentalen Ideen* (Berlin: de Gruyter 2005), 165–78.

53 Klimmek, *Kant's System*, 174; cf. Kant's discussion of the regulative use of the idea of thoroughgoing determination, B680–96. Cf. Longuenesse, *Human Standpoint*, 220. Wolff enunciates the principle in Dt. Log. §27; cf. Ontol. §229.

"the undetermined object of an empirical intuition" (B34), so that it can possess no further determinateness beyond what the understanding is able to give to it. Of course, if Hegel rejects Kant's transcendental idealism, he will also have to reject the notion that the manifold of sensibility is completely indeterminate in itself, receiving its form solely through the agency of the finite mind.[54] On the other hand, I have also been arguing that Hegel nevertheless wants to retain certain aspects that are associated with transcendental idealism, even as he *objectifies* them, so to speak, by interpreting them as features of things themselves. We may thus expect Hegel to affirm the *thoroughgoing underdetermination* of the finite sphere as a *metaphysical principle*, and, as I will argue, this is exactly what he does. In the following section, I take up the skeptical consequences of Hegel's views.

3.8. Hegel's unmitigated skepticism regarding the finite thought-determinations and the shortcomings of Kant's critique of metaphysics

Thanks to the work of scholars like Michael Forster, Robert Pippin, Klaus Vieweg, Kenneth Westphal, and more recently Paul Franks and Dietmar Heidemann, there is now a broad consensus that Hegel's sustained engagement with skepticism both ancient and modern is an essential component of his philosophy.[55] There are, however, different ways of interpreting Hegel's attitude toward skepticism in its various forms and modifications. One influential school of thought, going back to Robert Pippin, holds that Hegel conceived his idealism as a means of overcoming the "noumenal skepticism" introduced by Kant's doctrine of the thing-in-itself and the ideality of space and time. Whereas on this view neither Kant nor Fichte was able convincingly to establish "that the conditions for a possibly self-conscious experience of objects are genuinely objective," Hegel's achievement in the *Phenomenology* was to have provided "a 'deduction' of the absolute objectivity of the

---

54 In Chapter 6, we see in more detail how and why Hegel rejects this claim.
55 See Forster, *Hegel and Skepticism*; Pippin, *Hegel's Idealism*; Klaus Vieweg, *Philosophie des Remis: Der junge Hegel und das "Gespenst des Skepticismus"* (Munich: Fink 1999); Kenneth Westphal, *Hegel, Hume und die Identität wahrnehmbarer Dinge: Historisch-kritische Analyse zum Kapitel "Wahrnehmung" in der Phänomenologie von 1807* (Frankfurt am Main: Klostermann 1998); Franks, *All or Nothing*; Dietmar Heidemann, *Der Begriff des Skeptizismus: Seine systematischen Formen, die pyrrhonische Skepsis und Hegels Herausforderung* (Berlin and New York: de Gruyter 2007).

Notion (*both* the deduction of its basic structure and the deduction of its objectivity) without the transcendental-skeptical remainder of things in themselves."[56] On this account, the *Phenomenology* and by extension the *Logic* are essentially anti-skeptical endeavors. In the *Phenomenology*, Hegel is said systematically to "undercut" the realist conceptions that give rise to skepticism about our ability to know being as it is in itself, "outside" of our thought, thus overcoming skepticism. So even as Hegel skeptically demonstrates the conceptual tensions and defects of basic categories and conceptions of knowledge taken singly, he is also positively "sublating" them, revealing their necessary conditions in more complex and more adequate conceptions of knowledge that transmit their justification back to the other conceptions, rightly understood. To the extent this strategy succeeds, the necessity and objectivity of our most basic concepts will thereby have been established.

This interpretation makes the *Phenomenology*'s "self-consummating skepticism" look very much like the methodical skepticism of Descartes' *Meditations*, notwithstanding the profound differences in how Hegel and Descartes conceive the exact nature of the skeptical challenge.[57] Dietmar Heidemann draws attention to this similarity. To the extent that the *Phenomenology*'s "processual" skepticism pursues the positive goal of establishing a form of knowledge that proves immune to skeptical doubt, it belongs to the tradition of methodical skepticism inaugurated in the *Meditations*: doubt is the means of investigation, not its end. If however, a form of skepsis-resistant, speculative knowledge could be justified, "skepticism in its global orientation toward all previous forms of taking-to-be-true would itself have been overcome."[58]

However, this picture of a recursive justification redounding to all the forms of knowledge that have been subjected to skepticism in the course of arriving at "absolute knowing" needs to be qualified. Consider for instance what Hegel has to say about the *Phenomenology*'s

---

56 Pippin, *Hegel's Idealism*, 92, 93; cf. 99–109. McDowell's approach to Hegel is a variant of that pioneered by Pippin, though his realist orientation is clearly an important philosophical difference.

57 Pippin (*Hegel's Idealism*, 95–96) distinguishes between "Cartesian" and "Kantian" varieties of skepticism and rightly emphasizes Hegel's distance from Descartes' preoccupation with the problem of our knowledge of the external world. The sense in which his characterization of Hegelian skepticism can nevertheless be assimilated to Descartes' methodical skepticism is orthogonal to that in which the two philosophers diverge.

58 Heidemann, *Begriff des Skeptizismus*, 211.

"pathway of despair." It does not conform to what is usually understood by the word "doubt," he writes, namely "a shaking up of this or that presumed truth, followed by a return to that truth again, after the doubt has been appropriately dispelled – so that at the end of the process the matter is taken as it was in the first place" (GW 9:56/§78). But this, in a nutshell, is just what methodical skepticism does. It is essentially a means of justifying the beliefs it begins by casting into doubt, and though it might enrich our awareness of the grounds and interconnections of those beliefs, it hardly sets out to transform their content. Hegel's "self-perfecting skepticism," by contrast, is meant to produce "the conscious insight into the untruth of phenomenal knowledge for which the supreme reality is what is in truth nothing but the unrealized Concept" (*ibid.*).

In this context it is noteworthy and not a little surprising that Hegel himself routinely denies that the authentic skepticism of the ancients, which he takes as the only true and philosophically serious skepticism, is a form of *doubt* at all.[59] The German expression *Zweifel* (doubt), he says, "is always skewed and inappropriate when used of skepticism" (GW 4:204):

> Ancient skepticism does not doubt, but is certain of untruth; it does not wander aimlessly about with thoughts that leave open the possibility that this or that might still be true; rather it proves the untruth with certainty. Or its doubting is, for it, certainty, and does not have the intention of reaching truth; it leaves nothing undecided, but is decidedness in an absolute way, perfectly finished. (TW 19:362)

The *Phenomenology*'s "self-perfecting skepticism" (*sich vollbringender Skeptizismus*) and its "path of despair" (*Verzweiflung*) are to be understood in the same terms. What the *Phenomenology* aims for is not the overcoming of doubt, but the overcoming of misplaced certainty in what Hegel calls merely "phenomenal knowledge" (GW 9:55; cf. 69/§§78, 109).

Heidemann himself takes essentially the same view in his related discussion of Hegel's response to the so-called *five tropes of Agrippa*. Hegel follows Sextus Empiricus in his conviction that from within the framework of our ordinary conception of knowledge and justification, there

---

59 On Hegel's negative appraisal of modern (Cartesian and esp. Humean) skepticism, see Michael Forster, "Hegel on the Superiority of Ancient over Modern Skepticism," in H. F. Fulda and R.-P. Horstmann (eds.), *Skeptizismus und spekulatives Denken in der Philosophie Hegels* (Stuttgart: Klett-Cotta 1996), 64–82.

is no effective defense against Agrippa's skeptical onslaught. There are, however, two different possible responses to this state of things. Either one concedes that "the concept of knowledge proper to the understanding's finite thinking is deficient and thus in need of correction," in which case prospects for a revised conception within the framework of "finite thought" remain open. Alternatively, one concedes that "the concept of knowledge proper to the finite thought of the understanding is deficient," but explains this deficiency as arising from the fact that "finite cognition itself is intrinsically aporetic and antinomial in its very constitution." I agree with Heidemann that "Hegel argues for the second implication and takes up a skeptical position with regard to the understanding's epistemic potentials, since on his view the contradictions that the tropes reveal in deductively or inferentially justified cognition are both unavoidable and irresolvable."[60]

I take this to mean that even if we are willing to grant that Hegel succeeds in establishing a form of speculative knowledge immune to Pyrrhonian skepticism, the critical process of generating and justifying it does not *eo ipso* justify the internal coherence and objective validity of the finite forms of knowledge. For part of what sublation entails is a *transformation* of the content or intension of the forms thus criticized and sublated. Therefore even the relative validity or adequacy of those forms as moments of the Concept is bound up with a substantial shift in content, and hence what has come to be justified (*sit venia verbo*) is no longer the same concept or category that was in play for the finite understanding. Though the conclusion of the *Phenomenology* has often been taken to imply that Hegel pulls up his phenomenological "ladder" behind him, so to speak, so that it is available to be traversed in both directions, up and down, I suggest that the more consistent view (regardless of whether Hegel consciously held it or not) is closer to the ladder of Wittgenstein's *Tractatus* that we cast away after ascending by it, with no way back down but also no longing to descend. Granting then for the sake of argument that Hegel's genetic exposition of absolute knowing or of the absolute Idea succeeds, the resulting insight into speculative truth does not equip us with knowledge of why we were in fact always right in holding reality to conform to the forms of finite cognition, but only of the way those forms were themselves more or less distorted manifestations of the reality of the Concept.

---

60 Heidemann, *Begriff des Skeptizismus*, 174–75.

3.9. "The critical philosophy is an imperfect form of skepticism"

This analysis leaves no room for interpretations of Hegel as striving to vindicate, perhaps by means of some variety of transcendental argument, the necessity and objectivity of the categories that make up the finite thought of the understanding. Hegel simply does not view authentic, Pyrrhonian-style skepticism as a problem to be overcome, at least not in the sense that Kant presumably found Humean skepticism to be such a problem, or in the sense that contemporary epistemologists confront the problem of skepticism. By the same token, overcoming Kant's noumenal or transcendental skepticism is not the same thing as refuting doubts about the real objective import of the categories. This kind of doubt, which has its source in realist intuitions about the metaphysical difference between thought and being, is in fact a means of shoring up the forms of finite thought as a perhaps contingent, but nevertheless for us non-optional, indispensible conceptual scheme.

"*Philosophia critica ... imperfecta est Scepticismi forma*" (GW 5:227), Hegel states in his seventh habilitation thesis. That he should characterize transcendental idealism as a form of skepticism is not surprising: the gap opened between things in themselves and objective experience as constituted by the categories is the core of Kant's noumenal skepticism. But in light of the foregoing, we can now also see why Hegel describes the critical philosophy as an *imperfect* form of skepticism. As Kant himself argues, one powerful reason for distinguishing between mere appearances and things in themselves, and for restricting determinate cognition to the former, emerges from reflection on the antinomies of pure reason: for if the assumption of the transcendental ideality of the spatio-temporal objects of cognition is necessary and sufficient for resolving the contradictions that arise within reason itself in its pursuit of determinate knowledge of the unconditioned, then this fact speaks strongly, albeit indirectly, in favor of the truth of that assumption (cf. Bxx–xxi; 534–35).

Hence the result of distinguishing between things in themselves and appearances as comprehending only what is conditioned is to segregate a sphere in which the categories can be employed meaningfully and without contradiction from one in which they cannot be so employed, effectively insulating them from the contradictions that arise when the categories are taken to be ontological as well as epistemological forms. To Hegel's mind, this is a manoeuvre intended to maintain the empirically given sphere of the conditioned as internally consistent – a limiting condition on Kant's anti-skeptical doctrine of empirical realism. However, another, contrasting, non-Kantian critical strategy is conceivable. One could leave the transcendental distinction between appearances and things in themselves, which Kant correlates with the distinction between the conditioned and the unconditioned, to one side, and instead focus exclusively on the logical or metaphysical distinction between the conditioned and the unconditioned. The antinomies would then come into view as arising *within the categories of the conditioned* themselves as soon as we try to set them in determinate relation to the unconditioned to which they refer by virtue of the very meaning of the term "conditioned." In other words, the categories would make essential reference to a ground which they could not, however, make intelligible in their own terms; indeed, the attempt at substantive formulation of the unconditioned in terms of the categories renders it unintelligible. Without the framework of transcendental idealism and its constitutive reference to subjective, cognitive-psychological faculties, there is no longer any way to insulate the categories from the antinomies, and hence no way to maintain the limiting condition on Kant's anti-skeptical doctrine of empirical realism. This would be to embrace a *perfect* skepticism that Kant's critical philosophy qua transcendental idealism is designed to exclude.[61]

There can be no full-fledged dialectic in the framework of transcendental idealism. And since "metaphysics," in Hegel's critical use of the term, denotes commitment to the fundamental status and coherent content of the categories (finite thought-determinations), neither can there be a genuine and thoroughgoing critique of metaphysics in the framework of transcendental idealism. Thanks to transcendental idealism, the critical philosophy is just not that critical.

---

61 Cf. Arndt, *Dialektik und Reflexion*, 167–70.

4

SKEPTICAL IMPLICATIONS FOR THE FOUNDATIONS OF NATURAL SCIENCE

4.1. Introduction

This chapter continues the line of thought begun in Chapter 3, emphasizing the skeptical dimensions of Hegel's attitude to the forms of finite cognition. In the present chapter, though, I turn from general issues in metaphysics to the more concrete example of natural science. In section 4.2, the terms of Hegel's critique of empirical science are set out. In a nutshell, his view is that nature, as a sphere of finite things, is characterized by *self-externality*; that is, no thing within nature has its full determinateness by virtue of its own essence (Hegel's conception of the finite is anti-essentialist); nor, ultimately, should nature itself be regarded as a fully determinate reality, complete in itself. Rather, the natural world is truly incomplete; it has its ultimate determination not within itself, but in the reality of the Concept of which it is an ineliminable, but subordinate moment. Nature is in this sense self-external; indeed, it is the sphere of self-externality as such.

This "fact" about nature shows up in the form of certain questions that haunt scientific practice and the philosophy of science. In particular, current science has not yet succeeded in identifying uncontroversial natural kinds nor in formulating laws of nature that are in equal measure universal and explanatorily adequate. Taxonomic schemata, both in the life sciences and in the foundations of chemistry, are subject to ongoing revision (though the case of biological species is obviously more fluid than that of the periodic table of elements).[1] *Universal*

1 On some of the difficulties in identifying and classifying natural kinds in chemistry, see R. F. Hendry, "Elements, Compounds, and other Chemical Kinds," *Philosophy of Science* 73:5 (2006): 864–75; see also E. G. Marks and J. A. Marks, "Newlands Revisited: A Display of the Periodicity of the Chemical Elements for Chemists," *Foundations of Chemistry* 12 (2010): 85–93. I briefly discuss the case of biology below.

laws of nature are strictly instantiated only in highly artificial experimental situations; explanatory applications in the real world inevitably involve inexactitude, modification of their predicted effects due to the influence of other laws, *ceteris paribus* clauses in the formulation of prediction, and other kinds of qualification and relativity.[2] In section 4.3 I draw on work by Nancy Cartwright and others to point out the systematic as well as historical continuities between Aristotelian essentialism and the modern, "Newtonian," view of nature as a realm primarily of necessitating laws to which individual bits of matter are subject. I also address the specific features of Goethean science, which Cartwright sees as the first truly radical break in modernity with the tradition of Aristotelian essentialism. I suggest that Hegel participates in the Goethean revolution, but that unlike Goethe, he does not embrace the idea of nature as a fully determinate totality. Nature's limitations are the source of the limitations of natural science.

In Hegel's eyes, then, the classificatory and explanatory weaknesses in even our best theories are not, or are not merely, a reflection of the limitations of current science or even of the fundamental limitations of humans' ability to grasp the real structure of nature. They are indicative of a metaphysical indeterminacy in nature itself. Though this may at first glance appear to rest on the fallacy of arguing from ignorance ("We have not discovered truly universal exceptionless laws of nature; therefore there are none"), Hegel's position is more sophisticated than that. Within the more comprehensive metaphysics of the Concept, Hegel is able to provide an interpretation of why natural science is incompletable that does not make exclusive reference to the understanding as a purely subjective, human faculty. The details of his critique are the subject of section 4.4. In the concluding section I return to the discussion of McDowell's interpretation of Hegel, begun in Chapter 3. McDowell is right to suggest that empirical science is a

---

2 Regarding the artificiality of the experimental situations in which laws appear as strictly instantiated, consider Nancy Cartwright's concept of a "nomological machine" in *The Dappled World: A Study of the Boundaries of Science* (Cambridge University Press 1999), 49–74; Hegel acknowledges the artificiality of the circumstances necessary for identifying and instantiating universal laws at GW 12:216. An important aspect of Cartwright's thought, and one that is particularly relevant in the present context, is her *scientific realism* (e.g. 24–25). She resists constructivism and other forms of anti-realism while nevertheless denying that laws of nature express genuinely universal, that is, *global* features of the natural world. This aspect of her thought is relevant to me here because I also want to stress the ways in which Hegel may be considered a scientific realist, though one of an unorthodox kind, to be sure.

medium for actualizing rational freedom. According to Hegel, though, in the end it is not an adequate medium.

4.2. Relation-to-other, relation-to-self, self-externality: the terms of Hegel's critique of empirical science

Emphasis on Hegel's skepticism goes against a widespread approach that reads the *Phenomenology* (as well as the *Science of Logic, mutatis mutandis*) as a kind of transcendental argument. According to this transcendental approach, the book begins with the most minimal form of cognition (knowing that this spatio-temporal object before me is a tree, say) and successively uncovers the conditions of possibility of such knowledge in ever more complex modes of cognition, self-interpretation, and social interaction, reaching at last into the foundations of religion, art, and philosophy. This "transcendental" approach assumes (1) that beliefs like "This spatio-temporal item is a tree," or "Salt is white in color and cubic in shape," or "As bodies fall to earth, their velocity increases as the square of the time" *count as knowledge* in the sense relevant for Hegel even though our ordinary conceptions of why they are justified might be deeply mistaken. Furthermore, it is assumed (2) that the purpose of the *Phenomenology* is to show that *we can only possess real certainty regarding the truth of such beliefs* when we recognize that they also commit us to belief in certain speculative truths about the nature of concepts and knowledge in general. (Since different versions of the transcendental approach specify different contents for the underlying conditions of possibility, I will omit to specify the relevant concepts here.) I would contend, however, that even items such as Galileo's law of free fall do not fully count as knowledge in the sense relevant for Hegel. Neither the *Phenomenology* nor in particular the *Science of Logic* is intended as a transcendental deduction of the validity of (inter alia) empirical science. This section comprises a textual argument for attributing this strongly skeptical view to Hegel.

One place where we recognize Hegel's rather dim view of empirical science is the chapter on "Observing Reason" in the *Phenomenology*. As a shape of consciousness, observing reason is the initial manifestation of a more general attitude toward objectivity, namely "reason's certainty of being all reality," or as Hegel also puts it, "that all actuality is nothing other than it; its thinking is itself immediately actuality; its relation to actuality is therefore that of idealism" (GW 9:132/§232).

To identify the variety of idealism specific to observing reason as a distinct shape of self-consciousness, it is helpful to contrast the forms of idealism that Hegel assembles in the immediately preceding chapter under the title "Self-Consciousness." "The whole extent of the sensuous world is preserved" for shapes like stoicism, skepticism, the unhappy consciousness, and the "desiring" consciousness associated with the dialectic of master and servant; however, it is preserved "only as related to ... the unity of self-consciousness with itself; and for self-consciousness it [the sensuous world] is thus an indifferent subsistence [*ein Bestehen*] that is only *appearance* or *difference* and which has no being in itself" (GW 9:104/§167). The movement of this more primitive form of idealism is to negate the independent being of everything other than the self-conscious I, thereby exhibiting its lack of being-in-itself or, conversely, its merely derivative being as modification of consciousness. The movement of desire, for instance, is to consume the only apparently independent other, thus assimilating it to the self (see GW 9:103–5, 119–20/§§166–68, 201–4). The dialectical impasse peculiar to this form of idealism is that in the end it achieves no stable, objective expression of what it takes to be the truth, namely self-consciousness itself. It cannot therefore *realize* its truth, for in order to do so, it would be required to produce a stable, objective expression with which it can correspond.[3] Two striking instances of this failure are, again, the desiring and consuming master whose negative activity, in contrast to that of the servant, finds no positive expression in a product; and the skeptic, whose expression of the sovereignty of self-conscious thought consists wholly in exercising its "sophistry" on a steady stream of externally given contents, and which therefore remains sealed up in a paradoxical subjectivity that must contradict itself in order to remain true to itself (GW 9:109–16, 120/§§178–96, 205).[4]

In contrast to the negative idealism of self-consciousness, the *positive idealism* of reason manifests as the certainty that the sensuous world, properly approached, will reveal its intelligibility, rational order, and

---

3 This requirement is rooted in Hegel's notion of truth; cf. Longuenesse, *Hegel's Critique*, 24–27.

4 The seeming tension between Hegel's critical discussion of skepticism here and his identification of the *Phenomenology* itself as a form of skepticism is resolved by noting Hegel's distinction between various "modifications" of skepticism in its relation to philosophy: cf. GW 4:213 and 221–22, where Hegel criticizes the skeptic in terms similar to those of his critical exposition in the *Phenomenology*. For further discussion see Heidemann, *Begriff des Skeptizismus*, 120–29.

universal conformity to mind; that is, that the sensuous world *in its independence from consciousness* is homologous with, and hence a positive expression of, self-conscious thought. This initial characterization might seem to point to the rationalist tradition in Western thought, but Hegel makes it clear that empiricism is the historical movement corresponding to this shape of consciousness. His explanation for this initially surprising correlation sheds additional light on his relation to transcendental idealism:

> [T]he certainty of being all reality is at first only the pure category. In this initial recognition of itself in the object, reason finds expression in the *empty* idealism that takes reason only as it first appears to itself, and deludes itself that the complete reality [of reason] is revealed as soon as the pure "mine" of consciousness has been pointed out in all being and all things have been declared to be sensations and representations. It is bound, therefore, to be at the same time absolute empiricism, since in order to give filling to its empty "mine," i.e. to get hold of *difference* and all its development and formation, this reason requires an alien impulse prior to which there is no manifold of sensation or representation. (GW 9:136/§238)

As we saw above, Hegel charges transcendental idealism with having reduced the I to a mere representation that must be able to *accompany* all my other representations, thereby making them "mine." In Hegel's eyes, this is tantamount to having mistaken what is in truth a *concrete* universal for an *abstract* universal, as Hegel calls a feature that is merely common to a plurality of individuals.[5] The other side of this coin is that the significance of the categories is reduced to how they function in relation to the formal unity of self-consciousness: namely as the guarantee that all representations will be such as to be *accompanible* by the representation "I think," that is, such as to be integrated into the unity of self-consciousness and thereby "mine." Concomitant with this (in Hegel's eyes) formalistic, subjectivist understanding of the I and the categories, is the thesis that they rely for their content on a source outside and heterogeneous to the mind (GW 9:137/§238). In this sense Kant is an empiricist and Hegel will later group transcendental idealism together with Lockean empiricism as the *Encyclopedia*'s Second Attitude of Thought to Objectivity (ENC §§37–41).

---

5 See the discussion in section 4.4 below and esp. Robert Stern, "Hegel, British Idealism, and the Concrete Universal," in *Hegelian Metaphysics*, 143–76.

Two observations are in order here. First, we see that transcendental idealism forms the very matrix for Hegel's discussion of empiricism and empirical science in "Observing Reason." This suggests an acceptance of Kant as having, in all essentials, gotten it right about empirical science, though perhaps in terms Kant himself would be loath to recognize. As an "attitude of thought to objectivity," to borrow that phrase once again, empirical science embodies the view that, as cognizers, we can achieve full self-realization only by engaging directly with the experiential world. There, and nowhere else, lies the fulfillment of theoretical reason which, in its Kantian conception, Hegel frequently identifies with the I (e.g. GW 4:358–59; 15:14; ENC §45). Reason, qua conceptually constituted apperceptive spontaneity, achieves its actuality by discovering in the world, in the content of sensuous experience, the very conceptual structures that inform itself. To hearken back to McDowell's words above, "the way empirical thinking is beholden to the independent reality disclosed in experience ... is not, just as such, an infringement on the freedom of apperception. It constitutes what we might conceive, rather, as the medium in which that freedom is exercised."[6]

Observe secondly that although Hegel does equate this particular idealism of reason with the view that "things" are really "sensations and representations" and therefore "mine," his emphasis does not lie primarily on their being *mere* sensations and representations or on their being *just* mine. In contrast to with the negative idealism of self-consciousness, observing reason is decidedly optimistic about finding within sensuous experience an *objective expression of its own essence*. The *mine-ness* brought about by empirical science signifies not subjectification of the world so much as objectification of the mind. So to all intents and purposes, we could be dealing here with the McDowellian Kant who has been emancipated by Hegel from the restrictive "frame" of transcendental idealism. Also note, however, that while the McDowellian view of apperception's relation to experience solves problems analogous to those which positive reason solves vis-à-vis negative idealism, that very same view is here the start of a whole new set of problems. Consider the way Hegel continues the passage cited above:

---

6 McDowell, "Hegel's Radicalization of Kant," 74; see the discussion in the previous chapter.

This idealism therefore becomes the same kind of self-contradictory ambiguity as skepticism, except that, while the latter expresses itself negatively, the former does so positively. But it nevertheless fails to bring together its contradictory thoughts of pure consciousness as all reality, on the one hand, and the alien impulse or sensuous sensation and representation as an equal reality, on the other. Instead of bringing them together, it shifts back and forth between them, and is caught up in the two and stumbles into the spurious, namely sensuous, infinity … In order to reach this *other* that it holds to be *essential*, i.e. to be the in-itself, the pure reason of this idealism is therefore thrown back by its own self on to that knowing which is *not* a knowing of the true; in this way, it condemns itself of its own knowledge and volition to being *an untrue kind of knowing, and cannot let go of an opining [Meinen]*[7] *and perceiving [Wahrnehmen] that have no truth for it.* (GW 9:136/§238; final emphasis added)

At issue in this passage is clearly a *heterogeneity* between the form of pure consciousness on the one hand and the content of sensation and representation on the other. But how should we construe that heterogeneity? One way is in terms of the spontaneity of reason versus the receptivity of sensibility, or of concepts versus the non-conceptual content that renders them objectively determinate. We could then say that observing reason is caught in the *aporiae* of scheme–content dualism. But hasn't McDowell – and indeed observing reason itself – already overcome that problem? After all, the idea that in experience receptivity draws our conceptually constituted spontaneity into play, evincing a deep affinity with the very structures of reason itself, is supposed to be the answer to the heterogeneity problem that confronted Kant's rigorous dualism of activity/passivity, concept/intuition. And the optimism that empirical science will prove the intrinsic intelligibility of the experiential world, as it were by the deed, is the animating spirit of observing reason.

However, the heterogeneity that will become problematic for observing reason does not ultimately derive from those dualities, nor does Hegel articulate it in terms of them. He places the difficulties instead in a direct line of descent from the *Meinen* of sense certainty, through the dialectic of perception, down to skepticism. So looking back over this genealogy of observing reason, what other terms suggest

---

7 Hegel is playing here on the homophony of the German verb *Meinen* (to believe in the weakest sense of having a belief that is for the believer himself, i.e. subjectively, insufficiently justified) and the possessive pronoun *Meines* ("mine").

themselves for construing the problematic heterogeneity? Let us concentrate on a passage near the conclusion of "Perception":

> This determinateness, which constitutes the essential character of the thing and distinguishes it from all others, is itself determined in such a way that the thing is thereby in opposition to other things, but is supposed to be preserved [along with its determinateness] as being for itself. But it is only a thing (or a unit with being-for-itself) insofar as it does not stand in this relation to others; for in this relation what is posited is rather its continuity with others, and to be continuous with others is to cease to be for itself. It is precisely by virtue of its *absolute character* and its opposition to others that it *relates itself to others*, and it is essentially only this relating. Relation, however, is the negation of its independence, and thus it is really the essential property of the thing that causes it to perish [*zugrundegehen*]. (GW 9:78/§125)

What is at issue here is a heterogeneity that cuts through the metaphysical constitution of the thing-of-many-qualities itself, destabilizing it. On the one hand, the "thing" is a determinate *unit* or *individual* by virtue of its being-for-self; the thing's relation-to-self is here determined by what is commonly called its *essential property*. On the other hand, the thing is *determinate* by virtue of its opposition to all other things; in its relation to any other thing, *this* thing will differ by virtue of there being at least one pair of contradictory predicates, one of which applies to *this* thing, the other of which to the other. That predicate designates its essential property. But then its essential property may well differ according to which other thing happens to stand in relation to it, and this is to say that the thing's essential property is determined by its relation-to-other, not its relation-to-self. The thing's identity or relation-to-self is thus the very door by which difference or relation-to-other enters into it. The thing-of-many-properties is not such as to be able to integrate this heterogeneity so as to "be at one with itself in its other." This failure constitutes its finitude and makes it subject to the self-externality and passing-over into others (flux) that distinguishes finite structures from the Concept.

I suggest that this heterogeneity between relation-to-self and relation-to-other and the self-externality constituted by it is what ultimately underlies the concept/intuition, spontaneity/receptivity dualities that seem at first blush to be exclusively of interest in the passage from "Observing Reason." The many passages where Hegel characterizes sensibility and the forms of intuition in just such terms of self-externality support this suggestion (cf. GW 12:41–42, 226; ENC §§247A, 258).

The upshot of this line of interpretation is that Kant, precisely because of his commitment to the centrality of formal apperception, mistakenly took empirical science (especially mathematical physics) as the *exclusive* medium and the *appropriate* and *adequate* medium in which to actualize theoretical reason. Instead, Hegel would say, empirical science *as such* locks reason into an element heterogeneous to it, an element ruled by difference, finitude, relation-to-other and self-externality, and therefore an element which excludes identity and infinite relation-to-self in principle. Empirically oriented reason "condemns itself," as Hegel says in the passage above, "to being an untrue kind of knowing, and cannot let go of an opining and perceiving that have no truth for it." The untruth of opining and perceiving is not finally a result of transcendental idealism's commitment to the subjectivity of spatio-temporal appearances; rather, the objective phenomenality of spatio-temporal things, and hence the illusory nature of our knowledge of them, is a function of their metaphysical lack of ontological independence, unity, identity, and totality.[8]

4.3. The limitations of empirical science and the real nomological underdetermination of nature

This perspective informs Hegel's discussion of some of the central problems in the philosophy of science. Is nature divided up into distinct, non-vague natural kinds such that we could "cut it at the joints" if we could only identify the proper level of description and classificatory division? Or is all classification of natural phenomena merely nominal? Is inductive (universal) inference justified; does it lead to knowledge of natural kinds and laws? In practice, many if not all the natural laws we have so far been able to formulate are hedged by *ceteris paribus* clauses. What does that imply for the concept of a law of nature? And what is the status of branches of inquiry (such as biology or economics) that do not allow of laws even approaching strict

---

8 As Longuenesse rightly comments, "Hegel's goal is not modestly to follow the development of particular sciences. Nor is it ... to *ground* particular sciences. Rather, it is to call upon particular sciences to demonstrate the part they take in the existence of reason ... Hegel proposes so little to ground scientific discourses that on the contrary, his purpose is to dissolve their claim to objective validity, and thus to open the space for speculative philosophy" (*Hegel's Critique*, 37–38).

generality? These questions bear on the very foundations of natural science, and Hegel consistently takes a pessimistic stand on them. To this extent we may say that he espouses skepticism as to the possibility of adequate empirical theories in general. What qualifies his position as distinctively speculative is that he does not explain his pessimism or skepticism by reference to the limits of rational inquiry, but by reference to the ontological features of natural objects themselves. It is not that reason is not equal to the wealth and complexity of the natural world, but rather that nature does not measure up to the demands of reason.

In support of this contention, I would point first to Hegel's views on descriptive and classificatory sciences generally. The natural world seems to present scientific inquiry with "an inexhaustible supply of material for observation and description." In truth however,

> here at the boundary-line of the universal where an immense field seems to have opened up, [observation and description] have found only the limitations of nature and their own activity; it is impossible to know whether what seems to have being in itself is not merely something contingent. What bears in itself the impress of a confused or inchoate, feeble structure, barely developing out of rudimentary indeterminateness, cannot claim even to be described. (GW 9:140/§245)

Thus, one reason why empirical science is constantly driven out towards the boundaries of its seemingly well-established categories and classifications lies in their ultimately nominal character. In a closely related discussion in the *Science of Logic*, Hegel criticizes empirical science for having to be content with definitions that indicate no more than "*marks*, that is, determinations that are indifferent as regards their essentiality to the object and whose only purpose is rather to be *markers* for external reflection" (GW 12:213).[9]

---

9 This shortcoming is especially evident in zoological classifications: cf. GW 12:217–19. Classificatory schemes (e.g. that of Linnaeus) are exposed to competing schemes subject to constant revision as new species are discovered that do not clearly fit into the existing order, e.g. hybrids. We should not underestimate how massive this problem of taxonomic revision truly is. Ernst Mayr (*The Growth of Biological Thought: Diversity, Evolution, and Inheritance* [Cambridge, MA: Harvard University Press 1982], 246) makes the point that a taxonomist "can still productively spend his entire life doing nothing but describing new species and assigning them to appropriate genera. The diversity of organic nature seems to be virtually unlimited. At the present time [1982] about 10,000 new species of animals are described annually, and even if we accept the lowest of the estimates of undescribed species, it would take another two hundred years to complete the task of simply describing and naming all existing species."

There is therefore some truth to Clark Butler's contention that Hegel is a nominalist, although in this case as in so many others we must take care to specify the peculiarities of *Hegelian* nominalism.[10] Butler points to statements like this one from the lengthy *Zusatz* to §246 of the *Encyclopedia*: "In thinking things, we transform them into something universal; but things are singular and the Lion as such does not exist." Certain aspects of Hegel's treatment of "judgments of inherence" can also be read as supporting a nominalist interpretation.[11] On the other hand, Robert Stern provides a "substance-kind" analysis of Hegel's concept of universality, inspired by Aristotle, which accounts for Hegel's criticism of judgments of inherence like "The rose is red," while maintaining a central role for the universal.[12] Stern can draw on a rich arsenal of arguments to support his interpretation; however, the precise extent to which Hegel does have recourse to a basically Aristotelian essentialism, or even whether his own metaphysical and methodological commitments would allow him to, is open to question.

As this chapter proceeds, it will become evident how very far Hegel goes in mounting a fundamental critique of the classificatory enterprise of descriptive natural science – much further, presumably, than a philosopher committed to Aristotelian essentialism would permit herself to go. Even so, this critique must be understood in light of Hegel's other commitments, most specifically to his views on the indeterminateness, instability, and fragmentary character of the finite sphere. It may well be that substance-kind universals like "lion" do not in fact exist *in re*, *pace* Stern and Aristotle.[13] The denial that such universals exist either *in re* or *per se* is not necessarily equivalent to denying the

---

10   Clark Butler, "Hermeneutic Hegelianism," *Idealistic Studies* 14:2 (May 1985): 121–35, and more recently his argument in the introduction to G. W. F. Hegel, *Lectures on Logic: Berlin 1831*, trans. Clark Butler (Bloomington and Indianapolis, IN: Indiana University Press 2008), esp. xvii.

11   Cf. ENC §170 and the corresponding remarks in *Lectures on Logic: Berlin 1831*, 183–84: "Thus we say that the predicate *inheres* within the subject. The predicate is a determinate content within the subject taken as a totality .... The other side of the matter is that the predicate is universal in point of form. It has the determination of being universal. The universal now passes as what is substantive, as subsisting for itself." In personal communication Butler has indicated that he reads the reference to self-subsistence of the universal as a criticism of the Platonic theory of forms, and he stresses that Hegel never ceases to tie the purely logical concepts back to singular items of sense perception as that from which they have been abstracted.

12   Cf. Stern, *Structure of the Object*, 73–106.

13   But for an example of a committed essentialist who would nevertheless deny the existence of natural kinds at the level of descriptive biology see Ellis, *Philosophy of Nature*, 28–32.

existence and efficacy of any universals whatsoever; that is, Hegel may deny the reality of universals at the level of biological species and *a fortiori* at the level of non-specific properties like "red" or "small," without therefore qualifying as a nominalist in the traditional sense. As I am interpreting Hegel here, the robust existence of universals like "lion" or "rose" is compromised by metaphysical deficiencies in the finite sphere of nature. Nature falls short of the Concept partly owing to its poor nomological behavior, which in turn conditions the degree to which real universals are present and identifiable in it. But this need not entail unrestricted nominalism.

Now, we may certainly concede to an Aristotelian essentialist that a typically empiricist, pluralist view of objects, according to which objects are thrown together, as it were, out of ontologically independent elements, runs into trouble as soon as we try to put in to work in understanding scientific practice. If kind-substances and my concepts of them were really rooted in some kind of law-like conjunction of distinct elements, the prima facie nomological unruliness of nature would continuously be calling our identification of substance-kinds into question. This might not seem to be so much of a problem for anti-essentialist philosophers of science, but as Nancy Cartwright has persuasively argued, the presupposition of something closely akin to Aristotelian essences or substance-kinds (she speaks of "Aristotelian natures") is actually a necessary condition on our identification of law-like regularities.

Cartwright supplies a kind of counter-narrative about the way the specifically modern, "laws-of-nature" conception of the empirical world allegedly came to supplant the Aristotelian conception of the primacy of kinds or natures. According to what she calls the "official narrative," the scientific revolutionaries of the seventeenth century abandoned the Aristotelian use of "natures" to explain what goes on in the natural world, on the grounds that such explanations introduce scientifically useless, "occult" qualities that reproduce the *explanandum* in a purely tautological way. On the surface, the moderns replaced these natures and their occult qualities with the idea of *laws* decreed to nature by God. Laws, as van Fraassen puts the point, provided a link between God's decree and nature by way of the idea "that nature has its inner necessities, which are not mere facts, but constrain all mere facts into a unified whole. The theological analogy and dying metaphor of law provided the language in which the idea could be couched."[14]

---

14 Quoted in Cartwright, *Dappled World*, 80.

While this official narrative may capture the self-conception of the moderns and their contemporary heirs, Cartwright thinks it distorts what actually happened. Rather than a revolutionary break, she sees a largely unbroken tradition of relying on "natures" to do the explanatory work in physics. As a case in point, Cartwright adduces Newton's famous *experimentum crucis* in optics, throwing an interesting sidelight onto Goethe's rival conception of a theory of colors.[15] Newton's experiment is meant to clinch the argument that white light is in reality composed of rays of different color, each with its own characteristic degree of refrangibility. The experimental setup is such that, in an otherwise darkened environment, white light passes through two prisms; at the first it is broken into its (putatively) component colors, each exiting the prism at a different angle; at the second, by contrast, the separate component rays exit the prism unaltered and at the same angle as in the case of the first prism. Newton's inference is that the prism is acting in the same way in both cases, bending the rays of each color according to its specific refrangibility, the only difference being that in the white light entering the first prism they are mixed, and upon exiting have been separated out according to their degree of refrangibility. Light, Newton infers, is therefore generally composed of rays of different colors.

Goethe, whose influence on Hegel's conception of scientific methodology can hardly be questioned, objected to this inference as resting on a body of evidence too slim by far to support the generalization Newton draws from it.[16] Cartwright inquires into the differing background assumptions that underlie Newton's confidence. Her conclusion is that Newton is implicitly oriented toward the basically Aristotelian conception of fixed or essential *natures*: "Newton focuses on one special experiment and maintains that that experiment will pinpoint an explanation that is generalizable ... [H]e looks to a feature that is part of the inner constitution of light itself."[17] This "inner

---

15 Cf. Newton's First Letter to Oldenburg (February 6, 1672), in H. W. Turnbull, J. F. Scott, A. R. Hall and L. Tilling (eds.), *The Correspondence of Isaac Newton*, vol. 1 (Cambridge University Press 1959–77), 92–106.

16 Cf. Cartwright, *Dappled World*, 96; on the insufficient basis of Newton's generalizations see HA 14:156–58. On Goethe's influence on Hegel, see Eckart Förster, "Die Bedeutung von §§ 76, 77 der *Kritik der Urteilskraft* für die Entwicklung der nachkantischen Philosophie," *Zeitschrift für philosophische Forschung* 56 (2002): 170–90, 321–45, and *The Twenty-Five Years*, 358–62; on Goethe's method, esp. in reference to the theory of light and color, see 250–77.

17 Cartwright, *Dappled World*, 101.

constitution" corresponds, she thinks, to an Aristotelian-style essence or nature, that is, a thing with capacities to act and a tendency to act in those ways under appropriate circumstances. This allows Newton to "downplay the experimental context. The context is there to elicit the nature of light; it is *not an essential ingredient in the ultimate structure of the phenomenon* ... The connection between the natures and the behavior that is supposed to reveal them is so tight that Newton takes it to be *deductive*."[18]

I will return to Goethe's objections to Newton's procedures presently, as they bear directly on Hegel's own views. But in order fully to appreciate their significance, we must first consider a further aspect of the relation between laws and "natures."

Cartwright believes that the laws of nature, such as they are, are determined by the natures of the kinds of things that populate what she calls "the dappled world," rather than the other way around. However, she takes this to mean that the laws that manifest those natures constitute at best a loosely knit patchwork.[19] Laws, she argues, are at best descriptions of relatively idealized interactions between things under relatively artificial conditions designed to isolate and shield the interactions from the wider environment.[20] From the nomological perspective of the laws thus extracted, therefore, the real world, that is, the world as it appears when unconstrained by the experimental situation, is bound to seem messy since it is made up of a plurality of different kinds of things interacting according to their specific natures rather than according to universal laws. Cartwright gives numerous examples of such messiness and of the difficulties of establishing laws that are both universal in scope and truly explanatory in application. If natural science is chiefly concerned with the discovery and mutual integration of universal and necessary laws of nature, then it might well seem that we are so far removed from that goal as to have made hardly any progress at all since the time of Galileo.[21]

18 *Ibid.*, 102–3; emphases added; cf. HA 14:146–53.
19 *Ibid.*, 34.
20 Cartwright refers to such experimental situations as "nomological machines" (*ibid.*, 50). She affirms that such nomological machines give us genuine insight into the natures of the things that make up the world; however, she rejects the unreflecting extrapolation that the *world itself* is like a nomological machine, and embraces instead a worldview she calls metaphysical pluralism (33).
21 From this perspective, Kant's nightmare scenario, in which reason is confronted with a multiplicity of laws so dappled that we could not begin to grasp their interconnections, might be closer to the truth than he realized: cf. 20:209.

Here the persistence of Aristotelian-style natures comes in. If we choose to measure progress in terms of what we have learned about the nature of light, for example, or the nature of electromagnetism, the chemical elements, and so on, then we have indeed come a long way in the past few centuries. The laws of nature, circumscribed in scope and disconnected though they may be, do indeed seem to open windows onto the "inner constitution" of the kinds of things they concern. And this, again, is also the path to understanding how Newton can declare with a clear scientific conscience that a single experiment performed in a singularly artificial context can prove definitively that light is composed of rays.

When it comes to Aristotelian natures, Goethe turns out to have been by far the more radical modernist. His objection to Newton's theory is not merely that its evidential basis is too slim, too much tailored to unique experimental circumstances to support the kinds of inferences Newton makes. As Cartwright observes:

> Goethe's disagreement with Newton is not a matter of mere epistemological uncertainty. It is rather a reflection of deep ontological differences. For Goethe, all phenomena are the consequence of interaction between polar opposites. There is nothing in light to be isolated, no inner nature to be revealed. No experiment can show with a single experiment what it is in the nature of light to do. The empiricists of the scientific revolution wanted to oust Aristotle entirely from the new learning. I have argued that they did no such thing. Goethe, by contrast, did dispense with natures; there are none in his world picture.[22]

Hegel is closer to Goethe in this respect than he is to Newton or indeed to the mainstream of modern science. Granted, Goethe differs from Hegel in that his "intuitive method" of natural science proceeds from the bottom up, gradually identifying and individuating *Urphänomene* in their specific, limited totalities, whereas Hegel seems committed to the diametrically opposed conception of a rigorously top-down account that derives the particular and manifold from the structure of the Concept.[23] This difference appears less salient, though, when we realize that Hegel restricts the scope of truly rigorous science to the *a priori* unfolding of the structure of the Concept: he would not agree that the phenomena of nature are capable of a single, unified,

---

22 Cartwright, *Dappled World*, 103.
23 Cf. Förster, *The Twenty-Five Years*, 370.

rigorous derivation, for the precise reason that nature itself is not a single, unified, fully determinate totality.

Thus, the unruliness on the side of the classifications is itself a reflection of nature's own poor nomological behavior. Hegel is quite explicit about this:

> To an even lesser extent than the other spheres of nature does the animal world represent an independent, rational system of organization, nor can it maintain the forms as they would be determined by the Concept and preserve them from the imperfection and mixing of conditions that lead to adulteration, atrophy, and transition. This *weakness of the Concept in nature* as a whole subjects not only the formation of individuals to external contingencies ... but even the genera are exposed to changes in the external, universal life of nature. (ENC §368; emphasis added)[24]

In other words, nature's classificatory and nomological unruliness is a consequence of the deficient metaphysical constitution of Aristotelian essences or natural kinds. As *determinate* beings (*Daseiende, Existierende*), they exist in essential unity and community with their polar opposites, and are continuously driven to pass over into them as an expression of this constitutive unity (cf. GW 9:141–42/§§247–48). The character of reason, by contrast, is to maintain its identity in and through its unity with its other. These are the authentically Hegelian terms for the heterogeneity between formal apperception and the sensible manifold that plagues transcendental idealism. The essential character of reason is its *absolute determinacy*, that is, the fact (as far as Hegel is concerned) that it is fully determined and individuated exclusively by its relation to its own internal differentiations.[25]

Finite objects, on the other hand, are characterized by *relative determinateness*. They are determined and individuated exclusively by their (negative) relation to all the other determinate beings which they

---

24 Cf. GW 12:39 and, for an instance from Hegel's early career, GW 4:91–92. For discussion see Wolfgang Lefevre, "Die Schwäche des Begriffs in der Natur: Der Unterabschnitt 'Beobachtung der Natur' im Vernunft-Kapitel der *Phänomenologie des Geistes*," in A. Arndt, K. Ball, and H. Ottmann (eds.), *Hegel-Jahrbuch 2001: Phänomenologie des Geistes, Erster Teil* (Berlin: Akademie Verlag 2002), 157–71.

25 "Determinacy," as a *terminus technicus*, always entails some *relation*. If that relation takes place between the determinate entity and some other entity – if, that is, it consists in the entity's relation-to-other – we are dealing with a case of *finite determinacy*. If on the other hand the determinacy is constituted purely by the entity's relation-to-self, we have a case of *absolute determinacy*.

are not and yet which are essentially implicated in what they *are*. The result is that they are never fully determined and individuated since in order fully to express what they are, they must change and pass over into new shapes and conditions. In its manifestation as observation, description, and classification, reason (that is, absolute determinacy, relation-to-self) is immediately caught up in and contaminated with a heterogeneous element which it tries but fails to assimilate. Here, self-externality is ineluctable.

4.4. Hegel's critical analysis of the notion of "laws of nature"

The trajectory of Hegel's engagement with the philosophy of science points beyond nature and natural science themselves, which he grasps as metaphysically dependent stages in the self-actualization of the Concept. In a passage that recalls Schelling, Hegel explains that there are real analogies between the levels of mind (such as sensibility, understanding, reason) and natural phenomena:

> [I]t may turn out that the objective world exhibits mechanical and final causes; its actual existence is not the norm of the *true*, but rather the true is instead the criterion for deciding which of these existences is the true existence [of the objective world]. Just as the subjective understanding exhibits also errors in it, so the objective world exhibits also aspects and levels of truth that by themselves are still one-sided, incomplete and only relations of appearances. (GW 12:154)

For this reason, Hegel is disposed to treat persistent difficulties with the concept of causal laws of nature as reflections of metaphysical limitations inherent to natural objects as such. Whereas the work of empirical classification was driven along by reason's need to find its *totality* and internal *order* and differentiation expressed in an objective medium, the inductive search for law-like connections between appearances reflects reason's drive to find its inner *necessity* and *universality* objectified. Hegel sees no prospects for an enduring satisfaction of this "rational instinct" (GW 9:143/§250). "For observing consciousness, the *truth of the law* is found in *experience*, i.e. it is *there for it* in the form of *sensuous being*. But if the law does not have its truth in the Concept, it is a contingency, not a necessity, and so really not a law" (GW 9:142/§249).

In his discussion of biology, Hegel makes two further observations that cast doubt on the possibility of discovering *natural* exemplifications of universality and necessity. The first is that many or perhaps all of our expressions of laws of nature are hedged by various *ceteris paribus* clauses.

> The law as it first appears exhibits itself in an impure form, cloaked in single, sensuous forms of being; the Concept that makes up its nature is immersed in empirical material. The instinct of reason sets out to find out by experiment what happens under this or that set of circumstances. The result is that the law seems only to be all the more immersed in sensuous being. (GW 9:143/§251)

This process of multiplying and differentiating the circumstances that seem relevant to the law is Janus-faced. On the one hand, it purges the law's expression of any merely coincidental elements, leading to an increasingly precise formulation. Thereby, however, the law also becomes increasingly abstract and distant from the concrete circumstances that are the context and element of any *actual* instantiation of the law. On the other hand, the more thoroughly we consider the varying circumstances in which the law seems to manifest itself, the less unified the law appears to be in its actual operation, while more and more possible exceptions seem to arise.

This is the observation behind Nancy Cartwright's notion of the "dappled" character of the natural world. Many of the classic laws of physics seem to state facts about what necessarily happens, and they do indeed state facts; only, these facts concern highly idealized situations.[26] One example is Newton's law of universal gravitation: "Two bodies exert a force between each other which varies inversely as the square of the distance between them, and varies directly as the product of their masses."[27] As Cartwright points out, this "universal law" does not in fact apply to any and all two bodies whatsoever. For instance, Coulomb's Law states that two bodies exert a force between each other that varies inversely as the square of distance between them, and directly as the product of their *charges*.[28] So the actual behavior of any two charged, massive bodies will deviate from what either law would predict in isolation, while the real world is characteristically messy in the sense that any actual instance of causation will presumably be determined

---

26 See Nancy Cartwright, "Do the Laws of Physics State the Facts?," in J. W. Carrol (ed.), *Readings on Laws of Nature* (University of Pittsburgh Press 2004), 71–83. Cf. ENC §286A.

27 Quoted Cartwright, "Do the Laws of Physics," 73.

28 Cf. *ibid.*, 76.

by more than one (kind of) force. If the behavior of bodies in the real world results from the combined "action" of simple laws (though of course laws, as abstract objects, are not strictly speaking causally efficacious), and if the combined effect of such laws is not itself dictated by the laws taken separately, then a basic tension arises within the very concept of a law of nature: "In order to be true in the composite case, the law must describe one effect (the effect which actually happens); but to be explanatory, it must describe another. There is a trade-off here between truth and explanatory power."[29]

Cartwright's dilemma is also at the heart of Hegel's discussion in "Observing Reason" and in the closely related chapter on "Force and the Understanding." There the problem is that the putative law of nature is present in appearance, but that the very same appearance that manifests the law also exhibits any number of features that the law does not explain:

> In [the appearance] the law is present, but it is not the entire presence of the appearance; with every change of circumstance the law takes on a different actuality. Thus appearance retains for itself aspects that are not internal [to the law]; i.e. the appearance has not yet been posited in truth *as appearance*, as *sublated* being-for-self. This defect in the law must equally become manifest in the law itself ... To the extent that it is not *the* law, pure and simple, but rather *a* law, it exhibits determinateness; consequently, there are indefinitely *many* laws. But this plurality is itself a defect ... [The understanding] must therefore let the many laws collapse into *one* law. (GW 9:91–92/§150)

In contemporary terms, this response to the tangled multiplicity of the laws we require for actual explanation may be understood as appealing to the idea of a "covering law" or a "super law." Cartwright makes three critical points that are immediately relevant here. First of all, it is by no means clear that such laws are always available, or that they ever are. We must countenance the possibility that "nature may well be underdetermined; God failed to write laws for every complex situation."[30] Second, it is possible that super laws fail to be explanatory at all: "This is an old complaint against the covering law model of explanation: 'Why does the quail in the garden bob its head up and down in that funny way whenever it walks?' ... 'Because they all do.'"[31]

29 *Ibid.*, 75.
30 *Ibid.*, 80.
31 *Ibid.*

And third, while super laws may be explanatory by virtue of bringing our attention to broader patterns in nature, and for just that reason they may at the same time fail to shed any light on what, in a particular case, is actually going on in causal terms, and thus fail to explain anything in the basic sense of telling us how and why something is happening.

When we compare this with Hegel, the first and third observations appear to boil down to the single Hegelian point that there may well be pervasive underdetermination at both the macro-level (absence of suitable covering laws) and the micro-level (failure of the covering law to provide a sufficiently detailed explanation). And this points not simply to deficiencies in our explanatory abilities, but to a real lack of full *nomological* determination in nature itself.

The second of Cartwright's points cited agrees in substance with Hegel's charge that what we call causal explanation is at bottom tautological. Certainly Cartwright would not accede to this charge in the full generality Hegel wants to give it. But she does point to a danger inherent not only in the shrug-of-the-shoulders variety of everyday explanation ("Because they just do, that's all"), but in high-level scientific explanation as well, namely that it reproduce or reduplicate the *explanandum*, superficially conferring upon it a law-like or universalizing form in the *explanans*. Hegel calls attention to this tendency repeatedly, both in the *Phenomenology* and in the *Logic* (e.g. GW 12:304–5; 9:94–95/§§154–55). In "Observing Reason" he complains that laws frequently take this form:

> [F]or example, sensibility and irritability stand in an inverse ratio of their magnitude, so that as the one increases the other decreases; or better, taking the magnitude itself as the content, the greatness of something increases as its smallness decreases. – Should, however, a determinate content be given to this law, say, that the size of a hole *increases*, the more what it is filled with *decreases*, then this inverse relation can equally be changed into a direct relation and expressed in this way, that the size of the hole *increases* in direct ratio to the amount taken away – a *tautological* proposition, whether expressed as a direct or an inverse ratio. As so expressed, the proposition means simply this, that a quantity increases as this quantity increases. (GW 9:152–53/§271)

Granted, this representation of scientific explanation crosses the line from polemic into satire, but the point is well taken nonetheless. To the extent that law-like generalizations do more than record regularities (Hume's constant conjunction) and provide them with a quantitative formalization, they fail to do genuine explanatory work. "Why does this F change like this when that G does that?" "Because they all do." (Or rather, "Because they mostly do, except when …") Many of us will perhaps be inclined to view this as a failing of particular (or particular kinds of) explanations; Hegel seems to believe that, ultimately, it is the form all explanation must take. Within the boundaries of the natural world, the explanatory regress can no more be stopped than can be the proliferation of differing explanations and the multiplication of laws; at best, the problem is capped by a tautological super law more expressive of reason's demand for order and necessity than of nature's conformity to it. Why? Because nature ultimately has no "inside," no "ground" which, itself natural, would genuinely "explain" why things are as they are: "It is manifest that behind the so-called curtain that is supposed to conceal the inner world, there is nothing to be seen unless *we* go behind it ourselves, as much in order that we may see, as that there may be something behind there which can be seen" (GW 9:102/§165)[32] – and for Hegel, this something is not nature, but the Concept.

4.5. Natural science as a stage within the life of the Concept

The main business of this chapter has been to argue that empirical science is not (*pace* McDowell) a fully adequate medium for reason's actualization of its freedom, although it is a medium in which that task can begin. For reason cannot discover, in the objective medium of the natural world, adequate reflections or objectifications of a number of essential features of the Concept: totality, order (stable internal differentiation), universality, and necessity. In consequence, the Concept cannot here be "at one with itself in the other."[33]

---

32 Cf. Hegel's scathing remarks on Haller's poem "On the Infinite," GW 4:92; ENC §§140, 246.

33 In order to keep my discussion to a manageable length, I have omitted discussion of Hegel's views on a privileged phenomenon of nature, namely organic life, which Hegel repeatedly characterizes as the single most adequate realization of the Concept in the self-external sphere of nature (cf. GW 12:182–87; ENC §251/251A, and esp. ENC §337). Also, it should not be overlooked that Hegel interprets the human search for laws of nature as a manifestation of the life of the Concept itself in a decidedly non-metaphorical sense of *life*. Nevertheless, in regard to the ultimate underdetermination and incompleteness of nature as a level of reality, Hegel's views on organic life make no difference.

Thus, empirical natural science embodies reason to the extent that it succeeds in uncovering intimations of reason's native totality, order, universality, and necessity throughout nature. One can go further: empirical science is itself an aspect of the life of the Concept. Like organic life, empirical science is driven by a rational instinct to assimilate the superficially non-conceptual stuff of experience to its own rational form, experiencing thereby a kind of growth and maturation. Empirical science constitutes, as an instance of orchestrated human, social activity, the life of the Concept in its unconscious immediacy. The scientifically engaged mind does not self-consciously conceive its activity as the emergence and partial actualization of the level of reality that is reason or the Concept. It is therefore limited, like organic life, by the nature of the beings to which it is externally directed and on which it depends for its continuing subsistence. These are essentially determinate, finite, self-external, and hence necessarily incompletable beings. They share in the structures that reason finds in them, so scientific explanation is no mere imposition of human norms onto an unstructured or differently structured world; but they do not adequately actualize those structures, and so scientific explanation is an infinite task, not a sphere of satisfactory rational self-actualization.

Far beyond their present or foreseeable needs for securing and augmenting their material existence, human beings seek out laws of nature. We do this, according to Hegel, out of a rational instinct to actualize unconditioned reason, what McDowell calls apperceptive spontaneity. Therefore, as McDowell suggests, natural science is indeed a medium for actualizing rational freedom. According to Hegel, though, in the end it is not the adequate medium. Scientific endeavor is fraught with uncertainty and incompleteness; our best-founded theories appear to be mere fragments of a more perfect theory we may have no reasonable hope of attaining. If Max Weber is right, then our very purpose in the pursuit of science is to produce knowledge destined to become obsolete in exact proportion to its fruitfulness in suggesting new objects and avenues of research, new science.[34] Science is thus an infinite task in which the rational instinct can therefore find no lasting satisfaction.

This idea is familiar to us today, both through Weber and more generally as the idea of infinite progress toward consensus in an ideal

---

34 Cf. Max Weber, "Science as a Vocation," in *The Vocation Lectures* (Indianapolis, IN and Cambridge: Hackett 2004), 1–31.

scientific community. The idea was familiar to Hegel, too, not least in the guise of the "infinite progress" toward positing the I in nature for which he repeatedly criticized Fichte (cf. GW 4:46–48, 401; 21:226–27). Many of Hegel's contemporaries interpreted Kant's limitations on knowledge and his regulative ideals as meaning that theoretical reason was of its very essence an unceasing striving for scientific completion, and that the achievement of a complete and unified scientific edifice would in fact signal the *death of reason*. Obviously, Hegel disagreed. This variety of progressivism amounted for him to subjectivist skepticism: if our scientific knowledge of the world is subject to a continual process of growth and perfectibility, then our best current theory of how things are is at best only partially correct; and if progress is truly conceived as *infinite*, then in relation to the ultimate goal our best current theory is not much better than total ignorance, or at least there would no way for us to measure how far we have advanced in getting it right.

Hegel courageously accepted the idea that we will never complete empirical science, but he interpreted this failure as a reflection of the fact that nature itself is incomplete and, within its own sphere, incompletable. Which is to say again that he objectified a certain strand of Kantian skepticism: As Kant argues in regard to the First Cosmological Antinomy, the contradiction between the thesis of the natural world's totality and that of its infinity is moot, since what we ultimately mean by "the natural world" is the inclusive concept (*Inbegriff*) of appearances, and the idea of a totality or an infinity of appearances is out of place.[35] But if we join Hegel in dropping the frame of transcendental idealism while radicalizing the idea of the dialectic, the resolution of the cosmological antinomy applies to the objects themselves. The impossibility of completing science is the "spiritual" counterpart of nature's own intrinsic incompleteness, though not as a sign of her inexhaustible wealth, but of her insurmountable limitations.

Taken seriously, this implies denial that there can be any ultimately justifying foundation for claims to scientific knowledge of nature within finite cognition. Hegel, far from seeking any such ultimate grounding for the sciences, seems rather to explain them as conditioned by the finite nature of their very objects. This is the upshot of Hegel's reflections on skepticism and of the detailed analysis of his

---

35 Cf. B528–29; cf. also the discussion of Kant's revision of the Principle of Thoroughgoing Determination in Chapter 3.

views on the philosophy of science. Not only natural science, but the very realm of nature points beyond itself – to the Concept. Hegelian metaphysics is thus revisionary: the critique of finite cognition (part and parcel with his critique of traditional metaphysics) does not end with the rehabilitation of finite cognition from the point of view of the absolute Idea. Both the *Phenomenology* and the *Science of Logic* are by intention transformational. The forms and categories of finite cognition are changed in their very content so as become recognizable as subordinate forms of the Concept, and this requires that we change our view as to what features of reality those forms and categories actually pick out. This movement bears less resemblance to the methodical skepticism of Descartes which, in the end, leaves all our beliefs as they were before, than to the Platonic ascent out of the cave and into the light. It is supposed to change our mind.

THE METHODOLOGY OF FINITE COGNITION AND THE IDEAL OF MATHEMATICAL RIGOR

5.1. Introduction

Early modern philosophy was born of a new spirit of methodicalism: consider Bacon's *Novum Organon*, the quantitative and experimental procedures exemplified in Galileo's *Dialogues concerning Two New Sciences*, or Descartes' *Discourse on Method*. Correspondingly, what is most distinctively modern in Wolff's systematization of logic and metaphysics is its *methodological* commitment to the mathematical ideal, as Hegel recognizes in his discussion of it in the *Lectures on the History of Philosophy*: "logical consequence, method is the principal thing" (TW 20:122; cf. 153).[1] Hence any attempt to reject, to inherit, or to transform classical rationalist metaphysics must come to terms with its pretensions to having achieved a scientific philosophy on a par with mathematical demonstration.[2] This in turn requires an account of what is specific to mathematical and philosophical cognition, respectively, and of their respective places in the system of sciences. In this chapter I explore Hegel's conception of mathematical knowledge as a means to understanding the sense in which he could himself claim to have transformed philosophy into a science more rigorous even than geometry.

The background of the coming discussion is Jacobi's critical thesis that the mathematical ideal of knowledge leads necessarily to a particularly extreme version of formalism and thence to determinism

---

1 Cf. Honnefelder, *Scientia*, 296–98.
2 For a similar interpretation of Hegel's critique of mathematical cognition cf. Heinz Röttges, *Der Begriff der Methode in der Philosophie Hegels* (Meisenheim am Glan: Anton Hein 1981), 86–89; cf. also Rainer Schäfer, *Die Dialektik und ihre besonderen Formen in Hegels Logik. Hegel-Studien* Beiheft 45 (Hamburg: Meiner 2001), 178.

and nihilism.[3] A difficulty arises when we notice that Hegel seems to embrace Jacobi's thesis, even though he himself espouses a metaphysics that is explicitly committed to the *absolutely relational* view of finite things that we first encountered in Chapter 3. Is Hegel inconsistent in this respect? I argue that he is not. Once we understand his distinctive views on the nature of mathematical cognition and its relation to speculative science, we can also see the precise ways in which his own metaphysics of absolute relationality differs from the "formalism" criticized by Jacobi. Specifically, Hegel accorded a unique status to mathematics as the highest possible form that the Concept can take within the sphere of finite cognition. As I will show, Hegel's high regard for mathematics is not based on its intuitive and apodictic qualities; in this he differs markedly from Kant. Rather, he is drawn to a systematic property of mathematical investigation he calls "real definition." The significance of such real definitions is that, in a sense to be explored in the following, they *produce the external reality* of the relevant mathematical objects from their *concepts*. To this extent, they parallel the work of speculative science (in particular the *Science of Logic*), which consists in demonstrating the necessity with which the Concept undergoes a process of ideal logical genesis and self-realization.

At the same time, Hegel believes he can show both the ways in which the structure of the Concept is implicit in mathematical cognition, how it can be derived on the basis of an internal critique of mathematical cognition, and the specific ways in which mathematical cognition remains tied down within the limits of finite cognition. The ultimate goal of this chapter is therefore to explain how it is that Hegel can agree with Jacobi about the nihilistic implications of the demonstrative ideal of knowledge *within the sphere of finite cognition*, while also affirming the internal unity of mathematical cognition (properly understood) and speculative science.

---

3 Whether consciously or not, Jacobi belongs to the same tradition as the pietist attack on Wolff's mathematically oriented methodology: "The pietists' original attack was aimed at Wolff's identification of mathematical and philosophical method. Thus the pietists put forward a *magister* in Jena who called himself Volcmar Conrad Poppo; he published a work entitled *Spinozismus Detectus* in which he was so bold as to make a distinction between the mathematical and philosophical method and between a mathematical and a philosophical inference, in order then to assert that Spinozism lay concealed *formaliter* within the mathematical method and the mathematical syllogism" (Dt. Log., 95, n. 16). This criticism was part of the pietists' campaign against Wolff's alleged atheism, led by J. J. Lange.

5.2. Jacobi's critique of rationalism and the methodological ideal of the *mos geometricus*

In Chapter 2 I argued that Hegel follows Kant in denying that the unconditioned can be known by subsuming it under the categories or finite thought-determinations, and that *insofar* as pre-critical metaphysics is characterized by the attempt to do just that, Hegel also follows Kant in his rejection of that tradition. In the *Logic*, Hegel puts this by saying that "as for the *content* of [pre-critical] metaphysics, Kant has in his own fashion shown that it leads by strict demonstration to *antinomies*" (GW 12:229; first emphasis added). Kant's discovery was that certain *contents* (notably the world-whole, but also the soul and a necessary being) are beyond the limits of discursive thought, and that their necessary unknowability can be demonstrated using only the means available to discursive thought itself. By the same token, however, Kant may be said to accept uncritically that discursive thought and its method of demonstration possess exclusive cognitive legitimacy; his exclusion of certain contents (the unconditional) from the sphere of determinate cognition serves on Hegel's view to *insulate* discursive reason against inconsistencies that could call it into question. Hence in the passage just quoted Hegel goes on to say that Kant "did not reflect on the nature of such demonstration itself, which is bound up with finite content; but the one must fall with the other" (GW 12:229).

As framed by Hegel, Jacobi's importance lies in his critique of the finite, discursive rationality for which, within the scope of the sensible world, Kant seeks to guarantee empirical substance and objective content. According to Jacobi, discursive form tends inevitably toward formalism. Demonstration or deduction, he argues with some plausibility, is a procedure based on the construction of tautologies, propositions that are true necessarily, but also merely in virtue of their *form*. The systematic elaboration of human knowledge requires that the intrinsic qualities of the content given in experience be successively reformulated as relations, a process that (in the words of Jacobi's "Open Letter" to Fichte) transforms "content into form" (*die Sache in bloße Gestalt*), and makes "form into content, content into nothing" (FJHW II, 1:201).

Now Jacobi believes that, as a matter of fact, truly radical formalism is a conceptual impossibility. This view is especially evident in the second edition of the *Spinoza Letters*, where he argues that we can have no conception of an absolutely dependent entity:

Such an entity would have to be utterly passive, and yet it *could* not be passive; for whatever is not already something, cannot be made into something through mere *determination*; no properties can be produced, by virtue of relations, in something that has none in itself, indeed not even any relation would be possible with respect to such a thing. (FHJW I, 1:163)

However, despite its ultimate incoherence, Jacobi thinks that the encroachment of formalism on human life is itself the result of existential pressures on human survival. Rationality, he argues in Supplement VII to the *Spinoza Letters*,

is a property of humans ... an instrument they use ... Since our conditional existence rests on an infinity of *mediations*, an immeasurable field is opened to inquiry which we are forced to deal with for the very sake of our physical preservation. The objective of all these inquiries is to discover what *mediates* the existence of things. The things whose mediation we comprehend, that is, whose *mechanism* we have discovered, are those which we can ourselves produce when the means are in our hands. (FHJW I, 1:260)

Instrumental rationality, that is, the investigation of mechanisms, of means and ends, of inputs and outputs, is directed toward the formulation and subsequent exploitation of *functional relations*. Putting the matter this way helps to see why "mechanistic" explanation as Jacobi understands it has an inherent tendency toward formalism. Mechanistic explanation (as opposed to physically realized mechanisms) focuses on the *causal roles* played by the relevant components in a system, tending to identify them with those roles. Causal roles, however, are essentially relational, and their specification consists in an enumeration of the possible states of the entity, the states of that or other entities upon which these states regularly follow, and the states of that or other relevant entities to which they give rise.

The formalized procedure for characterizing causal roles is the Ramsey–Lewis method for defining theoretical terms: the theory is rewritten as an existentially quantified sentence in which all the theoretical terms are quantified out and then defined in terms of their causal or functional relations to each other.[4] It is generally agreed that theoretical terms, so defined, are multi-realizable; which is to

---

4 For a classic presentation of the procedure see David Lewis, "How to Define Theoretical Terms," in *Philosophical Papers*, vol. I (Oxford University Press 1983), 78–96.

say that the intrinsic properties (*qualities*) of any system instantiating the theory are defined purely in terms of extrinsic properties (*relations*), so that any object(s) that fulfill the causal role(s) thus specified fall under the definition, regardless of the qualities they might be thought of possessing *absolutely*, that is, outside of any relations. To put it in terms somewhat closer to those Jacobi would have used, objects come to be defined in terms of form, not in terms of their experiential qualities or *content*: We cannot comprehend, he writes, "what we are unable to construct ... When we say that we have scientifically investigated a quality, what we in fact mean is that we have reduced it to figure, number, position, and motion and dissolved it therein; which is to say: we have *objectively* annihilated the quality" (FHJW I, 1:258, n. 1).

In a posthumous paper, Lewis himself shows how causal role analysis, in its Ramsified form, gives rise to a variety of mitigated skepticism he calls "Ramseyan Humility."[5] Though he presents a couple of different arguments for the position, the crux of it seems to be this: all that we can capture in our theory, once it has been appropriately Ramsified, are the *relational* properties any occupants of the causal roles have to instantiate, and indeed we know those properties only by observation, that is, by the effects they have on us. However, there are, as Lewis argues, independent grounds for believing that those roles at least could have been occupied by altogether different *intrinsic* properties. There remains, therefore, an ineliminable contingency in the fact that *just these* observable properties are the ones that occupy the causal roles identified by our theory; and hence absolute limits are placed on the extent of our insight into why these properties (and not others) play the role that they do. One can bypass this skeptical implication only by asserting either (a) that the causal roles a property fulfills are essential to it, so that any property that plays that role is identical to the intrinsic property in question; or (b) that properties just are causal roles, that is, relations, and that there is nothing above and beyond those roles to worry about.

Rae Langton has argued that Ramseyan humility is very close to, and can indeed serve as an interpretation of, Kant's transcendental skepticism regarding "things in themselves" and his limitation of

5 David Lewis, "Ramseyan Humility," in D. Braddon-Mitchell and R. Nolan (eds.), *Conceptual Analysis and Philosophical Naturalism* (Cambridge, MA: MIT Press 2009), 203–22.

knowledge to the relational properties exhibited in the phenomena.[6] Broadly speaking, Langton's position is an epistemic version of structural realism, the view that all we can know of nature are the structural relations between phenomena, but that we can know these with perfect objectivity.[7] Other contemporary philosophers of science and mathematics, however, have embraced an *ontic* or *metaphysical* interpretation of structural realism according to which objects themselves, along with their properties and causal powers, are constituted solely by their position as nodes in a structure. Philosophers of this persuasion argue against their critics that structures can do all the metaphysical work traditionally reserved for substantival individuals, including individuation.[8] Now, in regard to *scientific* knowledge, Jacobi clearly subscribes to a form of *epistemic* structuralism *avant la lettre*. However, he sees its ontic counterpart as leading to a state of worldlessness (what Hegel will call "acosmism," e.g. ENC §50) in which neither qualities nor individual bearers of properties are acknowledged as irreducibly real and in which, consequently, the experiential content that constitutes the substance of our lived existence is nihilistically denied as illusionary. Rationality, made absolute, leads to formalism and thence to nihilism.

Therefore, Jacobi is best characterized as the critic of a certain strand of scientific realism that arose in the period of the scientific revolution, one chief proponent of which is of course Spinoza.[9] This is

6 See Rae Langton, "Elusive Knowledge of Things in Themselves," *Australasian Journal of Philosophy* 82 (2004): 129–36. For a more detailed presentation of her view see *Kantian Humility*. Lewis's essay is a response to Langton's ideas.

7 On the Kantian overtones of structuralist realism in the early twentieth century, see Barry Gower, "Cassirer, Schlick and 'Structural' Realism: The Philosophy of the Exact Sciences in the Background to Early Logical Empiricism," *British Journal for the History of Philosophy* 8:1 (2000): 71–106. Ramsey-sentences play a recurrent, central, and controversial role throughout the contemporary discussions of structural realism, both in its epistemic and ontic varieties. For an example, see the overview article by James Ladyman, "What is Structural Realism?," *Studies in the History and Philosophy of Science* 29:3 (1997): 409–24, esp. 411–13. Structural realism in the physical sciences initially arose as a response to the *anti-realist* contentions of those who saw either historical theory-change or the empirical underdetermination of physical theories as undermining traditional realist commitments.

8 Prominent representatives are James Ladyman (e.g. "On the Identity and Diversity of Individuals," *Proceedings of the Aristotelian Society, Supplementary Volumes* 81 [2007]: 23–43) and Steven French, "Structure as a Weapon of the Realist," *Proceedings of the Aristotelian Society* 106 (2006): 1–19.

9 For a critical account of ontic structural realism tracing it back to the scientific revolution, see Bas Van Fraassen, "Structure: Its Shadow and Substance," *British Journal for the Philosophy of Science* 57 (2006): 275–307.

the meaning of his sibylline question in *Beilage VII*, "Does man have reason: or·does reason have man?" When the efficacy of reason as a tool or instrument (*Werkzeug*) in the struggle for survival – the reason *we have* – seduces us into identifying the form of intelligibility produced by reason with being itself, that is, when the strategies of "mechanistic" or functional explanation are hypostatized as the very structures of reality itself, the result is an alienating and potentially oppressive ideology that divides the mind against itself – the reason that *has us*.[10]

Specifically, Jacobi sees fatalism, nihilism, and the denial of substantial individuality as implicit in every attempt to erect a metaphysical system of reason; in its most fully articulated form, this is supposed to be the rationalist ideology exemplified in Spinoza's *Ethics*. I have already indicated one way in which nihilism could arise from such an ideology, namely via the *formalism* inherent in functional analysis. A closely related source is the *holism* of functional analysis.[11] As I pointed out above, the complete Ramsification of a theory entails the interdefinability of its basic terms. Since the meaning of a term is formulable only in terms of its relations to the others, the effect is semantic holism: the meaning of each term consists in its relations to all the others. This holism, which is one of the essential characteristics of functional analyses, is thus a concomitant effect of transforming intrinsic properties into relational ones, and this is the same procedure that we saw to entail formalism.

If we go on to assume, as seems natural, that successful explanations of the functional variety also provide insight into *what* the functionally analyzed states and entities *actually are*, the path is paved to the metaphysical holism Jacobi attributes to Spinoza: "All individual things mutually presuppose and are related one another, so that no single one of them can either exist or be comprehended without all the others; that is to say, they form an inseparable whole, or to speak more correctly and more literally: *they exist altogether in a single, absolutely indivisible, infinite thing* [= Spinoza's substance], *and in no other way*" (FHJW I, 1:100).

This result is incompatible with the metaphysical individualism that Jacobi sees as underwriting personal free will; in other words, it entails

---

10 For discussion see Sandkaulen, "'Oder hat die Vernunft den Menschen?'."
11 See the concise discussion by Robert Cummins, "Functional Analysis," in N. Block (ed.), *Readings in Philosophy of Psychology*, vol. I (Cambridge, MA: MIT Press 1980), 185–90.

fatalism. Furthermore, since individuals are grasped not only as not possessing any non-relational, substantial reality of their own, but as being *differentially constituted*, that is, by negation and limitation within a network of functions, the position entails *nihilism*: "*Determinatio est negatio, seu determinatio ad rem juxta suum esse non pertinet.* Individual things, insofar as they exist in a determinate manner, are *non-entia* (FHJW I, 1:100).

Jacobi should therefore be understood as calling for a limitation of the scope of functional explanation – or rather, as insisting on the ineluctable evils that ensue when it is hypostatized as a metaphysical doctrine. Formulated thus, Jacobi's critique of metaphysics sounds very much like Kant's, and Hegel was obviously right to pair them as having together called attention to the untenable implications of pre-critical rationalist metaphysics. Yet the valence of Jacobi's critique differs in important ways from that of Kant. Hegel puts it this way:

> While Kant attacked the former metaphysics mainly from the side of its matter, Jacobi attacked it especially from the side of its **method of demonstration** and, with great clarity and profundity, he put his finger on precisely the point at issue, namely that such a method of demonstration is strictly bound to the cycle of rigid necessity of the finite and that *freedom*, i.e. the *Concept* and with it *everything that truly is*, lies beyond it and is unattainable by it. – According to Kant's result, it is the peculiar content of metaphysics that leads it into contradictions; the inadequacy of cognition is due to its *subjectivity*. Jacobi's result is that the inadequacy is due instead to the method and the whole nature of cognition itself, which only grasps a *concatenation of conditions and dependency* and thereby proves itself inadequate to what exists in and for itself and to what is absolutely true. (GW 12:229)

Even though Kant and Jacobi come to results that may be formulated identically (by saying, for instance, that discursive reason has by its very nature no theoretical purchase on the unconditioned), they represent two rather different approaches. Kant's transcendental critique focuses on the conditions of possibility of objective, discursive knowledge and is to that extent a constructive undertaking. Central to Jacobi's critique, by contrast, is the concern that scientific and instrumental rationality necessarily converge and that each is liable to distort and conceal the structures of lived experience in a practically detrimental way. Hegel appropriates both these strains of the critical project. Like Kant, he seeks to provide an account of the finite forms of thought and their role in constituting finite subjectivity. However, in his assertion that the forms of finite, discursive reason, when conceived as the exclusive and irreducible forms of cognition, gravely distort and conceal the true character of "freedom, that is, the concept and hence everything that truly is," he is much closer to Jacobi. It is the form of finite cognition as such that he seeks to criticize, not merely the illicit extension of that form to a content that necessarily destabilizes it.

5.3. Hegel's appropriation of Jacobi's critique: a problem and its solution

But what of the substance of Jacobi's critique? For Hegel finds appealing not merely the broad methodological gesture towards a fundamental critique of the instrumental rationality at work in pre-critical (and to Jacobi's mind, in post-critical, German idealist) rationalism; he also embraces Jacobi's charge that "every path of demonstration leads to fatalism" (FHJW I, 1:123).[12] More particularly, Jacobi alleges that (1) the essential role of tautologies ("identical propositions") in demonstrative reasoning, (2) the primacy of relations over intrinsic properties or qualities, and (3) the closely related primacy of the whole over the parts (semantic and especially metaphysical holism) are what entail fatalism and nihilism. And excepting (1), these are among the most striking features of Hegel's own system, which I think is best understood as a version of metaphysical structural realism. The very concept of the Concept is that of a complex of nested relations that are absolutely prior to any (by definition *finite*) relata.[13] The concept of absolute negativity is that of a self-referring procedure or process that originates the elements through whose relations it manifests itself, thereby also individuating itself as the *singulare tantum* it is. And the Hegelian absolute, "*das Absolut-Wahre*" cited above, is by definition

---

12 Of course it is easy to find passages in which Hegel directly repudiates Jacobi's views about the inner identity of rational demonstration and fatalism or nihilism (e.g. GW 15:12–13). However, he does so on the basis of a conception of the relation between mediation and immediacy that differs from the conception that characterizes finite cognition (from the standpoint of which Jacobi formulates his critique). In other words, it is consistent to recognize Hegel's denial of the necessary connection between rationalist metaphysics and fatalism/nihilism, while insisting that he shares Jacobi's (slightly reinterpreted) views on the nihilistic consequences of rationalist metaphysics *as conceived by finite cognition*.

13 Cf. Horstmann, *Ontologie und Relationen;* Christian Iber, *Metaphysik absoluter Relationalität* (Berlin and New York: de Gruyter 1990).

the whole, while the various individualities populating Hegelian science are *moments* that can claim neither determinateness nor existence outside that whole.

Hegel is therefore committed to precisely the doctrines that Jacobi identifies as the source of all evil in systematic metaphysics. This fact is entirely unproblematic for Jacobi's position, but it creates difficulties for Hegel, who quite explicitly embraces Jacobi's methodological critique of the rationalist tradition. How can this be other than a contradiction?[14]

The answer lies in the way Hegel identifies the limits of Jacobi's critique. The following passage is worth quoting at length:

> [I]n Jacobi's thought, the transition from mediation to immediacy has more the character of an external rejection and dismissal of mediation. To this extent, it is reflective consciousness itself which, isolated from rational intuition, isolates the mediating movement of cognition from that intuition ... Here we must distinguish between two acts. First there is finite cognition itself, which is concerned exclusively with objects and forms which do not exist in and for themselves, but are conditioned and grounded by something other than themselves. The very character of such cognition thus consists in mediation. The second type of cognition is the reflection just referred to, which recognizes both the first, subjective mode of cognition itself and its objects as not absolute. Thus on the one hand this second mode of cognition is itself mediated, for it essentially refers to the first mode of cognition, having it as its presupposition and object. On the other hand, though, it is the sublation of that first mode of cognition. Therefore ... it is a mediation which is itself the sublation of mediation, or in other words it is a sublation of mediation only to the extent that it is itself mediation. As the sublation of mediation, cognition is *immediate* cognition. (GW 15:11–12; emphasis added)

To sum this up in familiar terms, Hegel criticizes Jacobi for failing to have provided an *internal critique* of finite cognition. This way of putting it, while accurate, tends to gloss over the difficulty involved in saying what an internal critique of *finite cognition* actually entails. First of all, it is finite cognition itself which isolates the mediating movement of cognition from the "intuition of reason." In other words, when

---

14 In the Jena period he had been scathing in his criticism of Jacobi (e.g. GW 4:346–86). As early as 1807, however, Hegel had in private already begun to cultivate more amicable relations with Jacobi, and his positive assessment of Jacobi's philosophical significance becomes public in his appreciative review of vol. III of Jacobi's *Works* (1817).

Jacobi takes up the position of intuition or immediacy against mediation in order to formulate an "external" critique of the latter, Hegel sees him as *unconsciously* tied down to a position *internal* to finite cognition itself; for the rigid opposition of mediation and immediacy is, like other such oppositions, characteristic of finite cognition as such. So Jacobi's critical rejection of mediation is thwarted by a performative self-contradiction in that his external rejection of mediation is itself a gesture of mediated, finite cognition.

A second point is that concepts like "immediacy," "the unconditioned," "subjectivity," "God," and so on are formulable both from the perspective of finite cognition (mediation) and from the speculative standpoint. This, as we saw in Chapter 2, is the crux of Hegel's critique of pre-critical metaphysics: it rightly strives for knowledge of the unconditioned, but as formulated from the standpoint of finite cognition, and so it strives in vain. As we also saw, Kant recognizes the impossibility of carrying out the traditional metaphysical project on its own terms, but remains in crucial respects committed to the paradigm of finite cognition constitutive of that very project. Something similar is true of Jacobi. He recognizes that the standpoint of mediation (finite cognition), posited as absolute, erodes or distorts concepts as fundamental as those of freedom, individuality, personality, and the unconditioned status of the supreme being. But when he reasserts the "intuitive" conception of those terms against their rationalist distortions, he unwittingly articulates them in the form of finite cognition. Against the philosophies he finds implicated in his critique of rationalist ideology, "Jacobi urges not only the content, but also the *substantial form* of his rational intuition" (GW 15:13; emphasis added). Here "substantial form" is a term of art denoting a conception of objects as lacking any essential *internal* self-relation and hence as barren of the life and self-directed activity constitutive of freedom, individuality, and self-determining personality, which are of course Jacobi's central concerns. Hegel therefore concludes the passage above with this admonition:

> If cognition does not understand its immediacy in this way, it fails to grasp that it is only in this sense that it is the immediacy *of reason*, and not that of a rock. For natural consciousness, knowledge of God may well appear as merely immediate knowledge, and natural consciousness may see no difference between the immediacy with which it is aware of Spirit and the immediacy of its perception of a rock. But the business of philosophical knowledge is to recognize what the activity of natural

consciousness truly consists in, to recognize that its immediacy is a living, spiritual immediacy that only arises within a self-sublating process
of mediation. (GW 15:12)

Jacobi is here once again unconsciously tied down to a position within
finite cognition, and his unconscious commitment involves him in a
performative self-contradiction when he calls on the forms of finite
cognition in order to assert a content that is supposed to be beyond it.

A solution to our difficulty thus begins to take shape. Jacobi is right
to object to what we could call the *identity-logic* of demonstrative reasoning (which he sees as resting on the construction of tautologies), to
the primacy of *finite* relations over individual determinacy, and to
the *domination* of the parts by the whole; but he fails to see that these
are versions of identity, relationality, and holism as conceived from
the standpoint of finite cognition. Hegel will insist that his own conception of identity as entailing difference, his conception of absolute
relationality (constitutive self-relationality), and his conception of
organic holism not only are not subject to Jacobi's critique, but that
they are necessary if that critique is to be formulated in a way that is
true to Jacobi's intentions and immune to the kind of performative
self-contradictions in which he entangles himself on Hegel's view.

A third and final point emerges from consideration of the long passage from the *Jacobi Review*: the internal critique of finite cognition
demands a self-reflexivity that is lacking from Jacobi's critique. Hegel's
"second act" or "second mode" of cognition is a reflection on the first.
This idea is exemplified by both the *Phenomenology* and the *Science of
Logic*. Hegel takes up various "shapes" of natural consciousness and
"determinations" of finite cognition, respectively, and shows (a) that
neither they nor the forms of objectivity they imply are "absolute," and
(b) that they nevertheless prove to be (incomplete) manifestations of
the absolute Spirit or Idea when they are properly grasped. In other
words, and looking ahead to the coming discussion of geometric cognition, speculative science consists at least in part in explicating the
actual form of cognitive activity that gives rise to various levels of finite
determination, but which is reflected inadequately or in a distorted
manner by the determinations it gives rise to. This work of explication generally results in a determination of the form of the given
cognitive activity that differs from its manifest form and the form of
objectivity implied by it. What an activity like empirical science or
geometry, say, is in itself or for the speculative point of view, and what

it appears to be from the finite perspective, are two different things. Yet for Hegel's methodological alternative to Jacobi to work, the series of reinterpreted forms of cognitive activity must lead to some *penultimate* form, such that when this form is critically explicated, the resulting description coincides with the "second mode of cognition" itself. Assuming this to be the case, the consciousness of the speculatively accurate description of what that form of cognitive activity is in itself will *eo ipso* be consciousness of the *speculative* form of cognitive activity: methodological self-consciousness. And this is indeed how Hegel conceives the course taken by the *Logic*, as is well known.[15] This form of self-reflexivity is thus implied if an internal critique of finite cognition is to be possible.

The solution to the difficulty proposed above therefore comes to this. Hegel can consistently embrace Jacobi's methodological critique of traditional metaphysics if he can interpret it (a) as bearing on a specifically finite and thus distorted conception of identity, relationality, and holism, and (b) as failing to recognize the self-reflexive properties of cognition that generate a continuous transition from finite cognition to its speculative "sublation." As with Kant, Jacobi's critique of traditional metaphysics demonstrates the necessity of a completely altered view of logic or the nature of cognition, but halts blindly at the threshold to such a view. As I will now go on to argue, Hegel revisits the paradigm of rationalist methodology – the *mos geometricus* or geometric method – in order to show that when reconstructed from the point of view of his second mode of cognition it reveals its inner identity with the method of speculative science itself.

5.4. Hegel on the rigor of Euclidean geometry

Stated at its simplest, the claim I will argue for in the following is this: geometry is, for Hegel, the highest form of finite theoretical cognition, and speculative explication of this form shows that when geometric cognition becomes fully self-reflexive, surrendering the last vestiges of its self-externality, it thereby passes over into speculative, logical cognition. In other words, the self-overcoming of geometric cognition is paradigmatic for the relation between finite cognition and the second mode of

15 See Angelica Nuzzo, "The End of Hegel's Logic: Absolute Idea as Absolute Method," in D. G. Carlson (ed.), *Hegel's Theory of the Subject* (Houndmills: Macmillan 2005), 187–205.

cognition Hegel offers as an alternative to Jacobi's external juxtaposition of discursive reason and intuition, mediation and immediacy.

This result is doubly significant. With regard to Hegel's understanding of speculative methodology, it sheds valuable light on the relation between speculative logic and mathematics that Hegel himself emphasizes in several places. With regard to Hegel's relation to pre-critical, rationalist metaphysics, in turn, it shows how he would be able to understand his dialectical method as the authentic successor to the *mos geometricus* idealized by the Cartesians, by Spinoza, and by Wolff and his school.[16] Hegel joins Kant and Jacobi in rejecting the geometric method as inappropriate to philosophy; however, his reasons systematically diverge from theirs and place him in a considerably more *internal* relation to the methodology of rationalist metaphysics. Hegel's reasons for rejecting the geometric method are neither chiefly epistemic (as Kant's are) nor do they derive from specifically moral and metaphysical worries (as Jacobi's do); instead Hegel focuses on certain formal and architectonic features of the geometric method and shows how they can be systematically transformed to give rise to a speculative methodology with a claim to rigor equal to that of geometry, but better suited to the topic of speculative science, the Concept.

Hegel declares the "unfolding of thinking in its necessity," that is, speculative logic, to be uniquely capable of an exposition that is "strictly and immanently plastic," and asserts that a successful exposition of logic would in this respect surpass even mathematics (cf. GW 21:18).[17] In what does this rigorous and immanent plasticity of logic consist? We may best begin to approach this question by first considering another: in what does specifically mathematical rigor and immanence consist? For mathematics is the only science with which Hegel explicitly compares the science of logic at this level of methodological reflection.

Mathematics' exceptional status manifests itself inter alia in the fact that Hegel characterizes the *sublimity* of mathematics in terms that are nearly identical to his terms of praise for speculative philosophy.[18] Compare these two passages, the first of which is taken from Hegel's

---

16 On the paradigmatic character of the geometric order of demonstrations, cf. Wolff's Preface to the fourth edition of Dt. Met. §7.

17 Compare Hegel's specification of his methodological ideal of plasticity with Wolff's conception of scienticity, spelled out extensively in Disc. Prael. §§115–32. Also cf. the analysis in Honnefelder, *Scientia*, 301.

18 The importance of mathematics for Hegel should not be underestimated. Geometry was among his earliest intellectual interests (cf. Jaeschke, *Hegel-Handbuch*, 1) and he

discussion in the *Doctrine of the Concept* and the second from the preface to the 1832 edition of the *Doctrine of Being*:

[1] This science [i.e. mathematics], because of its abstract subject matter ... has an aura of sublimity about it, for in these empty silent spaces color is extinguished and the other sensuous properties have equally vanished, and further, the interests that appeal to living individuality is hushed. (GW 12:226).

[2] [T]he need to occupy oneself with pure thought presupposes a long road that the human spirit must have traversed; it is the need, one may say, of having already attained the satisfaction of necessary need, the need of freedom from need, of abstraction from the material of intuition, imagination, and so forth; from the material of the concrete interests of desire, impulse, will, in which the determinations of thought hide as if behind a veil. In the silent spaces where thought has come to itself and communes only with itself, the interests that move the life of peoples and individuals are hushed. (GW 21:12–13)

Not only is the characterization of the two sciences virtually identical; these two passages are the only ones in all of Hegel's published writings in which he speaks of *stille Räume* and *Schweigen des Interesses*. Perhaps the admonition that adorned the entranceway to Plato's Academy would also make a fitting epigraph for Hegel's *Science of Logic*: "Let no one unversed in geometry enter here."

We find these somewhat circumstantial observations confirmed when we consider the place of mathematics within the architectonic of the *Science of Logic*. Under the heading "Synthetic Cognition" in the *Logic*, Hegel provides a lengthy and detailed discussion of mathematics that can guide our reflections here. It is illuminating to observe in advance the place of this discussion in the architecture of the *Logic*: its location (*Doctrine of the Concept* 3.2.b.3) identifies it as the *highest form* of *finite theoretical* cognition ("the idea of the true"), directly at the transition to "the idea of the good" or finite *practical* cognition. The finitude of mathematical cognition can be directly inferred from its placement in the *second* of the three chapters

devoted intensive study to Euclid's *Elements* in the period leading up to his move from Frankfurt to Jena (cf. Johannes Hoffmeister [ed.], *Dokumente zu Hegel's Entwicklung* [Stuttgart-Bad Cannstatt: Fromann 1936], 288–300). On the relation of these fragments to Proclus' Neoplatonic philosophy of geometry, see Alan L. T. Paterson, "Hegel's Early Geometry," *Hegel-Studien* 39/40 (2005): 61–124. In 1805/6 he taught courses in arithmetic and geometry both in Jena and at the Nuremberg Gymnasium while he was working on the *Science of Logic*.

comprising the section on "The Idea": Hegel specifies elsewhere that within a given triad, the first and third can be considered *definitions* of the concept, while the second represents the concept in its externality or difference, that is, finitude (ENC §85). The "idea of the true" thus denotes the moment of difference or finitude in the Idea. That mathematical cognition is the highest form of finite theoretical cognition can in turn be directly inferred from its placement in the *third* subsection of Hegel's discussion of synthetic knowledge. For by the same rule again, Hegel's placement of mathematics (under the subtitle "The Theorem") identifies it as the completely mediated second *definition* of synthetic cognition, restoring at a higher level its initial or immediate definition, namely the category of definition.[19] Note the potentiated self-referentiality implied by this placement: the theorem represents the fully mediated, complete, second definition of synthetic cognition, the first definition of which was "definition." At the same time, in the broader context of the Idea, "Life" contains the first and the "Absolute Idea" the properly second definition of the Concept, which is of course the main topic of this third part of the *Logic* and the underlying theme of the *Logic* as a whole. Viewed thus, mathematical cognition (more specifically, the theorem) is the *definitive* form of theoretical cognition as it exists in the finite sphere (the sphere of difference), and is surpassed in the theoretical realm only by the infinite cognition of the absolute Idea.

Some readers are sure to find observations like this akin to numerology and about as meaningful. Be that as it may, Hegel's views on "metaphysical definitions" (ENC §85) are key to understanding the relative status of thought-determinations in the context of the *Logic* as a whole – its conceptual rhythm, so to speak – and, like musical rhythm, it is inseparable from *counting*. I will return to the subject in a less schematic way later when assessing the speculative status of mathematical cognition. For now the main point to hold on to is the exceptional status of mathematics among the finite modes of theoretical knowledge.

Turning now to the details of Hegel's discussion, we find specifically mathematic rigor to rest on the nature of mathematical definition, axiomatization, and demonstration.[20] I will address these in order,

---

19 On Hegel's concept of "second definitions" see below.
20 Cf. Kant's parallel discussion at B754–66.

taking (as Hegel does) Euclid's systematic presentation of geometry as my chief example.

In the first place, then, mathematics deals with well-defined objects. Geometric objects are like tools and other products made to serve human utility, in that they can be sufficiently nominally defined on the basis solely of the determinations explicitly posited in them.[21] This is not to say that such objects do not involve further essential determinations not included in the definition and discoverable only through mathematical research. As Hegel emphasizes, geometrical objects are abstract determinations of space, and when the features by which we define them are contemplated in the context of the structure of space itself, they reveal synthetic relations and laws (cf. GW 12:211). However, these further determinations, not originally posited in the definition of a triangle, say, as a trilateral plane figure, will not contradict or otherwise cancel this initial definition: the triangle is and remains what it is constructed to be. Contrast the case of natural objects, for which there is no sure criterion distinguishing what is essential and what non-essential to their definition.[22] As we know from the history of the empirical sciences, definitions of living species and genera are as liable to change as are those of fundamental forces of nature. The *vis viva* controversy is one case in point; ongoing modification to Linnaeus' taxonomy is another. Quarrels of this nature are exceedingly rare in mathematics. Especially, there is no room for verbal disputes; both the reference and the intensional content of the geometrical terms are transparent. This is not the case in empirical disciplines, where the intension of terms is liable to shift as a result of further observation (or be disputed in the first place), causing extension to shift (or deviate) accordingly. The well-defined nature of mathematical objects is therefore the first characteristic that distinguishes specifically mathematical rigor.[23]

Second, geometry rests on axioms. When chosen correctly, the axioms are indemonstrable within the system of inferences to be drawn from them. This means two things. For one, there can be no

---

21 Cf. GW 12:211–12 for Hegel's discussion of the superior definability of tools, artifacts, and geometrical objects in comparison with objects found in the natural world.

22 Cf. GW 12:212–13. As Kant remarks, "[A]n empirical concept cannot be *defined* at all, but only *made explicit*" (B755).

23 If we follow Kant, neither is a definition in the strict sense possible in philosophy (cf. B758). For Hegel's divergence from Kant on this issue, see below.

properly *mathematical* quarrel about the truth of the axioms. Relatively to geometry, its axioms are first principles constituting the very discourse of geometry. For another, it means the axioms are to be logically independent of one another: they must be chosen in such a way that no one of them can be proved on the basis of the others, for else they would not all be genuinely *first* principles.[24] Although Hegel does not draw attention to the fact, completeness is a related property of any well-chosen set of axioms: Every true geometrical proposition ought to be provable on the basis of the axioms that constitute the science. Together, these features of a well-chosen set of axioms guarantee that geometry forms a relative totality: first, that is, non-inferentially justified, true principles ground a system of inferences such that any true proposition that concerns the objects belonging by definition to the science can be rigorously demonstrated on the basis of those principles without recourse to any additional principles borrowed from outside the science. In addition to the precise definability of its objects, therefore, axiomatization is a second factor in the constitution of mathematical rigor.[25]

5.5. The deductive order of Euclidean geometry and the place of real definitions

The third aspect of mathematical rigor initially appears as a feature of order, that is, of the determinate sequence of propositions and demonstrations. Euclid's *Elements* have been hailed as the paradigm of the synthetic method, Hegel says, because "the order in the progression of its theorems" is such that "for each theorem the propositions required for its construction and proof are always found already proved" (GW

---

24 Hegel praises Euclid's wisdom in recognizing the indemonstrability of the fifth postulate, concerning parallel lines, within the purview of geometry; he insists, however, that a philosophical demonstration on the basis of the "concept" of parallels is possible. See GW 12:221.

25 Some may be inclined to find this discussion of geometry outdated in light of modern developments in mathematics. For instance, do not Gödel's incompleteness theorems show the impossibility of a formally complete axiomatic system? That would render the very ideal by which Hegel measures geometry empty. And does not the relativity of Euclidean geometry as revealed by the existence of non-Euclidean geometries compromise Hegel's commitment to Euclidean geometry as the pinnacle of finite theoretical cognition? Or again, has not modern mathematics and logic taught us the extent to which axiomatic systems are really just based on the arbitrary choices of certain conventions? Cogent responses can be given to each of these questions, but would require more space than is available here.

12:222). Hegel does not question the importance of exhibiting, in strict sequential form, the inferential relations that obtain among the various theorems. Interestingly, however, he seems to see it merely as a *concomitant* of properly mathematical rigor, not as a sufficient characterization of its essence. For consider the fact that, superficially at least, virtually any discipline can be served up in axiomatized form, yet without thereby attaining the rigor peculiar to mathematics. (In a footnote, Hegel directly quotes at length a passage from Wolff's *Principles of Architecture* that serves by itself as a satire on the mania for the *mos geometricus*: see GW 12:228n.) Kant would of course wholeheartedly agree with Hegel's point here, but he would give a different rationale for his critique: he would attribute the impossibility of generalizing the geometric method for use in non-mathematical disciplines to the impossibility of intuitive construction outside the realm of mathematics (cf. B762ff.). Hegel offers a different view.

In the case of empirical sciences in particular, Hegel points out, a presentation *more geometrico* begins, as mathematics does, with definitions and principles serving to individuate the specific field of discourse. It then goes on to an increasingly thorough individuation (*Vereinzelung*) and concretization of the objects specific to its field – again, as does mathematics. In the case of empirical sciences, however, individuation and concretization are effected by bringing in observed features of the relevant objects and subsuming them under the definitions and principles (GW 12:224). Here Kant might locate the crucial flaw in the fact that "experience teaches us what is, but it does not teach us that it could not be other than what it is"; in other words, empirical sciences will inevitably lack the element of necessity peculiar to mathematics as built on construction in *a priori* intuition (cf. B762).[26] Hegel places his emphasis elsewhere: the essential element of mathematical rigor lies according to him in the fact that here individuation and concretization of the objects are *not added* to the definitions and principles from an external source, but developed out of them. Whereas Kant stresses the aspect of apodictic certainty, Hegel puts weight on the self-contained character of mathematics and its

---

26 Hegel presumably has Kantians in mind when he dismisses constructibility in sensible intuition as the source of mathematics' particular excellence. We've "heard enough" about that, he says: "Against this shallowness we need only make equally shallow mention of the fact that no science comes about through intuition, but only *through thinking*" (GW 12:226; cf. GW 12:42).

ability to generate determinacy from within a closed system.[27] Despite the veneer of systematicity lent by the *mos geometricus*, therefore, empirical sciences that cast themselves in its mold are in truth rather more similar to aggregates.

Thus if we are to understand the nature of the rigor manifested in the formal organization (*formelle Konsequenz*) of the geometric method, we must look more carefully at the process of individuation and concretization Hegel calls "being determinate" (*Bestimmtsein*: GW 12:223).

To use Hegel's illustration, the subject of the first book of Euclid's *Elements* is the triangle, defined as a trilateral, rectilinear, plane figure.[28] The initial movement of the book is to isolate the triangle's *concept* from its *reality*. Hegel explains it this way: The initial definition of the triangle specifies it as three-sided. Proposition 1.4, however, demonstrates that two sides and the enclosed angle alone are sufficient to determine any triangle. In the language of geometry, these are theorems about *congruence* among triangles, but as Hegel plausibly notes, the comparison among individuals implied in terms like "congruence" and "coincidence" is at bottom a "necessary detour" (GW 12:223)[29] to the insight that any triangle, taken by itself, is fully determined in its existence by just these three factors, namely the two sides and the enclosed angle. This insight, Hegel goes on, is tantamount to the *reduction* of the "sensuous" triangle to its simplest conceptual determinations. Whereas the sensuous triangle needs three angles and three sides to be real, the conceptual triangle requires only two sides and one angle. Thus the concept of the triangle has been isolated from its (initially, seemingly) "superfluous" reality.[30]

27 Once again, cf. Wolff's conception of real definitions as those which immediately support the demonstration of the *reality* of the *definiendum*, by specifying (in the case of *a priori* definitions) how it can be produced (Dt. Log. §§41, 48–49). A closely related notion is that of the determinability of the predicates of a concept (or the properties of an object) by its definition (or essence) as the *criterion of truth* (Dt. Log. §524). Spinoza's conception is related (cf. TIE §95).

28 Cf. Euclid, *The Thirteen Books of the Elements*, vol. 1, trans. Sir T. Heath, 2nd edn. (New York: Dover 1956), 153f., esp. definition 19.

29 For Hegel's proof of 1.4, see Paterson, "Early Geometry," 105–7.

30 Paterson ("Early Geometry," 87), relates this notion of a superfluity of reality over and above the conceptual determination of the triangle to Proclus' idea that mathematical objects are essentially *simple* and hence non-spatial; the geometer's projection of them in imagination compromises that simplicity, while the demonstrations bring the mathematical objects back to their formal (Platonic) simplicity. He notes that for Hegel difference is essential to geometrical figures and is expressed in their essential spatiality; despite this important difference from Proclus, however, Hegel's emphasis

Note that this result may be said to conflict with the initial (nominal) definition of the triangle. That definition specified three sides; two sides are sufficient for the triangle's being determinate (its *Bestimmtsein*). So in a sense the definition contains more than is necessary for the determination of the triangle; it contains the concept of the triangle *and its reality* in a confused or undifferentiated ("immediate") manner.

Book I concludes with a demonstration of the Pythagorean theorem.[31] This famous theorem states that in a right triangle, the sum of the areas of the squares erected on the side subtending the acute angles equals the area of the square erected on the side subtending the right angle, the hypotenuse. There are some well-known alternatives to Euclid's demonstration of the theorem, some of which bring out the relation of the three squares by way of constructions that are simpler and more intuitive than the version in the *Elements*.[32] The peculiar rigor of Euclid's demonstration, however, lies for Hegel not in its intuitive certainty or its power to justify and convince (where Kant would place it), but in its special relation to the foregoing propositions and especially to the initial definition of the triangle. Hegel emphasizes that the theorem states an equation (*Gleichung*) of the three sides of the triangle (in algebraic notation, $a^2 + b^2 = c^2$), conditioned by the special self-identical (*sich-selbst-gleiche*) nature of the right angle.[33] In other words, over the course of Book I the *concept* of the triangle has been differentiated from its three-sided *reality*, and through a synthesis of the conceptual determinations of the triangle as explicated in the intervening theorems, its three-sided reality has been reproduced in a thoroughly conceptual form. The initial merely *nominal* definition that contained no distinct determination of the relation of the conceptual to the real has been restored on a higher level as a *real* definition capturing the real as contained within the conceptual. In Hegel's words, "This proposition [i.e. the Pythagorean theorem] is therefore the perfect, real definition of the triangle – at this point, of the right

on the conceptual unity and simplicity of figures places him in the Neoplatonic tradition (and distinguishes him markedly from Kant with this emphasis on the intuitive manifold).

31 See Euclid, *Elements*, 1.47. The last proposition, 1.48, is the converse of 1.47.

32 For details see Euclid, *Elements*, vol. I, 352–55.

33 Cf. GW 12:223–24. A right angle is formed by a straight line standing on a straight line in such a way as to make the adjacent angles equal. On this and the related topic of degrees of unity in geometrical figures, see Paterson, "Early Geometry," 76–79.

triangle, which is the simplest and most regular in its distinctions" (GW 12:223). He points to similar patterns in the following books on rectangles and circles. They all culminate, he says, in "*second* definitions" (GW 12:224).

It is helpful to compare Hegel's thought here with rationalist doctrines of definition. Traditionally, a satisfactory *nominal definition* was minimally required to be internally consistent, that is, to exhibit the *definiendum* as a logically possible object. However, not all logically possible objects are in fact really possible, Leibniz's example being the decahedron, a ten-faced regular Euclidean solid. Though the concept of a decahedron, as just defined, contains no contradiction, it is not in fact possible to inscribe such a solid in Euclidean space.[34] A *real definition*, by contrast, would exhibit the *definiendum* in such a way that its *real possibility* is manifest. For Leibniz, this is tantamount to a formulation of the essence of the thing in question:

> Essence is fundamentally nothing but the possibility of a thing under consideration. Something which is thought possible is expressed by a definition; but if this definition does not at the same time express its possibility then it is merely nominal, since in this case we can wonder whether the definition expresses anything real – that is, possible – until experience comes to our aid by acquainting us *a posteriori* with the reality (when the thing actually occurs in the world).[35]

One way of defining a thing so as to exhibit it as really possible is to provide a rule for constructing it; for by construction we bring the object into actual existence, and trivially, whatever is actual is possible. The classic example is the constructive definition of the circle as the figure generated by rotating, in a single plane, a line of finite length about a single point.[36]

But this is a minimal requirement on real definitions: Spinoza (as well as Leibniz in other places) requires furthermore that a real definition specify the essence in such a way that all the essential properties

---

34 Cf. Leibniz, *New Essays on Human Understanding*, trans. and ed. P. Remnant and J. Bennett (Cambridge University Press 1996), 293–94. My example is taken from Gideon Freudenthal, *Definition and Construction: Salomon Maimon's Philosophy of Geometry* (Berlin: Max Planck Gesellschaft für Wissenschaftsgeschichte 2006), 56–60.

35 Leibniz, *New Essays*, 293–84, quoted in Donald Rutherford, *Leibniz and the Rational Order of Nature* (Cambridge University Press 1998), 74.

36 Spinoza, TIE §96; cf. the notion of a causal definition in Leibniz, *Philosophical Essays*, trans. and ed. R. Ariew and D. Garber (Indianapolis, IN: Hackett 1989), 57; see also Kant, 14:23, 31.

of the substance may be derived from it.[37] This demand gives rise to a number of subtle and interesting difficulties regarding the question whether a constructive definition like that of the circle should also be considered as providing an adequate definition of its essence in relation to its properties.[38] But this is a question that we need not pursue here.

As far as can be inferred, Hegel's attitude to this tradition is characteristically complex. An immediately striking difference is that he effectively sides with the empiricist tradition when it comes to real definitions of substances (or what Hegel would think of as finite objects of nature). According to Locke, real definitions are possible in mathematics, but not in physics. For example, "the real composition of its [sc. gold's] sensible Parts, on which depend all those properties of Colour, Weight, Fusibility, Fixedeness, etc., which are to be found in it"[39] are unknowable to us and hence incapable of any but a nominal definition. Hegel would agree with this assessment, but for reasons that not only differ fundamentally from Locke's, but which are contrary to the rationalist tradition as well: as we saw in the last chapter, his views on the nature of the finite objects of experience entail anti-essentialism in regard to them, and this clearly implies that in no sense can a real definition be given of such objects in which no independent essence is to be discerned.

A further difference emerges when we consider the rationalist emphasis on the importance of *real possibility* (especially by Leibniz). In several places, Hegel criticizes the prioritization of possibility which, he says, "when taken in isolation from actuality and necessity ... is a mere abstraction and as such it is grounded in abstract *identity*, the *formal* unity of the understanding" (GW 15:15).[40] This stance is an expression of Hegel's general rejection of pre-critical metaphysics as one-sidedly caught up in *finite* thought-determinations and the objects or *entia* they constitute: the irreducibility and uniqueness of the finite

---

37 Cf. Spinoza, TIE §§95–97.
38 This question is at the center of Maimon's critique of Kant; see the discussion in Freudenthal, *Definition and Construction*, 60–65.
39 John Locke, *An Essay Concerning Human Understanding*, ed. P. H. Nidditch (Oxford University Press 1979), III, 4, §§19, 419, quoted in Freudenthal, *Definition and Construction*, 59.
40 Cf. GW 11:385–89, where Hegel seeks to demonstrate that "real possibility" is nothing other than the totality of actual conditions upon the existence of a finite object, and that real possibility is thus equivalent to actuality, but an actuality not of the finite object itself, but of *others*.

thought-determinations (categories) and the focus on the *ens* (*tò ón*) is what characterizes pre-critical metaphysics in its entirety, that is, as both general and special metaphysics, as *ontology*, and it is this exclusively ontological orientation of philosophy that Hegel's speculative logic is designed to overcome (cf. GW 21:48–49).

Nonetheless, Hegel's heavily modified concept of the real definition is recognizably indebted to that tradition. He preserves both the traditional constructive or generative aspect and the more stringent requirement that a real definition enable us to derive the thing's properties from its essence; indeed, he seems to be claiming that a real definition as he conceives it secures the reality of the thing precisely by delineating its concept. Of course Hegel speaks here in terms of reality and concept, not property and essence (a transformation that follows from his very different metaphysical standpoint), but the analogy is obvious.

To reiterate the main point, then, the sequential presentation of the inferential relations obtaining among the various truths of Euclidean geometry is not at the very core of its peculiar rigor. As Hegel indicates, the sequential arrangement subserves a deeper purpose, namely the manifestation of the identity of concept and reality. Whenever we frame a definition, we abstract from certain features of the *definiendum*, features that may be concomitants of every real instantiation of the *definiendum*, but which do not obviously serve to determine it conceptually. Thus a first difference between concept and reality emerges, a difference commonly referred to by saying that concepts are always, to some degree, abstract and less determinate than the real objects that fall under them. Upon further analysis we may find that certain components of our definition are strictly speaking superfluous. They are part of the *reality* of the *definiendum*, and they may in fact be its essential accidents; but they are not necessary to the *determination* of that reality. The *being-determinate* of the *definiendum* is distinct from its universal, conceptual essence or its *being-determined*, its *Bestimmung*. The full measure of rigor is lacking whenever these two sides – *Bestimmtsein* (reality) and *Bestimmung* (conceptuality) – are brought together in an external or merely additive way. Hegel believes that this will always be the case in empirical science, not only for the Kantian reason that the finite mind is dependent on the material of empirical intuition to receive the full being-determinate of the objects of experience, but also because *finite objects as such exhibit a separation between their conceptual determination and their real determinateness,* a separation that signifies not (only) a limit of finite human cognition, but (also) an ontological deficiency in the objects themselves. It is because of this separation and externality that they are exposed to destruction and passing away (cf. GW 12:213–19). Where it is possible, however, owing both to the mode of cognition and to the metaphysical constitution of the object of cognition, to derive the reality from the concept, there the full measure of scientific rigor is present.

This is what Hegel means by individuation and concretization. It is not something that can be achieved through "mere display" (GW 12:220) of putatively actual, spatio-temporal individuals. A "spatio-temporal individual" would be a veritable oxymoron in Hegelian terms, since spatio-temporal existence as such is a form of self-externality that fundamentally *hinders* individuation and full, internally determined concretization. We will see in the next section that it is this very connection to forms that themselves are essentially tied to the sensuous, that is, spatial, forms of external intuition that compromises the rigor of geometry. Nonetheless, geometry has a privileged status in Hegel's hierarchy of scientific disciplines. Alone among non-speculative sciences, geometry exemplifies the internal relation between "nominal" and "real" definition, concept and reality, universality and individuality. Its ability to arrange its propositions in a strict sequence of deductive priority is just the outward manifestation of the special relationship of universality and individuation that constitutes mathematical structures. Applied externally to any other kind of objects, it is illusory.

To conclude with a brief comparison between Hegel and Kant on this topic, we should note how little concerned Hegel is, in his positive discussion of geometry, with issues of apodictic certainty, intuitive constructability, and similar questions about the epistemology of mathematical knowledge. These questions dominate Kant's discussion in the *Critique of Pure Reason*. There Kant is at pains to spell out why the geometrical method can never be the legitimate form of philosophical knowledge, and why any pretension of such form "must divert philosophy from its true purpose, namely, to expose the illusions of a reason that forgets its limits, and by sufficiently clarifying our concepts to recall it from its presumptuous speculative pursuits to its modest but thorough self-knowledge" (B763). His discussion accordingly revolves around the distinction between intuition and the understanding, and focuses on the nature of the evidence attaching to single definitions, axioms, and demonstrations.

Hegel by contrast focuses almost exclusively on the systematic character of geometry. The axioms are chiefly of interest insofar as they make for a self-contained (immanent) and complete science. The theorems are exhibited as the medium for an individuation and concretization of the mathematical object, or in equivalent terms, as the material for its complete, real definition. We may, if we wish, couch Hegel's view in Kantian terms: geometry contemplates the universal (the definition) in the concretion of a single theorem; and not wholly unlike philosophy (both on Kant's and on Hegel's view), the really adequate definitions come in geometry, too, at the end of the work, not at its beginning (B759). But reformulations like these are mere play: the parallels with Kant serve in the end only to heighten awareness of how very different Hegel's orientation to mathematics finally is. Kant is oriented toward the epistemic qualities of mathematical cognition. Hegel is oriented toward mathematical cognition as a form of rational existence, namely, the existence of the Idea.

5.6. Geometry as a form of the rational existence of the idea

This last statement goes beyond the analysis of Hegel's text as just given. However, Hegel himself explicitly formulates the main thesis of his discussion of the category "theorem" in just such terms:

> *The unity of all the content-determinatenesses* is equivalent to the *Concept*; a proposition contained in it is therefore itself a definition again – not one, however, that expresses the Concept only as it is immediately taken up, but one that expresses it rather as developed into its determinate, real differences, or one that expresses the Concept's complete existence [*vollständiges Dasein*]. The two together, therefore, present the *Idea*. (GW 12:222)

The form of cognition exemplified by Euclid's treatment of geometry is thus itself the existence of the Concept in the most adequate form it can take within the sphere of finite theoretical consciousness. It may be helpful to contrast this with Hegel's remarks in the introductory discussion of the *Concept in General*. There he states that "the Concept, insofar as it has achieved such an *existence* [*Existenz*] that is itself free, is nothing other than *I* or pure self-consciousness" (GW 12:17). It is true that bare self-consciousness is already the existence (*Existenz*) of the

Concept, but Hegel defines existence in this sense as the "undifferentiated unity of essence with its immediacy" (GW 11:323): a determination clearly distinct from what he here calls the complete existence (*vollständiges Dasein*) of the Concept, namely, the Concept as it has "developed into its determinate, real differences." Therefore, to the extent that self-consciousness is a purely cognitive, theoretical being (it is of course also a *practical* being), it finds its fullest realization in the systematization of knowledge *more geometrico*, with the qualification, as always, that this is said of *finite* cognition. More precisely, then, to the extent that the Concept can realize itself under conditions in which the subject of cognition is distinct from its object, axiomatized geometry is its highest theoretical realization. (As we will soon see, it is the features constitutive of geometry's finitude as a form of cognition that Hegel brings into play in his critique of mathematical cognition.)

The richer significance of Hegel's positive treatment of mathematics in the *Logic* becomes apparent when we take a step back and view the whole work as a series of increasingly adequate *definitions of the absolute*. In the *Encyclopedia* version of the *Logic*, Hegel explains that:

> [T]he logical determinations in general, can be regarded as the definitions of the absolute, as *metaphysical definitions of God*. More specifically, only the first simple determination within a given sphere, and then the third, which is the return out of difference and into simple relation-to-self, can always be regarded this way. For, to define God metaphysically means to express his nature in *thoughts* as such. But logic comprises all thoughts as they are while still in the form of thoughts. (ENC §85)

Accordingly, Hegel points to Being as such a definition (ENC §86R), to Nothing (ENC §87R), to Measure (ENC §107), to the Concept (ENC §160A), and to the Idea (ENC §213R).[41] Of the Idea he says, "The definition of *the absolute*, that it is the *Idea*, is itself absolute. All previous definitions return to this one" (ENC §213R).

In what sense is this final definition absolute? A couple of answers immediately suggest themselves. Since all the previous definitions turn out to "return into," that is, to be in some sense reducible to this one, it can be said to be absolute. We can give this first answer

---

41 In the Major Logic he also designates the Infinite as the "second definition" of the absolute after Being: see GW 11:78.

more content by contrasting the Idea with the relatively one-sided thought-determinations that lead up to it. The Idea, Hegel insists, is not "an idea *of something*"; so in this sense it is not relative. It does entail a set of relations: the Idea in its self-diremption (*als urteilend*) "particularizes itself into the *system* of determinate ideas: ideas, however, that are only this, the process of returning into the One Idea, into their truth" (ENC §213R). But as this formulation shows, the relations it implies are all internal to itself; they are aspects of its self-relation, and to have no relation except to oneself is to be absolute.

These initial answers are helpful in that they specify absoluteness as equivalent to self-relation and (as I will be supposing for the remainder of my discussion) self-referentiality.[42] However, this is a specification of the absolute Idea as the *content* of the definition; it is not thereby also a specification of the definition as such. Yet it is the definition itself that Hegel characterizes as absolute. Why?

To answer this question, let us return to Hegel's discussion of geometry, armed now with the notion of absoluteness as self-referentiality. As I indicated before, Hegel places that discussion under the heading "Synthetic Cognition," a section that begins with an analysis of nominal definitions and ends with what Hegel calls the real (*reelle*) definition. It should now be obvious that this section thematizes precisely the thought-determination that Hegel uses to characterize the advance through the *Logic* as a whole: what the *Logic* provides are definitions of the absolute, and the central theme of "Synthetic Cognition" is definition as a cognitive form. In the context of Hegel's own treatment of speculative logic, therefore, his discussion of synthetic cognition represents *the first instance of self-reference*. This is not to say that self-reference as such has not been thematized in foregoing chapters. But self-reference has not been *instantiated* in the work prior to this point. Hegel's discussion of synthetic cognition (i.e. real definition) is a thematization of what the *Logic* itself is meant to achieve, and it is a thematization that occurs in *immanent* reflection, not in the external reflection of scholia, asides, and other forms of digression. By turning

42 Alan L. T. Paterson compares Hegel's and Gödel's views on the self-referential nature of mathematical concepts in "Does Hegel Have Anything to Say to Modern Mathematical Philosophy?" *Idealistic Studies* 32:2 (2002): 143–58. Although mathematical objects are implicitly self-referential, mathematics as such provides no logic of self-referentiality. Paterson's focus is different from that of the present chapter, but suggests independent confirmation of the approach taken here.

back upon itself, therefore, the exposition of the *Logic* has at this point become *absolute*.

Despite its importance, this observation still does not get us all the way to an answer why the definition of the absolute is itself absolute. Hegel's thematization of the real definition is indeed the first instance of self-referentiality in the *Logic*, but it is not the last. To be exact, it is the *penultimate* instance of self-referentiality, the ultimate instance being the reflection on the dialectical method that constitutes the bulk of the concluding chapter on the absolute Idea. The absolute Idea, as the *ultimate* definition of the absolute, instantiates self-referentiality both formally and in terms of its content. Formally, that is, in terms of the referential relation, what the Idea refers to is *itself*. Moreover, in terms of content, that is, in terms of the constitution of its referent, self-referentiality is instantiated: the absolute Idea, in thematizing itself, thematizes self-referentiality; an additional level of self-consciousness has thereby been introduced, and it is just this level that the *mos geometricus* essentially *lacks*.

Let us break down this somewhat compact thought. I will begin once more from the discussion of geometry, but this time around I will emphasize the ways in which it *fails* to instantiate self-referentiality, rather than the ways it succeeds in doing so. As a *matter of fact*, we could say, Hegel's thematization of real definition in the section on "Synthetic Cognition" is self-referential. Why? Because he characterizes the *Logic* itself as a series of definitions of the absolute. Therefore, to thematize the cognitive *form* of definition is to thematize the pivotal *form* of the *Logic* itself. This is an aspect of its success. On the other hand, geometry as a form of human cognition is obviously not about itself as conceptual activity. It is about spatial relations, which are the very antithesis of self-internality essential to the Concept, the Idea, and Spirit. Thus *what* Hegel thematizes in the section on "Synthetic Cognition" *fails* to be self-referential. His thematization is, *as a matter of fact*, self-referential; yet what is thematized – geometry, real definition – is not self-referential, even though it is itself the same *fact* that the Concept is: it is, so to speak, the *factual existence* (*Dasein*) of the Concept, but in an unselfconscious form.

What the absolute Idea brings to this fact of systematic, synthetic cognition is the self-consciousness of science as the existence of the Concept. Both the form and the content of its thematization are explicitly self-referential.

5.7. Preliminary result of this discussion: geometrical cognition, speculative cognition, and the structure of the Hegelian concept

What this discussion has shown is, in the first instance, that Hegel accords a uniquely high status to geometry within the sphere of finite theoretical cognition, and why he does so. I have also indicated some of the ways in which geometry fails to be fully self-referential and hence remains subject to a degree of the self-externality that characterizes the finite realm in general and finite cognition in particular. In the next section, I will go on to say more about the aspects of self-externality peculiar to geometrical objects and geometrical cognition. At this point, however, I would like to draw attention to the link between Hegel's views on geometry and the two modes of cognition he offers as a methodological alternative to Jacobi's critique of discursive reason.

As we saw in the opening section of this chapter, Hegel seeks to appropriate Jacobi's critique of (what Hegel calls) finite cognition, while reinterpreting it so as to argue that Jacobi's rejection of metaphysical relationalism (structuralism) and holism no longer need extend to these concepts in their properly speculative form. Hegel can do this because he understands relationality as essentially self-relationality ("absolute relationality"), and holism as an organological structure in which the self-relating Concept generates its own reality, one that is only seemingly composed of "indifferent" parts or individuals. Furthermore, Hegel suggests that insight into structures of this speculative kind can be attained through an internal or self-referential critique of finite cognition.

Hegel's explication of geometrical cognition is an important application of these ideas. To the extent that his account is plausible, he is able to show that this exceptional form of finite theoretical cognition exhibits the self-reflexivity or absolute relationality he associates with speculative cognition (the second mode of cognition discussed above), and that the hallmark of Euclidean rigor lies in the relation of concept and reality achieved by real definitions. Furthermore, he is able to indicate the determinate ways in which this finite mode of cognition fails to realize the fully self-referential structure of speculative cognition; it is self-reflexive in form only, but not also its referential content. Hegel's analysis is thus an important test case for the methodological alternative he offers to Jacobi: finite cognition can be criticized at a fundamental level and its ability to *articulate "absolute truth"* strictly denied, while at the same time being capable of a systematic transformation that exhibits its inner identity with and dependence on the "second" or speculative mode of cognition. To the extent that Hegel applies this method to the form of cognition taken as paradigmatic by pre-critical, rationalist metaphysics, Hegel can also plausibly claim to have vindicated his methodology as the authentic successor to that of "the former metaphysics," rather than merely rejecting it or abstractly negating it, as Kant and Jacobi do.

My discussion of geometry has also produced a second, unanticipated result. For what has emerged from it is the highly determinate structure identified by Horstmann as that of the Hegelian Concept. For the absolute Idea is related to itself *precisely by way of* being related to a second term, namely the determinate form of thought represented by the *Logic*, just as the second mode of cognition is related to the first in the *Jacobi Review*. Echoing the distinction introduced just above, we may call this the *formal* moment of its self-relation. At the same time, this second term (the *Science of Logic* as executed by the speculative logician) is related to itself in precisely the same manner: in the chapter on the "Absolute Idea," the "object" of the *Logic* is the very method that constitutes the *Logic*. The self-referentiality of the *Logic* is thus potentiated or redoubled. The implicit, formal self-relation instantiated in geometrical cognition becomes in turn the explicit object of self-referential reflection in the cognition of the absolute Idea, contentual self-relation. I will accordingly refer to these two levels of self-relation as the formal and the contentual level.

Now it should be clear from our previous discussion of geometrical cognition that formal relation-to-self is mediated by the cognitive relation to the objects of geometry. Geometrical cognition relates to itself by relating to specifically geometric objects. These objects, however, do not in their turn exhibit any relation-to-self; they are purely self-external. Geometrical cognition is therefore infected by this self-externality in its object and cannot for this reason return entirely into itself in its relation to the object. This qualifies geometrical cognition as a partially inadequate, finite realization of the Concept. But let us consider the cognition of the Idea, which arises through an internal critique of geometrical cognition and which will instantiate the contentual relation-to-self. The cognition of the Idea is constitutively related to geometrical cognition as its specific, finite other. Since that other formally instantiates relation-to-self, the cognition of the Idea relates to itself by relating to an other whose formal structure is isomorphic to its own. The content level (absolute Idea) is thus constituted by virtue of having a formal self-relation as its object or content: form gives rise to content. And since the object of the cognition of the Idea is structured in the same way as itself, its relation to that object constitutes a full return into self, in Hegel's terms a relation of infinitude or infinite relation-to-self.

Note, however, that the moment of finitude or self-externality is not thereby erased from the Hegelian infinite. Finite cognition is a constitutive moment of the (infinite) cognition of the Idea, and reference to finite, self-external, non-absolute objects of knowledge is thus an ineliminable, albeit subordinate and by nature evanescent moment of the Idea's self-cognition. To say that a moment is "evanescent" or "vanishing" (*verschwindend*) does not imply that it is ever finally *vanished*, erased, or eliminated. Its constitutive character is to be *vanishing*, not to be *nothing*. This is trebly significant in respect to Hegel's philosophical predecessors Spinoza, Jacobi, and Fichte. It marks an important difference with respect to Spinoza insofar as it signals a rejection of his *acosmism*, which we saw above to be one facet of his nihilism. For the finite is never fully nothing, a sum of *non-entia*; at the level of *formal* self-relation it represents an unsublatable moment. With regard to Jacobi, it signals a rejection of formalism, which we also saw to be a facet of the nihilism with which Jacobi charges rationalist metaphysics. For the fact that the formal, finite relation-to-self remains a constitutive moment of the absolute relation both maintains the finite, (self-)external content at the formal level and reinstates a *sui generis* non-finite, absolute content at the contentual level of relation-to-self. And with regard to Fichte, finally, it signals an acknowledgment of the *progressus infinitus*, Fichte's idea that the finite I infinitely strives to posit the non-I as identical with itself, so as to restitute its own infinitude as the absolute I, but that the full satisfaction of that striving is impossible lest the rug be pulled from under the conditions of self-consciousness (an essential feature of the I: cf. GA I, 2:399–404, 408). It is well known that Hegel rejected Fichte's idea as installing an infinite finitude and thereby destroying the speculative idea of absolute unity at its core.[43] The structure that we have analyzed here, however, does hold a place for the perennial recurrence of a self-external, finite content that cannot vanish lest the foundation crumble on which the higher-level self-relation of philosophical cognition is built. In other words, the

---

43 Cf. GW 4:399, 406–8; 21:123, 126–31, 138–39.

progressus infinitus is retained, but as a subordinate, vanishing, yet nonetheless indispensible moment.[44]

We have therefore come to see Hegel's views on geometrical cognition and his methodological response to Jacobi as facets of a far more comprehensive structure. For the structure that they instantiate (the structure of the Concept) has fundamental significance both for the methodology of finite cognition and its relation to speculative knowledge, and for the central concern to respond to the metaphysical challenge of nihilism. It is of the utmost importance to recognize that the structure of the Concept is indistinguishable from the method Hegel implements in appropriating and surmounting Jacobi's critique of systematic, rationalist metaphysics. And as I emphasized in Chapter 1 above, the structure of the Concept is itself the structural expression of the logical dynamic of absolute negativity.

5.8. Hegel's critique of the geometric method

Before leaving Hegel's treatment of geometry in the *Science of Logic*, it is worth our while to consider in more detail the ways it fails to overcome its status as finite cognition. To put it in the broadest perspective, Hegel's critique of the geometric method or deductivist science more generally is integral to answering the equally sweeping claims by Kant and Jacobi that scientific cognition of the absolute is impossible. For both men equate scientific cognition with deductivism, the ideal of which is realized in the axiomatized system of the *mos geometricus*. Immanent critique of this mode of cognition with the aim of providing an alternative is therefore instrumental in securing Hegel's more fundamental stance on the possibility of speculative science. As comparison with the original text quickly reveals, the discussion of geometry culminates in the passage quoted above in which Hegel identifies Jacobi and Kant as those who put an end to the method of rationalist metaphysics: for Hegel, too, this intra-philosophical debate on methodology forms the immediate context of his treatment of mathematics.

However, there is also a more specific story to be told here. Kant had rejected the geometrical method as an appropriate form for

---

44 Here it seems to me that Hegel would concede the "positive significance" of the negativity of the finite qua evanescence which, according to Arndt, he rejects because no speculative use can be made of it: see Arndt, *Dialektik und Reflexion*, 198.

philosophy on the grounds that philosophy is a discursive discipline concerned with the adequate analysis and elucidation of given categories, whereas mathematics has a superior source of evidence in *a priori* intuition and can define its objects into existence (B751). While it is true that the foundational character of transcendental philosophy confers upon it a dignity unmatched by the sciences whose possibility it explains, we must also recognize the deflationary tendencies in Kant's characterization of the "discipline of pure reason" (B740–822) as a whole. Mathematics, he says, "presents the most splendid example of the successful extension of pure reason, without the help of experience" (B740). Transcendental philosophy, by contrast, constitutes an essentially negative "discipline" of pure reason: its job is to reject error by establishing the limits of what can be known scientifically; it does not present an extension of pure reason without the help of experience. On the contrary, precisely in its positive results, namely the determination of the conditions of possibility of experience, transcendental philosophy is necessarily guided by that very possibility *as given* (cf. B811). To this extent, critical philosophy is a science even more dependent than those whose possibility it grounds, since mathematics depends in no way on the possibility of experience and would be as rigorous and splendid even if no world whatsoever existed beyond the mind. The conclusion of the First Critique is therefore a "humiliation of human reason" (B823) in its pure theoretical employment; it is positive only as representing an exercise of autonomy in reason's own self-limitation.

As my discussion in the preceding section indicates, Hegel too rejects the *mos geometricus* as an appropriately philosophical mode of cognition. Unsurprisingly, though, Kant's deflationary tendencies are absent from Hegel's rationale. As the placement of geometry inside the second moment of the Idea shows, it is only the highest form of *finite* theoretical cognition. Recall that only the first and third moments are "definitions" of the absolute, while the second represents its self-externalization in the sphere of difference: the constitutive lack of self-conscious identification of the Concept with its form of existence qua geometry marks it as self-external. This self-externality infects all aspects of geometry, as I will go on to explain. The mind's relation to a non-minded kind of objects basically compromises geometry in its degree of rigor, immanence, plasticity, and (as Hegel understands it) freedom. These virtues are to be met with in their full measure only in a successfully realized system of speculative science.

In what follows, I will spell out Hegel's critique of geometry in more detail. This will equip us to understand the respects in which he agrees with Kant and Jacobi in their rejection of rationalist metaphysics; but more importantly, it will prepare us for a discussion of Hegel's own alternative methodology.

As I indicated above, Hegel's criticisms of geometric cognition can be summed up under the heading of self-externality, but what that means in detail differs somewhat from point to point. To begin with the relation of geometric cognition to its own procedures, Hegel criticizes the fact that in a typical (Euclidean) demonstration we begin with an auxiliary construction whose purpose we discern only in retrospect, having understood the proof and its conclusion. It represents objectivity without subjectivity. As he puts it, we must "blindly" obey the directives for a construction as long as "the purpose motivating it is yet to be declared"; until we see what that purpose is, the work of construction remains for us a "meaningless act" (GW 12:225). Hegel formulates this criticism in similar terms in his comparison of geometry and speculative science in the Preface to the *Phenomenology*:

> As regards cognition, we do not, in the first place, have any insight into the necessity of the construction. It does not arise from the concept of the theorem; it is rather imposed, and the instruction to draw precisely these lines where infinitely many others could be drawn must be blindly obeyed without our knowing anything except that we believe that this will be to the purpose in carrying out the proof. In retrospect, this expediency also becomes evident, but for that very reason it is an external expediency because it becomes evident only after the proof. (GW 9:32–33/§44)

Given Hegel's own extensive practical experience with geometrical proof, he would have been familiar with both perspectives first-hand: that of the geometer who is from the outset "in the know" as to the purpose of the auxiliary construction, and that of the student of geometry who must follow the teacher's directives in hopes that it will all make sense in the end. Anyone familiar with the rhetorical organization of Euclidean proofs, with their strict canon of general enunciation, the setting out of an instantiating figure, the auxiliary construction, followed by demonstration and finally re-enunciation of the proposition, is likely to recognize his own experience in Hegel's description. One can easily have the feeling of "going along" with the constructive directions, somewhat the way one goes along with certain kinds of jokes that are highly stereotypical in structure: the rationale of what one is required to imagine is both hidden and promised (by the very genre of discourse) to be revealed in short order. It is not an exaggeration to say that, for a moment, the audience of the proof or the joke, as the case may be, willingly relinquishes its freedom and places itself in the hands of another, namely in expectation of a payoff in restored transparency and insight at the point when laughter sets in or the geometer inscribes his QED.

In a sense Hegel might be said to be overly scrupulous in criticizing geometry for what is, after all, an aspect of almost every didactic relationship, and in the case of geometry moreover is a sacrifice of perfect transparency and freedom that is so voluntary, so momentary, and so benign as hardly to count as an instance of unfreedom at all. His scrupulousness attests, however, to the unique character of speculative logic as he conceives it: "The exposition of no subject matter can be in and for itself strictly and immanently plastic, as is that of thinking in its necessary development ... in this respect, the science of logic must surpass even mathematics, for no subject matter intrinsically possesses this freedom and independence" (GW 21:18). Hegel's criticism of geometry sheds light on this positive methodological ideal. The exposition of "thinking in its necessary development" makes no demands on the student of logic whose meaning is not immediately evident. Insight is never to be deferred to a later stage of the exposition. The activity and forward movement of thinking is to be guided by a purely immanent purposiveness; any moment that points beyond itself to a fulfillment seemingly different from itself must itself play a role in generating the form of that fulfillment: its purpose must not exist outside of it as a given and already determined end. In the terms of subjective experience, the speculative logician must at no moment have the feeling of giving himself over to external guidance or of performing an activity whose content remains opaque to him.[45]

In short, therefore, the *first way* in which geometrical cognition can be said to be "external" is by virtue of the *self-externality* it finds within

---

45 What Hegel embraces as a methodological *norm* directly mirrors the autopoietic nature of the *object* of the speculative method as he conceives it. Francisco Varela's metaphor of "laying down a path in walking" is apt in this context: cf. Thompson, *Mind in Life*, 180). Also see Wolfgang Welsch, "Absoluter Idealismus und Evolutionsdenken," in K. Vieweg and W. Welsch (eds.), *Hegels Phänomenologie des Geistes. Ein kooperativer Kommentar zum einem Schlüsselwerk der Moderne* (Frankfurt: Suhrkamp-Verlag 2008), 655–88.

itself: performing actions (belonging to the auxiliary construction) whose meaning and purpose are unknown to the cognitive subject of those actions is a way of being external-to-self within one's very actions; to describe such actions as a form of blind obedience is just a way of emphasizing this moment of alienation, however fleeting and benign it may be.

The *second*, closely related way that geometrical cognition fails to overcome a certain externality is that it remains *external to the object* of cognition. Whereas the auxiliary construction represents a moment of objectivity without subjectivity, the actual demonstration represents a moment of "subjective act lacking in objectivity" (GW 12:225). Given the virtually paradigmatic objectivity of mathematical cognition, Hegel's remark may initially seem jarring. What he means by it, though, turns out to be exactly what is ordinarily taken to be its superior objectivity over against the arbitrariness of subjective thought.

To take an example, a typical Euclidean proof leads from a proposition containing analytically unrelated predicates (e.g. the property of being the set of prime numbers and the property of being infinite), through some kind of preliminary construction (in this case, the multiplication of the members of a set purporting to be the set of all prime numbers, and the addition of one unit to the resulting product), to a demonstration (by way of what is now called the unique-prime-factorization theorem or the fundamental theorem of arithmetic) that there can be no largest prime number.[46] Now as Hegel would point out, neither the construction of a putatively complete set of prime numbers and the operations following upon it, nor even the fact that any non-prime integer can be factorized into a unique set of powers of prime numbers, *generates* the truth of the proposition that there are infinitely many prime numbers. On the contrary, because prime numbers are what they are, the fundamental theorem of arithmetic is true.

What Hegel calls the "nerve of the demonstration" is, as he says, "something in which the connectedness [i.e. the content to be proved] *appears* and is *external*" (GW 12:225; cf. GW 9:32/§43). In the case of Euclid's proof that there is no greatest prime number, the strategy is indirect: a contradiction is generated from the assumption that a complete finite list of primes could be provided. But this contradiction falls wholly on the side of *our* thinking: it does not belong to the

46 Cf. Euclid, *Elements*, IX.20.

affirmative essence of prime numbers, and it certainly plays no role in their generation. The observation that alternative proofs exist for many propositions leads to a similar conclusion. The fact that there are alternative ways of bringing someone to see the truth of the theorem means that the conditions of its intelligibility are distinct from the ontological conditions of the relation (*Verhältnis* or *Verknüpfung*) that forms the content of that theorem. This is precisely what Hegel means when he calls geometric cognition a "subjective act lacking in objectivity." For cognition to be objective in the full, speculative sense in which Hegel wants to use that term, it must be directly involved in the *genesis* of the cognitive object. But Hegel believes that the objects in whose genesis thinking is directly involved are the pure thought-determinations, and in the final analysis it is thought itself in its self-production which is the exclusive "object" of truly "objective" thinking.

As we are about to see, Hegel does not in fact accord the objects of mathematics full reality. What is more important right now, though, is to grasp the meaning of the genetic-productive conception of objectivity in the context of Hegel's broader methodological concerns. I have already indicated one way in which mathematics exhibits close affinities with speculative logic: it produces *real definitions* of its objects. As was indicated above, we recognize the presence of this traditional concept of the real definition in Hegel when we recall that, on his conception, a real definition demonstrates how the reality of the *definiendum* (in our example, the three-sidedness of the triangle) is contained in its concept. Nonetheless, this conception is heavily modified in comparison to the traditional one: it dispenses with the properly *constructive* aspect of the classical formulation, it relocates the real definition to the properly *demonstrative* part of science, and it invites us to consider *reality* purely in terms of the *individuation* and concretization of conceptual components rather than in terms of *instantiation*.

This point comes out more clearly, perhaps, in Hegel's parallel discussion of mathematics and speculative philosophy in the Preface to the *Phenomenology*. There, too, he takes the Pythagorean theorem as his example and points out that it is not the triangle itself that divides itself up in the construction and carries out the proof:

> In philosophical cognition, too, the coming to be of determinate being [*Werden des Daseins*] is distinct from the coming to be of essence

> [*Werden des Wesens*] or of the inner nature of the object [*Sache*]. But ...
> philosophical cognition contains both, whereas mathematical cog-
> nition sets forth only the coming to be of *determinate being*, i.e. the
> coming-to-be of the *being* of the nature of the object in *cognition* as
> such. (GW 9:32/§42)

In other words, geometry brings about a real definition of its object,
that is, it demonstrates how the simplest conceptual determination of
the (right) triangle entails or "passes over into" its existent determinateness as a three-sided figure, a determinateness whose immediate
existence for cognition is the nominal definition of the triangle as a
trilateral plane figure. What geometry cannot show is why the simple
conceptual determination of the triangle appears by way of the manifold determinations that are ultimately reunited in its real definition.
At bottom, the whole play of externalization into distinct components
(i.e. the relations thematized over the course of a book of the *Elements*)
and reintegration (i.e. the real or "second" definition at the close of a
book) is contingent upon the subjective activity of the geometer.

At the same time, however, this very subjective activity, taken in
itself, is a mirror of the self-directed, generative-productive activity by
which the Idea gives itself existence. Speculative logic, by taking a step
back, as it were, and grasping the nature of the activity that leads to
geometrically real definition (the self-referentiality discussed above),
can bring about a real definition in a higher sense:

> [It] also unites these two distinct movements [sc. the coming to be
> of existence and of essence]. The internal genesis or the coming to
> be of substance is an unbroken transition into outer existence, into
> being-for-other, and conversely, the coming to be of existence is how
> existence is by itself taken back into essence. In this way, the movement
> is the duplex process and coming to be of the whole. (GW 9:32/§42)

The ultimately simple thought here is that the Idea comes into existence only by grasping itself as the source of the plurality of determinations and by grasping its own nature as necessitating at once both the
emergence of those determinations as separate, and their recognition
as internally identical aspects of itself, the Idea. The geometrically real
definition carries out only the first half of this double movement: it
grasps the existence of the triangle for cognition in its three-sidedness,
for instance, as necessitated by the nature of the triangle. But owing to
the specific nature of the mathematical object it cannot grasp why it
should figure in such a process of cognition at all. Hegel believes that

the real definition achieved by speculative science goes geometry one better: it exhibits the essence of its "object" (the absolute Idea) by actually bringing it into existence in a process of self-reflective resumption of cognition into itself. Speculative science is thus directly involved in the genesis of its object.

There is one further aspect of geometric cognition's self-externality that must be addressed before going on to a brief discussion of the specific self-externality of the geometric *object*. It consists in the status of geometric axioms as *relative* first principles. That is, the geometer treats the axioms as first principles whose truth is not subject to debate within the science of geometry proper. From a perspective internal to the practice of geometry, the axioms are thus absolute; they are treated as self-evidently true and incapable of further demonstration. On Hegel's view, however, the axioms of geometry are synthetic propositions, and as such they are in need of a demonstration that will mediate the elements synthetically combined in them: he believes in fact that they can be demonstrated in the more fundamental science of logic (cf. GW 12:221–22). In Hegelian terms, geometry has its "truth" in another science, namely in speculative logic. Now when something that is essentially relative to another is treated as absolute, it is treated as "indifferent" (*gleichgültig*) – Hegel's technical term for this state of affairs. And a term that is indifferent to that other in which it has its truth or being, is (again in Hegel's technical terms) external to it. Insofar as its own truth or being lies in that other, it is external to itself in being external to that other. And this is the case with geometry and mathematics generally: it is constrained, qua mathematics, to treat as indifferent what is dependent on another; it treats as *absolute* first principles what are in fact only *relatively* first principles. And in this sense mathematical cognition is self-external.[47]

We turn now from the self-externality of geometric cognition to the self-externality of geometric objects. Geometry is the science of space, spatial relations, spatial magnitudes. Space as such is for Hegel "the abstract universality of [nature's] self-externality [*Außersichsein*] – its unmediated indifference" (ENC §254; cf. GW 12:226). The objects of

---

47 Hegel's view is notably similar to Plato's (cf. *Republic* 533c). The scientific status of geometric "axioms" was already a subject of debate in classical antiquity. For an account of the genesis of the concept of axioms in its relation to dialectical thought in antiquity, see Árpád Szabó, "Die Anfänge des Euklidischen Axiom-Systems," *Archive for the History of the Exact Sciences* 1 (1960/62): 37–106, esp. 67–70. Also cf. GW 4:208, 216–17.

geometry are thus infected with an ineliminable self-externality. From this fact several consequences immediately follow.

First, the objects of geometry are fundamentally "*begrifflos*" (GW 12:226) – "void of concept" in the Hegelian sense that their very nature excludes the self-internality (*Insichsein*) that is an essential feature of the Concept as self-relation and infinite return to self. Thus despite the fact that the conceptual movement represented by the geometrically "real definition" is the closest *formal* analogue of the realization of the Concept (i.e. the Idea) in the sphere of finite theoretical cognition, its *content* is the very antithesis of the Concept. Thought cannot find itself in the content of geometry, even though geometry is de facto the highest finite realization of finite theoretical cognition.

A second, closely related consequence is the deficient mode of geometrical evidence. Space, as the highest possible abstraction from the natural, sensuously given world, is a "non-sensuous sensuous" (GW 12:226) as Hegel says: an object of sensibility that has been stripped of all its sensuous qualities, leaving only the purely formal determinations. Above, I underscored the fact that Hegel speaks of the "silent spaces" of abstract thought, untouched by human interest, only in connection with speculative science and geometry. Yet geometry remains inferior to speculative logic because what it *abstracts from* are the sensuous qualities of objects defined by their self-externality. Such abstraction is powerless to effect a *metabasis eis allos genos* in the objects of geometry: they remain sensible and self-external even at the outer limit of abstraction and formalization. The role of intuition in geometric demonstration is concomitant with this fact. For this very reason, Hegel bucks the Kantian tradition that makes intuition the defining feature of geometry's cognitive superiority to purely discursive sciences (cf. GW 12:226). On the contrary, he argues: the link with sensible intuition preserves an ineliminable moment of self-externality in geometrical thought, thereby compromising it as a medium for adequately realizing and manifesting the "conceptual" structure of being. Oddly enough, in the perspective of speculative science, geometry's intuitive evidence is a cognitive failing, not a cognitive strength.

A third consequence of the self-externality of geometric objects is that they cannot instantiate the *concrete identity* peculiar to the pure thought-determinations that form the content of speculative logic. The inner identity of the thought-determinations with the Idea is manifested in the forms of transition specific to the three "spheres" of the logic: Being, Essence, and the Concept. In Being, the determinations "pass over" into one another (*Übergehen ins Andere*); in Essence, they "shine into" each other (*Scheinen ins Andere*); and in the Concept they reveal themselves to be developments into and out of each other (*Entwicklung*: cf. ENC §161/161A). In contrast to the dialectical transitions that characterize speculative logic, geometry knows only "formal inferences" (*formelles Schließen*) by way of the "formal identity" (*formelle Identität*) of the geometric space-determinations:

> Geometry is a science of *magnitude*, and hence *formal* inference is the one most appropriate to it; since it treats the quantitative determination alone, abstracting from anything qualitative, it can confine itself to *formal identity*, the unity void of concept which is equality and belongs to external, abstractive reflection ... It is only because the space of geometry is the abstract emptiness of mutual externality that it is possible for figures to be drawn in its indeterminateness in such a way that their determinations remain perfectly at rest outside one another with no immanent transition to the opposite. The science of these determinations is therefore plainly and simply the science *of the finite* which is compared according to magnitude and has for its unity the external one of equality. (GW 12:226–27)

When Hegel talks here of the merely "formal" inference and quantitative comparison, he must be referring to the fourth figure of the syllogism of determinate being (*Dasein*), the so-called mathematical inference: "When two things or determinations are equal to a third, they are equal to one another" (GW 12, 104–6). He notes that this inference, which is recognized as a self-evident axiom in mathematics, has as its ultimate consequence the elimination of difference between subject and predicate: when logic is conceived on the model of the mathematical inference, it can be reduced to a purely mechanical routine of substitution designed to reveal equalities, making inference into "a totally empty and tautological construal of propositions" that could as easily be carried out by a calculating machine (GW 12:110).

The last result is of special significance. The overarching purpose of discussing Hegel's views on geometry has been to illuminate his appraisal of Jacobi and Kant as epochal critics of the rationalist method of philosophical cognition. We have seen that Hegel diverges from Kant's appraisal of geometry in virtually every point, praising it for its self-contained immanence and totality, rejecting it for its various aspects of self-externality and its link with sensible intuition as a source of certainty. So although Hegel also rejects the *mos geometricus* as an appropriate form of philosophical cognition, his reasons for doing so are very different from Kant's. This last result shows, on the other hand, how similar Hegel's reasons are to Jacobi's reasons for rejecting the model of axiomatized geometry. In its discursive (non-intuitive, non-constructive) aspects, geometry relies on the modes of reasoning (deduction, tautology, finite relationality) that Jacobi perceived as a source of formalism and hence, ultimately, nihilism. In his critique of geometry, Hegel appears to share Jacobi's judgment, or at least to hold a view with distinct affinities to that of Jacobi. As we have seen, though, the difference lies in Hegel's conviction that geometry qua finite cognition can also be reconstructed from a speculative point of view as adumbrating the structures of a non-finite form of cognition, a form of cognition immune to the formalistic and nihilistic consequences Jacobi feared.

6

DIE SACHE SELBST: ABSOLUTE NEGATIVITY AND HEGEL'S SPECULATIVE LOGIC OF CONTENT

6.1. Introduction

In the previous four chapters of this book I have mainly been concerned to explore Hegel's critique of finite cognition in its three basic forms as (pre-critical) metaphysics, natural science, and mathematics. I would now like to turn to Hegel's more positive view of finite cognition as a moment within the unfolding of the Concept with an indispensable role to play in the identification of subject and substance. At the center of this chapter is the thesis that the problematic relation between Kant's transcendental apperception and the sensible manifold, on the one side, and between Spinoza's monist substance and its determinateness in the finite modes, on the other, are strictly analogous problems. Indeed, I will argue that they are but two manifestations of one identical problem, namely the proper analysis of determinate intentional content, and that Hegel's logic of absolute negation provides a unified solution to this problem.

In order to describe these twin problems in a way that highlights their interconnections both with one another and with Hegel's unified approach to solving them, I draw on the scholastic terms "formal" and "objective reality" that Descartes introduced into modern philosophical discourse. I have chosen here to prefer these terms over more conventional terms of our time such as "intentional content," "representational content," or "intrinsic properties," for example, mainly because they suggest a basic affinity between these categories as specifications of the common term "reality." Over the course of this chapter, I will show that this affinity grounds what Kant referred to as "transcendental affinity" and that this grounding is necessary in order to give a satisfying account of determinate, *relatively* mind-independent reality and our access to it as intentional beings.[1] At the end of the chapter, I will draw some conclusions regarding the sense in which Hegel can and cannot be said to be engaged in a realist project of naturalizing intentionality.

6.2. The traditional concepts of formal and objective reality and their usefulness for analyzing Hegel's talk of substance and subject

In keeping with my overall thesis that the basic goals and problems of pre-Kantian rationalism continue to form an important backdrop for Hegel's thinking, I would like to set the stage for this chapter by calling on two important terms from the rationalist tradition, namely, *formal* and *objective reality*. In the sense in which I will be employing them, the terms have their origin in the philosophy of Descartes and signify, to a first approximation, the being of a substance taken in itself (formal reality) and the being peculiar to mind-dependent representational content (objective reality).[2] Thus, whatever exists possesses a determinate degree of formal reality: the highest degree if it exists as a substance (and here an infinite substance possesses a higher degree of formal reality than a finite one); essential and non-essential properties possess a lesser degree, and their various modes and the modes of modes possess the least (discounting problematic entities such as

---

1 In speaking of "relatively" mind-independent reality I mean that reality exists independently of any individual finite mind, but not independently of the existence of any mind at all.

2 Cf. Descartes' clarification of the terms in his reply to the first set of objections in CSM 1:74. The terms "formal" and "objective reality" can of course be traced back further than Descartes: he appropriates them from a metaphysical tradition reaching back to thinkers such as Henry of Ghent, John Ockham, and Duns Scotus, with whose views Descartes would have been familiar through Suarez. But Descartes' use of these terms deviates from that of the scholastic metaphysicians, unsurprisingly in view of the shift in his conception of mind and cognition. For an extensive analysis of the similarities and differences, see T. J. Cronin, *Objective Being in Descartes and in Suarez*. Analecta Gregoriana 154 (Rome: Gregorian University Press 1966). Notably, J. C. Doig offers an exclusively extra-mental interpretation of objective reality in Suarez that is for obvious reasons in sharp contrast to Descartes' understanding of the concept (see J. C. Doig, "Objective Being in Descartes and Suarez," *New Scholasticism* 51 [1977]: 350–71). This is intriguing in view of the interpretation of Hegel that I will be developing over the course of this chapter: I use the concepts of formal and objective reality as part of an account of the underlying homogeneity of the extra-mental and intra-mental realms, which entails emphasis on the extra-mental character of objective reality in certain of its Hegelian moments.

shadows or cold, which should be considered as mere privations with no positive reality of their own).[3] In this sense, ideas also possess formal reality in that they are modes of thinking substance (*res cogitans*); ontologically speaking, they are on a par with modes of material substance like determinate shape or position. Differently from all other formal realities, however, modes of thinking substance are further individuated by their representational content, that is, their objective reality. Representational content, too, comes in varying degrees, as Descartes himself indicates: the degree of formal reality possessed by the mind-independent referential object of the idea, if it actually exists, should be understood as an indicator of the degree of objective reality attaching to the idea.[4] Here the number of the predicates or "realities" constituting the essence of the intentional object are an important measure, especially when they are defined by affirmative qualities, in which case they are called *perfections*. (Descartes famously introduces the objective reality of God in this manner as a crucial step in the Trademark Argument of Meditation III.)[5] Hence one very important feature of the concept of objective reality is its potentiality for exhibiting a certain *parallelism* with formal reality, both in terms of its content (in which case we have *adaequatio rei et intellectus*) and in terms of its ordering by degree (in which case the epistemic dignity of the cognition is measured in terms of the metaphysical status and hence explanatory scope of the referent).

3 Cf. the work done by these distinctions in Descartes' proof of the existence of a supreme being in Meditation III. It will soon become relevant to note that their *parallelism* with degrees of objective reality is equally crucial in that argument. Descartes spells out this parallelism at CSM 2:116–17. Spinoza is similarly explicit: see PPC 1a4; cf. TW 20:139, where Hegel makes reference to this passage. Hegel discusses the Trademark Argument (which he considers to be a typical example of the "metaphysical" approach to speculative questions), including the concepts of formal and objective reality, at TW 20:139–45. Hegel finds it to be of greatest significance in Descartes' argument that the *first* attribute of God is that he is the cord (*Band*) that binds cognition and truth or being (TW 20:144–45).

4 See once again CSM 2:116–17.

5 This ultimately scholastic conception of positive or affirmative "realities" as "perfections" will continue to play an implicit role even in Kant's construction of the theoretical concept of God in the Transcendental Ideal section of the First Critique, where the *ens realissimum* is introduced by way of the idea of a *complete* set of all *non-negative* predicates: cf. B601–7. It is important to note in this connection that despite his sharp criticism of ontotheology, Kant casts no doubt on the legitimacy of the conception of positive realities from which it is constructed; it even appears to retain a function within transcendental philosophy, as argued, e.g., in Longuenesse, *Human Standpoint*, 211–35.

The extent to which Hegel was influenced by the details of Descartes' metaphysics and epistemology is questionable.[6] However, there can be no such question with regard to Descartes' most original successor, Spinoza, whose thought played an undisputed role in the formation of post-Kantian idealism. But one of Spinoza's most distinctive doctrines, the parallelism of ideas and things, is unintelligible without the notion of formal and objective realities. "The order and connection of ideas is the same as the order and connection of things" (E2p7). As Spinoza goes on to explain in the scholium:

> When I said that God is the cause, e.g., of the idea of a circle only inso-far as he is a thinking thing, and of a circle only insofar as he is an extended thing, my reason was simply this, that the formal being of the idea of a circle can be perceived only through another mode of thinking as its proximate cause, and that mode through another, and so ad infinitum, with the result that as long as things are considered as modes of thought, we must explicate the order of the whole of Nature, or the connection of causes, through the attribute of thought alone; and insofar as things are considered as modes of extension, again the order of the whole of Nature must be explicated thought the attribute of Extension only. (E2p7s)

Here the immediate claim is that, qua *formal reality*, ideas stand in causal relations to ideas while extended things stand in causal relations to extended things, and that despite the lack of causality across attributes (Thought/Extension), the causality within each attribute is of the same nature as that in any other.[7] But even to formulate the associated claim that "a circle existing in Nature and the idea of the existing circle – which is also in God – are one and the same thing, explicated through different attributes" (E2p7s), it is necessary to pre-sume the *objective reality* of the circle that individuates God's idea of a circle as his idea *of* a circle. The parallelism in question is thus three-fold: *causal parallelism* in the formal reality of Thought and Extension,

---

6 See, e.g., Hegel's dismissive remark in the *Lectures on the History of Philosophy* (TW 20:127).

7 Cf. E2p36: "Inadequate and confused ideas follow by the same necessity as adequate, or clear and distinct ideas." This obviously cannot be *logical* necessity since part of what it means for an idea to be confused is for it to fail to exhibit the distinct components that constitute its inferential relations to other ideas. So it seems plausible to take Spinoza to mean causal necessity, which of course fits with his overall discussion in this part of E2 of ideas in terms of bodily interactions.

respectively, and (in the optimum case) *representational parallelism* between objective reality and referents in formal reality (TW 20:176).

Presumably, Hegel has in mind this doctrine when he credits Spinoza with having given appropriate form to Descartes' conception of God as the unity of thought and being, the guarantor that the objective reality of any clear and distinct perception adequately corresponds to a formal reality (cf. TW 20:157). The fundamental idea of Cartesian metaphysics, he writes, is this:

> (a) To move from self-certainty to truth, to cognize being in the concept of thinking. In this thinking: "I think," I am a single individual; thinking is present merely as something subjective, and being is not demonstrated as contained with the concept of thinking, there is no transition to separation in general. (b) The negative of being for self-consciousness is also present; and this negative term, unified with the positive I, is posited as unified in itself in a third term, in God. In God, thinking and being is the same; being is precisely in the negative, in the concept, in God's being thought of [*Gedachtsein*]. (TW 20:145)

The principle that, by virtue of God's perfection, clear and distinct perceptions are necessarily true plays a crucial role in Descartes' proof of an external, material world. Descartes argues that the presentations of sense, whose content is chiefly composed of extended things, are external to the essence of the thinking I, which is constituted by the intellect's exercise of self-conscious judgment; sense presentations must therefore arise from a source external to pure self-consciousness.[8] The veridicality of sense presentations, namely the truth that what appears to me are in themselves ("formally") extended substances and not merely properties caused by the "eminent" reality of a non-extended substance, is guaranteed by God's perfection. But this tie is external to mind and body, as Hegel notes, and Descartes gives no account of how it is that the sense presentations mediated by the body can be present to intellectual, judgmental self-consciousness in the first place.[9]

Spinoza's dual-aspect monism lays the groundwork (though merely the groundwork) for a more satisfying account. However, there is still

---

8 Cf. CSM 2:54–55.

9 Note the similarities between Descartes' prioritization of the faculty of judgment in self-consciousness and his separation of that faculty from sense and imagination, on the one hand, and Kant's doctrine of the role of judgment in transcendental apperception and his separation of understanding and sensibility, on the other. The problems that arise from this separation will play a role in the following.

some question as to how his doctrine of parallelism is to be interpreted. Like Spinoza (and Descartes as well, on the interpretation given above), Hegel is committed to the identity of thought and being.[10] But of course *unlike* Spinoza, Hegel will insist on the primacy of subjective self-determination and the relative underdetermination of traditional conceptions of causality, which (as I argued in Chapter 4) Hegel believes to be inadequate even for the cognition of nature, much less subjectivity. So one helpful way of framing his intellectual engagement with Spinoza is to ask how it might be possible to hold on to a monistic identity of thought and being (subject and substance) without falling either into determinism or into a metaphysics of substance and attribute that Hegel finds inherently question-begging.[11] (This description of Hegel's philosophical program converges with the one given in Chapter 5.)

In order to have terms in which to explore this question without presupposing any specific solution to it, I therefore propose to use the Cartesian expressions "formal" and "objective reality." As I have now indicated, I think this proposal finds at least partial justification in the philology. But the real justification will emerge in the course of the interpretation in which I put them to use. The advantage of the Cartesian expressions is that they make salient the notion that being and thought are determinants of the same underlying determinable, "reality," without prejudicing the decision as to whether or not they are unified in that determinable. To illustrate what I mean, "vertebrate" and "invertebrate" are determinants of the same underlying determinable, "animal," but there is no animal that is somehow both vertebrate and invertebrate, thus unifying those determinants as aspects of itself. By contrast, "shape" and "size" are determinants of the same underlying determinable, "extension," and they are so by

---

10 For the relevant interpretation of the Cartesian *cogito*, see ENC §64; cf. GW 15:8. For revealing instances of Hegel's treatment of Spinoza's "extension" and synonymous with "being," see his discussion of the concept of "reality" in the *Science of Logic*: GW 21:99–102; also see TW 20:177.

11 Briefly, Hegel's reason for rejecting the substance-attribute model as a satisfactory basis for conceiving the unity of thought and being is that Spinoza has no principled way of introducing the distinction. "Attribute" is defined at E1d4 as "that which the intellect perceives of substance as constituting its essence." As Hegel points out, this definition seems to presuppose a finite intellect external to substance that perceives its essence in a determinate, but therefore limited way. This begs the question (1) of the origin and existence of such an intellect and (2) of the metaphysical status of the attributes themselves, e.g. are they real or ideal? Are they really one or really many? Cf. TW 20:169–73.

jointly inhering in every extended thing, thus enjoying a certain kind of unity within it.

It is to be expected that Hegel's unity of thought and being will be of a *sui generis* kind and different from either of the determinate-determinable relations just exemplified. Just how that relation is to be conceived is the subject of this chapter. I will suggest, however, that just as the Cartesian terms "formal" and "objective" determine *realitas* (whose closest German equivalent would be *Sachhaltigkeit*), their Hegelian counterparts "substance" and "subject" are to be understood as determining what Hegel emphatically but elusively refers to as *die Sache selbst.*

6.3. Kant, the structure of apperception, and the problematic relation of the sensible manifold to objective reality

Descartes himself does not spend a lot of time thinking about the sense in which formal and objective reality are determinants of the common determinable, reality, except to conceive truth as the correspondence of formal and objective reality in a clear and distinct idea.[12] This is precisely what Hegel criticizes in the passage above when he says that Descartes locates their unity in God as a "third term" external to mind and world. Kant, however, makes an important further contribution to what we might call the Cartesian theory of truth. His interest lies with the analysis of the conditions under which it is possible for there to be any such reality as objective reality in the Cartesian sense. What, Kant is effectively asking, are the conditions of possibility for objective reality?[13] He departs, superficially at least, from the Cartesian conception in Meditation III, for instance, according to which objective reality is *caused* by formal reality, the latter taken now as answering roughly to Kant's things in themselves.[14] Objective reality, as the content of thinking, comes to be viewed as constituted at the most basic level by the forms of thinking itself (the categories). How so? Well, the first precondition of objectivity, that is, the character of being an *object* or the

---

12 His perhaps most direct statement of the principle occurs in the Synopsis of the *Meditations*: CSM 2:11.

13 I am not the first reader to try to bring Kant's concept of objectivity into closer proximity to the scholastic and Cartesian conceptions: see, e.g., Hans Wagner, "Realitas objectiva (Descartes–Kant)," *Zeitschrift für philosophische Forschung* 21 (1967): 325–40. See also the discussion of this topic in Chapter 2.

14 This statement has to be qualified in an important respect, as I will indicate below.

content of a representation, is that there be a *difference for me* (for consciousness) between myself and what I am conscious of. Obviously, the object I am conscious of cannot be *causing* this difference since it cannot be constituted *as* an object prior to the difference. Kant suggests that the difference arises as an act of spontaneity. This act seems not to be further explicable; indeed, that is the point of characterizing it as spontaneity. However, he does introduce the notion (albeit with less than full methodological transparency) that this act of spontaneity is performed in a determinate number of modes which (for reasons that, once again, he fails to make fully transparent) he conceives as forms of combining an originally given manifold.

Hence the difference constituting the original possibility of objectivity, that space in which determinate objects can come to be for me, their *Da-Sein* if you will, is necessarily determinate in respect to one or more of these modes of combination. So objectivity in general arises from an original act of spontaneity, namely the positing of a difference, such that that difference is formally determined in respect to one or more of the modes in which the original act is performed.[15] Therefore, to be objective reality (i.e. representational content) necessarily entails that the content manifest those formal determinations in which spontaneity itself first takes on determinate shape. So this self-determining of spontaneity is at least partially constitutive of content or objective reality.

Now, we mustn't sweep under the carpet the difficulty attaching to the notion of an original manifold and its combination. It is clear that Kant requires this notion if he is to account for the material determinacy of content. And it is also true that, in regard to the material factor of determinacy, he holds on to the Cartesian relation of causality between formal and objective reality. But this is a notorious source of obscurity in Kant's doctrine of transcendental idealism that I do not wish to dwell on just here. (I will return to it anon.)[16]

The more promising point right now is that objectivity as such may tentatively be conceived as something like a *property* of the formal reality that is the act of spontaneously positing a difference: the original

---

15 On this notion of a spontaneous act and its dual role in Kant's theory of self-consciousness and noumenal causality, see Watkins, *Metaphysics of Causality*, 272–82. I return to this idea below.

16 For an overview of positions on the role of Kant's things-in-themselves and their relation to appearances, see Karl Ameriks, "Kantian Idealism Today," *History of Philosophy Quarterly* 9:3 (1992): 329–42.

difference of thinking and what is thought. Objective reality is thus an aspect of the spontaneity of – *the I*. One has to be very careful in expressing this relation since at this level of abstraction it is easy to stray into nonsense. With that cautionary remark in place, though, I would like to suggest that this view is tantamount to a reduction of objective reality, heretofore grasped as an independent determinant of reality, to the status of being *the* unique determinant of the formal reality of thought, namely, its reduction to an aspect of its spontaneity.

At the very same time, however, we must also re-emphasize that the formal reality of thinking also requires a difference over against its objective reality, and that difference has to show up for it *as* a difference. Simply put, thinking must be self-conscious, that is, aware of itself as distinct from its content. In order for that difference to be there *for thinking*, thinking must be there *for itself*, and indeed these are merely two ways of looking at the same undivided awareness.

On the face of it, this is a fairly obvious thing to notice. As is well known, Karl Leonhard Reinhold thought he could make of it a self-evident first principle, his Principle of Consciousness: "In consciousness, the subject distinguishes the representation from the subject and the object and relates the representation to both."[17] However, a second glance reveals an unobvious complication. For this difference to be there *for thinking* is for object-consciousness and the spontaneity of thought itself to belong to representational content, that is, objective reality. So what I cautiously described as a "reduction" of objective reality to formal reality in the case of thinking, immediately entails what we might describe as the *absorption* of formal reality into objective reality. Here at the latest it must be clear that the relation of objective and formal reality cannot be adequately grasped in terms of substance and attribute. Whatever the ultimate meaning of a "reduction" of objective reality to the formal reality of self-conscious spontaneity, the relation of the two cannot be grasped on the model of thing and property.

We cannot therefore simply distribute the determinations "objective" and "formal reality" across the terms "representational content" and "thinking," respectively, in a one-to-one manner. Since the formal reality of thinking immediately entails consciousness of thinking as a correlate of consciousness of content in general, the formal reality of thinking (spontaneity) cannot properly be said to be the basis or

17 Reinhold, *Beyträge* 1:167.

"substance" of the determination or property as which I had tentatively characterized objective reality just above. For the thinking could not emerge into existence (could not be *there*) if it were not itself already constituted as objective reality. The formal reality of thinking is formal reality precisely insofar as it is objective reality. Indeed, being object-ive, that is, being content for itself, is the condition for it being real in any sense whatsoever. Thinking is *essentially* self-conscious.

Now, these are the familiar twists and turns of self-consciousness as conceived by post-Kantian idealists. The main point to hold on to here is that the formal reality of the I (thinking, spontaneity) is metaphysically dependent on (let's say: posited by) its objective real-ity, while at the same time the objective reality of content as such is metaphysically dependent on (posited by) the spontaneity that is the formal reality of thinking. There appears to be a kind of circle or flip-flopping here such that the formal reality of thinking is identi-cal to its objective reality just insofar as it differs from its objective reality, and vice versa. As we saw in the earlier chapters of the book, this flipping is precisely the structure of the Concept, the dynamic of absolute negativity.

6.4. The sensible manifold and the concept of truth as correspondence

Rather than going on now directly to talk about Hegel, I would like to back up for a moment to survey what I have said up to this point, with a view to characterizing Kant in relation to Descartes. Descartes, fol-lowing an instinctive insight or perhaps merely adhering to existing terminology, grasps the formal and the objective as two determinants of what he calls *reality* and what I think can be most tellingly referred to in our context by the German word *Sachhaltigkeit*. He does not, how-ever, ask how they come to be in relation or in what their relation con-sists. Spinoza does implicitly pose this question and answers by saying they are just two aspects of a single, infinite substance. But this answer indicates no more than a direction for inquiry. Their mere determi-nation as "attributes" of a common "substance" tells us nothing about why the two terms are or must be related, nor really anything about their relation itself. In particular, Spinoza has nothing to say about the intentionality or content-fulness of objective reality in virtue of which its relation to at least one other attribute (extension) is that of representation. In this respect he has no more to say than Descartes, although by uniting them in a single ultimate being he creates a basis for approaching the question.

Kant, on the other hand, both poses this question and suggests the answer that objectivity is a *metaphysical condition* of the formal reality of the I, a condition posited and fulfilled by the spontaneous act of differentiation that is thinking in its most original emergence. Accordingly, the forms of objectivity are the forms constitutive of thinking in its formal reality and they are also the forms that determine (measure) the objective validity of any determinate claim to knowledge.

What I dubbed the "Cartesian theory of truth" is of course affected by Kant's suggestion. For Kant, as for Descartes, truth lies in the adequate correspondence between objective and formal reality. With the important and puzzling exception of the material factor of objective content (Kant's sensible manifold), which bears vestiges of the old causal theory,[18] the only *formal* reality at stake in the determination of truth is the formal reality of thinking itself. So however one ends up spelling out the meaning of this claim, truth – from the Kantian standpoint as reconstructed here – is going to have to lie in the correspondence of thinking with itself.

How so? And how can we disregard the formal reality that is (it would seem) causally involved in the objective reality of the material factor of knowledge? Well, because the objectivity (*stricto sensu*) of knowledge lies wholly with its categorial self-determination: categorial determinations which are constituted by the act of spontaneity in its positing of difference. (Compare Hegel's criticism of Descartes, above, for not having "made the transition to separation.") Objectivity in this sense defines the whole space within which possible decisions of truth and falsity are situated; the manner in which that space is materially filled out cannot therefore be *ultimately* decisive for the determination of truth because truth is not *ultimately* a relation between thinking and the manifold but between thinking qua formal reality and thinking qua objective reality.[19]

---

18 This legacy is manifest in Kant's original formulation of the transcendental project in the letter to Herz from February 21, 1772 (10:124–35, esp. 130). Forster, who makes use of this letter, suggests the idea that representations can and must be caused in various ways remains crucial even for the critical Kant: see Michael Forster, "Kant and Skepticism," in Brady Bowman and Klaus Vieweg (eds.), *Die freie Seite der Philosophie: Skeptizismus in Hegelscher Perspektive* (Würzburg: Königshausen und Neumann 2006), 149–70, here 165.

19 This idea bears close similarity to the view of Longuenesse in *Hegel's Critique*, 24–27. It is a crucial moment in the analysis of Hegel's concept of truth, but for the reasons I am

Admittedly, there is something immediately and obviously dissatisfying about this conclusion and Kant himself would surely have rejected it out of hand. (Whether his own reasons for rejecting it would be cogent is another question.) Truth indeed consists *as a matter of definition* in the correspondence of objective and formal reality,[20] and that correspondence may indeed lie wholly within the self-relation of thinking. But *as a matter of fact*, the criterion for deciding the truth of any determinate knowledge claim depends on the material determination of the objective and formal reality, and on the degree to which they correspond.[21] Objectivity, one should say, is the mere possibility of truth, not something that could itself be true. The sensible manifold with its obscure, supposedly causal relation to objectivity must play some decisive role after all.

The particular difficulty posed is that the sensible manifold as the material factor in determining objective reality has nothing to which it obviously corresponds, not on Kantian premises anyway. Objective reality in its non-material (categorial) determinations *just is* the formal reality of thinking. Correspondence in this case is not mysterious, notwithstanding the dialectical "flip-flopping" we observed above. The sensible determinateness of objective reality, though, is a different matter. For one thing, it is thoroughly contingent in a way the forms of its combination (the categories) are not. These forms of combination are, to repeat, themselves the formal reality of thinking, and there is a determinate number of them, a number determined by some unifying principle in the nature of thinking itself. Hence their necessity in relation to thinking: it is the necessity of identity. The sensible manifold by contrast exhibits indefinite variety and seems not to be expressive of thinking as such; it is the peculiarly non-intellectual factor in objectivity. Furthermore, Kant's basic doctrine precludes the possibility of becoming determinately aware of any correspondence between the sensible manifold and the properties of things in themselves whose causal expression they are (at least on some plausible interpretations).

Upon reflection, this doctrine is itself nothing more than the concession that the very idea of *comparing* an objective reality with a

---

about to spell out in the main text, it is not sufficient by itself because it provides no account of the determinate material content of any real knowledge: cognition's agreement with itself cannot, after all, take merely the form A = A (cf. GW 11:260–65).

20 This claim can be made without qualification for Kant (cf. B82 and, in relation to the notion of truth as it relates to transcendental idealism, B236). Hegel clearly also holds a version of the correspondence theory (cf. GW 12:26).

21 Kant makes this point explicitly in his discussion of the definition and criterion of truth (B82).

formal reality "outside" it, of which it is the effect, is nonsense. To echo Hegel's criticism in the Introduction to the *Phenomenology*, were we to conceive objective reality as a kind of *medium* through which we are in touch with something external to or independent of that medium, be it causally or otherwise, then we could obviously never compare that medium with anything that is in principle unavailable to thought except through that medium (cf. GW 9:53/§73).

From a different point of view one might in turn object that, if the sensible manifold is truly *given*, be it as an effect or as an independent existence in itself, then the very idea of content (objective reality) and hence of correspondence is rendered empty. As many philosophers have underscored (not least among them Descartes), the content-correspondence relation is in no way assimilable to either resemblance or causality. This is, the reader will recall from the discussion of E2p7 above, part of the meaning of Spinoza's doctrine of parallelism: causal relations may link ideas to ideas and extended things to extended things, they may even be *identical* causal relations on both sides; there is no causality across attributes, however, and hence causality is useless (on this understanding) for explaining the relation of representation that defines objective reality.

Lastly, it remains mysterious why, if the sensible manifold is a given existence, the mere combining of its elements should render it into an objective reality, any more than binding sticks into a bundle makes them, in and of itself, a sign. It is by no means obvious that combination (or Kant's "synthesis") is a sufficient or even a necessary condition for objectivity in the sense of representational content, or how it could be.

Nevertheless, simply to jettison the material determinateness of objectivity is clearly no alternative. A full account of the inner relation between formality and objectivity, being and thought, as determinations of (as it now appears) a single *realitas* or *Sachhaltigkeit*, requires something more and other than what we find in orthodox Kantianism. In other words, the theory of content (objective reality) as we have taken it up here implies a theory of truth as correspondence; but such a theory, it is beginning to seem, may not be completable on Kantian principles.

6.5. Hegel's hypothesis: the extra-mental reality of Conceptual structure

The reader should note that despite the fact that the discussion so far has brought into play concepts such as spontaneity, thinking, (self-) consciousness, representation and objectivity, and truth, the focus has not been epistemological in the narrow sense. That is, questions about certainty, verification, justification, and so on have consistently been left aside. The real focus here is metaphysical. *What is* the spontaneity of thinking? *What is* representation in its formal and objective reality? *What is* self-consciousness and what is it consciousness of? *What is* truth and how can the requirement for determinateness be understood and fulfilled? This focus will remain throughout the rest of this chapter, too; even so, the discussion will soon turn more strongly to the activity of knowing (cognition). The point to bear in mind, and a point that goes to the heart of what makes Hegel a difficult thinker, is that his philosophy of the Concept or absolute negativity, constitutes a *metaphysics of knowing*. This is also his deepest difference over against Kant and an important source of his sometimes scathing remarks about him. In particular, the psychologism with which he reproaches Kant ought to be understood as a response to the *aporiae* that arise when the activity of knowing is conceived as an essentially subject-bound activity that nevertheless makes essential reference to a truth that is partially subject-transcendent.

One helpful way of looking at Hegelian speculative science is to see it as starting with a certain analysis of the "logic" of knowing (i.e. the "dialectical" identity of formal and objective reality presented above), and then positing it as a structure/dynamic absolutely prior to the subjective acts of knowing that make up finite cognition. This structure/ dynamic is that of the Concept/absolute negativity. In this way, Hegel believes he can both explain the *possibility of truth* (that is, the correspondence between formal and objective reality), the *relative impossibility* of grasping it from the point of view of finite cognition, and *the necessity of finite cognition* as an agent in the full actualization of the structure/ dynamic in question. This is the source both of his profound rejection of the modes of finite cognition and his unparalleled elevation of human cognitive activity to something on the level of a metaphysical event. It will be helpful to keep these remarks in mind during the following discussion, as a general point of orientation.

Above, I presented the dialectical flip-flopping of what I called thinking in its absolute spontaneity. That act, I said, has as its immediate result the positing of a difference such that the "space" in which the I can become aware of an object is thereby opened. This is an analytic implication of thinking, where "thinking" has the status of an item of primitive introspective acquaintance. Since this difference has to be present to thinking *as difference*, thinking, in acting to posit that difference, must also be conscious of itself. In a word: consciousness is indivisibly self-consciousness. Since "being conscious" is here serving to characterize what is called objective reality, we must therefore say that the formal reality of thinking is actual only as objective reality. They posit each other mutually, differing only in being identical, differing only so as to be identical.

Despite its superficially paradoxical character, this dialectical structure takes its plausibility from the experience of self-consciousness itself, which is as intimate and undeniable to each of us as it is acknowledged to be vexing and elusive as an object of discourse. Yet when we approach the structure of self-consciousness from the perspective of a theory of truth and content (the correspondence of formal and objective reality), it appears discomfittingly incomplete. It seems not only not to clarify the *source* of materially determinate objective reality; it seems even to preclude the possibility of there being such material determinacy, a consequence we likewise know from experience to be false.

I would like to suggest that Hegelian philosophy, in one of its fundamental aspects, is a measure taken to remedy this *aporia*. The measure consists in embracing the dialectical structure whose saving plausibility derives from the experience of consciousness itself, but only in order to identify that structure as having a reality beyond and in some sense prior to its unfolding in consciousness. To speak this way is at once unavoidable and inconvenient. For just as the difference between formal and objective reality itself reveals its full significance only in being taken back into a kind of flickering or flip-flopping identity, so too will the suggestion of a reality beyond or prior to consciousness prove to shed its most intense light in the moment of its rejection.

The measure consists in supposing that the structure/dynamic analyzed above as that of *thinking*, is the structure of *all reality* (a recurring *terminus technicus* in the *Phenomenology*, particularly).[22] This is precisely to say that the structure belongs equally to formal and objective reality and that it gives rise to the very distinction between them. If objective reality is best characterized as *Inhaltlichkeit* (contentfulness) and formal reality as *Sachhaltigkeit* (substantiality), this structure that underlies both terms and the difference between is what Hegel calls *die Sache*

---

22 The first significant occurrence in the body of the work is at GW 9:131, at the transition from self-consciousness to reason; after that it comes to play an important role in characterizing shapes of consciousness and marking their advance.

selbst, variously (but sometimes misleadingly) translated as "the matter at hand" or "the thing itself."

One of the most compact, but also most conspicuous of Hegel's presentations of this idea is to be found in the Preface to the *Phenomenology,* which was intended to introduce both that work and the projected second volume that would have included both the speculative logic and the philosophies of nature and spirit (cf. GW 9:446–47). Despite its length and the breadth of topics it addresses, the Preface can justly be said to be devoted to the exposition of the single idea that substance is subject, and to the methodological consequences of that idea.

That "the true shape in which truth exists can only be the scientific system of truth" (GW 9:11/§5); that "the true is the whole" (GW 9:19/§20); that speculative philosophy must recognize and strive to fulfill the understanding's (i.e. finite cognition's) demand for a "ladder" (GW 9:23/§26) to the standpoint of science – these are each a direct consequence of the conception upon which, as Hegel says, "everything turns," namely, that "the true must be grasped and expressed not as *substance,* but equally as *subject*" (GW 9:18/§17). Hegel's criticisms of his philosophical contemporaries – both those who eschew discursive reason in favor of either religious faith or intellectual intuition as well as those who cement themselves into the supposedly secure bastion of common sense allied with the unassailable truths of mathematics, empirical and pure natural science, and history – also flow from this central conviction. It is therefore important to understand exactly what it signifies.

"Substantiality," Hegel tells us, is a form that characterizes *the immediate* as such, be it the immediacy *of* knowing or immediacy as it is *for* knowing (GW 9:18/§17). To grasp "the true" or the absolute as *merely* substantial is thus to grasp it either as pure being (e.g. with the Eleatics, with Spinoza, or as Schelling does when he conceives the absolute as an "indifference point") or as a pure or absolute I in the manner of the early Fichte. The former is immediacy *for* knowing (objectivity in one-sided abstraction from its being known). The latter is the immediacy *of* knowing: the spontaneity of self-positing in one-sided abstraction from the *difference* with which self-positing is identical. (This, to reiterate, is a concomitant of the duality of formal/objective reality that goes into the self-constitution of thinking.) In both cases, objective reality is reduced to, or rather eliminated in favor of, formal reality pure and simple, be it the formal reality of the given or that of spontaneity. In this Hegel would seem to follow Jacobi's critical diagnosis of Fichtean idealism as "inverted Spinozism" (cf. Jacobi's *Sendschreiben an Fichte* [FHJW II, 1:195]). On the other side, the ecstatic identification with nature, substance, or the "*Sein in allem Dasein*," if such can indeed be achieved, is the death of the self, longing for which Schelling, in the *Letters on Dogmatism and Criticism*, recognizes as one source of his own and his contemporaries' enthusiasm for Spinoza.[23] More importantly yet, to conceive of oneself as constituted originally in the (alleged) pure self-identity of an absolute I is also to negate the self and be plunged into nihilism (as Fichte himself appears to acknowledge at the end of Book II of *The Vocation of Man*, although he develops this as a consequence of reducing formal to objective reality: cf. GA I, 6:249–52).

We must grasp, therefore, that Hegel's rejection of immediacy, that is, the "form of substantiality" (GW 15:13), is motivated by metaphysical concerns with the constitution of selfhood as well as by the epistemological concerns that have frequently been identified as the sole motivation behind it. The two sets of concerns are in fact intimately linked. To take the decisive case as an example, Hegel's criticism of intellectual intuition as the proposed methodological basis of speculative science certainly has to do with the question whether and how such intuition (assuming it to be possible, as Hegel seems to acknowledge) could serve to justify claims to science and allow scientific knowledge to be appropriated in a universal, public sphere devoid of esotericism.[24] Paired with this question, however, is Hegel's certainty that as a form or mode of consciousness, intuition necessarily imparts to the object of knowing the form of a self-identical "substantial" thing that is immediate *in the metaphysical sense*. The subjectivity of substance cannot be "apprehended and expressed" in an intuitive mode, despite what its advocates may say about the intentional content of their knowledge.[25] For we cannot merely *see* or intuit the self-differentiating structure of subjectivity; as the structure/dynamic of *thinking*, that structure can

---

23 Cf. SW I, 1:208; also see his letter to Hegel of February 4, 1795, where he insists that "our highest goal is the destruction of personality" (HBr 1:22).

24 For Hegel's acknowledgement of the possibility of intellectual intuition see, e.g., GW 9:19; 15:10; on the epistemological difficulties of this alleged faculty, see Kenneth Westphal, "Kant, Hegel, and the Fate of 'the' Intuitive Intellect," in S. Sedgwick (ed.), *The Reception of Kant's Critical Philosophy: Fichte, Schelling, and Hegel* (Cambridge University Press 2000), 283–305. The imperative that science must be capable of being appropriated universally by the understanding (i.e. finite cognition) is stated at GW 9:15–16.

25 Cf. once again GW 15:9, 10–11, 13.

only be *thought*. But this specific epistemological concern is not in the first instance motivated by worries over justification, but by the sense that intuition as a mode of awareness systematically distorts the *Sache* of speculative science. Rather like optical illusions and other cases of systematically non-veridical perception, where the content of perception persists in spite of our belief in its non-veridicality, intellectual intuition *presents* the absolute in the non-veridical form of (mere) being or substance, despite the philosopher's protestations about the subjectivity of the absolute. But if the absolute depends for its actualization on being *veridically present in consciousness*, as I am suggesting Hegel believes, intuition must be abandoned as an inadequate means to this dually epistemological and metaphysical end (GW 9:18/§§17–18).

The key assumption here is that the formal reality of the absolute depends on its objective reality, or more specifically on its being present as an objective reality *of the right kind*, one that veridically presents it or adequately corresponds to it. This is what Hegel means by "the true" or "speculative truth." Now this constitutes a new turn in the dialectical structure of thinking sketched above. There the formal reality of thinking depended on its objective reality, that is, on self-consciousness. No further restraints were placed on the manner in which formal reality must be present to itself, and one could as well imagine it to be sheer presence in inner sense, as Kant sometimes seems to allow. By contrast, what is now being said is that "the true" depends, for its formal reality or existence, on being present to consciousness as an objective reality of a certain character and with certain determinations. (Note that this is the aspect of material determination that led to *aporiae* when we first encountered it above.) With Hegel we can say, equivalently, either that "the scientific system of truth" is the only shape in which the true exists (i.e. has formal reality), or that qua subject the true is, *in itself*, in-and-for-itself, but that it is *actual* only in coming to be in-and-for-itself *for itself*. Intuition, however, is not a shape in which this can come to pass.

This brings us to the heart of Hegel's theory of representational content, which I first touched on in Chapter 2. Least controversially, the formal reality of thinking depends on its objective reality, for the reasons set out above. Somewhat more controversially, the formal reality of thinking depends on the presence of specific form-determinations in its objective reality, roughly corresponding to the Kantian categories or forms of understanding that Hegel calls finite thought-determinations. Most controversially, *all reality* ("the true," "the absolute") depends on the emergence of a difference between formal and objective reality such that formal reality *exists* just to the extent that it is *posited* in and through its objective reality, in other words as an object of knowing. In the more familiar terms of the history of philosophy, we might say that whole of reality is mind-dependent: idealism. The characterization is accurate, but potentially misleading insofar as the "Conceptual" structure exemplified in this *objectivation* of formal reality is extra-mental; that is, it is not bounded by the cognitive activity of finite subjects, but rather constitutes the space in which such subjects come to find themselves over against a world of finite things. As I will now go on to argue, this is the heart of Hegel's solution to the problem of the sensible manifold and the material determinateness of objective reality.

6.6. Hegel versus Spinoza and Kant: towards a more satisfying model of determinate substance and determinate consciousness

The most important thing to keep in mind in the following is that Hegel does not set out to derive the sensible manifold in its contingency, unless by this we mean the necessity of contingency as such.[26] Rather, the question throughout is how to think the material determinateness of objective reality *as objective*, that is, as constituting representational content, instead of being *merely* formal (nonrepresentational) reality with no fully intelligible role to play in the determinate cognition we obviously know to depend on it. The solution is going to be that formal reality as such (what Hegel calls "being" [*Sein*] or "substance") is by its very constitution determined to become objective reality; that is, the sensible manifold is *nothing but* the guise in which the necessary passing over of being-in-itself (substance) to being-for-itself (subject) is actualized. In Hegel's gnomic utterance, "The supersensible is therefore *appearance qua as appearance*" (GW 9:90/§147).[27]

---

26 Cf. Dieter Henrich, "Hegels Theorie über den Zufall," *Kantstudien* 50 (1958/59): 131–48; also see Konrad Utz, *Die Notwendigkeit des Zufalls: Hegels spekulative Dialektik in der Wissenschaft der Logik* (Paderborn: Schöningh 2001).

27 The conception I develop in the following shares features with Andreas Arndt's concept of "objective reflexion" in Hegel and post-Hegelian philosophy; see *Dialektik und Reflexion*, 164ff. As Arndt emphasizes, Hegel interprets the structure of reflection (what I am describing here as the dynamic genesis of objective content) as *ideal* but, crucially, objective in contrast to the "mental" reflection of finite subjects.

Hegel introduces the cell-form of this movement in sections 53 and 54 of the Preface: "The movement of being [*des Seienden*] consists partly in becoming other to itself and **thereby its own immanent content**; partly in taking back into itself this unfolding or this its determinate being [*Dasein*], i.e. it makes itself into a *moment* and simplifies itself into determinateness" (GW 9:38/§53; emphasis in bold added). Taking *Seiendes* to signify "substance" or whatever has the form of immediacy, this means that substance actualizes itself or has *existence* (*Dasein*) in being other than itself, that is, not-substance. Within the framework that Hegel has set up in the Preface, "not-substance" is co-extensive with "subjectivity," the latter being originally constituted as the positing of a *difference*. So what is being said is, inter alia, that the actuality of substance is its differentiation from itself or its existence (presence, *Dasein*) as subjectivity.

This is a difficult thought and not one that can be expected to be received as self-evident or even especially plausible. There are, however, a few things to be said in its favor. The first is that it associates the conception of thinking as the self-positing of difference (the original possibility of objective reality, as I argued above) directly with the notion that substance or being is the same self-positing of difference. Being, it might be said, is here conceived as numerically identical with the formal reality of thinking. This does not quite prove anything, but does indicate a coherence of this conception of being or substance with a conception of subjectivity that can be arrived at independently of it. The introjection, if you will, of this structure into substance is the germ of an explanation of the layered character of particulars as bare particulars on one level and bearers of properties on the other – an explanation that will ultimately assimilate the substance-attribute structure of "things" to the structure of intentionality.

Second, the original *determinateness* of being, the idea that substance is necessarily or essentially qualified by attributes (the view Hegel criticizes in Spinoza!), is built into this conception: substance is originally determinate in being *different* over against something other than itself. At least within a traditional, rationalist framework of metaphysics, this is one of the strong points of Hegel's conception. In contrast to Spinoza, for example, the difficulty of the determinateness and hence difference or plurality of attributes need not arise. This is a difficulty for Spinoza because he introduces the plurality of attributes by appealing to the perception some external intellect has of the essence of substance (E1d4). This raises the question whether the difference of attributes is merely ideal and hence in some sense external to substance (which for Spinoza is God). If so, this would have the discouraging consequence that God would be internally indeterminate. Alternatively, that difference might be grasped as *internal* to substance. In this case, divine unity and simplicity is rendered problematic at the least.[28] On the Hegelian conception, by contrast, the original determinateness of substance *just is* the existence of the intellect that finds itself outside (infinite) substance and therefore finite: in Hegel's technical terms, the determinateness of substance is identical to the existence of the *understanding* or *finite cognition*.

Third, then, and by the same token, the objective reality of substance, its being-for-consciousness, is identified with its *Dasein* in the threefold sense of actuality, concrete existence, and determinate being. The picture that emerges is one in which the material determinateness of objective reality – its content, or what it is *of* – is given immediately with this objective reality since objective reality itself constitutes, as a matter of metaphysical necessity, the determinateness of substance. However, it constitutes that determinateness not in the sense of a subjective, arbitrary act of thinking, but in the sense that objective reality or thinking itself, by virtue of its own metaphysical constitution *just is* the determinateness of substance or formal reality.

This last point can once again be clarified by reference to Spinoza. As I discussed at the beginning of this chapter, E2p7 famously enunciates the identity of the order and connection of ideas with that of extended things. As I pointed out, this proposition is both enriched and made problematic by the fact that ideas themselves constitute a formal reality, that of the attribute *cogitatio*, which by nature is

28 Noa Shein, "The False Dichotomy between Objective and Subjective Interpretations of Spinoza's Theory of Attributes," *British Journal for the History of Philosophy* 17:3 (2009): 505–32, has recently argued for the possibility of mediating between these views. Shein puts Hegel in the subjectivist camp, and rightly so; however, Hegel does not fall prey to the objections to the subjective interpretation since what he is urging is not primarily an epistemological interpretation. If one were to say, "Since the attributes are relative to the finite intellect, and the finite intellect cannot know God as he is in himself, the attributes cannot be an objective aspect of God's nature," then it could easily be disputed that Spinoza means finite intellect in E1d4 at all, and also that it is out of tune with the rest of Spinoza's philosophy to restrict knowledge in the way the interpretation suggests. (The latter would clearly also be out of tune with Hegel's philosophy.) But Hegel is asking (1) for a metaphysical account of the origin of the finite intellect within the infinity of the divine substance, and (2) for a deeper account of what it could mean for an infinite intellect (Hegelian "reason") to have perspective on itself as required by Spinoza's definition.

representational. Now to proclaim an identity in kind between causal links among ideas on the one hand and extended things on the other is by no means trivial. Even so, given the uniqueness of substance on Spinoza's monistic account, it is hardly a surprising consequence. The really hard problem is to understand the relation of ideas qua object-ive reality to extended things, in virtue of which they represent them (to consciousness). That kind of parallelism would be truly exciting. But if all Spinoza's basic conception warrants is the identity of ideas and extended things qua formal reality, then his position would in effect coincide with the position Donald Davidson championed as "anomalous monism."[29]

On the face of it, this may seem an odd thing to say. After all, Davidson posits only token-identity between physical and mental events, guar-anteeing that laws of nature (for which regularities between *types* is required) cannot be mapped onto the mind. In this way, anything that could count as a substantial psycho-physical determinism is precluded. Here Spinoza obviously differs from Davidson, at least as regards his intentions. However, if his doctrine of parallelism was confined merely to the relations among ideas and extended things respectively, and only insofar as they are regarded in their formal reality, then it would segregate the content-determinations of ideas (their objective reality) from the psycho-physical laws he is looking for. Clearly, this would undermine the neo-Stoic epistemological realism Spinoza intends, opening the door instead to the Cartesian skepticism he meant to obviate.[30] This would be a dissatisfying result all round.

Once again, however, these difficulties do not arise on the Hegelian conception. Spinoza's substance-attribute model of the absolute and the parallelism associated with it is replaced by some-thing like an emergentist account,[31] according to which the counter-part to Spinoza's "order of ideas," understood as objective reality, is an actualization of the formal reality of the Hegelian counterpart to "substance," representing what Hegel calls its "unfolding" or grad-ual self-determination. Owing to the processual character of this

29 Donald Davidson, "Mental Events," in *Essays on Actions and Events* (Oxford University Press 1980), 217–24.

30 Davidson obviates that kind of skepticism in his own fashion by taking issue with scheme–content dualism and offering an externalist account of the (self-) ascription of propositional attitudes: see "On the Very Idea of a Conceptual Scheme," in *Inquiries into Truth and Interpretation* (Oxford University Press 1984), 183–98.

31 Cf. Hegel's use in the Preface, unusual for its time, of the term *emergieren* (GW 9:39).

self-determination, there is room here both for error and skepticism as well as for truth and the full speculative identity between thought in its objective reality (representational content) and the formal reality of substance.

Returning to the main line of argument, then, Hegel's hypothesis is that substance exists and is actual ("*ist da*" in the complex meaning of this Hegelian locution, which includes the component of determinateness) as objective reality or thinking.[32] We can flesh this out by considering the "second part" of the moment of being or immediacy, namely its "taking its unfolding or existence back into itself" so as to reduce itself to a "moment" and "simplify itself into determinateness." Strictly speaking, this is not of course a second *part* or *phase* of the movement, but a second aspect or way of describing it.

The self-positing of difference which lets objective reality emerge *as the sole and actual determinateness* of substance is, as noted above in my discussion of spontaneous thought and the structure of self-consciousness, a difference that is present to spontaneity as the difference that it is: the very existence of rational spontaneity is constituted by its determinative activity, and that determinative activity per se constitutes objective reality, in which spontaneity is in turn present to itself *both* as distinct from representational content *and* as identical with the content which is its consciousness of self.

In the midst of this highly abstract structural description, we can touch familiar ground by drawing once again on Kantian terminology. Self-conscious spontaneity is originally present to itself in and through the activity of objective determination, as Kant indicates somewhat elliptically at B153–5. Yet as Eric Watkins brings out clearly, the spontaneous activity of which we are aware in the non-sensible, purely intellectual consciousness of apperception is itself fully indeterminate:

> On Kant's account, there is something very special about the self or at least about our mode of conscious access to it. Since it is not a directly observable object, but rather, insofar as we can be aware of it at all, issues in an activity rather than a determinate state of an object, it is not something that can be described by using the same concepts that apply to the *determinate* states of external objects ... [A]s a consequence of this fact, the self or the synthetic activity that we are aware of in self-consciousness is neither a *determinate* phenomenon nor a noumenon.[33]

---

32 On the tight link between determinateness and *Dasein*, see GW 21:96–98.
33 Watkins, *Kant and the Metaphysics of Causality*, 280; emphasis added.

At the same time, however, the spontaneous activity here attributed to a substantial self that is meant somehow to be distinct from this activity, consists precisely in the *creation* of *determinate* objective contents of representation and it is accessible to awareness exactly insofar as it engages in this activity of determination. One can of course hold on to Kant's distinctions in this context between activity and passivity, on the one hand, and between an indeterminate substance and its determinate effects, on the other. This way of describing apperceptive awareness of spontaneity accords, however uneasily, with our common-sense, categorially structured perception of external objects. Yet I think it is fair to observe, in a Hegelian spirit, that the introduction of these terms (themselves laden with metaphysical assumptions) obscures the actual structure or dynamic of spontaneous self-determination. It conceals the way in which the substantial I that is here presupposed as the source of spontaneous activity and as indifferently capable of acting or not, really only exists as anything determinate at all through the mediation of its own spontaneous positing of determinate objectivity and hence also of itself as distinct therefrom. Hegel's logic of autonomous negation allows him to describe this dynamic and the structure that represents it.

Kant's methodologically uncontrolled introduction of distinctions is meant, in effect, to tame the paradoxical structure of apperception. Even as we partially abstract from his terms, however, we can still recognize Kant's account of apperception as an important source of plausibility for Hegel's terse description of the movement by which *substance* (*Seiendes* in the passage quoted above) posits itself as *content*. Echoing Kant, we may say that it is by being categorized and rendered into thought, understanding, that substance "returns into itself" as a simple determinateness and posits itself as (its own) content. We must nevertheless be careful to respect the fact that Hegel renders his description of that movement in terms that make no reference to mental operations. An interpretation sympathetic to his intentions will see in this movement a template not merely for the genesis of self-consciousness (the Kant-problem), but equally for the genesis of determinate substantiality (the Spinoza-problem). Hegel's bold thesis is that determinateness in general can and must be spelled out in terms of the relation between formal and objective reality (substance and subject), that this relation is the source of all determinateness including that of its own relata.

6.7. Self-determination and the absolutely negative spontaneity of the Concept

We now have what is basically the whole story about the relation between formal and objective reality that I have used to frame my analysis of Hegel's project and to situate it in the broader context of rationalist metaphysics and Kant's transcendental idealism. All that is missing are two crucial pieces: first, why does this "movement" of determination get started in the first place: in Leibniz' words, why is there something rather than nothing? And second, how is this a solution to the problem of the sensible manifold or the material determinateness of objective reality?

The elements for answering the first question are contained in section 54 of the Preface. There Hegel begins by setting out a fundamental relation of synonymy between the three terms substance (*Sein*), self-identity (*Sichselbstgleichheit*), and immediacy. To be is to be self-identical and identity is to be conceived as non-relationality or, to the extent that it belongs in the class of relations generally, as the negation of relation as such; this last point is what justifies the equation of being and identity with immediacy.[34] Accordingly, the negation of self-identity is to be understood as synonymous with the negation of being or substance; the further negation of immediacy that is also entailed by this synonymy is also independently plausible, on the grounds that to be mediated and hence in some regard ontologically dependent is *not to be*, that is, not to exist with the independence (immediacy) characteristic of *substances*. Properties, whose existence is mediated by their relation of inherence in a substance, cannot be said not to have any being *at all*, but they certainly have a lesser degree of being than the substances in which they inhere. Mediation, Hegel says, is the "dissolution" of an existence or determinate being (*Dasein*: GW 9:40/§55).

In a step he does not bother to justify, Hegel asserts that self-identity is pure abstraction and that pure abstraction is what thinking is; therefore, he infers, substance is identical in its essence to thinking. This assertion is by no means arbitrary or ad hoc. The context that motivates it has in fact been playing an important role throughout the discussion

---

34 The reasoning is that identity must be counted as a relation because it is the negation of a relation (namely, that of difference), and the negation of a relation is itself a relation. Cf. Colin McGinn, *Logical Properties* (Oxford University Press 2000), 12, who introduces this argument in response to those who, like the early Wittgenstein, deny that identity is a relation.

so far. Recall first that the *form* of substantiality is equally common both to an object of thought such as Spinozist substance or Schelling's indifference point, on the one hand, and to the Fichtean absolute I, on the other. We should conceive the presence of this form of substantiality within thought as a reflection or projection of the dialectical structure of thinking itself. That structure, recall further, is the expression of the fact that the formal reality of the act of spontaneity depends for its constitution on its objective reality or the presence of its difference to itself. The self-positing of the formal reality of thinking, that is, the positing of the "absolute" I, is (as the early Fichte would say) the result of an "intellectual intuition" or "absolute abstraction" from difference or mediation. As just stated, however, difference or mediation is inseparably bound up with the objective reality that is part of the very constitution of the I, and so it is internal to the I as well. So thinking the I as self-identical is to render it falsely into the form of a substance. By the same token, then, the act of absolute abstraction that Fichte (to a certain extent rightly) sees as integral to the act of self-constitution, just is the positing of the substantial form (i.e. self-identity, immediacy). The point is that this positing as self-identical is (a) conditioned by the difference and mediation here under discussion, and more importantly (b) itself the direct, if unwitting, expression of the unity of the Concept to which that difference and mediation belong by virtue of absolute negativity. Fichte's error, from the Hegelian point of view, is to have grasped the elements of this dynamic relation in the categories of finite cognition.

Now, paradoxically, in the absolute abstraction from difference and objective reality, I cease to exist as a self, as an I. This seems to be the common conviction of Fichte and Schelling (as indicated before) as well as of Hegel. For it coincides with an utter negation of determinateness and one cannot, after all, be a self without being any particular self. So the possibility of the formal reality of the I in its self-identity and immediacy is at once also the negation of the I. Similarly, the positing of substance in its self-identity and immediacy, in abstraction from the difference that constitutes thinking *and all determinateness*, renders it indeterminate and thus tantamount to nothing, and this of course is his recurring criticism of Spinoza's nihilism, acosmism, or inability to derive particularity and determinateness from within substance as he understands it.[35] For Hegel, this state of affairs means that

---

35 Hegel is thus very close to Jacobi in this aspect of his Spinoza-critique, as his remarks in GW 15:10–11 and his discussion of acosmism (e.g. ENC §§50, 151; TW 20:163,

the positing of self-identity (or synonymously: substantiality) is an *absolute negation* of it. Not surprisingly, in light of the foregoing, this absolute negation is, immediately and for itself, precisely the self-positing of difference that was imputed to being at the outset as the movement inherent in it. Absolute negation is thus the source of determinacy, subjectivity, existence (*Dasein*).

That is the answer to the first question about how the whole story of determinate content is supposed to get started. The final step is now to consider how this move can also explain the existence of the sensible manifold as the material determination of objective reality.

6.8. Hegel, Schellingian *Naturphilosophie*, and the solution to the problem of the sensible manifold

In this section I am going to follow what may initially appear to be a roundabout path through some of the basic features and problems of Schellingian *Naturphilosophie*, in order to arrive at an understanding of just how Hegel can claim fully to accommodate the material determinateness of the sensible manifold without falling either into an insane deductivism about contingent empirical facts (contra early Schelling, for example) or into a reductive physicalism or determinism about the internal relation between cognition and natural processes (contra Spinoza). As we will see, this path will quickly lead us to some of the most relevant implications of his philosophy for contemporary metaphysics and epistemology: the integration of intentionality and naturalism in a view that preserves our epistemic contact with the world while balancing the limitations of (finite) cognition with a robust commitment to knowledge of the unconditioned.

I emphasized above that Hegel does not take it upon himself to deduce particular qualities. If he ever was in the business of trying to deduce individuals like Krug's quill pen, he had gotten out of it

---

171, 191) show, and there are systematic reasons to follow Jacobi and Hegel in the charge of nihilism against Spinoza: see Michael della Rocca, "Rationalism, Idealism, Monism, and Beyond," in Eckart Förster and Yitzhak Melamed (eds.), *Spinoza and German Idealism* (Cambridge University Press 2012), 7–26. As I suggested in Chapter 5, however, part of what Hegel rejects in Jacobi is his complementary, but structurally identical positing of particularity "in substantial form," which prevents him from advancing beyond the conceptual framework he thus shares with Spinoza and rendering him helpless to distance himself from it in any conceptually determinate fashion.

by the time of the *Phenomenology*.[36] The philosopher's task is rather
to deduce (1) the necessity of appearance in general (i.e. that everything that *is* must by necessity appear), such that (2) the contingent
qualities that materially determine appearance (the sensible manifold) are from the beginning constituted as having objective import
or signification (in other words, they should be shown to be, *by their
very nature*, embedded in a structure of intentionality) and (3) as having time, space, and the thought-determinations (Kant's categories)
as their form-determinations. This third aspect of the task may be
considered as already partially completed by Kant. To the extent that
the form-determinations of objective reality just are determinations
of the formal reality of the act of spontaneity in which the self posits
itself in its difference from the object of thought, they are built into
that object from the beginning. Similarly, the first aspect of the task
has effectively been carried out above: to the extent that substance
(being) gains determinateness as such only through its movement of
differing from itself in objective reality or consciousness, the necessity of appearance has also been deduced. What is left, therefore, is
to explain why that appearance is a *concrete, natural world* of sensuous
determinations rather than a purely formal and to that extent empty
self-consciousness.

   This task is the most difficult that Kant's idealist successors dared to
undertake. Fichte sought to deduce sensation by way of his theory of the
oscillation (*Schweben*) of imagination between the opposite extremes
of I and non-I: every point at which the mind posits the opposition as
such, it leaves what he calls a "trace" (*Spur*) of that oscillation, and this
trace is what shows up in consciousness "as a something, as a possible
material" (GA I, 3:147; cf. GA I, 2:434–46). Schelling, in the *System of
Transcendental Idealism*, follows Fichte in the essentials: "The incomprehensibility of the production (creation) of matter even with respect to
its material vanishes in light of this explanation. All material is merely
the expression of a balance of opposing activities that mutually reduce
each other to a mere substrate of activities" (SW I, 3:400).[37]

---

36 Henrich makes this point in "Hegels Theorie über den Zufall." For Hegel's reply to
   Krug's challenge to deduce his quill pen, see GW 4:174–87, where he still seems to hold
   such a deduction possible in principle. Some of Hegel's remarks in the *Phenomenology*
   (GW 9:65, 70) make clear that he has given up his earlier stance on the possibility of
   deducing sensuous individuals.
37 While Schelling's construction is clearly influenced by Fichte's theory of imaginative
   oscillation, he is also following the Kant's precedent in constructing matter from

Schelling explicitly identifies this "stuff" or substrate with sensation (I, 3:404), the nature and necessity of which he thus finds intelligible. The general fact that the I always already finds itself limited and determined by something which in natural consciousness appears as external and alien to the self (namely, matter) is explicable from Schelling's transcendental perspective as the result of the self's own activity of self-constitution. Schelling admits, however, that "limitation in general leaves the determinate limitation completely open, even though both arise through one and the same act. Both together, that the determinate limitation cannot be determined by the limitation in general, and that it nevertheless arises at the same time and by the same act, make it incomprehensible and inexplicable for philosophy" (1,3:410).

W. T. Krug, who refers to this passage, was right to object that this incomprehensibility is a sign that something is amiss with the transcendental idealism of Fichte and Schelling, who believe it is possible to dispose with things in themselves and supply the full material determinateness of experience from within the I.[38] Schelling's increasing insistence (in opposition to Fichte, who will soon break with him over this very issue)[39] that transcendental idealism must be complemented by a philosophy of nature that explains the emergence of subjectivity from basic forces of matter, may be viewed as a response to this difficulty: the self always already finds itself over against a concrete world of sensuous appearances that, rightly understood, constitute the external history of its own emergence.

Now the point of rehearsing the outlines of this strand of post-Kantian philosophy from Fichte to Schelling is to suggest that Hegel essentially agrees with Schelling's *naturphilosophische* strategy for deriving the material determinations of objective reality from a source that is external to the *finite* subject. The fact that Hegel included *Naturphilosophie* as part of his system of science from his first years in Jena (1801/2) till the last edition of the *Encyclopedia* (1830) shows as much. His quarrel with Schelling focuses exclusively on the methodological details

opposing forces of attraction and repulsion. There is no doubt that Schelling recognized the deep structural analogy between Kantian matter and Fichtean imagination. Cf. Förster, *The Twenty-Five Years*, 230–46.

38 Wilhelm Traugott Krug, *Briefe über den neuesten Idealismus* (Leipzig: Müller 1801), 22–24.

39 See the correspondence between Fichte and Schelling in Walter Jaeschke (ed.), *Der Streit um die Gestalt einer ersten Philosophie (1799–1807)*, vol. II (Hamburg: Meiner 1993), esp. 216, 222–30.

of this strategy. The difficulties lie (1) in explaining the emergence of subjectivity (i.e. objective reality as such), which is essentially *difference*, on the basis of an absolute conceived as *indifference*; (2) in the systematic non-veridicality of intuition as a form of awareness of subjectivity, due to intuition's essentially "substantial form"; and finally (3) the formalism of the epigones that Hegel perceived as the inevitable fate of *Naturphilosophie* as long as it remained tied to an inadequate methodological basis.[40]

The first two points of criticism have already been discussed above. It is the critique of formalism that will take us the rest of the way to Hegel's theory of the material determinateness of objective reality.

As with the critique of Schellingian intuitionism, the critique of formalism also has both an epistemological and a metaphysical aspect. The epistemological aspect concerns the alleged arbitrariness and superficiality with which *Naturphilosophie* was being practiced by Schelling's followers, and its exclusive reliance on analogical reasoning – a form of argument Hegel elsewhere treats as closely allied with induction and hence unsuitable in rigorously *a priori* contexts (cf. GW 12:113–18; ENC §190). More to the present point, however, is that the source of this formalism lies in an insufficient theory of the *genesis of content* (*objective reality*). Because Schelling can give no account of why the indifferent absolute should differentiate itself, neither can he account for (a) why there should be a sphere of nature that (b) presents itself as the material object of some mind. It is well and good to assume the opposing activities of self-consciousness on the one hand and the opposing forces of matter on the other, and to posit an analogy between them; Hegel need have no problem accepting that. But to interpret this parallelism as more than brute coincidence, some account is required of why this twofold, polar duality arises in the first place. In short, there has to be an account of why precisely the complex structure of the *Hegelian Concept* arises, for as I outlined in Chapters 1 and 5, the structure of the Concept is precisely this unity of two polar relations unfolding in and through each other.

By this point in the overall account of Hegel's philosophy it should come as no surprise that he believes himself to be in a more advantageous position for explaining this structure and the necessity

---

40 Hegel explicitly limits the aim and scope of his Schelling critique in §52 of the Preface to the *Phenomenology*.

that generates it, *owing to the theory of absolute negativity*. In order to be determinate at all and thus not to be nothing, substance (being) must become other than itself by "passing over" into objective reality (thought). This positing of difference (which Hegel accordingly refers to as *determinate negation*) is radical. It is the self-positing of the absolute as the absolutely other: multiplicity, contingency, in short a qualitative manifold whose only common denominator is its objectivity (i.e. embeddedness in the structure of intentionality into which being is "unfolding" itself). Nonetheless, as the *self*-positing of the absolute, this manifold is also the immediate expression of the absolute negativity as which it emerges.

Hegel repeatedly emphasizes the essentially negative, restless character of the manifold as a constant passing over and passing away; he would regard the notion of a purely positive manifold as a contradiction in terms. Indeed, this is precisely how he derives the concept of time:

> Space is immediately existing quantity in which everything maintains a positive subsistence [*Bestehen*] and even the limit is present in the form of positive subsistence; that is the shortcoming of space. Space is this contradiction of having negation in it [*an ihm*], but in such a way that this negation disintegrates into indifferent subsistence. Therefore, since space is only this internal negation of itself, the self-sublation of its moments is the truth of space; now, time is precisely the existence [*Dasein*] of this continually self-sublation ... it is the negation of the negation, self-relating negation. (ENC §257A)

Hegel uses this idea of the immanent negativity of the *eo ipso temporal* manifold in order to link it directly to a further element within the dynamic of absolute negativity, namely the positing of a purely self-identical, affirmative pole. Things do not come to be and pass away *in* time, he asserts; rather time itself is this coming to be and passing away, and he therefore characterizes time as "das *seiende Abstrahieren*" (ENC §258R), the concretely existing process of abstraction. This means two things. On the one side, the temporal process must be seen as the emergence of something radically indeterminate in itself, something abstract, namely, the purely self-identical pole of being with no internal differentiation. On the other side, the fact that this affirmative pole is continuously being posited (by abstraction) as the concomitant of negation should be seen as a manifestation of the absolutely negative logic of the Concept itself:

The reason why the finite is perishable and *temporal* is that, unlike the concept, it is not in itself total negativity; rather, although it has this negativity in itself as its universal essence, the finite is one-sided and does not conform to it and therefore stands to it in the relation of a *power* to which it is subject. But the Concept ... is absolute negativity and freedom in and for itself, and time is therefore not a power it wields nor is the Concept in time and something temporal, but rather *the Concept* is itself the power of time, which is only this negativity as externality. (ENC§258R)[41]

Now as we saw in Chapter 1, one of the most striking aspects of the unfolding of the logic of autonomous negation is that the two poles, affirmation-identity and negation-difference, truly fall asunder to appear as two fully disparate, merely externally related terms. This *dis*integration of the structure is not a flaw in its logical construction, but a highly significant moment in its dynamic that will absorb Schelling's idea of an essential but incomprehensible limitation. I would like to consider this feature from three different perspectives.

First, this logically necessitated disintegration of the Conceptual structure is what Hegel evokes in the *Science of Logic* by the metaphor of the Idea "freely releasing" itself into an existence of spatio-temporal contingency: "For the sake of this freedom, the *form of* [the Idea's] *determinateness* is just as absolutely free – the *externality of space and time* existing absolutely for themselves and without subjectivity" (GW 12:253). At the conclusion of the *Phenomenology* he chooses a related metaphor of sacrifice: "The self-knowing Spirit knows not only itself but also the negative of itself, or its limit: to know one's limit is to know how to sacrifice oneself. This sacrifice is the externalization in which Spirit displays the process of its becoming Spirit in the form of *free contingent happening*, intuiting its pure Self as time outside of it, and equally its Being as space" (GW 9:433/§807). This metaphor takes up in a very precise way the Schellingian idea of a limitation that is posited necessarily, but posited as completely contingent in its concrete qualities. I would suggest, however, that Hegel improves on Schelling's conception here by incorporating this free, contingent, external happening into the unfolding logic of absolute negation as one of its logically derivable moments.

The second point follows directly on the first. As an *objective reality* this logically incorporated moment of disintegration is present in the form

---

41 Cf. Arndt's critical remarks on this passage in *Dialektik und Reflexion*, 188.

of *sensuous consciousness* (GW 9:432/§806), with which Hegel begins the *Phenomenology*. The dialectic of sense certainty is set into motion by the assumption, on the part of consciousness, that it confronts being as a positive manifold of substantial determinateness. Over the course of Hegel's highly compact exposition of the dialectic, sensuous conscious-ness is induced to recognize that its own experience is characterized by a disintegration or diremption of its object into two radically disparate poles: an unstable manifold of radically insubstantial – *nichtige* (GW 9:69/§109) – determinations on the one side, and an abiding, substan-tial, but wholly abstract and indeterminate unity – pure being – on the other. This is precisely the concretely existing process of abstraction as which Hegel characterizes time in the passage quoted above. In a cer-tain sense, the Concept and its character of self-relation is completely lost and absent in this opening movement of the book. The realm of sense particulars is completely lacking in necessary connection (cf. GW 9:71/§111), and the affirmative unity of the Concept has been occluded by an empty, internally undifferentiated notion of being. But that is just what it means for Spirit to have "sacrificed" or "freely released" itself, and at a more literal level it is the expression of the structural disinte-gration that is built into the dynamic of absolute negativity.

If we look carefully we can discern here the problem of the manifold that we have been tracking throughout this chapter. On the one hand there is the problem of how the manifold is related to (Spinozistic) substance as its own determination; in Hegel's words, "Substance, taken by itself, would be intuition devoid of content, or the intuition of a content which, as determinate, would be only accidental and would lack necessity" (GW 9:431/§803). In other words, the manifold appears here, paradoxically, as the *necessary* concomitant of substance, but as wholly *outside its essence*. The qualitative relationship between substance and any *positive* determination is therefore fundamentally *contingent*, while its only *necessary* determination is fundamentally *nega-tive*, that is, to emerge as the "abstraction" of the process of coming to be and passing away constituted by its contingent positive determin-ations. On the other hand, this same falling asunder is expressed as a quasi-Fichtean "I" that also lacks any essential relation to the sensible manifold through which it is individuated.[42] For the "truth" of sense

---

42 I work out this interpretation in more detail in Brady Bowman, "Spinozist Pantheism and the Truth of Sense Certainty," *Journal of the History of Philosophy* 52 (2012): 85–110; see also Bowman, *Sinnliche Gewißheit*.

certainty, the sensible manifold has no role to play as materially determinate content.

This brings me to the third and final point. In this situation of disintegration, which for finite subjectivity is the situation in which it first becomes aware of itself, it can seem as though we were dealing with an empty substantiality or subjectivity, on the one hand, and a purely external manifold, on the other, with no account of the vital relation we know them from experience to have: "Knowledge would seem to have arrived at things, at the difference from itself, and at the difference of manifold things, without comprehending how and whence they came" (GW 9:431/§803). Hegel suggests that we switch perspectives and consider the restless negativity of the manifold itself as the beginning of the internal (self-) relation that seems to be lacking. The logic of absolute negation allows him to do this.

Hegel insists both that time is the non-conceptual existence of the Concept itself (e.g. GW 9:429/§801) and that time is the form in which the "I" is sensuously present to itself (GW 9:429/§801). Both the emptiness of the absolute that emerges in sense certainty and the apparent insubstantiality or nullity of the sensible manifold are traces or symptoms that this merely determinate, external-relational negativity is not yet the "terrific power" (GW 9:27/§32) of the absolutely negative Concept itself. In its presence in actuality, absolute negativity is *neither* subject *nor* substance (taken in this merely determinately negative sense), *but the finite understanding's freely initiated act of cognizing the manifold.* Viewed from the proper perspective, there is really no difference between the infinite Idea's "free release" of itself and the finite understanding's free decision to understand what is originally present to it as the sensible manifold. Of course, the knowing of such finite things by the finite understanding is not the knowing of speculative science; that decision to understand can find no finite satisfaction. But neither is it an activity situated outside the essence of the Idea and its speculative knowledge of itself; it is the object of Spirit's self-knowledge:

> Spirit ... has shown itself to us to be neither merely the withdrawal of self-consciousness into its pure inwardness, nor the mere submergence of self-consciousness into substance, and the non-being of its difference; but Spirit is *this movement* of the Self which empties itself of itself and sinks itself into its substance, and also, as Subject, has gone out of that substance into itself, making the substance into an object and a content at the same time as it cancels this difference between objectivity and content. (GW 9:431/§804)

It may seem that, after the moments of identity-affirmation and difference-negation have fallen asunder, the act of positing their relation as the Concept's own relation-to-self is just that: *an act of positing*, a *postulation*. There is a sense in which that appearance is not deceiving. It is up to the finite understanding *actually to achieve* that self-relation within the process of the manifold. This is a task, indeed an infinite task; the manifold resists unification and complete determination *essentially*. And yet the assumption of the task is itself the activation or actualization of a structure that guarantees the process of the manifold an absolute meaning and value in and for itself as the life of the absolute. This is why Hegel can say that the absolute "is essentially a result, that only in the end is it what it truly is; and that precisely in this consists its nature, namely, to be actual, subject, the spontaneous becoming of itself" (GW 9:19/§20).[43]

6.9. Hegel's speculative logic of content: from appearance to reality, and back again

The necessity of appearance in general or objective reality, as materially determined by a contingent, sensible manifold of qualities in space-time and conforming to the pure thought-determinations is demonstrated in the abstract in the *Science of Logic*. Speculative logic can therefore accurately be described as a *logic of content*; not however (or at least not exclusively) as a transcendental logic of the categorial content that finite subjectivity is constrained by its own nature to think, but as a metaphysical logic of what has to be there to be thought, and of the way that thought has to be there for determinacy to arise.[44] Of course, once it is clearly seen which problem Hegelian philosophy undertakes to solve, this distinction can be recognized as a mere difference in emphasis.

There is an interesting moral to this story that I would like to bring out by way of conclusion. Hegel envisions speculative philosophy as an account of the dual necessity of appearance or objective reality and a finite understanding that posits itself as a substantial self or formal

43 I therefore believe that Hegel's own conception of finite cognition and its relation to the absolute is actually already much closer to the conception with which Arndt wants to replace it and in regard to which he criticizes Hegel for having refused even to acknowledge it: cf. *Reflexion und Dialektik*, 220–30.

44 In this my interpretation differs from that of Pirmin Stekeler-Weithofer, *Hegels Analytische Philosophie: Die Wissenschaft der Logik als kritische Theorie der Bedeutung* (Paderborn, Munich, etc.: Schöningh 1992).

reality confronted on the other side by the formal reality of a substantial world – a thing in itself in the midst of other things in themselves. Such an account evades the formalism that hampered other incarnations of Kantian and post-Kantian idealism, in that it conceives formal and objective reality (substance and subject) as the merely apparently distinct sides of a Möbius strip-like fundamental reality: the Concept, absolute negativity, *die Sache selbst*. Self and world, subject and substance, are indeed distinct *moments* of the movement through which that reality unfolds, yet not such that the gap between form and matter, thought and sensation, knowing and nature that troubles Kantianism could open between them.

John McDowell has persuasively argued that Kant can be saved from psychologism and subjectivism only by rejecting transcendental idealism: the forms of intuition and conception must be understood to be the forms of the very things themselves if our beliefs are truly to count as knowledge. We must cease to think of objective reality as mere appearance as the Kantian framework requires us to do. McDowell sees Hegel's idealism as just such a radicalization of Kant.[45]

One aim of this book has been to argue that McDowell's compelling suggestion is practicable only by adopting a position at least as strong as that which informs Hegel's speculative dialectic. For that is what provides the theory of content required not only for the variety of realism favored by McDowell but also for any genuinely tenable conception of self-consciousness (at least any that starts with Kant). But if the speculative dialectic is the condition on which Kantian subjectivism and psychological formalism can alone be overcome, this has far-reaching consequences for the metaphysical status of those very finite things our knowledge is meant to reach.

After sketching his theory of absolute negativity as the source of all form and content in sections 54–55 of the Preface, Hegel turns in the latter part of section 55 to a discussion of Platonic realism. The significance that he should do so at all and the significance of what he has to say about it can hardly be exaggerated:

> Above we indicated the significance of the *understanding* with respect to the self-consciousness of substance; we can now see clearly from what has just been said its significance with respect to its [the understanding's] determination as something substantial [*als Seiender*]. – Determinate

---

45 McDowell, "Hegel's Radicalization of Kant"; cf. Chapter 3.

being [*Dasein*] is quality, self-identical determinateness or determinate simplicity, a determinate thought; this is the understanding of [i.e. the understanding *inhering in*] determinate being. It is thereby *Noûs*, as Anaxagoras first recognized the essence of things to be. Those who came after him comprehended [*begreifen*] the nature of determinate being more determinately as *eidos* or *idea*; that is, as *determinate universality*, as *kind* ...

Precisely because determinate being is determined as kind, it is a simple thought; *Noûs*, simplicity, is substance. By virtue of its simplicity or self-identity, it [substance] appears fixed and enduring. But this self-identity is no less negativity; therefore, that fixed determinate being passes over into its dissolution. Determinateness at first seems to be constituted only by relating to an *other*, and its movement thus seems imposed on it by an external power; but having its being-other in itself and being self-movement is just what is entailed by the *simplicity* of thinking itself. For this simplicity of thinking is the self-moving and self-differentiating thought, and its own interiority, the pure Concept. In this way then, understanding [or intelligibility: *Verständigkeit*] is a becoming, and as this becoming it is rationality [*Vernünftigkeit*]. (GW 9:40/§55)

I have quoted this lengthy passage in nearly its entirety because it expresses at once both Hegel's embrace of the realism that identifies objective insight with the formal reality or essence of what exists, and his demotion of the finite form and content of the known to a mere moment in the emergence of speculative truth. How so?

The "simple thoughts" Hegel refers to are moments in the unfolding, that is, in the absolute negativity of substance, that is, its self-positing as subject or objective reality. Now the core of self-positing as subject consists in the dialectic sketched out in my first discussion of sections 53–54 above. The formal reality or substantiality of the subject is posited only in and through its objective reality, that is, its appearance or presence to itself. This movement, in the final analysis, is all there is: it is *all reality* or *die Sache selbst*. While this is on the one side the key to grasping the full material and formal determinateness of objective reality – the point McDowell rightly urges against transcendental idealism – on the other side it entails that formal reality, the things themselves we justly take ourselves to know, are mere *appearance*, that is, *merely* objective reality. And the way we know this, according to Hegel, is by their dialectic, their passing-over and seeming or *Scheinen*, their dissolution. Indeed, Hegelian science consists in nothing other than the attempt to demonstrate precisely this fact and to exhibit its structure as "the Concept" or "the Idea."

The path to a robust realism beyond the *aporiae* of transcendental idealism therefore turns out to be a path that leads through that realism to what Robert Stern has called Hegel's *idealism of the finite*: the doctrine that the concrete world of seemingly rigid and permanent things is *nothing in itself*, that it has its ground in the deeper structure or movement Hegel calls the Concept or, equivalently, absolute negativity. Or to reverse the dictum cited above: the thing in itself is the appearance *as appearance*, that is, substance on its way to subjectivity.

Once spelled out, this radical doctrine reveals its distance from common sense, which as Hegel says must view speculative philosophy as being like an attempt to walk upside down (cf. GW 9:23). But if this book has been successful, I hope to have shown that just such a radical doctrine is required if the major stations of modern philosophy from Descartes through Spinoza to Kant are to be brought together within a single conceptual space and reconciled with the facts of our immediate experience of consciousness.

7

ABSOLUTE NEGATION AND THE
HISTORY OF LOGIC

7.1. "The true is the whole"

"The true is the whole" (GW 9:19/§20) is among the most eminently quotable of Hegelian *dicta*. But, we may ask, the whole *what*? Seemingly the most obvious is the answer, the whole *system*: "The true shape in which truth exists, can only be the scientific system of such truth" (GW 9:11/§5). Again, however, the answer leaves open the precise nature of the unity and totality that characterizes a system on Hegel's conception. So what is the authentically Hegelian conception of systematic unity and totality? The answer suggested by this book is that the system, in its fundamental and paradigmatic shape, is the dynamic of absolute negativity.[1] As a philosophical conception, absolute negativity can claim to delineate the process of organic self-differentiation and self-identification to a degree that is extraordinary for a purely discursive medium. Its logical unfolding allows for precise indication of its beginning and ending, and the clearly discernible phases of that unfolding allow us to distinguish characteristically different moments or configurations of its basic elements, which in turn can serve in the dialectical analysis of a host of more concrete phenomena. Furthermore, one of the unique features of the dynamic of absolute negativity is that among the phases through which it unfolds, the very disappearance of the overall shape, its vanishing by turns into simple

---

1 The intimate connection between negativity and systematic totality in Hegel is clearly recognized by Jean Hyppolite: *Logic and Existence*, trans. L. Lawlor and A. Sen (Albany: SUNY Press 1997), e.g. 97–101, and esp. 105–26, where Hyppolite discusses the differences between "speculative negation" and the "empirical negation" which he closely associates with Bergson and thus with traditional positive asymmetricalism. On the importance of this work in setting the agenda for French philosophy of difference see Lawlor's remarks in the Introduction, x–xiv.

undifferentiated unity and radically disparate multiplicity, and into manifestations of constitutively non-totalizable spheres like that of nature, are as it were *calculated in*. In the virtuosic hands of its inventor, this makes absolute negativity into a powerful conceptual resource.

Thus, the true is the unfolding of absolute negativity. The true *exists* in the shape of *its* scientific system. The special resonance of this formulation should be unmistakable. In the terms introduced in Chapter 6, truth may be said to be the adequate correspondence of formal and objective reality. There we saw that this relation, which is the condition of possibility for there being what we call *knowledge*, is a peculiarly complex and superficially paradoxical *metaphysical* state of affairs. Objective reality was described as the way in which formal reality achieves existence and determinateness – its way of positing itself as other than itself – while formal reality, in turn, was itself accordingly to be grasped as the emergence of objective reality. In this way, objective reality took on an extra-mental existence, or at least turned out not to be the exclusively intra-mental existence it was for Descartes and to some extent for Kant. Therefore, when Hegel speaks of the true *existing* in the shape of *its* system, we must not understand him to be talking merely about the way we must organize our (seemingly external) *knowledge* of the truth. The absolutely negative structure of the Hegelian true does, of course, mean that knowledge of the truth is *necessitated* by the truth, in other words that truth cannot go unknown; knowledge of the true enters into it, so to speak, as one of its metaphysical constituents.[2] More than that, however, it means that existence itself, what Hegel calls *Dasein* or determinate being, is structured at its core *as* truth. Intentionality, or the internal relation of objective and formal reality, is the structure of all being. To call one last time on the saying of Anaxagoras, "*Noûs*, thought, is the principle of the world ... the essence of the world is to be defined as thought" (GW 21:34). This thought is the thought of absolute negativity.[3]

From this metaphysical perspective on truth and knowledge, cognition ceases to appear as a narrowly mental, skull-bound process,

---

2 This difficult idea of knowledge (i.e. true thoughts) as being *necessitated* by truth is not peculiar to Hegel; it surfaces more recently, and controversially, in David M. Armstrong's theory of truth: see *Truth and Truthmakers* (Cambridge University Press 2004), 5–9.

3 Cf. Hegel's statement, "Things are a proposition" (*die Dinge sind ein Urteil*): ENC §§167–68.

becoming instead a deep and pervasive feature of the world; its place within the whole can therefore no longer be a narrowly epistemological question of certainty and justification. I say, "its place *within* the whole," for even as Hegel identifies it with the principle and essence of the world, its absolutely negative character also entails that it go out of itself and posit itself as a moment over against the whole of itself, and hence that it also exist in a guise of constitutive self-externality and incompleteness. This is finite cognition. Over the course of this book we have accordingly seen how Hegel mounts a systematic critique of finite cognition that does not treat it merely as a set of systematically false or distorted beliefs. Rather, when finite cognition comes to grasp itself most explicitly, namely in the *a priori* sciences of (pre-critical) metaphysics, pure natural science, and mathematics, the characteristic failings it exhibits reveal themselves to be symptoms of its *determinately* negative character and its origin in the structure of absolute negativity.

Thus, as we saw in Chapter 2, traditional metaphysics and category theory, even in their Kantian incarnation, fail to give a unified account of the categories and their real applicability: a convincing unifying principle is (on Hegel's view) lacking, and the dialectical contradictions that arise from the application of the categories to the real (i.e. the unconditional) can only be avoided by undermining the concept of knowledge itself (transcendental idealism and the problematic notion of "knowing" something that is *mere appearance*). Speculative science, by contrast, can draw on the concept of absolute negativity to generate a systematically unified list of categories and explain both their objective applicability and their inherent limitations in articulating the unconditional totality represented by the structure of absolute negativity and the Concept.

Pure natural science comes up against difficulties in the attempt to unify nature into a single whole by formulating a consistent system of deterministic laws of nature. Rather than attribute these difficulties to the finitude of the human understanding, pure and simple, Hegel suggests that we grasp finite cognition and nature as metaphysically correlative terms. On this view, nature as the object of finite cognition is intrinsically self-external, and its self-externality systematically prohibits its being whole or complete. Hence the incompletability of natural science. By drawing on the concept of absolute negativity, speculative science can explain this incompletability by interpreting the basic structure of nature (namely self-externality) as a moment with the total structure of the Concept or, equivalently, as a moment in the unfolding *whole* of absolute negativity.

We saw axiomatic Euclidean geometry to be the highest form of finite cognition. In deriving real definitions of its objects, geometry is able to achieve limited or finite totalities superior to anything available in traditional metaphysics or natural science. These real definitions show how the concept and the reality of their privileged objects (e.g. the triangle) are distinct aspects of a single whole in which the concept itself separates itself from the reality and then reproduces it from within. Herein, geometry is very much like speculative science. However, the geometrical method can never become a full-fledged model for philosophical cognition because it exhibits a variety of forms of self-externality that prevent it from achieving the degree of self-contained totality speculative science demands. By working out the ways in which geometrical cognition both intimates and falls short of the full structure of absolute negativity, Hegel shows its affinities with, and differences from, an authentic whole.

Finally, both Spinoza's model of the absolute as substance and Kant's model of the mind as a spontaneity dependent on external, non-intentional "stuff" for its content run into analogous problems. Neither can give an account of wholeness: Spinoza cannot explain why substance externalizes itself in determinate attributes and finite modes; Kant cannot explain why sensibility and understanding work together to produce a cognitive whole, the unity of consciousness. By analyzing both these two problems and Hegel's approach to the Concept and absolute negativity in the traditional terms "objective reality" and "formal reality," the resources are generated for resolving those difficulties and producing an integrated theory of intentionality and nature, mind and world, *subject* and *substance*.

Hence the *Problematik* in which Hegel's critique of finite cognition gains shape and philosophical interest is embedded in or, rather, is identical to the theory of absolute negativity and the metaphysics of the Concept.

7.2. Hegel's place in the history of thought on negation

Given the novelty and importance of the concept of negativity in Hegelian philosophy, it is natural to ask about Hegel's place in the history of philosophical thought on negation. In his exhaustive survey of that history, Lawrence Horn divides the gamut of theories into *symmetricalist* and *asymmetricalist* streams of thought.[4] Symmetricalists are those who hold that affirmation and negation are logically equip-rimordial acts, neither one reducible to the other; they are dualists. As prominent advocates of symmetry, Horn names Frege, Royce, Ayer, and Geach, noting that Wittgenstein's loyalties are unclear, while both Aristotle and Russell go back and forth between symmetrical-ism and asymmetricalism.[5] This latter, asymmetricalist camp is made up of those who hold that of the two acts affirmation and negation, one is more basic and the other (in one way or another) reducible to it. Horn puts Parmenides, Plato, Spinoza, Kant, Goethe, Freud, and the British neo-Hegelians in this camp.[6] Horn does not hesitate in equating asymmetricalism with commitment to the priority of affirm-ation and the derivative or eliminable status of negation. Accordingly, when he counts Hegel, too, among the asymmetricalists, it is because he takes Hegel to believe that "every significant negation is a deter-mination or limitation; significant negation must always occur on a positive ground."[7] Horn does not consider the possibility of an asym-metricalism that prioritizes negation. However, if such a position may be termed inverse or negative asymmetricalism, this is precisely the description that best suits Hegel's theory of absolute negativity. In this, Hegel forms a unique class of his own.

For the sake of accuracy and completeness it should be noted, first, that theories both of symmetry and asymmetry come in many shapes and varieties and can hardly be reduced to any single set of arguments beyond their common, defining convictions. Second, both of Horn's two camps are confronted by certain difficulties, while each also has a number of arguments going in its favor. The basic problem for sym-metry is that to be on a par with affirmative judgments, which make reference to (positive) facts, negative judgments would seem to require negative facts as their proper referents. Yet "never shall this prevail," as Parmenides said, "that things that are not *are*."[8] Thus begins the long history of asymmetricalism, one early high point of which is Plato's

4 See Horn, *Negation*, 1–5, 45–79.
5 *Ibid.*, 46.
6 *Ibid.*, 65–67. Armstrong could also be added to this list: see *Truthmakers*, 53–81, as well as his early formulation of the theory in *A Combinatorial Theory of Possibility* (Cambridge University Press 1989), 92–97.
7 Horn, *Negation*, 64; cf. 90–91.
8 Fragment 294 (quoted in Plato, *Sophist* 242a): cf. G. S. Kirk, J. E. Raven and M. Scofield, eds., *The Presocratic Philosophers*, 2nd edn. (Cambridge University Press 1983), 248; cf. fragment 293, *ibid.*, 247.

attempt in the *Sophist* to equate negation or non-being (*to mê on*) with difference or otherness (*to heteron*).[9] An alternative strategy, to be found in Bacon, for example, is to assimilate negation ("is not") to error ("is false that ...").[10]

The asymmetricalist reaction, however, is plagued by problems of its own. Plato's response appears to be either inadequate or circular, as Horn notes: if "other" is not able to perform all the logical tasks assigned to "not," the reduction is inadequate; if "other" can take on all those tasks, then it is itself negative in nature.[11] Neither does negation as falsity appear to have a leg to stand on. Horn cites a polemical example from Geach: "'Do not open the door!' is a command on the same level as 'Open the door!' and cannot be paraphrased as 'Let the statement that you open the door be false!'"[12] Nor is there any guarantee that for every negative statement an unequivocal affirmative counterpart can be identified.[13] To top it off, it is not even always clear how to tell which sentences are negative and which are affirmative.[14]

As we will see, Hegel's negative asymmetricalism will address a number of these difficulties. Before I proceed, though, I should also note that its symmetry or asymmetry vis-à-vis affirmation is not the only question about negation over which philosophers have split. At least since Aristotle, the distinction between so-called "external" or propositional negation ("a is not b") and "internal" or term negation ("a is not-b") and the relation between the two have been a source of recurring puzzlement to logicians, and the ramifications throughout logical theory are on a par with those concerning symmetry.[15] Aristotelians, past and present (e.g. George Englebretsen),[16] insist on the logical irreducibility and

---

9 As others have noted, Hegel's view of negation as being-other is closely related to the view expressed in the *Sophist*; but Hegel clearly also goes beyond anything to be found in Plato when he conceives both of negation and of otherness as capable of self-relation: Plato would hardly have countenanced the idea that something can be the other of itself. See Henrich, "Formen der Negation," 245–56, esp. 250; see also Iber, *Absolute Relationalität*, 223.

10 Horn, *Negation*, 56–59.

11 *Ibid.*, 50–51.

12 *Ibid.*, 59.

13 *Ibid.*, 53.

14 Horn (*ibid.*, 32) invites us to consider this paradigm from Frege and try to sort the propositions into the negative and affirmative: "a. Christ is immortal; b. Christ lives forever; c. Christ is not immortal; d. Christ is mortal; e. Christ does not live forever."

15 Cf. Horn's overview, *ibid.*, 5–23.

16 See George Englebretsen, *Logical Negation* (Assen, Netherlands: Van Gorcum 1981). For the closely related distinction between predicate *denial* propositional *negation*, see

primacy of term negation, whereas those in the Stoic tradition (notably Frege, in modern times) insist on the primacy of propositional negation. The relevance of this dispute for understanding Hegel has been shown by Paul Redding.[17] Over against McDowell's and especially Brandom's appropriation of Hegel, he emphasizes the Aristotelian elements in Hegel's concept of negation, a feature which sets Hegelian logic apart from the post-Fregean logic Brandom and others build on, thus raising the question whether it can be wholly assimilated to the philosophical program for which they seek to appropriate it. A thoroughgoing comparison of Redding's approach with my analysis here is a *desideratum*, the fulfillment of which promises further insight into Hegel's place in and contribution to the history of logic. The two approaches may turn out to be complementary. In this chapter, however, I will focus exclusively on the issue of symmetry and asymmetry.

As I indicated above, I think Horn's characterization of Hegel as an asymmetricalist is accurate only under the additional qualification that we view him as a negative asymmetricalist, a possible stance that Horn himself does not consider. It will prove illuminating, however, if we first consider some of the evidence for counting Hegel among more traditional, positive asymmetricalists, since this perception has shaped many interpretations of Hegel's concept of determinate negation, despite their having seldom been formulated explicitly in these terms.

When determinate negation is introduced by Hegel for the first time in print, in the methodological Introduction to the *Phenomenology*, he casts it in the following terms:

> [T]he exposition of untrue consciousness in its untruth is not a merely negative movement ... Skepticism ... only ever sees pure nothingness in its result and abstracts from the fact that this nothingness, when determined, is the nothing *of that from which it has resulted*. For it is only when it is taken as the nothingness of that from which it emerges, that it is in fact the true result; in that case it is itself a determinate nothingness and has a *content* ... [W]hen the result is conceived as it is in truth, as *determinate* negation, a new form has thereby immediately arisen, and in the negation the transition has been made. (GW 9:57/§79)[18]

Fred Sommers, "Predictability," in M. Black (ed.), *Philosophy in America* (Ithaca, NY: Cornell University Press 1965), 262–81.

17 See Paul Redding, *Analytic Philosophy and the Return of Hegelian Thought* (Cambridge University Press 2007).

18 Note how closely Hegel associates negation, i.e. the relation of negativity, with the idea of *content*. In light of the preceding chapter, we should recognize that in this

This often-cited passage makes one thing clear: negation, properly understood, is supposed to reveal a positive content intimately connected with it. In light of what we know of Hegelian dialectic, it is indeed plausible to say that the positive content that is said to result from determinate negation is really the more adequate, more concrete shape of consciousness from which the negated shape is merely an abstraction and which it *presupposes as its own positive basis.* So Hegel could plausibly be interpreted as espousing a version of the presuppositionality thesis, that is, the thesis that every negative judgment presupposes a positive judgment as its semantic basis.[19] On the other side, however, one may well find puzzling the locution: "the *nothing* of that from which it has resulted." Clearly, the idea that a nothing or negation somehow *belongs to* a shape of consciousness is not easy to square with traditional asymmetricalism, and I will return to this difficulty presently.

For the moment, though, let us continue to bring the asymmetricalist aspects of determinate negation into sharper focus. Determinate negation, dialectic, and the Hegelian notion of experience are closely wedded concepts. Especially in the *Phenomenology*, dialectical movement is characterized by the fact that determinate negation gives rise to a new, affirmatively true (*wahr*) object, and Hegel explicitly equates the dialectic with "what is ordinarily understood by experience" (GW 9:60/§87). Now this equation is valid only with an important qualification meant to correct the vulgar conception according to which the experience of the untruth of our initial concept is occasioned by a further, distinct object "which we happen to find by coincidence and externally" (GW 9:60/§87). Dialectical experience, says Hegel, consists in the emergence of the new object *from the initial object itself,* and is thus free from the contingency and externality that characterize the vulgar concept of experience.[20] Note, however, that this qualification bears strictly on the underlying *identity* of the first and the second "object" and the consequent *necessity* of the transition in thought from the one

often-cited passage, Hegel is not asserting merely that when we negate something we are, at least implicitly, appealing to or even bringing about some positive state of affairs. He must also have in mind his *speculative theory of content* as metaphysically constituted through absolute negativity.

19 On the presuppositionality thesis, see Horn, *Negation,* 63–73.

20 This difference is linked to that between "empirical negation" and "speculative" negation introduced by Hyppolite in his comparison of Hegel with Bergson: see note 1 above.

to the other. For on the other hand Hegel embraces that aspect of the vulgar conception according to which the negative experience (the experience of the untruth of the first object) is immediately and for itself the positive experience of a second, presumably "true" object. In Hegel's own phraseology, difficult to render in English, the experience is had or "made" *an dem (anderen) Gegenstand* (GW 9:60/§87). I understand this to mean that it is by way of or in the form of positively experiencing some (different) state of affairs and affirming it as in some sense true or real, that we come to negate our former view of things as false or as based on the perception of a merely apparent state of affairs. The experience of untruth is immediately identical with the experience of a contradictory or otherwise incompatible truth, where the valence is such that the truth-experience explains or constitutes the untruth-experience. Negation would thus appear to reduce to affirmation or at least strongly to presuppose it.[21]

Hegel's remarks here are reminiscent of Spinoza's dictum that "truth is the standard both of itself and of falsity" (E2p43s). The similarity is unlikely to be coincidental. Spinoza's remark is found in his discussion of the proposition that "a true idea in us is one which is adequate in God insofar as he is explicated through the human mind" and hence that whoever "has a true idea knows at the same time that he has a true idea, and cannot doubt its truth" (E2p43). The core idea in this discussion is the affinity of the human mind with the mind of God *insofar as the human mind "perceives things truly"* (E2p43; emphasis added). This same idea is central both to Hegel's *Phenomenology* and to the *Logic*: Absolute knowledge and the absolute idea, respectively, as the *terminus ad quem* of a literally *gradual* ascent to truth mark the point of coincidence between the human mind and the active, intellectual nature of the absolute itself (insofar as the latter explicates *itself* through the human mind, as one might add to complete the analogy to Spinoza's text).[22] But Spinoza's deity, inasmuch as it is defined as

---

21 This would put Hegel in the same camp as Kant, who is quite explicit in his view that negations always reduce to limitations or privations, which in their turn immediately coincide with positive states of affairs that are merely represented in terms of negative predicates (cf. B601–4). In a similar vein, Kant teaches that the proper use of negative judgments is merely to prevent error (B737; cf. B97). Stekeler-Weithofer seems to attribute a substantially similar view to Hegel: see, e.g., *Hegels analytische Philosophie*, 110, on Hegel's concept of Becoming; traces of the error-theory of negation are also recognizable on pages 67, 92.

22 Cf. E5p36. There is reason to believe that Hegel continued to share Schelling's view that speculative science is in the most literal sense the absolute's very own

absolutely infinite, must be construed as thoroughgoing affirmation, wholly without negation. Adequate ideas, then, as the mark and standard of truth, are wholly affirmative in character, and falsity or negation strongly presuppose it.

Yet now we must again take notice of the difficulty mentioned above, that for Hegel *das Nichts* or negation is somehow part of the make-up of the new, affirmatively grasped object. This does not sit well with asymmetricalist eliminativism regarding negation. If negation is somehow built into affirmation or absolute position (being), then it cannot be eliminated in favor of it. As I have tried to show in Chapter 6, Hegel appeals to his theory of absolute or self-reverting negation in order to account for the fact that (formal) reality comes to be posited as content in the first place, that it "unfolds" itself into objective reality, that is, into thought. I also suggested that we could follow rationalist metaphysicians such as Descartes and Spinoza in conceiving objective reality as coming in degrees proportional to the degree of reality contained in the formal reality of its referent. This idea can be adapted to Hegel as follows. The degree of objective reality represented by a given conceptual content is measured by the extent to which that content *represents* the dynamic of absolute negation from which it arises, rather than merely *exhibiting* or manifesting that dynamic as one to which it is subject in its passing-over, reflecting or *Scheinen*, and so on. In equivalent structural terms, the greater the extent to which the relations constituting the Concept are explicit in the representational content of objective thought, the *truer* that content will be.

Viewed in these terms, determinate negation represents (in the first instance) a subordinate relation within the dynamic of absolute negation, just as finite cognition represents (in the first instance) a subordinate phase in the unfolding of speculative knowledge of the Concept.[23] The fact that determinate negation exhibits traits of positive asymmetricalism is therefore rooted in the deeper fact that

self-consciousness, which is realized therein by degrees approaching to adequacy (cf. Beiser, *German Idealism*, 573–95; cf. also Hegel's approval of the idea in Plotinus that "God's essence is thought itself and present in thought" [TW 19:444]). By now it should be clear that this is a compact way of expressing the relation between formal and objective reality that was worked out in the preceding chapter.

23 The qualification "in the first instance" is meant to signify that both determinate negation and finite cognition will, in the final instance, themselves fully represent the structure of absolute negativity; it is, after all, as finite cognizers that we become aware of speculative truth.

it surfaces out of absolute or autonomous negation. The varieties of positive asymmetricalism – namely, the alternating explanations of negation in terms of otherness (Plato), limitation (Spinoza, Kant), or falsity (Bacon) – are thus all equally adumbrated by Hegel's notion of determinate negation. However, determinate negation exhibits these forms of positive asymmetricalism not because Hegel advocates any of these reductionist approaches to negation, but because the logic of absolute negation serves as a unifying ground of otherness, self-differentiation, and hence limitation, and of the generation of object-ive reality or the intentionality which is, of course, the original ground of possibility for misrepresentation.[24] And for this reason I think that Horn's characterization of Hegel needs to be emended: Hegel is a negative asymmetricalist for whom negation is the basic fact to which affirmation and determinate negation must ultimately be reduced. In the history of thought about negation, Hegel therefore occupies a *sui generis* position.

7.3. Autonomous negation and classical logic

In this section I will address a question closely related to Hegel's place in the history of philosophical thought about negation, namely the relation of absolute or "autonomous" negation to classical logic. Henrich's reconstruction of autonomous negation relies from the outset on classical logic, for example, on the classical concept of neg-ation as a monadic operator requiring a term subject to negation, on a modified version of the Law of Double Negation, on the classical identity relation, and not least on the Principle of Non-Contradiction. Without these assumptions, the dynamic of autonomous negation could not get started. But doesn't this represent a serious difficulty for Hegel since he clearly sees autonomous negation as a primitive methodological operation for generating all the content of classical

---

24 It is significant that Hegel analyzes illusion or misrepresentation (*Schein*) prior to his thematization of the structures of "subjective logic" or thought. He seems to approach intentionality from the point of view of an originally extra-mental differ-entiation of formal and objective reality, rather than approaching misrepresentation on the basis of presuppositions about intentionality. The place of an account of mis-representation for theories of intentionality has been underscored by Fred Dretske, "Misrepresentation," in R. J. Boghdan (ed.), *Belief: Form, Content, and Function* (Oxford: Clarendon Press 1986), 17–36.

logic, including identity and contradiction?[25] If the dialectical logic of autonomous negation is parasitical upon classical logic, presupposing it in its very formulation, this would seem to defeat Hegel's claim to be working out a "completely altered view of logic."

In order to reply to this charge, we should first observe that the appearance that autonomous negation is parasitical upon classical logic is *in part* an artifact of Henrich's reconstruction of the procedure, which I have used as a starting point for my interpretation of Hegel's philosophy. That we make use of classical logic in order to *reconstruct* the concept of absolute negativity does not *eo ipso* entail that absolute negativity is rooted in classical logic. As far as it goes, however, this reply is bound to appear superficial. The role of classical logic in articulating the logic of autonomous negation cannot be external to that logic in the way it might be external to an account of purely natural phenomena, for example.

We should therefore acknowledge that classical logic does indeed set limitations on Hegel's presentation of speculative science. In part, these limitations play a positive role: classical logic constitutes a parameter for every discursive representation of knowledge and Hegel's is no exception. As he himself acknowledges, "the dialectical movement likewise has propositions for its parts or elements" (GW 9:45/§66), and an unmediated break with the "logic of the finite understanding" would simply render that movement unintelligible, indeed unrepresentable. We as finite cognizers could not even become aware of the kind of dynamic Hegel means to describe by absolute negativity if we did not always already have the classical logic of the understanding at our disposal. In this sense, classical logic sets parameters for Hegelian logic as it does for any discursive concatenation of propositions.

On the other hand, classical logic itself is plagued by certain limitations, some of which have been the subject of philosophical debate since antiquity. These limitations are probably most evident in the

---

25 This observation may be behind de Boer's decision to disregard Henrich's analysis of negation in Hegel (*On Hegel*, 222, n. 1). Against Henrich's approach, she argues that propositional negation (i.e. the form of negation I identified above as characteristic of Stoic and Fregean logic) cannot be the source of Hegel's conception, and that Hegel is interested in concepts such as "not," "nothing," and "double negation" chiefly in order to show that they inadequately express the speculative negation he has in mind. In one regard I fully agree with this criticism, for reasons that I will spell out in this section. At the same time, however, I contend that the unity of Hegel's conception of absolute negation only becomes perspicuous when we start with Henrich's analysis.

so-called paradoxes of material implication and the logical status of contradiction, but surface also in discussions of bivalence and more generally in questions concerning the correct representation of natural language and human rationality.[26] The ramifications of these problematic features of classical logic are far-reaching. So while we can no more jump over classical logic than we can our own shadow, we must not for that reason accept it as having ultimate authority and objective validity. We might therefore look at the role of classical logic in Hegelian dialectic in analogy with three-dimensional representations of Minkowski space: there is a very real sense in which *we cannot imagine* the space of general relativity; it is nonetheless evident, however, that we are perfectly capable of using *what we can imagine* (our ordinary, three-dimensional perceptual space) as a means to working out and even effectively representing to ourselves the full complexity of general relativity. The relation of dialectical to classical logic is the same.

This suggestion can be made more concrete when we turn to Hegel's otherwise notoriously obscure account of the "speculative sentence" (GW 9:42–46/§§60–66). Rainer Schäfer has provided a convincing account of the speculative sentence.[27] His basic idea is to understand the speculative sentence as a dynamicized counterpart to Hegel's early definition of the Absolute as the identity of identity and difference, comprising three distinct moments. First, the propositional form exhibits a *distinction* between the subject and the predicate, which Hegel plausibly describes as manifesting "the determinate sense [*Sinn*]" (GW 9:43/§61) and content of the subject-term. In ordinary sentences, this difference is purely external; for example, "The rose is red" predicates redness of the rose, but many things other than the rose are red, while the rose also exhibits many properties besides its redness. In the case of the speculative sentence, by contrast, the subject "fills its content" and "ceases to go beyond it, and cannot have further predicates or accidents" (GW 9:43/§60). In other words, the properly speculative proposition exhibits an *identity* between the

---

26 The paradoxes of material implication were first discovered in the context of Stoic logic (see Sextus Empiricus, *Adversus Mathematicos*, 8.109–17); the closely related principle *ex falso quodlibet* is traditionally (but falsely) attributed to Duns Scotus; see William Kneale and Martha Kneale, *The Development of Logic* (Oxford University Press 1962), 128–37, 280–97.

27 Cf. Schäfer, *Dialektik*, 177–93. I closely adhere to the details of Schäfer's account, though I will indicate some respects in which my interpretation differs from his.

content of subject and predicate, and this is the second moment, in which the initial self-externality of subject and predicate is sublated. The third moment, which Hegel calls the "rhythm" (GW 9:43/§61) of the speculative proposition, is the unity of the first two, contrary moments.

Here is Hegel's compact description: "Formally, what has just been said can be expressed thus: the nature of judgment or the proposition as such, which involves the distinction of subject and predicate, is destroyed by the speculative proposition, and the proposition of identity [i.e. the tautology] which the former becomes, contains the counter-thrust against that relation" (GW 9:43/§61). The dynamic of absolute negation is easy to discern here. As in the act of "absolute abstraction" described in Chapter 6, the "identical sentence" itself is what is supposed to bring about the difference, the *Gegenstoß* to the relation of identity. What in Hegelian terms starts out by looking like a substantial form or form of immediacy (A = A), is revealed to be a result of self-reverting negation that immediately gives rise to a difference that constitutes the determinateness and thus the essence or identity of the substance-term (that is, the grammatical subject).

Schäfer explains the source of the dynamic that is manifest in the speculative sentence by assuming that Hegel "replaces" the grammatical subject with the cognitive subject, which is suited to be a source of movement.[28] Based on the interpretation I developed in Chapter 6, this assumption is extraneous. The movement present in the speculative sentence is the self-movement attributed above to the absolute, self-reverting negation or *Gegenstoß* internal to "substantial" identity as such; the unfolding of that negation just is constitution of the symmetrical structures of self-consciousness and representational content on the one side, substance and accidence (attribute) on the other. However, this correction does not affect Schäfer's main point. The self-movement of absolute negation brings with it, as Schäfer clearly recognizes, a fundamental difficulty as to its adequate mode of exposition:

> Propositions and judgments are not able to express the dialectical, internally self-reverting movement of the grammatical subject to the predicate and from the predicate as essential predicate, as Concept, back to the grammatical subject that reveals itself in this movement as subjectivity. In sentences, only one direction of movement can be presented at a time. Hence there cannot actually be a speculative sentence

28 *Ibid.*, 183.

as a sentence. The speculative sentence as such strives beyond itself to another sentence which in turn tends beyond itself to yet another sentence expressing the unity of the two preceding sentences. Identity, difference, and the resulting identity of identity and non-identity are broken up into at least three sentences.[29]

Schäfer plausibly suggests that this difficulty motivated Hegel to work out the theory of the speculative syllogism he ultimately presented in the *Science of Logic*. In our present context, this sheds light on the relation of absolute negativity to classical logic. For one, it shows that Hegel's most sustained work on classical formal logic, which of course in his day was largely identical with syllogistic, grew out of the difficulties associated with providing a cogent exposition of absolute negativity; the doctrine of the speculative sentence did not therefore disappear after the *Phenomenology*, it was merely transmuted into the doctrine of the speculative syllogism that it naturally implied. More importantly, however, Schäfer rightly insists that even with the distribution of the movement of negativity across multiple sentences, the movement still cannot be genuinely represented because those sentences ultimately remain just that: "a rigid form" of mutually external subjects and predicates.

Hegel recognized that the means of classical logic, taken by themselves, are insufficient for a genuinely adequate representation of absolute negation. While it remained Hegel's express goal to give thoroughly discursive or at least thoroughly *linguistic* expression to speculative science in such a way as to rehabilitate the Platonic ideal of "philosophical demonstration" (GW 9:45/§65), the extent to which he succeeded remains open to question. As Schäfer himself points out, Hegel's critique of Schellingian intuitionism depends for its ultimate cogency on Hegel's ability to provide a fully discursive alternative.[30] Neither the speculative sentence nor the speculative syllogism nor yet the *Logic's* opaque conception of "original words" (GW 12:237) unambiguously achieve that aim.[31]

Classical logic may thus be seen on the one hand to limit Hegel's logic of autonomous negation in a positive sense, by constituting the parameters for a propositional representation of absolute negativity in

29 *Ibid.*, 188.
30 *Ibid.*, 190–91.
31 *Ibid.*, 189. Also see the insightful comments in de Boer, *On Hegel*, 152–54.

which the movement itself is indirectly present as what might be called a *para-propositional* unity.[32] By the same token, however, classical logic places real limits on Hegelian science in the sense of limiting what it can directly present in the way of "philosophical demonstration." There may simply be no perfectly controlled procedure for constructing the para-propositional unities Hegel originally called speculative propositions and later came to describe as the speculative syllogism.

This is of course a long-standing complaint against Hegelian dialectic by more classically minded philosophers. But while one ought not to seek to evade the charge, it should also be recognized that the lack of a purely formal procedure does not imply that Hegelian demonstrations do not proceed on a principled basis or that they are lacking in rigor. As I suggested in the previous chapter, absolute negativity should be regarded as a fruitful, systematic hypothesis; it is to be assessed on the basis of the rational intuitions it manages to integrate and the philosophical problems it manages to bring within the scope of a unified philosophical approach. It cannot lay claim *a priori* to any greater justification than other great philosophical hypotheses from Plato's theory of forms through Leibniz' monadology to the modal realism of David Lewis; by the same token, neither can it be dismissed out of hand along with the characteristic lines of questioning and avenues of research it opens.

Whatever the decision on that question, however, the charge that absolute negation is parasitical upon classical logic is not ultimately damaging. The relation between the logic of autonomous negation and classical logic is not one of competition to be more or less fundamental in terms of generating and grounding a single order of discourse. We do not use classical logic to *generate* the logic of autonomous negation the way we use the natural numbers, say, to generate the rational numbers and to construct models of the non-denumerable infinities that constitute the reals. The relation is rather more like that

---

32 The term "meta-propositional" might have seemed a more apt expression in that the Greek preposition "meta" has the sense either of something's going beyond or coming after something else or of its somehow traversing the other and stretching across it. I have chosen the slightly less apt preposition "para" (alongside of) because in the usage of modern logic, "meta" has come to signify a notion that is incompatible with what I wish to convey. A "meta-language" is a higher-order language used to talk about a lower-level language. Hegel's "speculative sentence" by contrast is not about any other sentences; it is a peculiar kind of (absolutely negative) unity that can be represented only through the means of propositional structures which, taken in themselves, necessarily distort it.

between the real numbers and the representation of motion: we pre-suppose them in order to be able to explore a dimension of concrete reality that is partially isomorphic with them. And, as I hinted above, a similar analogy might hold between classical and dialectical logic on the one hand, and three-dimensional space and Minkowski space on the other: classical logic is a means, not a foundation.[33]

7.4. Conclusion: absolute negativity and Hegel's "completely altered view of logic"

The concept of absolute negativity, and the "completely altered view of logic" associated with it, has a fourfold significance in Hegelian phil-osophy: metaphysical, methodological, critical, and existential. By way of conclusion, I will discuss each of these aspects in turn.

One of the most significant developments in post-Kantian phil-osophy was the rise of a non-mechanistic philosophy of nature and the vitalized Spinozism that was associated with it. Its earliest public manifestation was probably Herder's dialogue on Spinoza in *God: Some Conversations* (*Gott. Einige Gespräche*), published in 1787. Goethe's inves-tigations into plant and morphology (1790) and, somewhat later, into the nature of color (*c.* 1805ff.) were a seminal example of a new, thor-oughly non-Newtonian approach to nature that drew explicit inspir-ation from Spinoza. The generation of Schelling and Hegel could take full advantage of burgeoning research in chemistry, theories on electricity and magnetism, and empirically fueled speculation on their function in organic and even mental life.[34] Schelling's early attempts at systematic integration of these developments into a unified phil-osophy of nature and mind seem almost inevitable in retrospect, and

---

33 Hegel's "completely altered view of logic" is therefore not to be compared to the non-classical logics that proliferated in the twentieth century. "Dialectical" logic does not range alongside fuzzy logic, dialetheic logic, many-valued logic, etc., as an application-specific tool of analysis. For critical discussion of attempts to assimilate Hegel's dialectic to multivalued logic or paraconsistent logic, see Klaus J. Schmidt, "Formale Logik und Dialektik in Hegels Seinslogik," in H. Oosterling and F. de Jong (eds.), *Denken Unterwegs: Philosophie im Kräftefeld sozialen und politischen Engagements. Festschrift für Heinz Kimmerle* (Amsterdam: Grüner 1990), 127–44.

34 On the character of Romantic science and its institutional framework in Jena see Paul Ziche and Olaf Breidbach (eds.), *Naturwissenschaften um 1800. Wissenschaftskultur in Jena-Weimar* (Weimar: Hermann Böhlaus Nachfolger 2001); see also Paul Ziche "Naturforschung in Jena zur Zeit Hegels. Materialien zum Hintergrund der spekula-tiven Naturphilosophie," *Hegel-Studien* 32 (1997): 9–40.

Hegel's embrace of the project was anything but a passing flirtation, as demonstrated by the abiding place of *Naturphilosophie* in his mature thought.

Commitment to the systematic necessity and viability of a "speculative physics" distinguishes Schelling and Hegel from Kant and first-wave post-Kantians like Reinhold and Fichte, who could plausibly view themselves as engaged in a project continuous with that of Kant. Unlike those transcendental idealists, who (for all intents and purposes) identified finite subjectivity as the exclusive source of structure in the objective world, Schelling and Hegel were committed to a view on which the things of nature themselves make a substantial contribution to the structure of experience.[35] This view finds distinct expression in the architecture of Schelling's system at the time when Hegel arrived in Jena. The *terminus a quo* of his transcendental idealism is what he calls the "absolute act" of self-consciousness; its *terminus ad quem* "the entire nexus of the objective world and all the determinations of nature" (SW I, 3:398). Conversely, the *terminus a quo* of *Naturphilosophie* is a dynamic opposition between two fundamental tendencies of nature, expansion and contraction; its *terminus ad quem* the "construction of the ideal series" of the intellectual faculties and their categories from organic nature, all the way to the "construction of the absolute center of gravity in which, as the two highest expressions of indifference, *truth* and *beauty*, coincide" (SW I, 10:211). Transcendental idealism traces the unfolding of mind into nature, *Naturphilosophie* the unfolding of nature into mind, a symmetry that is possible on the basis of a deep structural analogy between the two realms. But is it anything more than an analogy?

In Chapter 1, I showed with Henrich that the relation-to-other that arises within the dynamic of absolute negation can "only be maintained with negation's relation-to-self if the other is in turn itself negation. But this means that the opposite of autonomous double negation must itself be double negation. Double negation can be conceived as self-relation only if it is conceived twice over."[36] The dynamic of absolute negation gives rise to a relation that it introjects into itself, thereby doubling or mirroring that relation in a more complex relational structure: the Concept. If we consider absolute negation for a

---

35 Cf. Hegel's critique of Kant and Fichte on this account in GW 4:332, 394, 396.
36 Henrich, "Hegels Grundoperation," 219.

moment as akin to a mathematical function, we might say that part of the very logic of that function is that it be fed into itself as its one unique argument, thereby giving rise to its doubling as its unique value. The virtue of Hegel's conception of absolute negativity is that it represents the mind–nature or subject–substance duality (1) as a relation that obtains between elements which, on each side, are themselves structured as unities of relation-to-self/relation-to-other, rather than as the "simple" relation of self-consciousness (relation-to-self), on the one side, to an "other" that has no internal structure save that which self-consciousness confers upon it in an act of positing or "synthesis." Rather than a relation between self-consciousness and an object, we have a relation between self-consciousness and an internally relational duality that can usefully be thought of in terms of Spinoza's distinction between *natura naturans* and *natura naturata*. (2) Moreover, Hegel's conception of absolute negativity represents this relation as arising *necessarily* within a single dynamic, such that no third term outside the unfolding of mind and nature (no Schellingian indifference point) is required to ground the unity of the process. (3) Lastly, Hegel's conception of absolute negativity thereby represents the relation between mind and nature as an originally and essentially "objective," that is, *intentional* relation, as I argued in Chapter 6. At the level of metaphysics, therefore, absolute negativity has some very desirable consequences.

Those consequences are ramified at the level of methodology. As I have argued repeatedly in this book, the dynamic of absolute negation constitutes distinct phases or moments. Onto these Hegel can map the individual "thought determinations" that go to make up his list of categories and the forms of concept, proposition, syllogism, and other more concrete forms of cognition in the *Science of Logic*. At the same time, the unified nature of that process allows him both to *order* that list in a unique sequence and to display the thought determinations as dependent aspects of a single, basic, self-explicating process. Thus both with respect to the procedures of speculative science and with respect to the basic account of how those procedures are to be justified, absolute negativity solves numerous problems in a single move.

Obviously, a philosophy such as that of Schelling and Hegel, that seeks its principle "outside" of consciousness and finite cognition, will diverge from the manifest image of the world that characterizes natural consciousness. Therefore, an effective *critique* of finite cognition is required if speculative cognition is to be brought into determinate relation to it. Schelling and Hegel saw the desirability of such a critique early on, and devoted their *Critical Journal of Philosophy* to exactly that purpose (cf. GW 4:117–20, 127–28). An important failing of their early critical strategy, however, was not to have accounted sufficiently for the existence of finite cognition which, after all, cannot be external to the Absolute if the latter is to have a legitimate claim to absoluteness. Rhetorical and justificatory concerns aside, the concrete features of finite cognition have to be explicable in terms of speculative cognition; it has to be possible to understand finite cognition and its limits from within the standpoint of speculative cognition, so as to make the latter accessible from within the standpoint of the former (cf. GW 9:22–23/§26).[37] This is an important test of the real scope of speculative cognition.

Chapters 2 through 5 of this book were largely devoted to Hegel's critique of finite cognition. I tried to show how he is able to interpret finite cognition in its most explicit theoretical manifestations – metaphysics, pure natural science, and mathematics – as corresponding to the structure of absolute negativity and to distinct moments within its dynamic. Specifically, I sought to show how Hegel is able to demonstrate features of self-externality in those sciences while offering a speculative aetiology for them. Thus in respect to the idea of immanent critique, as well, absolute negativity is a foundational concept inasmuch as the more familiar and seemingly more classically assimilable concept of *determinate negation* requires the more demanding notion.

Hegel's speculative approach to logic and epistemology is inseparable from the social, political, ethical, and existential dimensions that characterize the other areas of his thought. This point must be emphasized because, of course, the more politically, historically, and existentially oriented Hegel – the Hegel of the *Lectures on Aesthetics*, on the *History of Religion*, the *Philosophy of Right*, and parts of the *Phenomenology of Spirit* – has long enjoyed recognition in the English-speaking world as an enduring source of insight and innovative potential for ongoing research in a variety of disciplines, not just for philosophy. This has definitely not been the case with Hegel's speculative logic and metaphysics, however.[38] One guiding interest of this book has been to argue

---

37 Cf. Fulda, *Problem einer Einleitung*, 297–301.
38 Cf. Allen Wood: "Speculative logic is dead; Hegel's thought is not," in *Hegel's Ethical Thought* (Cambridge University Press 1990), Introduction, 4.

that Hegel the logician, metaphysician, and systematician, the Hegel of the *Logic* and the famous Preface to the *Phenomenology*, is both inseparable from that other, social-politically minded Hegel, and that this Hegel, too, remains a vital source of insights for contemporary philosophy not in spite of his continuity with a pre-Kantian tradition in metaphysics, but in good part because of it.

WORKS CITED

Primary sources: classical German philosophy

Baumgarten, Alexander Gottlieb. *Metaphysica*, 7th edn. Magdeburg: Hemmerde 1779.

Fichte, J. G. *Gesamtausgabe der Bayerischen Akademie der Wissenschaften*, ed. Reinhard Lauth, Hans Jacobs, Hans Gliwitzky, and Erich Fuchs. Stuttgart: Frommann-Holzbog 1964–.

Goethe, Johann Wolfgang von. *Werke*, ed. Erich Trunz. Munich: C. H. Beck 1981.

Hegel, Georg Wilhelm. *Briefe von und an Hegel*, ed. Johannes Hoffmeister, 4 vols. Hamburg: Meiner 1952.

The Difference between Fichte's and Schelling's System of Philosophy [...], trans. H. S. Harris and Walter Cerf. Albany: State University of New York Press 1977.

Encyclopedia of the Philosophical Sciences in Basic Outline. Part 1: Science of Logic, trans. and ed. Klaus Brinkmann and Daniel Dahlstrom. Cambridge University Press 2010.

Faith and Knowledge [...], trans. H. S. Harris and Walter Cerf. Albany: State University of New York Press 1977.

Gesammelte Werke, ed. Academy of Sciences of Nordrhein-Westfalia, in cooperation with the Deutsche Forschungsgemeinschaft. Hamburg: Meiner 1968–.

Heidelberg Writings. Journal Publications, trans. and ed. Brady Bowman and Allen Speight. Cambridge University Press 2009.

Lectures on Logic: Berlin 1831, trans. Clark Butler. Bloomington and Indianapolis, IN: Indiana University Press 2008.

Relationship of Skepticism to Philosophy, Exposition of its Different Modifications and Comparison to the Latest Form with the Ancient One, trans. H. S. Harris, in George di Giovanni (ed.), *Between Kant and Hegel: Texts in the Development of Post-Kantian Idealism*. Albany: State University of New York Press 1985.

Science of Logic, trans. George di Giovanni. Cambridge University Press 2010.

Werke in zwanzig Bänden, ed. Eva Moldenhauer and Karl Markus Michel on the basis of the 1832–45 edn. Frankfurt am Main: Suhrkamp 1969–.

Hoffmeister, Johannes (ed.). *Dokumente zu Hegel's Entwicklung.* Stuttgart-Bad Cannstatt: Fromann 1936.

Hölderlin, Friedrich. *Sämtliche Werke, Kleine Stuttgarter Ausgabe,* ed. Friedrich Beißner. Stuttgart: J. G. Cottasche Buchhandlung Nachfolger 1944.

Jacobi, Friedrich Heinrich. *The Main Philosophical Writings and the Novel Allwill,* trans. and ed. George di Giovanni. Montreal and Kingston: McGill-Queen's University Press 1994.

Werke. Gesamtausgabe, ed. Klaus Hammacher and Walter Jaeschke. Hamburg: Meiner/Frommann-Holzboog 1998–.

Kant, Immanuel. *Critique of Pure Reason,* trans. Norman Kemp Smith. London: Macmillan 1929.

Gesammelte Schriften. Akademie Ausgabe. Berlin: Reimer, later de Gruyter 1900–.

Krug, Wilhelm Traugott. *Briefe über den neuesten Idealismus.* Leipzig: Müller 1801.

Leibniz, Gottfried. *New Essays on Human Understanding,* trans. and ed. Peter Remnant and Jonathan Bennett. Cambridge University Press 1996.

Philosophical Essays, trans. and ed. Roger Ariew and Daniel Garber. Indianapolis, IN: Hackett 1989.

Reinhold, Karl Leonhard. *Beyträge zur Berichtigung bisheriger Mißverständnisse der Philosophen,* vol. I, *Das Fundament der Philosophie betreffend.* Jena: Widtmann und Mauke 1791.

Briefe über die Kantische Philosophie. Mannheim: Bender 1789.

Über das Fundament des philosophischen Wissens. Jena: Mauke 1791.

Schelling, Friedrich Wilhelm Joseph. *Sämmtliche Werke,* ed. Karl Friedrich August Schelling. Stuttgart: Cotta 1856–61.

System of Transcendental Idealism, trans. Peter Heath. Charlottesville: University Press of Virginia 1978.

Spinoza, Baruch de. *The Collected Works of Spinoza,* trans. Edwin Curley. Princeton University Press 1985.

Complete Works, ed. M. L. Morgan, trans. S. Shirley. Indianapolis, IN: Hackett 2002.

A Spinoza Reader: The Ethics and Other Works, ed. and trans. Edwin Curley. Princeton University Press 1994.

Wolff, Christian. *Discursus Praeliminarius de Philosophia in Genere: Einleitende Abhandlung über Philosophie im Allgemeinen,* ed. and trans. Günter Gawlick and Lothar Kriemendahl. Stuttgart-Bad Cannstatt: Fromann-Holzboog 1996.

Gesammelte Werke, ed. J. École, H. W. Arndt, Ch. A. Corr, J. E. Hofmann, and M. Thomann. Hildesheim, Zurich, and New York: Georg Olms 1965–.

Secondary literature and other primary sources

Allais, Lucy. "Kant, Non-Conceptual Content, and the Representation of Space." *Journal of the History of Philosophy* 47:3 (2009): 383–413.

Altman, Alexander. *Moses Mendelssohns Frühschriften zur Metaphysik.* Tübingen: Mohr-Siebeck 1969.

Ameriks, Karl. *Kant and the Fate of Autonomy: Problems in the Appropriation of the Critical Philosophy.* Cambridge University Press 2000.

"Kantian Idealism Today." *History of Philosophy Quarterly* 9:3 (1992): 329–42.

"Recent Work on Hegel: The Rehabilitation of an Epistemologist?" *Philosophy and Phenomenological Research* 52:1 (March 1992): 177–202.

Armstrong, David M. *A Combinatorial Theory of Possibility.* Cambridge University Press 1989.

Truth and Truthmakers. Cambridge University Press 2004.

Arndt, Andreas. *Dialektik und Reflexion: Zur Rekonstruktion des Vernunftbegriffs.* Hamburg: Meiner 1994.

"Figuren der Endlichkeit: Zur Dialetik nach Kant," in Annett Jubara and David Bensler (eds.), *Dialektik und Differenz: Festschrift für Milan Prucha.* Wiesbaden: Harrassowitz Verlag 2001, 91–104.

Bacon, Francis. *The New Organon,* ed. Lisa Jardine and Michael Silverthorne. Cambridge University Press 2000.

Baum, Manfred. *Die Entstehung der Hegelschen Dialektik.* Bonn: Bouvier 1986.

Baumanns, Peter. *Kants Theorie der Erkenntnis: Durchgehender Kommentar zu den Hauptkapitel der "Kritik der reinen Vernunft."* Würzburg: Königshausen und Neumann 1994.

Beiser, Frederick. *The Fate of Reason: German Philosophy from Kant to Fichte.* Cambridge, MA: Harvard University Press 1987.

German Idealism. The Struggle against Subjectivism 1781–1801. Cambridge, MA: Harvard University Press 2002.

The Romantic Imperative: The Concept of Early German Romanticism. Cambridge, MA: Harvard University Press 2003.

Blackall, Eric A. *The Emergence of German as a Literary Language.* Cambridge University Press 1959.

Bowman, Brady. *Sinnliche Gewißheit: Systematische Vorgeschichte zu einem Problem des Deutschen Idealismus.* Berlin: Akademie-Verlag 2003.

"Spinozist Pantheism and the Truth of Sense Certainty." *Journal of the History of Philosophy* 52 (2012): 85–110.

Brandom, Robert. *Tales of the Mighty Dead: Historical Essays in the Metaphysics of Intentionality.* Cambridge, MA: Harvard University Press 2002.

Burge, Tyler. "Philosophy of Language and Mind: 1950–1990." *Philosophical Review* 101 (1992): 3–51.

Butler, Clark. "Hermeneutic Hegelianism." *Idealistic Studies* 14:2 (May 1985): 121–35.

Cartwright, Nancy. *The Dappled World: A Study of the Boundaries of Science.* Cambridge University Press 1999.

"Do the Laws of Physics State the Facts?," in John W. Carrol (ed.), *Readings on Laws of Nature.* University of Pittsburgh Press 2004, 71–83. (Originally published in *Pacific Philosophy Quarterly* 61 [1980]: 64–75.)

Cronin, T. J. *Objective Being in Descartes and in Suarez.* Analecta Gregoriana 154. Rome: Gregorian University Press 1966.

Cummins, Robert. "Functional Analysis," in Ned Block (ed.), *Readings in Philosophy of Psychology,* vol. 1. Cambridge, MA: MIT Press 1980, 185–90.

Davidson, Donald. *Essays on Actions and Events.* Oxford University Press 1980.

Inquiries into Truth and Interpretation. Oxford University Press 1984.

de Boer, Karin. *On Hegel: The Sway of the Negative*. Basingstoke, Palgrave Macmillan 2010.

de Vleeschauwer, Herman Jean. "La Génese de la Méthode Mathématique de Wolf." *Revue Belge de la Philologie et d'Histoire* 11:3–4 (1932): 651–77.

della Rocca, Michael. "Rationalism, Idealism, Monism, and Beyond," in Eckart Förster and Yitzhak Melamed (eds.), *Spinoza and German Idealism*. Cambridge University Press 2012, 7–26.

Descartes, René. *The Philosophical Writings*, trans. John Cottingham, Robert Stoothoff, and Dugald Murdoch. Cambridge University Press 1984.

di Giovanni, George. "Editor's Presentation," in di Giovanni (ed.), *Karl Leonhard Reinhold and the Enlightenment*. Dordrecht, Heidelberg, etc..: Springer 2010, 1–12.

"The First Twenty Years of Critique: The Spinoza Connection," in Paul Guyer (ed.), *The Cambridge Companion to Kant*. Cambridge University Press 1992, 417–48.

"The Unfinished Philosophy of Friedrich Heinrich Jacobi," in Friedrich Heinrich Jacobi: The Main Philosophical Writings and the Novel Allwill. Montreal and Kingston: McGill-Queen's University Press 1994.

Doig, J. C. "Objective Being in Descartes and Suarez." *New Scholasticism* 51 (1977): 350–71.

Dretske, Fred. "Misrepresentation," in R. J. Boghdan (ed.), *Belief: Form, Content, and Function*. Oxford: Clarendon Press 1986, 17–36.

Ellis, Brian. *The Philosophy of Nature: A Guide to the New Essentialism*. Montreal and Kingston: McGill-Queen's University Press 2002.

Englebretsen, George. *Logical Negation*. Assen, Netherlands: Van Gorcum 1981.

Erdmann, Johann Edouard. *Versuch einer wissenschaftlichen Darstellung der neueren Philosophie*. Stuttgart: Fromann 1932.

Euclid, *see* Heath, Sir Thomas.

Fisher, Mark and Eric Watkins. "Kant on the Material Ground of Possibility: From 'The Only Possible Argument' to the 'Critique of Pure Reason.'" *Review of Metaphysics* 52:2 (1998): 369–95.

Förster, Eckart. "Die Bedeutung von §§ 76, 77 der *Kritik der Urteilskraft* für die Entwicklung der nachkantischen Philosophie." *Zeitschrift für philosophische Forschung* 56 (2002): 170–90, 321–45.

Kant's Final Synthesis: An Essay on the Opus postumum. Cambridge, MA: Harvard University Press 2000.

The Twenty-Five Years of Philosophy, trans. B. Bowman. Cambridge, MA: Harvard University Press, 2012.

Forster, Michael, *Hegel and Skepticism*. Cambridge, MA: Harvard University Press 1989.

"Hegel on the Superiority of Ancient over Modern Skepticism," in Hans Friedrich Fulda and Rolf-Peter Horstmann (eds.), *Skeptizismus und spekulatives Denken in der Philosophie Hegels*. Stuttgart: Klett-Cotta 1996, 64–82.

Hegel's Idea of a Phenomenology of Spirit. University of Chicago Press 1998.

"Kant and Skepticism," in Brady Bowman and Klaus Vieweg (eds.), *Die freie Seite der Philosophie: Skeptizismus in Hegelscher Perspektive*. Würzburg: Königshausen und Neumann 2006, 149–70.

Franks, Paul. *All or Nothing. Systematicity, Transcendental Arguments, and Skepticism in German Idealism*. Cambridge, MA: Harvard University Press 2005.

"From Kant to Post-Kantian Idealism." *Proceedings of the Aristotelian Society, Supplementary Volumes* 76 (2002): 229–46.

Franz, Michael. *Schelling's Tübinger Platon-Studien*. Göttingen: Vandenhoek & Ruprecht 1996.

French, Steven. "Structure as a Weapon of the Realist," *Proceedings of the Aristotelian Society* 106 (2006): 1–19.

Freudenthal, Gideon. *Definition and Construction: Salomon Maimon's Philosophy of Geometry*. Berlin: Max Planck Gesellschaft für Wissenschaftsgeschichte 2006.

Fulda, Hans Friedrich. "Hegels Dialektik als Begriffsbewegung und Darstellungsweise," in Rolf-Peter Horstmann (ed.), *Seminar: Dialektik in der Philosophie Hegels*. Frankfurt am Main: Suhrkamp 1978, 124–74.

"Ontologie nach Kant und Hegel," in Dieter Henrich and Rolf-Peter Horstmann (eds.), *Metaphysik nach Kant?* Stuttgart: Klett-Cotta 1987, 44–82.

Das Problem einer Einleitung in Hegels Wissenschaft der Logik, 2nd edn. Frankfurt am Main: Klostermann 1975.

Ginsborg, Hannah. "Kant and the Problem of Experience." *Philosophical Topics* 34:1/2 (2006): 59–106.

"Was Kant a Nonconceptualist?" *Philosophical Studies* 137:1 (2008): 65–77.

Gower, Barry. "Cassirer, Schlick and 'Structural' Realism: The Philosophy of the Exact Sciences in the Background to Early Logical Empiricism." *British Journal for the History of Philosophy* 8:1 (2000): 71–106.

Grier, Michelle. *Kant's Doctrine of Transcendental Illusion*. Cambridge University Press 2001.

Grüne, Stefanie. *Blinde Anschauung: Die Rolle von Begriffen in Kants Theorie sinnlicher Synthesis*. Frankfurt am Main: Klostermann 2009.

Hanna, Robert. "Kant and Nonconceptual Content." *European Journal of Philosophy* 13:2 (2005): 247–90.

"Kantian Non-Conceptualism, Rogue Objects, and the Gap in the B-Deduction." *International Journal of Philosophical Studies* 19:3 (2011): 397–413.

Harris, William Torrey. *Hegel's Logic. A Book on the Genesis of the Categories of the Mind. A Critical Exposition*. Chicago: S. C. Griggs 1890.

Heath, Sir Thomas (ed. and trans.). *The Thirteen Books of the Elements*, 2nd edn. New York: Dover 1956.

Heidegger, Martin. *Sein und Zeit*. Tübingen: Max Niemeyer 2001.

Heidemann, Dietmar. *Der Begriff des Skeptizismus: Seine systematischen Formen, die pyrrhonische Skepsis und Hegels Herausforderung*. Berlin and New York: de Gruyter 2007.

Hendry, Robin Findlay. "Elements, Compounds, and other Chemical Kinds." *Philosophy of Science* 73:5 (2006): 864–75.

Henrich, Dieter. *Between Kant and Hegel: Lectures on German Idealism*, ed. David S. Pacini. Cambridge, MA: Harvard University Press 2003.

"Formen der Negation in Hegels Logik." *Hegel-Jahrbuch* (1974): 245–56.

"Hegels Grundoperation," in Ute Guzzoni, Bernhard Rang, and Ludwig Siep (eds.), *Der Idealismus und seine Gegenwart. Festschrift für Werner Marx*. Hamburg: Felix Meiner 1976, 208–30.

"Hegels Logik der Reflexion," in *Hegel im Kontext*. Frankfurt: Suhrkamp 1970, 95–157.

"Hegels Logik der Reflexion (neue Fassung)." *Hegel-Studien* Beiheft 18 (1978): 204–324.

"Hegels Theorie über den Zufall." *Kantstudien* 50 (1958/59): 131–48.

Selbstverhältnisse: Gedanken und Auslegungen zu den Grundlagen der klassischen deutschen Philosophie. Stuttgart: Reclam 1982.

Hoffmeister, Johannes (ed.). *Dokumente zu Hegels Entwicklung*. Stuttgart: Fromann 1936.

Honnefelder, Ludger. *Scientia transcendens: Die formale Bestimmung der Seiendheit und Realität in der Metaphysik des Mittelalters und der Neuzeit (Duns Scotus – Suarez – Wolff – Kant – Peirce)*. Hamburg: Meiner 1990.

Horn, Lawrence R. *A Natural History of Negation*. Stanford: Center for the Study of Language and Information (CSLI) 2001. (Originally published University of Chicago Press 1989.)

Horstmann, Rolf-Peter. *Die Grenzen der Vernunft: Eine Untersuchung zu Zielen und Motiven des Deutschen Idealismus*. Frankfurt am Main: Anton Hain 1991.

Ontologie und Relationen. Hegel, Bradley, Russell und die Kontroverse über interne und externe Beziehungen. Königstein im Taunus: Athenäum 1984.

Horstmann, Rolf-Peter (ed.). *Seminar: Dialektik in der Philosophie Hegels*. Frankfurt am Main: Suhrkamp 1978.

Houlgate, Stephen. *The Opening of Hegel's Logic: From Being to Infinity*. West Lafayette, IN: Purdue University Press 2006.

Hyppolite, Jean. *Logic and Existence*, trans. Leonard Lawlor and Amit Sen. Albany: State University of New York Press 1997.

Iber, Christian. *Metaphysik absoluter Relationalität*. Berlin and New York: de Gruyter 1990.

Jaeschke, Walter. *Hegel-Handbuch: Leben-Werk-Wirkung*. Stuttgart: Metzler 2003.

Jaeschke, Walter (ed.). *Der Streit um die Gestalt einer ersten Philosophie (1799–1807)*, 2 vols. Hamburg: Meiner 1993.

Jaeschke, Walter and Birgit Sandkaulen (eds.). *Friedrich Heinrich Jacobi: Ein Wendepunkt der geistigen Bildung der Zeit*. Hamburg: Meiner 2004.

Kirk, G. S., J. E. Raven, and M. Scofield (eds.). *The Presocratic Philosophers*, 2nd edn. Cambridge University Press 1983.

Klimmek, Nikolai. *Kant's System der Transzendentalen Ideen*. Berlin: de Gruyter 2005.

Kneale, William and Martha Kneale. *The Development of Logic*. Oxford University Press 1962.

Koch, Anton Friedrich. "Die schlechte Metaphysik der Dinge. Metaphysik als immanente Metaphysikkritik bei Hegel." *Internationales Jahrbuch des Deutschen Idealismus* 5 (2007): *Metaphysics in German Idealism*. Berlin and New York: de Gruyter 2008, 189–210.

Kreines, James. "Hegel's Metaphysics: Changing the Debate." *Philosophy Compass* 1:5 (2006): 466–80.

Ladyman, James. "On the Identity and Diversity of Individuals." *Proceedings of the Aristotelian Society, Supplementary Volumes* 81 (2007): 23–43.

"What is Structural Realism?" *Studies in the History and Philosophy of Science* 29:3 (1997): 409–24.

Langton, Rae. "Elusive Knowledge of Things in Themselves." *Australasian Journal of Philosophy* 82 (2004): 129–36.

Kantian Humility: Our Ignorance of Things in Themselves. Oxford University Press 1998.

Laywine, Alison. *Kant's Early Metaphysics and the Origins of Critical Philosophy.* North American Kant Society Studies in Philosophy 3. Atascadero, CA: Ridgeview 1993.

Lefevre, Wolfgang. "Die Schwäche des Begriffs in der Nature: Der Unterabschnitt 'Beobachtung der Natur' im Vernunft-Kapitel der *Phänomenologie des Geistes*," in Andreas Arndt, Karol Ball, and Henning Ottmann (eds.), *Hegel-Jahrbuch 2001: Phänomenologie des Geistes, Erster Teil.* Berlin: Akademie Verlag 2002, 157–71.

Lewis, David. "How to Define Theoretical Terms," in *Philosophical Papers*, vol. 1. Oxford University Press 1983, 78–96.

"Ramseyan Humility," in David Braddon-Mitchell and Robert Nolan (eds.), *Conceptual Analysis and Philosophical Naturalism.* Cambridge, MA: MIT Press 2009, 203–22.

Locke, John. *An Essay Concerning Human Understanding*, ed. Peter H. Nidditch. Oxford University Press 1979.

Longuenesse, Béatrice. *Hegel's Critique of Metaphysics.* Cambridge University Press 2007.

Kant on the Human Standpoint. Cambridge University Press 2005.

Lowe, E. J. *The Four-Category Ontology: A Metaphysical Foundation for Natural Science.* Oxford University Press 2006.

A Survey of Metaphysics. Oxford University Press 2002.

Malabou, Catherine. *The Future of Hegel. Plasticity, Temporality, and Dialectic.* New York: Routledge 2005.

Marks, E. G. and J. A. Marks. "Newlands Revisited: A Display of the Periodicity of the Chemical Elements for Chemists." *Foundations of Chemistry* 12 (2010): 85–93.

Mayr, Ernst. *The Growth of Biological Thought: Diversity, Evolution, and Inheritance.* Cambridge, MA: Harvard University Press 1982.

McDowell, John. "Hegel's Idealism as a Radicalization of Kant," in *Having the World in View: Essays on Kant, Hegel, and Sellars.* Cambridge, MA: Harvard University Press 2009, 69–89.

Mind and World. Cambridge, MA: Harvard University Press 1994.

McGinn, Colin. *Logical Properties.* Oxford University Press 2000.

Newton, Isaac, *see* Turnbull *et al.* (eds.).

Nuzzo, Angelica. "The End of Hegel's Logic: Absolute Idea as Absolute Method," in David G. Carlson (ed.), *Hegel's Theory of the Subject.* Houndmills: Macmillan 2005, 187–205.

Paterson, Alan L. T. "Does Hegel Have Anything to Say to Modern Mathematical Philosophy?" *Idealistic Studies* 32:2 (2002):143–58.

"Hegel's Early Geometry." *Hegel-Studien* 39/40 (2005): 61–124.

Pinkard, Terry. "How Kantian was Hegel?"*Review of Metaphysics* 43:4 (June 1990): 831–38.

Pippin, Robert. "Hegel and Category Theory." *Review of Metaphysics* 43:4 (June 1990): 839–48.

Hegel's Idealism. The Satisfactions of Self-Consciousness. Cambridge University Press 1989.

Pozzo, Riccardo. "Ploucquet – Hegel – Hamilton: Problem- und Wirkungsgeschichte." *Hegel-Studien* 26 (1991): 449–56.

"Zu Hegels Kantverständnis im Manuskript zur Psychologie und Transencendentalphilosophie aus dem Jahre 1794," in Martin Bondeli and Helmut Linneweber-Lammerskitten (eds.), *Hegels Denkentwicklung in der Berner und Frankfurter Zeit.* Munich: Fink 1999, 15–29.

Rand, Sebastian. "The Importance and Relevance of Hegel's Philosophy of Nature." *Review of Metaphysics* 61:2 (2007): 379–400.

Redding, Paul. *Analytic Philosophy and the Return of Hegelian Thought.* Cambridge University Press 2007.

Reich, Klaus. *Kants einzigmöglicher Beweisgrund zu einer Demonstration des Daseins Gottes: Ein Beitrag zum Verständnis des Verhältnisses von Dogmatismus und Kritizismus in der Metaphysik.* Leipzig: Meiner 1937.

Rockmore, Tom. *Hegel, Idealism, and Analytic Philosophy.* New Haven, CT: Yale University Press 2005.

Rosenkranz, Karl. *G. W. F. Hegel's Leben.* Berlin: Duncker & Humboldt 1844.

Röttges, Heinz. *Der Begriff der Methode in der Philosophie Hegels.* Meisenheim am Glan: Anton Hein 1981.

Rutherford, Donald. *Leibniz and the Rational Order of Nature.* Cambridge University Press 1998.

Sandkaulen, Birgit. "Das, Was oder Wer? Jacobi im Diskurs über Personen," in W. Jaeschke and B. Sandkaulen (eds.), *Friedrich Heinrich Jacobi: Ein Wendepunkt der geistigen Bildung der Zeit.* Hamburg: Meiner 2004, 217–37.

Grund und Ursache: die Vernunftkritik Jacobis. Munich: Fink 1999.

"'Oder hat die Vernunft den Menschen?' Zur Vernunft des Gefühls bei Jacobi." *Zeitschrift für philosophische Forschung* 49:3 (1995): 416–29.

"Die Ontologie der Substanz, der Begriff der Subjektivität und die Faktizität des Einzelnen: Hegels reflexionslogische 'Widerlegung' der Spinozanischen Metaphysik." *Internationales Jahrbuch des Deutschen Idealismus* 5 (2007): *Metaphysics in German Idealism.* Berlin and New York: de Gruyter 2008, 235–75.

"System und Systemkritik: Überlegungen zur gegenwärtigen Bedeutung eines fundamentalen Problemzusammenhangs," in Sandkaulen (ed.), *System und Systemkritik: Beiträge zu einem Grundproblem der klassischen deutschen Philosophie.* Würzburg: Königshausen und Neumann 2006, 11–34.

Schäfer, Rainer. *Die Dialektik und ihre besonderen Formen in Hegels Logik. Hegel-Studien* Beiheft 45. Hamburg: Meiner 2001.

Schmidt, Klaus J. "Formale Logik und Dialektik in Hegels Seinslogik," in Henk Oosterling and Frans de Jong (eds.), *Denken Unterwegs: Philosophie im Kräftefeld sozialen und politischen Engagements. Festschrift für Heinz Kimmerle.* Amsterdam: Grüner 1990, 127–44.

Schonfeld, Martin. *The Philosophy of the Young Kant: The Pre-Critical Project.* Oxford University Press 2000.

Sedgwick, Sally. *Hegel's Critique of Kant: From Dichotomy to Identity.* Oxford University Press 2012.

Sextus Empiricus. *Outlines of Skepticism*, ed. R. G. Bury. Cambridge, MA: Harvard University Press 1933.

Shein, Noa. "The False Dichotomy between Objective and Subjective Interpretations of Spinoza's Theory of Attributes." *British Journal for the History of Philosophy* 17:3 (2009): 505–32.

Smith, Norman Kemp. *A Commentary to Kant's Critique of Pure Reason.* New York: Humanities Press 1962.

Sommers, Fred. "Predicability," in Max Black (ed.), *Philosophy in America.* Ithaca, NY: Cornell University Press 1965, 262–81.

Stekeler-Weithofer, Pirmin. *Hegels Analytische Philosophie: Die Wissenschaft der Logik als kritische Theorie der Bedeutung.* Paderborn, Munich, Vienna, and Zurich: Schöningh 1992.

Stern, Robert. *Hegel, Kant, and the Structure of the Object.* London and New York: Routledge 1990.

Hegelian Metaphysics. Oxford and New York: Oxford University Press 2009.

Szabó, Árpád. "Die Anfänge des Euklidischen Axiom-Systems." *Archive for the History of the Exact Sciences* 1 (1960/62): 37–106.

Thompson, Evan. *Mind in Life: Biology, Phenomenology, and the Sciences of Mind.* Cambridge, MA: Harvard University Press 2007.

Trendelenburg, Friedrich Adolf. *Die logische Frage in Hegels System: Zwei Streitschriften.* Leipzig: Brockhaus 1843.

Turnbull, H. W., J. F. Scott, A. R. Hall, and L. Tilling (eds.). *The Correspondence of Isaac Newton.* Cambridge University Press 1959–77.

Utz, Konrad. *Die Notwendigkeit des Zufalls: Hegels spekulative Dialektik in der Wissenschaft der Logik.* Paderborn: Schöningh 2001.

Van Cleve, James. *Problems from Kant.* Oxford University Press 1999.

Van Fraassen, Bas. "Structure: Its Shadow and Substance." *British Journal for the Philosophy of Science* 57 (2006): 275–307.

Vieweg, Klaus. *Philosophie des Remis: Der junge Hegel und das "Gespenst des Skepticismus."* Munich: Fink 1999.

Wagner, Hans. "*Realitas objectiva* (Descartes–Kant)." *Zeitschrift für philosophische Forschung* 21 (1967): 325–40.

Watkins, Eric. *Kant and the Metaphysics of Causality.* Cambridge University Press 2005.

Weber, Max. *The Vocation Lectures.* Indianapolis, IN and Cambridge: Hackett 2004.

Welsch, Wolfgang. "Absoluter Idealismus und Evolutionsdenken," in Klaus Vieweg and W. Welsch (eds.) *Hegels Phänomenologie des Geistes. Ein kooperativer Kommentar zum einem Schlüsselwerk der Moderne.* Frankfurt: Suhrkamp-Verlag 2008, 655–88.

Westphal, Kenneth. *Hegel, Hume und die Identität wahrnehmbarer Dinge: Historisch-kritische Analyse zum Kapitel "Wahrnehmung" in der Phänomenologie von 1807.* Frankfurt am Main: Klostermann 1998.

Hegel's Epistemological Realism: A Study of the Aim and method of Hegel's Phenomenology of Spirit. Dordrecht, Boston, and London: Kluwer, 1989.

"Kant, Hegel, and the Fate of 'the' Intuitive Intellect," in Sally Sedgwick (ed.), *The Reception of Kant's Critical Philosophy: Fichte, Schelling, and Hegel*. Cambridge University Press 2000, 283–305.

Wolff, Michael. *Die Vollständigkeit der kantischen Urteilstafel: mit einem Essay über Freges Begriffsschrift*. Frankfurt am Main: Klostermann 1995.

Wood, Allen. *Hegel's Ethical Thought*. Cambridge University Press 1990.

Kant's Rational Theology. Ithaca, NY: Cornell University Press 1978.

Wundt, Max. *Die deutsche Schulphilosophie im Zeitalter der Aufklärung*. Hildesheim: Georg Olms 1964. (Originally published Tübingen: Mohr 1945.)

Geschichte der Metaphysik. Berlin: Junker and Dünnhaupt 1931.

Ziche, Paul. "Naturforschung in Jena zur Zeit Hegels. Materialien zum Hintergrund der spekulativen Naturphilosophie." *Hegel-Studien* 32 (1997): 9–40.

Ziche, Paul and Olaf Breidbach (eds.). *Naturwissenschaften um 1800. Wissenschaftskultur in Jena-Weimar*. Weimar: Hermann Böhlaus Nachfolger 2001.

INDEX